1907

ESSAYS

OF

WILLIAM GRAHAM SUMNER

EDITED, WITH PREFACES, BY
ALBERT GALLOWAY KELLER

AND
MAURICE R. DAVIE

IN TWO VOLUMES

VOLUME II

ARCHON BOOKS
1969

SBN: 208 00628 1
LIBRARY OF CONGRESS CATALOG CARD NUMBER: 69-12415

CONTENTS

VOLUME II

PREFACE

THE essays in this second volume, falling as they do within the range of economics and politics, date from an earlier period in Sumner's life. They are not for that reason the less timely; that they may make reference to runaway horses rather than to scorching automobiles is a matter of no moment. There are hoary errors and follies which, apparently, cannot be finally eliminated by experience, but recur under new names, or even under the old ones, and must be embraced, suffered from, exposed, and rejected over and over again.

Sumner's unrelenting, though often lonely, championship of hard money and free trade deserves recalling for the same reason that a military strategist studies the campaigns of doughty fighters of the past. If his assaults upon state interference are ever to repay re-reading, it is in the present period of emotional and muddled "experimentation." In an age of yearning after collectivism, the antidote of a powerful statement by a hard-hitting individualist is a good thing to have at hand; for it will be needed, later on, even if crowded to the back of the medicine-closet, for a time, by patented narcotics and stimulants that are sure to produce a morning after.

The reason why Sumner's positions will eventually be vindicated is because they are the result of the hardest kind of study, over many years, by a realist with insight. He had an appreciation of the inevitabilities — of those deep-lying laws of society's life and evolution which cannot be altered a whit by condemnatory resolutions, nor escaped by artful dodging, nor even melted away by the dropping of warm tears. He was as eager to make human life more abundant as any of the modern world-beatifiers, with their caught-up, bright ideas; and he was wholly disinterested, as are not all the economic and political medicine-men. But he did no wishful thinking; and, as he wanted no meddling by uncredentialed "experts," his views became a target for the epithet, "*Laissez-faire*" — a term of honor when it has connoted a tendency to put off action until one knows where he is going. Sumner knew well enough that there are times when one must act without much knowledge or without taking time belatedly to amass and analyze neglected facts; but to make headlong action a policy for all occasions was to him an evidence of witlessness.

The trouble with the "planners" and benefactors of society in the present is that they prefer intuition to tuition. When people are sufficiently disillusioned as regards such leadership, by suffering, they can acquire much tuition from certain of the "old" masters. That morning after is sure to come.

A. G. Keller

New Haven
June 26, 1934

ESSAYS OF
WILLIAM GRAHAM SUMNER

SKETCH OF WILLIAM GRAHAM SUMNER[1]

WILLIAM GRAHAM SUMNER was born at Paterson, New
Jersey, October 30, 1840. He is the son of Thomas Sumner, who came to this country from England in 1836,
and married here Sarah Graham, also of English birth.
Thomas Sumner was a machinist, who worked at his
trade until he was sixty years old, and never had any
capital but what he saved out of a mechanic's wages.
He was an entirely self-educated man, but always pro-
fessed great obligations to mechanics' institutes and other
associations of the kind, of whose opportunities he had
made eager use in England. He was a man of the
strictest integrity, a total abstainer, of domestic habits
and indefatigable industry. He became enthusiastic-
ally interested in total abstinence when a young man in
England, the method being that of persuasion and mis-
sionary effort. He used to describe his only attempt to
make a speech in public, which was on this subject,
when he completely failed. He had a great thirst for
knowledge, and was thoroughly informed on modern
English and American history and on the constitutional
law of both countries. He made the education of his
children his chief thought, and the only form of public
affairs in which he took an active interest was that of
schools. His contempt for demagogical arguments and
for all the notions of the labor agitators, as well as for
the entire gospel of gush, was that of a simple man with

[1] *The Popular Science Monthly*, June, 1889, XXXV, 261-268.

sturdy common-sense, who had never been trained to
entertain any kind of philosophical abstractions. His
plan was, if things did not go to suit him, to examine
the situation, see what could be done, take a new start,
and try again. For instance, inasmuch as the custom
in New Jersey was store pay, and he did not like store
pay, he moved to New England, where he found that he
could get cash. He had decisive influence on the convictions and tastes of the subject of this sketch.

Professor Sumner grew up at Hartford, Connecticut,
and was educated in the public schools of that city. The
High School was then under the charge of Mr. T. W. T.
Curtis, and the classical department under Mr. S. M.
Capron. These teachers were equally remarkable, although in different ways, for their excellent influence
on the pupils under their care. There was an honesty
and candor about both of them which were very healthful in example. They did very little "preaching,"
but their demeanor was in all respects such as to bear
watching with the scrutiny of school-children and only
gain by it. Mr. Curtis had great skill in the catecheti-
cal method, being able to lead a scholar by a series of
questions over the track which must be followed to come
to an understanding of the subject under discussion.
Mr. Capron united dignity and geniality in a remarkable
degree. The consequence was that he had the most
admirable discipline, without the least feeling of the irk-
someness of discipline on the part of his pupils. On the
contrary, he possessed their tender and respectful
affection. Mr. Capron was a man of remarkably few
words, and he was a striking example of the power that
may go forth from a man by what he is and does in the
daily life of a schoolroom. Both these gentlemen employed in the schoolroom all the best methods of teaching

now so much gloried in, without apparently knowing that they had any peculiar method at all. Professor Sumner has often declared in public that, as a teacher, he is deeply indebted to the sound traditions which he derived from these two men.

He graduated from Yale College in 1863, and in the summer of that year went to Europe. He spent the winter of 1863–1864 in Geneva, studying French and Hebrew with private instructors. He was at Göttingen for the next two years, studying ancient languages, history, especially church history, and biblical science. In answer to some questions, Professor Sumner has replied as follows:

"My first interest in political economy came from Harriet Martineau's 'Illustrations of Political Economy.' I came upon these by chance, in the library of the Young Men's Institute at Hartford, when I was thirteen or fourteen years old. I read them all through with the greatest avidity, some of them three or four times. There was very little literature at that time with which these books could connect. My teachers could not help me any, and there were no immediate relations between the topics of these books and any public interests of the time. We supposed then that free trade had sailed out upon the smooth sea, and was to go forward without further difficulty, so that what one learned of the fallacies of protection had only the same interest as what one learns about the fallacies of any old and abandoned error. In college we read and recited Wayland's 'Political Economy,' but I believe that my conceptions of capital, labor, money, and trade, were all formed by those books which I read in my boyhood. In college the interest was turned rather on the political than on the economic element. It seemed to me then, however, that the war, with the paper money and the high taxation, must certainly bring about immense social changes and social problems, especially making the rich richer and the poor poorer, and leaving behind us the old ante-war period as one of primitive simplicity which could never return. I used to put this notion into college compositions, and laid the foundation in that way for the career which afterward opened to me.

"I enjoyed intensely the two years which I spent at Göttingen. I had the sense of gaining all the time exactly what I wanted. The professors whom I knew there seemed to me bent on seeking a clear and comprehensive conception of the matter under study (what we call 'the truth') without regard to any consequences whatever. I have heard men elsewhere talk about the nobility of that spirit; but the only *body* of men whom I have ever known who really lived by it, sacrificing wealth, political distinction, church preferment, popularity, or anything else for the truth of science, were the professors of biblical science in Germany. That was precisely the range of subjects which in this country was then treated with a reserve in favor of tradition which was prejudicial to everything which a scholar should value. So far as those men infected me with their spirit, they have perhaps added to my usefulness but not to my happiness. They also taught me rigorous and pitiless methods of investigation and deduction. Their analysis was their strong point. Their negative attitude toward the poetic element, their indifference to sentiment, even religious sentiment, was a fault, seeing that they studied the Bible as a religious book and not for philology and history only; but their method of study was nobly scientific, and was worthy to rank, both for its results and its discipline, with the best of the natural science methods. I sometimes wonder whether there is any one else in exactly the same position as I am, having studied biblical science with the Germans, and then later social science, to mark the striking contrast in method between the two. The later social science of Germany is the complete inversion in its method of that of German philology, classical criticism, and biblical science. Its subjection to political exigencies works upon it as disastrously as subjection to dogmatic creeds has worked upon biblical science in this country.

"I went over to Oxford in the spring of 1866. Having given up all my time in Germany to German books, I wanted to read English literature on the same subjects. I expected to find it rich and independent. I found that it consisted of second-hand adaptation of what I had just been studying. I was then quite thoroughly Teutonized, as all our young men are likely to be after a time of study in Germany. I had not undergone the toning-down process which is necessary to bring a young American back to common sense, and I underrated the real services of many Englishmen to the Bible as a religious book — exactly the supplement which I then needed to my German education. Ullmann's 'Wesen des Christenthums,' which I had read at Göttingen, had steadied my religious faith, and I devoted myself at Oxford to the old Anglican divines and to the standard books of the Anglican communion. The only one of these which gave me any pleasure or profit was Hooker's 'Ecclesiastical Polity.' The first part of this book I studied with the greatest care, making an analysis of it and reviewing it repeatedly. It suited exactly those notions of constitutional order, adjustment of rights, constitutional authority, and historical continuity, in which I had been brought up, and it presented those doctrines of liberty under law applied both to church and state which commanded my enthusiastic acceptance. It also presented Anglicanism in exactly the aspect in which it was attractive to me. It re-awakened, however, all my love for political science, which was intensified by reading Buckle and also by another fact next to be mentioned.

"The most singular contrast between Göttingen and Oxford was this: at Göttingen everything one got came from the university, nothing from one's fellow-students. At Oxford it was not possible to get anything of great value from the university; but the education one could get from one's fellows was invaluable. There was a set of young fellows, or men reading for fellowships, there at that time, who were studying Hegel. I became intimate with several of them. Two or three of them have since died at an early age, disappointing hopes of useful careers. I never caught the Hegelian fever.

I had heard Lotze at Göttingen, and found his suggestions very convenient to hold on by, at least for the time. We used, however, in our conversations at Oxford, to talk about Buckle and the ideas which he had then set afloat, and the question which occupied us the most was whether there could be a science of society, and, if so, where it should begin and how it should be built. We had all been eager students of what was then called the 'philosophy of history,' and I had also felt great interest in the idea of God in history, with which my companions did not sympathize. We agreed, however, that social science must be an induction from history, that Buckle had started on the right track, and that the thing to do was to study history. The difficulty which arrested us was that we did not see how the mass of matter to be collected and arranged could ever be so mastered that the induction could actually be performed if the notion of an 'induction from history' should be construed strictly. Young as we were, we never took up this crude notion as a real program of work. I have often thought of it since, when I have seen the propositions of that sort which have been put forward within twenty years. I have lost sight of all my associates at Oxford who are still living. So far as I know, I am the only one of them who has become professionally occupied with social science."

Mr. Sumner returned to the United States in the autumn of 1866, having been elected to a tutorship in Yale College. Of this he says:

"The tutorship was a great advantage to me. I had expected to go to Egypt and Palestine in the next winter, but this gave me an opportunity to study further, and to acquaint myself with church affairs in the United States before a final decision as to a profession. I speedily found that there was no demand at all for 'biblical science'; that everybody was afraid of it, especially if it came with the German label on it. It was a case in which, if a man should work very hard and achieve remarkable results, the only consequence would be

that he would ruin himself. At this time I undertook the
translation of the volume of Lange's 'Commentary on Second
Kings.' While I was tutor I read Herbert Spencer's 'First
Principles' — at least the first part of it — but it made no
impression upon me. The second part, as it dealt with evolution, did not then interest me. I also read his 'Social Statics'
at that period. As I did not believe in natural rights, or in
his 'fundamental principle,' this book had no effect on me."

Mr. Sumner was ordained deacon at New Haven in
December, 1867, and priest at New York, July, 1869.
He became assistant to Dr. Washburn at Calvary
Church, New York, in March, 1869. He was also editor
of a Broad Church paper, which Dr. Washburn and some
other clergymen started at this time. In September,
1870, he became rector of the Church of the Redeemer
at Morristown, New Jersey.

"When I came to write sermons, I found to what a degree my
interest lay in topics of social science and political economy.
There was then no public interest in the currency and only a
little in the tariff. I thought that these were matters of the
most urgent importance, which threatened all the interests,
moral, social, and economic, of the nation; and I was young
enough to believe that they would all be settled in the next
four or five years. It was not possible to preach about them,
but I got so near to it that I was detected sometimes, as, for
instance, when a New Jersey banker came to me, as I came
down from the pulpit, and said, 'There was a great deal of
political economy in that sermon.'

"It was at this period that I read, in an English magazine,
the first of those essays of Herbert Spencer which were afterward collected into the volume 'The Study of Sociology.'
These essays immediately gave me the lead which I wanted,
to bring into shape the crude notions which had been floating
in my head for five or six years, especially since the Oxford
days. The conception of society, of social forces, and of the

science of society there offered was just the one which I had
been groping after but had not been able to reduce for myself.
It solved the old difficulty about the relation of social science
to history, rescued social science from the dominion of the
cranks, and offered a definite and magnificent field for work,
from which we might hope at last to derive definite results for
the solution of social problems.

"It was at this juncture (1872) that I was offered the chair
of Political and Social Science at Yale. I had always been
very fond of teaching and knew that the best work I could
ever do in the world would be in that profession; also, that
I ought to be in an academical career. I had seen two or three
cases of men who, in that career, would have achieved distinguished usefulness, but who were wasted in the parish and
the pulpit."

Mr. Sumner returned to New Haven as professor in
September, 1872. Of the further development of his
opinions he says:

"I was definitely converted to evolution by Professor
Marsh's horses some time about 1875 or 1876. I had re-read
Spencer's 'Social Statics' and his 'First Principles,' the second
part of the latter now absorbing all my attention. I now read
all of Darwin, Huxley, Haeckel, and quite a series of the natural scientists. I greatly regretted that I had no education in
natural science, especially in biology; but I found that the
'philosophy of history' and the 'principles of philology,' as I
had learned them, speedily adjusted themselves to the new
conception, and won a new meaning and power from it. As
Spencer's 'Principles of Sociology' was now coming out in
numbers, I was constantly getting evidence that sociology, if
it borrowed the theory of evolution in the first place, would
speedily render it back again enriched by new and independent evidence. I formed a class to read Spencer's book in the
parts as they came out, and believe that I began to interest
men in this important department of study, and to prepare

them to follow its development, years before any such attempt was made at any other university in the world. I have followed the growth of the science of sociology in all its branches and have seen it far surpass all the hope and faith I ever had in it. I have spent an immense amount of work on it, which has been lost because misdirected. The only merit I can claim in that respect is that I have corrected my own mistakes. I have not published them for others to correct."

The above statement of the history of Professor Sumner's education shows the school of opinion to which he belongs. He adopts the conception of society according to which it is the seat of forces, and its phenomena are subject to laws which it is the business of science to investigate. He denies that there is anything arbitrary or accidental in social phenomena, or that there is any field in them for the arbitrary intervention of man. He therefore allows but very limited field for legislation. He holds that men must do with social laws what they do with physical laws — learn them, obey them, and conform to them. Hence he is opposed to state interference and socialism, and he advocates individualism and liberty. He has declared that bimetallism is an absurdity, involving a contradiction of economic laws, and his attacks on protectionism have been directed against it as a philosophy of wealth and prosperity for the nation. As to politics he says:

"My only excursion into active politics has been a term as alderman. In 1872 I was one of the voters who watched with interest and hope the movement which led up to the 'Liberal' Convention at Cincinnati, that ended by nominating Greeley and Brown. The platform of that convention was very outspoken in its declarations about the policy to be pursued toward the South. I did not approve of the reconstruction policy. I wanted the South let alone and treated with patience. I lost my vote by moving to New Haven, and was contented to let it go that way. In 1876 I was of the same opinion about the South. If I had been asked what I wanted done, I should have tried to describe just what Mr. Hayes did do after he got in. I therefore voted for Mr. Tilden for President. In 1880 I did not vote. In 1884 I voted as a Mugwump for Mr. Cleveland. In 1888 I voted for him on the tariff issue."

A distinguished American economist, who is well acquainted with Professor Sumner's work, has kindly given us the following estimate of his method and of his position and influence as a public teacher:

"For exact and comprehensive knowledge Professor Sumner is entitled to take the first place in the ranks of American economists; and as a teacher he has no superior. His leading mental characteristic he has himself well stated in describing the characteristics of his former teachers at Göttingen; namely, as 'bent on seeking a clear and comprehensive conception of the matter or "truth" under study, without regard to any consequences whatever,' and further, when in his own mind Professor Sumner is fully satisfied as to what the truth is, he has no hesitation in boldly declaring it, on every fitting occasion, without regard to consequences. If the theory is a 'spade,' he calls it a spade, and not an implement of husbandry. Sentimentalists, followers of precedent because it is precedent, and superficial reasoners find little favor, therefore, with Professor Sumner; and this trait of character has given him a reputation for coldness and lack of what may be called 'humanitarianism,' and has rendered one of his best essays, 'What Social Classes Owe to Each Other,' almost repulsive in respect to some of its conclusions. At the same time, the representatives of such antagonisms, if they are candid, must admit that Professor Sumner's logic can only be resisted by making their reason subordinate to sentiment. Professor Sumner is an earnest advocate of the utmost freedom in respect to all commercial exchanges; and the results of his experiences in the discussion of the relative merits and advantages of the systems of free trade and protection have been such that probably no defender of the latter would now be willing to meet him in a public discussion of these topics."

THE POWER AND BENEFICENCE
OF CAPITAL [1]

SOME years ago I listened to an address by a social agitator who said: "I can get along with anybody in my audiences except these mean, stingy, little fellows who have saved up a few hundred dollars in the savings bank and then have borrowed enough more to build a little house of two tenements, one of which they rent. When I begin to talk about interest, and rent, and Henry George, they get up and go out by the whole seat-full at a time." The statement was the most eloquent recognition I ever heard of the power and beneficence of capital. It has always remained in my memory as a confession by an opponent of the education effected by savings and of the benefit conferred on society by savings banks. I make it the text for the remarks which I will address to you on this occasion.

We hear a great deal in these days about social discontent. It seems to be taken for granted that discontent is a sufficient proof of grievance which third parties are bound to take cognizance of and redress. It might be argued with far greater plausibility that discontent is a proof of prosperity. If you look around the world today you will find that discontent is greatest where the chances are greatest. A man who has never had anything or a chance to get anything is not discontented; he rests contented with what he has always been accustomed to. Let him enjoy an opportunity and win something and the effect will be to excite his wish to win more. There is

[1] Proceedings of The Savings Banks Asso. of New York, 1899, 77-95.

more discontent in one house in the United States or in England than in the whole Russian Empire. Discontent exists, then, where there are opportunities, and it is a stimulus to take advantage of opportunities. In that case it is an agency which produces achievement and drives on what we call progress. In other cases discontent is a result of conviction that opportunities have been lost and that it is too late to recover them. Then again, discontent is the twin sister of envy, when it is seen that others have profited better by opportunities. In no case does discontent, as a naked fact, prove anything, and when the details are known it never is proof of a grievance.

Our social philosophers, however, as I have said, assume that discontent is a legitimate and imperative demand for a remedy. They treat it as a social phenomenon, and the remedies which they propose are societal, that is, they are in the nature of devices and regulations which call for the action of the agencies of society. So far as these social philosophers get their way, we find that it is legislation which is set at work, and this legislation imposes tasks on functionaries and institutions. The net final and certain result is new burdens on taxpayers. Discontent is not diminished; it is generally increased. If you get a report of the operation of any of these devices which have already been adopted you will find it full of criticism, perhaps of derision, of the device. It is pointed out how crude the notion was; how ignorant of the conditions; how irrelevant to the purpose in view.

I will not now, however, dwell upon this aspect of social measures to cure discontent; what I am now more interested in is the education exerted by all this philosophy and all these devices on the people on whom they are brought to bear. The social philosophy which has been in fashion for a century past has educated us in the notion that we ought all to be "happy" (as the phrase goes) on this earth, and that, if we are not so, we ought to cry out, and then that somebody is bound to come and take care of us. Liberty, equality, and happiness have been declared to be natural rights, which is interpreted to mean that they were laid in our cradles as our endowment for the battle of life. Every human being, on this theory, comes into the world with an outfit and a patrimony of metaphysical, if not of physical, goods. This doctrine is, of course, very popular and the men who preach it are sure of popular applause and political power. Tell a man that just because he has been born, he ought to have and enjoy all the highest acquisitions of civilization without labor, self-denial, or study, and that he is a victim of injustice if he does not possess all those good things, and he will be sure to be delighted. Some of these grand old eighteenth-century dogmas which lie on the borderline between politics and social philosophy have been found very much in the way in our own history of the last twelve months. They have been pushed aside as out of date. Perhaps we may get an incidental advantage from recent history if we can throw them all overboard together, but it is more likely that the buncombe element in them has too much value for political purposes to be sacrificed, and so we shall see that retained. We may be very sure that all these theories of world beatification can produce nothing but disillusion and disappointment for those who put faith in them, and disintegration for the society in which they are current. The human race never received any gratuitous outfit of any kind whatever; no heathen myth ever was more silly and empty than such a notion; talk about the "boon of nature" and the "banquet of life" and the "free gift of land" is more idle than fairy tales. We can speak nowadays with some positive knowledge about the primitive condition of the human race on earth, assuming now that the facts about the primitive condition of man have some bearing on our modern social controversies. We know that the human animal is, by nature, more helpless in the face of nature than many other animals, and that nature did not start the human animal off with any other rights than those of all the other animals. The human race came upon this globe with no outfit at all. The mere task of existing and continuing here was so great that the human race was taxed to the utmost to meet it. The obvious proof of that is that large groups of men have, in innumerable instances, utterly perished from the face of the earth. These are facts of knowledge at the present time and so far as I know they are not disputed by anybody.

I have already intimated that these facts about the primitive order of things have very little value for modern social controversies. Their value lies in quite another direction. If we men have, to any extent, conquered the task of existence, if we have risen to some command over nature, and if we have created a domain of rights between ourselves, it is by civilization that we have done it. The good things were not given to us gratuitously at the outset; they are the product of the toil and suffering of mankind. They belong at the end, not at the beginning. The people who are nowadays examining the product and passing judgment on it are only betraying their own ignorance and folly. They are quite dissatisfied with it; they write books, hold conventions, and pass resolutions about how we ought to change it, and they draft ideas about how they would like to recon-

struct it. If we arrive at some correct idea of what
society is and what civilization is, we shall regard all such
speculations as more absurd than witchcraft or astrology.
We are the children of the society in which we were born.
It makes us. We are products of the civilization of our
generation. Only a handful of men can react upon the
society and the age in which they live so as to modify it
at all. They are the very *élite* of the human race, and
after all what they can do is only infinitesimal. Civilization means the art of living on this earth. All men have
always been trying to learn it, and all that now is in the
order of society is the product of this struggle of ages.
It pours along in a mighty flood which bears us all with
it; in it are all the efforts, passions, interests, and strife
of men. It is the play of these upon each other which
produces the heaving and swaying of the flood and determines its vast modifications of direction. If you come
to a faint understanding of this, the man with a scheme
in his pocket for the "reorganization of society" is made
to appear very ridiculous.

The instrumentality by which, from the beginning,
man has won and held every step of this development of
civilization, is capital. Some people talk about ideas
and philosophy which, they think, have ruled the affairs
of men. The ideas are only secondary. The philosophy,
when it has acted as a cause, has taken the form of dogma,
and has done harm as often as good. We may take
illustrations in proof from the present time. There is a
dogma afloat that labor alone makes wealth, so that the
whole product should belong of right to the laborer.
Another dogma is that limiting the hours of labor would
make work for more laborers, and another is that any
wealth which one man accumulates is so much taken
from some or all other men. Another is that all increase

in the value of land or franchises is due to the social organization and activity, and, therefore, should not go to the holders. These dogmas are all false, but they are of great scope. They are great fighting dogmas because they serve interests. It is for this reason that they win acceptance, because the great reason for inventing dogmas, principles, and phrases is to use them in controversy. These dogmas, therefore, which I have mentioned will, if adopted as the norm of legislation, produce destructive convulsions in society and nothing else. In the meantime the social development is going on by slow accretions which nobody notices; they are won by adjustments between the interests of men who meet new problems every day and solve them as well as they can under the conditions prevailing. These adjustments are all made by means of capital, because the interests are all matters of capital, and all the readjustments are secured by capital. In their turn they favor the creation of capital, because the readjustments which serve interests always mean attempts to win a given result by a smaller expenditure of labor and capital.

Others think that "organization" is the great force which has made civilization; they think that organization is arbitrary and subject to manipulation, and consequently it is upon the organization that they bring their efforts to bear. Organization has, of course, been a commanding phenomenon in the development of civilization. A student of that development is not likely to disregard organization. For myself, I am convinced that much is yet to be gained by better appreciation of the element of organization. But organization is only the *mode* under which the work of life goes on. It is not a force — it never can force anything. It has to do with the smoothness and harmony of the operations. In human society, in its lower forms, organization has always produced itself spontaneously and automatically and has, therefore, just suited itself to the case. It has sometimes become traditional and dogmatic, and for that reason it has become a hindrance, preventing necessary readjustments. Then societal convulsions and revolutions have occurred. In civilized society organization is equally spontaneous and automatic. In the civil organization some element of arbitrary action has become possible, and this it is apparently which has caused the notion that societal organization is a thing subject to conventions and resolutions. In regard to the civil organization, however, the chance of some arbitrary action has only introduced an element of risk and peril, just as an intelligent being runs the risk of going wrong where an instinctive being never has to face any question at all. All attempts so far made to extend the domain of policy in social matters have resulted only in doubt and in warnings of danger; the proposition to adopt a policy of organization can never do anything but disturb the harmony of the societal system which is its greatest advantage. They never will really change the societal organization, for it is already controlled by the mighty forces of interest. For instance: if so-called trusts are now a real step in the evolution of the industrial organization, a legislative policy of sweeping and destructive opposition to them is vain, and after producing great confusion and animosity and loss, will have to be abandoned. The case of department stores is similar and more simple and obvious. If the wages organization is suited to the present conditions of industry, it is quite useless to try to invent any organization of labor to supersede it. On the other hand, we may, from this case, see how the organization changes, for if the interests of men are not served by the wages organization they will seek to modify it in the detail in which it is unsatisfactory, whence it may follow in time that some different organization will be gradually evolved to take its place. Harmony of action, with the highest possible satisfaction of interests, is the point of equilibrium towards which the organization is always tending. Those men nowadays who can foresee the next steps to be taken to advance on this line are the great generals of the modern industrial army. If the organization is bad, it can waste and impede the effort; if it is good, it can allow the effort to reach its maximum result under the conditions. That is the sum of all that can be said about organization.

We must return then to the proposition already made. If men are not now in beastliness and utter want, it is by virtue of labor and self-denial. Labor and self-denial have been embodied in useful things, that is, capital. The things won on the one stage have become new instrumentalities on the next stage. It is not strange that the growth has been so slow, especially in its earlier stages, when we see how hard the struggle has been, and how much it has been at war with human nature. It is only when we have gained some conception of the painful and toilsome effort by which every step has been won, that we can estimate at its full value the civilization which we have inherited; but then, too, we are driven to believe that we never can gain anything more except by the same means. The great reason why the advance of civilization has been so slow is that it has never gone forward steadily. Its progress has been broken up. It has been broken up by ignorance and superstition, which is, of course, simply saying that it never could go on faster than men's knowledge at that stage could carry it. It has also been broken up by passion, and by strife over ques-

tions of policy. All this remains just the same now as it
ever was. Discord, strife, and war break up the orderly
and co-operative effort to reach a higher satisfaction of our
interests — which seems to be alone worthy of intelligent
and civilized men. The ignorance, folly, and strife destroy
capital; the orderly and well-organized efforts to satisfy,
create and preserve capital. The presence of capital
does not insure the extension of civilization, for the
capital may be wasted by error or it may be employed
entirely in an increase of population; but an extension
of civilization without an increase of effective capital or
a diminution of members is impossible.

It may seem to you that the course of thought on which
I have so far led you was somewhat too academical or
philosophical for this occasion, but I am now ready to
return to the orator and the savings bank depositors
whom I mentioned at the outset. The facts and ideas
which I have presented to you show that the savings
bank depositor is a hero of civilization, for he is helping
in the accumulation of that capital which is the indispensable prerequisite of all we care for and all we want to do
here on earth. The more convinced you are that the
notions and devices which are offered to us by social
speculators as the means of social progress are all vain,
and that the whole effort to find some means of easily
making everybody happy is a waste of time, the more you
will be thrown back on the industrial virtues as the only
moral resources at our command which enable us men to
fight the battle of life with success. The industrial virtues
are industry, frugality, prudence, and temperance. We
cannot, however, deny the presence of another element
which is powerful in determining our success — the element
of good or ill fortune. It is true that men have fortune,
or destiny, or Divine Providence at hand as a convenient

agency on which to throw the blame for the consequences
of their own acts, especially for those acts which are
violations of the industrial virtues; but when all is said
in correction of the popular abuse of luck, it is useless to
deny that good or ill fortune may make or mar the success
of men in spite of their most careful endeavors. This
element, however, is irrational; there is an element in
it of which we are ignorant. Therefore, it is beyond our
command and we have to submit to it and make the best
of it. Our only means of dealing with it, where we can
do so, is to meet it co-operatively as we do in insurance.

Returning, then, to the industrial virtues, I repeat that
they are our only moral resource for winning success in
the battle of life. The greater the disadvantages under
which one starts in life, the higher the value of these
virtues for winning the first foothold and making the
first step to something better. There is reason for profound faith in any device which is proposed for societal
improvement if, upon strict analysis, we can find that it
will touch the springs of industrial virtue and raise the
industrial virtues to higher activity. There is no ground
for faith in any device which does not stimulate those
virtues. It is not necessary to add that if devices which
are proposed are found upon examination to stimulate
envy or vanity, or fondness for talk, or a desire to live
by one's wits, they are only mischievous. It is not easy
for us to form estimates of each other's virtues, especially
when we look at each other in classes, but the savings
bank depositor, as a type, gives the surest and most concrete evidence of the industrial virtues. He must be
industrious, frugal, prudent, and temperate. He is a
capitalist; he is getting in hand that power which, as I
have said, has created and now upholds all civilization.
He is winning a share in its power. He is getting the

upper hand of the tasks of life. He is fortifying himself against bad luck and disaster. He is developing his own character by the self-denial and the persistent pursuit of a selected purpose which he is obliged to practise. You find nowhere else such guarantees of sound judgment, sober reason, and moderate temper as are offered by the fact of saving. There is no other guarantee of good citizenship which is so simple and positive, and at the same time so far-reaching, as the possession of savings. The seats-full of savings bank depositors who went out of the lecture proved it.

The old classical saying was: he who has wife and children has given pledges to fortune. He has opened avenues by which misfortune can reach him through other lives. But capital is the chief means of protecting those dependents; it gives education to the children and puts them on a higher plane for the battle of life than that on which their parents stood. It is right to conceive of the human race on this earth as engaged in an endless battle with the conditions of existence, striving so to modify them that men may get more out of their lives in the way of satisfaction of the possibilities of human nature. For a century past the current popular notion has been that the way to win the battle is to "raise the lower classes." The notion seems to be that the vicious criminal and poverty-stricken classes are a certain number of human beings who are miserable or harmful. It is thought that, if this number can be cured of social disease, all will be well. This notion is based on childish misconceptions as to what society is and as to the nature of social disease. Projects to abolish poverty are worthy of an age which has undertaken to discuss the abolition of disease. Why not abolish death and be as gods once for all? Why not resolve that everybody shall be good and happy? Why not vote that everybody shall have whatever he wants? Why trifle with details? If these agencies can get us any-thing, they can just as well get us everything. The trouble with creation out of nothing is not to make a universe; it is to make an atom of star-dust. If, then, we turn away from all these notions and devices and try to understand the case of man on earth just as it is, we find that our task always is to do the best we can under the conditions in which we are and with the means which we possess. Then it appears that capital is the means with which we do it and that it is by capital spent on the education and training of the rising generation that we keep up that advancing fight against the ills of life to which I have referred. I do not suppose that the savings bank depositors who left the lecture knew much about all this, but that class of men have a way of their own of getting at things. The possession of capital gives an acuteness of insight into whatever affects capital; men who have tried saving have not much patience with rhetoric and dogmatism about how to get on in life, and we know how acute they become in perceiving that the upshot of the schemes is to make them share their savings with those who have never done any saving. I suppose that when the savings bank depositors got up and left the lecture, it was an expression of this impatience.

I never saw a poem about the savings bank depositor. Poems are all written about heroes, kings, soldiers, and lovers; there are plenty of poems about glory, and love, and ambition, and even about poverty, but saving is passed by as sordid and mean — utterly unpoetical. It has always been thought noble to spend and mean to save, which only shows how far we are yet, with all our boast-ing, preaching, and discussing, from sound standards of judgment about the operations of society. It has, however, always been recognized that, among subjects of dramatic interest and power, the hero struggling against adversity with fortitude and perseverance is one of the grandest. In our modern commercial and unadventurous life, you will hardly find nobler examples of it than those seats-full of people who, after saving a little to make a beginning, had built two tenement cottages the mortgages on which they were trying to pay off.

Some people will answer that they see the utility and even the moral grandeur of savings by poor people, but that they dread and disapprove of accumulation. If the savings bank depositor saves enough to pass on up into the class of large and independent investors and finally to enter the class technically known as "capitalists," our social philosophers withdraw their sympathy and respect from him and denounce him because he is rich. Savings banks would then seem to be useful institutions because they are vicious only up to a certain point. Savings banks are the most efficient institutions for aggregating capital which we possess. That is the most useful function which they perform, when we regard them from the standpoint of society, not of the individual depositor. In fact, we must believe that, if the motives of thrift could be made to actuate the population far more widely than they now do, resources of capital could be found in the increased savings of the mass of the population of which we have at present but little idea. Savings are like taxes: if you want big results you must look to the aggregation of millions of small sums from the whole population, not to the aggregate of a few big sums from the millionaires.

In this connection the movement of the current rate of interest, regarding that rate as a stimulus to saving, is a very interesting and important phenomenon. If we knew more about the causes of the fluctuations of the

interest rate we should gain a deeper insight than we now
possess into some of the operations of the industrial
system; especially we should gain a text which we very
much need for the effects of legislation and taxes. The
rate at present favors the borrower, not the depositor.
If such a tendency of the rate was a result of an accumulation of capital more rapid than the extension of enterprise,
it would no doubt be advantageous; it would bring
about a reaction which would produce readjustments
and would be ultimately healthful. I find it difficult to
conceive of an increase of capital in excess of the extension
of enterprise, under the circumstances of industry and of
public temper which characterize our society. The fact
that the interest rate is as low here as in Western Europe,
or even lower, seems to me to be abnormal and even
irrational. It seems to me to point to errors of legislation. Our people have been congratulating themselves
for two years on an enormous balance of trade in our favor.
We have had large crops of cereals when other people
had small ones, and so we have sold the whole at high
prices; and the consequence is that we have paid our debts,
have got out of bad times into good ones, have dispelled
our political anxieties, and have capital out in Europe.
But when we try to draw home our credits we find that
our rate of interest falls — within a year we have seen it
fall a full point. I find one statesman quoted in a newspaper as saying: "If present conditions continue, it looks
as if all the gold in the world will come into the United
States." That is probably the most grotesque notion
that could enter anybody's head. It seems clear that the
fluctuation which we have experienced does not correspond
to the normal action of the forces which should produce
the rate of interest, and that the effects of it are not
subject for congratulation. A higher rate than that now

prevailing would give tone to the money market; it would be a benefit to small investors; it would remove perils which threaten speculation, and would lessen the dangers of discount banking; it would be a benefit to enterprise by giving greater steadiness and sobriety, especially as to the future; it would restore the relation which should exist between a new country and old ones. How can things be in a normal and healthful condition when we cannot earn greater interest on capital in a new country than what people will bid for it in old ones?

I was led to notice the rate of interest because I was speaking of the possible increase in the accumulation of capital which might be produced if the motives of saving could be stimulated throughout the mass of the people. By the side of the facts to which I have referred, and which are sometimes interpreted as showing that the formation of capital at present outstrips the extension of enterprise, there are other facts which show enormous demand for capital on account of unprecedented extensions of enterprise. It is idle folly to meet these phenomena with wailings about the danger of the accumulation of great wealth in few hands. The phenomena themselves prove that we have tasks to perform which require large aggregations of capital. Moreover, the capital, to be effective, must be in few hands, for the simple reason that there are very few men who are able to handle great aggregations of capital. This is also the reason why the attempts to execute great enterprises by the state or municipality, that is, by elected officers, especially in a democratic republic, are sure to be wasteful and comparative failures. The men who are competent to organize great enterprises and to handle great amounts of capital must be found by natural selection, not by political election. It is plainly childish to attack those elements of a case which are essential to it. If the aim is to establish tests and guarantees, or regulations, then there is room for discussion, but it is evident folly to say that we want a certain result and then to say that we will not consent to the most fundamental conditions of what we want. The aggregation of large amounts of capital in few hands is the first condition of the fulfilment of the most important tasks of civilization which now confront us. If, therefore, the view which I have suggested is correct — that, in spite of some present appearances to the contrary, there is to be, in the near future, a greatly increased demand for capital — then a great increase of the popular desire to save would be contributory to the present needs of society.

I have suggested, in this paper, that the savings bank depositor gets an education and development of character from the practise of saving. He gets a point of view and a way of looking at things which are substantially the same as those of all capitalists. The seats-full of savings bank depositors whom I mentioned at the outset incurred the ire of the agitator because they showed this. He was addressing poor men and men of the wages class, to which they belonged, but instead of responding to his class appeal as he wanted them to do, they showed the sentiments of the capitalist class. Hence his dissatisfaction with them. We have had experience of the political value and importance of the same conservative sentiments and property interests of the small capitalists. It is a matter for regret that the savings bank depositor does not know more about the investment of his own savings. If he knew, so to express it, where his money is, how it is being used, how the interest which he receives is won, and what is the nature of the political risks and perils to which his savings may be exposed, the social and political consequences would be most beneficial.

I once also heard another orator who was dilating upon the ills of life declare that the great cause of human woe was the "devil of interest." There is no doubt that interest is an awful devil. Your feeling towards this devil, however, depends on whether you are working for him or he is working for you. If you are working for him, especially if you have bound yourself to terms which are imprudent, beyond your strength, and full of gambling risk, then he is an awful taskmaster. You dare not eat, or sleep, or play. Pay-day seems to come every other day. Instead of winning release by work, you may see your load grow bigger and bigger, in spite of all you do, until you come to ruin. Therefore, when you are going to work for him, which we all have to do sometimes, you must be sure that you undertake only what you can accomplish within the conditions in which you find yourself. But if the devil of interest is working for you, he will work while you eat, and sleep, and play, and while you work to earn more. You must be careful to have him well harnessed and to give him proper superintendence and directions. Then, if time seems to you to slip away rapidly, and if old age comes on apace, the devil of interest will give you the only consolation you can get for your failing powers. When you turn to your savings bank book you will see that your capital is increasing just as rapidly as the flight of time, and that it will be ready to support your existence when your ability to work gives out. I have spoken about the power and beneficence of capital to maintain civilization; this last is its power and beneficence to guide the fate and sustain the happiness of the individual.

THE PHILOSOPHY OF STRIKES [1]

THE progress in material comfort which has been made during the last hundred years has not produced content. Quite the contrary: the men of to-day are not nearly so contented with life on earth as their ancestors were. This observation is easily explainable by familiar facts in human nature. If satisfaction does not reach to the pitch of satiety, it does not produce content, but discontent; it is therefore a stimulus to more effort, and is essential to growth. If, however, we confine our study of the observation which we have made to its sociological aspects, we perceive that all which we call "progress" is limited by the counter-movements which it creates, and we also see the true meaning of the phenomena which have led some to the crude and silly absurdity that progress makes us worse off. Progress certainly does not make people happier, unless their mental and moral growth corresponds to the greater command of material comfort which they win. All that we call progress is a simple enlargement of chances, and the question of personal happiness is a question of how the chances will be used. It follows that if men do not grow in their knowledge of life and in their intelligent judgment of the rules of right living as rapidly as they gain control over physical resources, they will not win happiness at all. They will simply accumulate chances which they do not know how to use.

The observation which has just been made about individual happiness has also a public or social aspect which is important. It is essential that the political institutions,

[1] *Harper's Weekly*, September 15, 1883

the social code, and the accepted notions which constitute
public opinion should develop in equal measure with the
increase of power over nature. The penalty of failure to
maintain due proportion between the popular philosophy
of life and the increase of material comfort will be social
convulsions, which will arrest civilization and will subject
the human race to such a reaction toward barbarism as
that which followed the fall of the Roman Empire. It
is easy to see that at the present moment our popular
philosophy of life is all in confusion. The old codes are
breaking down; new ones are not yet made; and even
amongst people of standing, to whom we must look to
establish the body of public opinion, we hear the most
contradictory and heterogeneous doctrines about life and
society.

The growth of the United States has done a great deal
to break up the traditional codes and creeds which had
been adopted in Europe. The civilized world being divided
into two parts, one old and densely populated and the other
new and thinly populated, social phenomena have been
produced which, although completely covered by the same
laws of social force, have appeared to be contradictory.
The effect has been to disturb and break up the faith of
philosophers and students in the laws, and to engender
numberless fallacies amongst those who are not careful
students. The popular judgment especially has been dis-
ordered and misled. The new country has offered such
chances as no generation of men has ever had before. It
has not, however, enabled any man to live without work,
or to keep capital without thrift and prudence; it has not
enabled a man to "rise in the world" from a position of
ignorance and poverty, and at the same time to marry
early, spend freely, and bring up a large family of children.

The men of this generation, therefore, without distinction of class, and with only individual exceptions, suffer

from the discontent of an appetite excited by a taste of luxury, but held far below satiety. The power to appreciate a remote future good, in comparison with a present one, is a distinguishing mark of highly civilized men, but if it is not combined with powers of persevering industry and self-denial, it degenerates into mere day-dreaming and the diseases of an overheated imagination. If any number of persons are of this character, we have morbid discontent and romantic ambition as social traits. Our literature, especially our fiction, bears witness to the existence of classes who are corrupted by these diseases of character. We find classes of persons who are whining and fault-finding, and who use the organs of public discussion and deliberation in order to put forth childish complaints and impossible demands, while they philosophize about life like the *Arabian Nights*. Of course this whole tone of thought and mode of behavior is as far as possible from the sturdy manliness which meets the problems of life and wins victories as much by what it endures as by what it conquers.

Our American life, by its ease, exerts another demoralizing effect on a great many of us. Hundreds of our young people grow up without any real discipline; life is made easy for them, and their tastes and wishes are consulted too much; they grow to maturity with the notion that they ought to find the world only pleasant and easy. Every one knows this type of young person, who wants to find an occupation which he would "like," and who discusses the drawbacks of difficulty or disagreeableness in anything which offers. The point here referred to is, of course, entirely different from another and still more lamentable fact, that is, the terrible inefficiency and incapability of a great many of the people who are complaining and begging. If any one wants a copyist, he will be more saddened than annoyed by the overwhelming applications for the position. The advertisements which are to be found in the newspapers of widest circulation, offering a genteel occupation to be carried on at home, not requiring any previous training, by which two or three dollars a day may be earned, are a proof of the existence of a class to which they appeal. How many thousand people in the United States want just that kind of employment! What a beautiful world this would be if there were any such employment!

Then, again, our social ambition is often silly and mischievous. Our young people despise the occupations which involve physical effort or dirt, and they struggle "up" (as we have agreed to call it) into all the nondescript and irregular employments which are clean and genteel. Our orators and poets talk about the "dignity of labor," and neither they nor we believe in it. Leisure, not labor, is dignified. Nearly all of us, however, have to sacrifice our dignity, and labor, and it would be to the purpose if, instead of declamation about dignity, we should learn to respect, in ourselves and each other, work which is good of its kind, no matter what the kind is. To spoil a good shoemaker in order to make a bad parson is surely not going "up"; and a man who digs well is by all sound criteria superior to the man who writes ill. Everybody who talks to American schoolboys thinks that he does them and his country service if he reminds them that each one of them has a chance to be President of the United States, and our literature is all the time stimulating the same kind of senseless social ambition, instead of inculcating the code and the standards which should be adopted by orderly, sober, and useful citizens.

The consequences of the observations which have now been grouped together are familiar to us all. Population tends from the country to the city. Mechanical and technical occupations are abandoned, and those occupations which are easy and genteel are overcrowded. Of course the persons in question must be allowed to take their own choice, and seek their own happiness in their own way, but it is inevitable that thousands of them should be disappointed and suffer. If the young men abandon farms and trades to become clerks and bookkeepers, the consequence will be that the remuneration of the crowded occupations will fall, and that of the neglected occupations will rise; if the young women refuse to do housework, and go into shops, stores, telegraph offices and schools, the wages of the crowded occupations will fall, while those of domestic servants advance. If women in seeking occupation try to gain admission to some business like telegraphing, in competition with men, they will bid under the men. Similar effects would be produced if a leisure class in an old country should be compelled by some social convulsion to support themselves. They would run down the compensation for labor in the few occupations which they could enter.

Now the question is raised whether there is any remedy for the low wages of the crowded occupations, and the question answers itself: there is no remedy except not to continue the causes of the evil. To strike, that is, to say that the workers will not work in their chosen line, yet that they will not leave it for some other line, is simply suicide. Neither can any amount of declamation, nor even of law-making, force a man who owns a business to submit the control of it to a man who does not own it. The telegraphers have an occupation which requires training and skill, but it is one which is very attractive in many respects to those who seek manual occupation; it is also an occupation which is very suitable, at least in many of its branches, for women. The occupation is therefore capable of a limited monopoly. The demand that women should be paid equally with men is, on the face of it, just, but its real effect would be to keep women out of the business. It was often said during the telegraphers' strike that the demand of the strikers was just, because their wages were less than those of artisans. The argument has no force at all. The only question was whether the current wages for telegraphing were sufficient to bring out an adequate supply of telegraphers. If the growing boys prefer to be artisans, the wages of telegraphers will rise. If, even at present rates, boys and girls continue to prefer telegraphing to handicraft or housework, the wages of telegraphers will fall. Could, then, a strike advance at a blow the wages of all who are now telegraphers? There was only one reason to hope so, and that was that the monopoly of the trade might prove stringent enough and the public inconvenience great enough to force a concession — which would, however, have been speedily lost again by an increased supply of telegraphers.

Now let us ask what the state of the case would be if it was really possible for the telegraphers to make a successful strike. They have a very close monopoly; six years ago they nearly arrested the transportation of the country for a fortnight; but they were unable to effect their object. More recently the freight-handlers struck against the competition of a new influx of foreign unskilled laborers, and in vain. The printers might make a combination, and try to force an advance in wages by arresting the publication of all the newspapers on a given day, but there are so many persons who could set type, in case of need, that such an attempt would be quite hopeless. In any branch of ordinary handicraft there would be no possibility of creating a working monopoly or of producing a great public calamity by a strike. If we go on to other occupations we see that bookkeepers, clerks, and salesmen could not as a body combine and strike; much less could teachers do so; still less could household servants do so. Finally, farmers and other independent workers could not do it at all. In short, a striker is a man who says: "I mean to get my living by doing this thing and no other thing as my share of the social effort, and I do not mean to do this thing except on such and such terms." He therefore proposes to make a contract with his fellow-men and to dictate the terms of it. Any man who can do this must be in a very exceptional situation; he must have a monopoly of the service in question, and it must be one of which his fellow-men have great need. If, then, the telegraphers could have succeeded in advancing their wages fifteen per cent simply because they had agreed to ask for the advance, they must have been far better off than any of the rest of their fellowmen.

Our fathers taught us the old maxim: Cut your coat according to your cloth; but the popular discussions of social questions seem to be leading up to a new maxim: Demand your cloth according to your coat. The fathers thought that a man in this world must do the best he could with the means he had, and that good training and education consisted in developing skill, sagacity, and thrift to use resources economically; the new doctrine seems to be that if a man has been born into this world he should make up his mind what he needs here, formulate his demands, and present them to "society" or to the "state." He wants congenial and easy occupation, and good pay for it. He does not want to be hampered by any limitations such as come from a world in which wool grows, but not coats; in which iron ore is found, but not weapons and tools; in which the ground will produce wheat, but only after hard labor and self-denial; in which we cannot eat our cake and keep it; in which two and two make only four. He wants to be guaranteed a "market," so as not to suffer from "overproduction." In private life and in personal relations we already estimate this way of looking at things at its true value, but as soon as we are called upon to deal with a general question, or a phenomenon of industry in which a number of persons are interested, we adopt an entirely conventional and unsound mode of discussion. The sound gospel of industry, prudence, painstaking, and thrift is, of course, unpopular; we all long to be emancipated from worry, anxiety, disappointment, and the whole train of cares which fall upon us as we work our way through the world. Can we really gain anything in that struggle by organizing for a battle with each other? This is the practical question. Is there any ground whatever for believing that we shall come to anything, by pursuing this line of effort, which will be of any benefit to anybody? If a man is dissatisfied with his position, let him strive to better it in one way or another by such chances as he can find or make, and let him inculcate in his children good habits and sound notions, so that they may live wisely and not expose themselves to hardship by error or folly; but every experiment only makes it more clear that for men to band together in order to carry on an industrial war, instead of being a remedy for disappointment in the ratio of satisfaction to effort, is only a way of courting new calamity.

STRIKES AND THE INDUSTRIAL ORGANIZATION [1]

ANYONE who has read with attention the current discussion of labor topics must have noticed that writers start from assumptions, in regard to the doctrine of wages, which are as divergent as notions on the same subject-matter well can be. It appears, therefore, that we must have a dogma of wages, that we cannot reason correctly about the policy or the rights of the wages system until we have such a dogma, and that, in the meantime, it is not strange that confusion and absurdity should be the chief marks of discussion carried on before this prime condition is fulfilled.

Some writers assume that wages can be raised if the prices of products be raised, and that no particular difficulty would be experienced in raising prices; others assume that wages could be raised if the employers would be satisfied with smaller profits for themselves; still others assume that wages could be raised or lowered according as the cost of living rises or falls. These are common and popular assumptions, and have nothing to do with the controversies of professional economists about the doctrine of wages. The latter are a disgrace to the science, and have the especial evil at this time that the science cannot respond to the chief demand now made upon it.

If the employer could simply add any increase of wages to his prices, and so recoup himself at the expense of the consumer, no employer would hold out long against a strike. Why should he? Why should he undertake loss,

[1] *Popular Science News*, July, 1887.

worry, and war, for the sake of the consumers behind him? If an employer need only submit to a positive and measurable curtailment of his profits, in order to avoid a strike and secure peace, it is probable that he would in almost every case submit to it. But if the employees should demand five per cent advance, and the employer should grant it, adding so much to his prices, they would naturally and most properly immediately demand another five per cent, to be charged to the consumers in the same way. There would be no other course for men of common sense to pursue. They would repeat this process until at some point or other they found themselves arrested by some resistance which they could not overcome. Similarly, if wages could be increased at the expense of the employer's gains, the employer who yielded one increase would have to yield another, until at some point he decided to refuse and resist. In either case, where and what would the limit be? Whenever the point was reached at which some unconquerable resistance was encountered, the task of the economist would begin.

There is no rule whatever for determining the share which any one ought to get out of the distribution of products through the industrial organization, except that he should get all that the market will give him in return for what he has put into it. Whenever, therefore, the limit is reached, the task of the economist is to find out the conditions by which this limit is determined.

Now it is the character of the modern industrial system that it becomes more and more impersonal and automatic under the play of social forces which act with natural necessity; the system could not exist if they did not so act, for it is constructed in reliance upon their action according to ascertainable laws. The condition of all social actions and reactions is therefore set in the nature of the forces which we have learned to know on other fields of scientific investigation, and which are different here only inasmuch as they act in a different field and on different material. The relations of parties, therefore, in the industrial organism is such as the nature of the case permits. The case may permit of a variety of relations, thus providing some range of choice.

A person who comes into the market, therefore, with something to sell, cannot raise the price of it because he wants to do so, or because his "cost of production" has been raised. He has already pushed the market to the utmost, and raised the price as high as supply and demand would allow, so as to win as large profits as he could. How, then, can he raise it further, just because his own circumstances make it desirable for him so to do? If the market stands so that he can raise his price, he will do it, whether his cost of production has increased or not. Neither can an employer reduce his own profits at will; he will immediately perceive that he is going out of business, and distributing his capital in presents.

The difficulty with a strike, therefore, is, that it is an attempt to move the whole industrial organization, in which all the parts are interdependent and intersupporting. It is not, indeed, impossible to do this, although it is very difficult. The organization has a great deal of elasticity in its parts — an aggressive organ can win something at the expense of others. Everything displaces everything else; but if force enough is brought to bear, a general displacement and readjustment may be brought about. An organ which has been suffering from the aggression of others may right itself. It is only by the collision of social pressure, constantly maintained, that the life of the organism is kept up, and its forces are developed to their full effect.

Strikes are not necessarily connected with violence to either persons or property. Violence is provided for by the criminal law. Taking strikes by themselves, therefore, it may be believed that they are not great evils; they are costly, but they test the market. Supply and demand does not mean that the social forces will operate of themselves; the law, as laid down, assumes that every party will struggle to the utmost for its interests — if it does not do so, it will lose its interests. Buyers and sellers, borrowers and lenders, landlords and tenants, employers and employees, and all other parties to contracts, must be expected to develop their interests fully in the competition and struggle of life. It is for the health of the industrial organization that they should do so. The other social interests are in the constant habit of testing the market, in order to get all they can out of it. A strike, rationally begun and rationally conducted, only does the same thing for the wage-earning interest.

The facts stare us plainly in the face, if we will only look at them, that the wages of the employees and the price of the products have nothing to do with each other; that the wages have nothing to do with the profits of the employer; that they have nothing to do with the cost of living or with the prosperity of the business. They are really governed by the supply and demand of labor, as every strike shows us, and by nothing else.

Turning to the moral relations of the subject, we are constantly exhorted to do something to improve the relations of employer and employee. I submit that the relation in life which has the least bad feeling or personal bitterness in it is the pure business relation, the relation of contract, because it is a relation of bargain and consent and equivalence. Where is there so much dissension and bitterness as in family matters, where people try to act by sentiment and affection? The way to improve the relation of employer and employee is not to get sentiment into it, but to get sentiment out of it. We are told that classes are becoming more separated, and that the poor are learning to hate the rich, although there was a time when no class hatreds existed. I have sought diligently in history for the time when no class hatreds existed between rich and poor. I cannot find any such period, and I make bold to say that no one can point to it.

THE INFLUENCE OF COMMERCIAL CRISES ON OPINIONS ABOUT ECONOMIC DOCTRINES [1]

ANY ONE who follows the current literature about economic subjects will perceive that it is so full of contradictions as to create a doubt whether there are any economic laws, or whether, if there are any, we know anything about them. No body of men ever succeeded in molding the opinions of others by wrangling with each other, and that is the present attitude in which the economists present themselves before the public. Like other people who engage in wrangling, the economists have also allowed their method to degenerate from argument to abuse, contempt, and sneering disparagement of each other. The more superficial and self-sufficient the opinions and behavior of the disputants, the more absolutely they abandon sober arguments and devote themselves to the method I have described. As I have little taste for this kind of discussion and believe that it only degrades the science of which I am a student, I have taken no part in it. In answer to your invitation, now, what I propose to do is to call your attention to some features of the economic situation of civilized nations at the present time with a view to establish two points:

1. To explain the vacillation and feebleness of opinions about economic doctrine which mark the present time, and

2. To show the necessity, just at this time, of calm and sober apprehension of sound doctrine in political economy.

At the outset let me ask you to notice the effects which

[1] An address before The Free Trade Club, New York City, May 15, 1879.

have been produced during the last century by the developments of science and of the industrial arts. Formerly, industry was pursued on a small scale, with little or no organization. Markets were limited to small districts, and commerce was confined to raw materials and colonial products. Producer and consumer met face to face. The conditions of the market were open to personal inspection. The relations of supply and demand were matters of personal experience. Production was carried on for orders only in many branches of industry, so that supply and demand were fitted to one another, as we may say, physically. Disproportionate production was, therefore, prevented and the necessity of redistributing productive effort was made plain by the most direct personal experience. Under such a state of things, much time must elapse between the formation of a wish and its realization.

Within a century very many and various forces have been at work to produce an entire change in this system of industry. The invention of the steam engine and of the machines used in the textile fabrics produced the factory system, with a high organization of industry, concentrated at certain centers. The opening of canals and the improvement of highways made possible the commerce by which the products were distributed. The cheapening of printing and the multiplication of means of advertising widened the market by concentrating the demand which was widely dispersed in place, until now the market is the civilized world. The applications of steam power to roads and ships only extended further the same development, and the telegraph has only cheapened and accelerated the means of communicating information to the same end.

What have been the effects on industry?

1. The whole industry and commerce of the world have been built up into a great system in which organization has become essential and in which it has been carried forward

and is being carried forward every day to new developments. Industry has been growing more and more impersonal as far as the parties to it are concerned. Our wants are satisfied instantaneously and regularly by the coöperation of thousands of people all over the world whom we have never seen or heard of; and we earn our living daily by contributing to satisfy the wants of thousands scattered all over the world, of whom we know nothing personally. In the place of actual contact and acquaintance with the persons who are parties to the transactions, we now depend upon the regularity, under the conditions of earthly life, of human wants and human efforts. The system of industry is built upon the constancy of certain conditions of human existence, upon the certainty of the economic forces which thence arise, and upon the fact that those forces act with perfect regularity under changeless laws. If we but reflect a moment, we shall see that modern industry and commerce could not go on for a day if we were not dealing here with forces and laws which may properly be called natural because they come into action when the conditions are fulfilled, because the conditions cannot but exist if there is a society of human beings collected anywhere on earth, and because, when the forces come into action, they work themselves out, according to their laws, without possible escape from their effects. We can divert the forces from one course to another; we can change their form; we can make them expend themselves upon one person or interest instead of upon another. We do this all the time, by bad legislation, by prejudice, habit, fashion, erroneous notions of equity, happiness, the highest good, and so on; but we never destroy an economic force any more than we destroy a physical force.

2. Of course it follows that success in the production of wealth under this modern system depends primarily on the correctness with which men learn the character of

economic forces and of the laws under which those forces act. This is the field of the science of political economy, and it is the reason why it is a science. It investigates the laws of forces which are natural, not arbitrary, artificial, or conventional. Some communities have developed a great hatred for persons who held different religious opinions from themselves. Such a feeling would be a great social force, but it would be arbitrary and artificial. Many communities have held that all labor, not mental, was slavish and degrading. This notion, too, was conventional, but it was a great social force where it existed. Such notions, either past or present, are worth studying for historical interest and instruction, but they do not afford the basis for a science whose object is to find out what is true in regard to the relations of man to the world in which he lives. The study of them throws a valuable sidelight on the true relations of human life, just as the study of error always throws a sidelight upon the truth, but they have no similarity to the law that men want the maximum of satisfaction for the minimum of effort, or to the law of the diminishing return from land, or to the law of population, or to the law of supply and demand. Nothing can be gained, therefore, by mixing up history and science, valuable as one is to the other. If men try to carry on any operation without an intelligent theory of the forces with which they are dealing, they inevitably become the victims of the operation, not its masters. Hence they always do try to form some theory of the forces in question and to plan the means to the end accordingly. The forces of nature go on and are true only to themselves. They never swerve out of pity for innocent error or well-intentioned mistakes. This is as true of economic forces as of any others. What is meant by a good or a bad investment, except that one is based on a correct judgment of forces and the other on incorrect judgment? How would sagacity,

care, good judgment, and prudence meet their reward if
the economic forces swerved out of pity for error? We
know that there is no such thing in the order of nature.

I repeat, then, that the modern industrial and commercial system, dealing as it does with vast movements which
no one mind can follow or compass in their ramifications
and which are kept in harmony by natural laws, demands
steadily advancing, clear, and precise knowledge of economic laws; that this knowledge must banish prejudices
and traditions; that it must conquer baseless enthusiasms
and whimsical hopes. If it does not accomplish this, we
can expect but one result — that men will chase all sorts
of phantoms and impossible hopes; that they will waste
their efforts upon schemes which can only bring loss; and
that some will run one way and some another until society
loses all coherence, all unanimity of judgment as to what
is to be sought and how to attain to it. The destruction
of capital is only the least of the evils to be apprehended
in such a case. I do not believe that we begin to appreciate
one effect of the new civilization of the nineteenth century,
viz., that the civilized world of to-day is a unit, that it
must move as a whole, that with the means we have devised of a common consent in regard to the ends of human
life and the means of attaining them has come also the
necessity that we should move onward in civilization by a
common consent. The barriers of race, religion, language,
and nationality are melting away under the operation of
the same forces which have to such an extent annihilated
the obstacles of distance and time. Civilization is constantly becoming more uniform. The conquests of some
become at once the possession of all. It follows that our
scientific knowledge of the laws which govern the life of
men in society must keep pace with this development or
we shall find our social tasks grow faster than our knowledge of social science, and our society will break to pieces

under the burden. How, then, is this scientific knowledge to grow? Certainly not without controversy, but certainly also not without coherent, steady, and persistent effort, proceeding on the lines already cut, breaking new ground when possible, correcting old errors when necessary.

3. It is another feature of the modern industrial system that, like every high organization, it requires men of suitable ability and skill at its head. The qualities which are required for a great banker, merchant, or manufacturer are as rare as any other great gifts among men, and the qualities demanded, or the degree in which they are demanded, are increasing every day with the expansion of the modern industrial system. The qualities required are those of the practical man, properly so called: sagacity, good judgment, prudence, boldness, and energy. The training, both scientific and practical, which is required for a great master of industry is wide and various. The great movements of industry, like all other great movements, present subordinate phenomena which are apparently opposed to, or inconsistent with their great tendencies and their general character. These phenomena, being smaller in scope, more directly subject to observation and therefore apparently more distinct and positive, are well calculated to mislead the judgment, either of the practical man or of the scientific student. In nothing, therefore, does the well-trained man distinguish himself from the ill-trained man more than in the balance of judgment by which he puts phenomena in their true relative position and refuses to be led astray by what is incidental or subsidiary. If, now, the question is asked, whether we have produced a class of highly trained men, competent to organize labor, transportation, commerce, and banking, on the scale required by the modern system, as rapidly as the need for them has increased, I believe no one will answer in the affirmative.

4. Another observation to which we are led upon notic-

ing the character of the modern industrial system is that
any errors or follies committed in one portion of it will
produce effects which will ramify through the whole system. We have here an industrial organism, not a mere
mechanical combination, and any disturbance in one part
of it will derange or vitiate, more or less, the whole. The
phenomena which here appear belong to what has been
called fructifying causation. One economic error produces
fruits which combine with those of another economic error,
and the product of the two is not their sum, nor even their
simple product, but the evil may be raised to a very high
power by the combination. If a number of errors fall together the mischief is increased accordingly. Currency and
tariff errors constantly react upon each other, and multiply and develop each other in this way. Furthermore, the
errors of one nation will be felt in other nations through
the relations of commerce and credit which are now so
close. There is no limit to the interest which civilized
nations have in each other's economic and political wisdom,
for they all bear the consequences of each other's follies.
Hence when we have to deal with that form of economic
disease which we call a commercial crisis, we may trace
its origin to special errors in one country and in another,
and may trace out the actions and reactions by which the
effects have been communicated from one to another until
shared by all; but no philosophy of a great commercial
crisis is adequate nowadays unless it embraces in its scope
the whole civilized world. A commercial crisis is a disturbance in the harmonious operation of the parts of the industrial organism. During economic health, the system
moves smoothly and harmoniously, expanding continually,
and its health and vigor are denoted by its growth, that is,
by the accumulation of capital, which stimulates in its
turn the hope, energy, and enterprise of men. Industrial
disease is produced by disproportionate production, a

wrong distribution of labor, erroneous judgment in enterprise, or miscalculations of force. These all have the same effect, *viz.*, to waste and destroy capital. Such causes disturb, in a greater or less degree, the harmonious working of the system, which depends upon the regular and exact fulfillment of the expectations which have been based on coöperative effort throughout the whole industrial body. The disturbance may be slight and temporary, or it may be very serious. In the latter case it will be necessary to arrest the movement of the whole system and to proceed to a general liquidation, before starting again. Such was the case from 1837 to 1842, and such has been the case for the last five years. It is needless to add that this arrest and liquidation cannot be accomplished without distress and loss to great numbers of innocent persons, and great positive loss of capital, to say nothing of what might have been won during the same period but must be foregone.

The financial organization is the medium by which the various parts of the industrial and commercial organism are held in harmony. It is by the financial organization that capital is collected and distributed, that the friction of exchanges is reduced to a minimum, and that time is economized, through credit, between production and consumption. The financial system furnishes three indicators — prices, the rate of discount, and the foreign exchanges — through which we may read the operation of economic forces now that their magnitude makes it impossible to inspect them directly. Hence the great mischief of usury laws which tamper with the rate of discount, and of fluctuating currencies which falsify prices and the foreign exchanges. They destroy the value of the indicators, and have the same effect as tampering with the scales of a chemist or the steam-gauge of a locomotive.

In the matter of prices we have another difficulty to contend with, which is inevitable in the nature of things.

We must choose some commodity to be the denominator of value. We can find no commodity which is not itself subject to fluctuation in its ratio of exchange with other things. Great crises have been caused in past times by fluctuations in the value of the commodities chosen as money, and such an element is, no doubt, at hand in the present crisis, although it had nothing to do with bringing it about. It follows that any improvement in the world's money is worth any sacrifice which it can possibly cost, if it tends to secure a more simple, exact, and unchanging standard of value.

The next point of which I wish to speak is easily introduced by the last remark; that point is the cost of all improvement. The human race has made no step whatever in civilization which has not been won by pain and distress. It wins no steps now without paying for them in sacrifices. To notice only things which are directly pertinent to our present purpose: every service which we win from nature displaces the acquired skill of the men who formerly performed the service; every such step is a gain to the race, but it imposes on some men the necessity of finding new means of livelihood, and if those men are advanced in life, this necessity may be harsh in the extreme. Every new machine, although it saves labor, and because it saves labor, serves the human race, yet destroys a vested interest of some laborers in the work which it performs. It imposes on them the necessity of turning to a new occupation, and this is hardly ever possible without a period of distress. It very probably throws them down from the rank of skilled to that of unskilled labor. Every new machine also destroys capital. It makes useless the half-worn-out machines which it supersedes. So canals caused capital which was invested in turnpikes and state coaches to depreciate, and so railroads have caused the capital invested in canals and other forms to depreciate. I see no exception to the rule that the progress won by the race is always won at the expense of some group of its members.

Any one who will look back upon the last twenty-five years cannot fail to notice that the changes, advances, and improvements have been numerous and various. We are accustomed to congratulate each other upon them. There can be no doubt that they must and will contribute to the welfare of the human race beyond what any one can now possibly foresee or measure. I am firmly convinced, for my opinion, that the conditions of wealth and civilization for the next quarter of a century are provided for in excess of any previous period of history, and that nothing but human folly can prevent a period of prosperity which we, even now, should regard as fabulous. We can throw it away if we are too timid, if we become frightened at the rate of our own speed, or if we mistake the phenomena of a new era for the approach of calamity, or if the nations turn back to mediæval darkness and isolation, or if we elevate the follies and ignorances of the past into elements of economic truth, or if, instead of pursuing liberty with full faith and hope, the civilized world becomes the arena of a great war of classes in which all civilization must be destroyed. But, such follies apart, the conditions of prosperity are all provided.

We must notice, however, that these innovations have fallen with great rapidity upon a vast range of industries, that they have accumulated their effects, that they have suddenly altered the currents of trade and the methods of industry, and that we have hardly learned to accommodate ourselves to one new set of circumstances before a newer change or modification has been imposed. Some inventions, of which the Bessemer steel is the most remarkable example, have revolutionized industries. Some new channels of commerce have been opened which have changed the character and methods of very important branches of commerce. We have also seen a movement of several nations to secure a gold currency, which movement fell in with a large if not extraordinary production of silver and altered the comparative demand and supply of the two metals at the same time. This movement had nothing arbitrary about it, but proceeded from sound motives and reasons in the interest of the nations which took this step. There is here no ground for condemnation or approval. Such action by sovereign nations is taken under liberty and responsibility to themselves alone, and if it is taken on a sufficiently large scale to form an event of importance to the civilized world, it must be regarded as a step in civilization. It can only be criticized by history. For the present, it is to be accepted and interpreted only as an indication that there are reasons and motives of self-interest which can lead a large part of the civilized world to this step at this time.

The last twenty-five years have also included political events which have had great effects on industry. Our Civil War caused an immense destruction of capital and left a large territory with millions of inhabitants almost entirely ruined in its industry, and with its labor system exposed to the necessity of an entire re-formation. Part of the expenditures and losses of the war were postponed and distributed by means of the paper currency which, instead of imposing industry and economy to restore the losses and waste, created the foolish belief that we could make war and get rich by it. The patriotic willingness of the nation to be taxed was abused to impose taxes for protection, not for revenue, so that the industry of the country was distorted and forced into unnatural development. The collapse of 1873, followed by a fall in prices and a general liquidation, was due to the fact that every one knew in his heart that the state of things which had existed for some years before was hollow and fictitious. Confidence failed because every one knew that there were no real grounds for confidence. The Franco-Prussian war had, also, while it lasted, produced a period of false and feverish prosperity in England. It was succeeded by great political changes in Germany which, together with the war indemnity, led to a sudden and unfounded expansion of speculation, amounting to a mania. Germany undoubtedly stands face to face with a new political and industrial future, but she has postponed it by a headlong effort to realize it at once. In France, too, the war was followed by a hasty, and, as we are told, unwise extension of permanent capital, planned to meet the extraordinary demand of an empty market. In England the prosperity of 1870–1872 has been followed as usual by developments of unsound credit, bad banking, and needless investments in worthless securities.

Here then we have, in a brief and inadequate statement, circumstances in all these great industrial nations peculiar to each, yet certainly sufficient to account for a period of reaction and distress. We have also before us great features of change in the world's industry and commerce which must ultimately produce immeasurable advantages, but which may well, operating with local causes, produce temporary difficulty; and we have to notice also that the local causes react through the commercial and credit relations of nations to distribute the evil.

It is not surprising, under such a state of things, that some people should lose their heads and begin to doubt the economic doctrines which have been most thoroughly established. It belongs to the symptoms of disease to lose confidence in the laws of health and to have recourse to quack remedies. I have already observed that certain phenomena appear in every great social movement which are calculated to deceive by apparent inconsistency or divergence. Hence we have seen the economists, instead of holding together and sustaining, at the time when it was most needed, both the scientific authority and the positive truth of their doctrines, break up and run hither and thither, some of them running away altogether. Many of them seem to be terrified to find that distress and misery still remain on earth and promise to remain as long as the vices of human nature remain. Many of them are frightened at liberty, especially under the form of competition, which they elevate into a bugbear. They think that it bears harshly on the weak. They do not perceive that here "the strong" and "the weak" are terms which admit of no definition unless they are made equivalent to the industrious and the idle, the frugal and the extravagant. They do not perceive, furthermore, that if we do not like the survival of the fittest, we have only one possible alternative, and that is the survival of the unfittest. The former is the law of civilization; the latter is the law of anti-civilization. We have our choice between the two, or we can go on, as in the past, vacillating between the two, but a third plan — the socialist desideratum — a plan for nourishing the unfittest and yet advancing in civilization, no man will ever find. Some of the crude notions, however, which have been put forward surpass what might reasonably have been expected. These have attached themselves to branches of the subject which it is worth while to notice.

1. As the change in the relative value of the precious metals is by far the most difficult and most important of the features of this period, it is quite what we might have expected that the ill-trained and dilettante writers should have pounced upon it as their special prey. The dabblers in philology never attempt anything less than the problem of the origin of language. Every teacher knows that he has to guard his most enthusiastic pupils against precipitate attempts to solve the most abstruse difficulties of the science. The change in the value of the precious metals which is going on will no doubt figure in history as one of

the most important events in the economic history of this century. It will undoubtedly cost much inconvenience and loss to those who are in the way of it, or who get in the way of it. It will, when the currency changes connected with it are accomplished, prove a great gain to the whole commercial world. The nations which make the change do so because it is important for their interests to do it. Now, suppose that it were possible for those who are frightened at the immediate and temporary inconveniences, to arrest the movement — the only consequence would be that they would arrest and delay the inevitable march of improvement in the industrial system.

2. The second field, which is an especial favorite with the class of writers which I have described, is that of prognostications as to what developments of the economic system lie in the future. Probably every one has notions about this and every one who has to conduct business or make investments is forced to form judgments about it. There is hardly a field of economic speculation, however, which is more barren.

3. The third field into which these writers venture by preference is that of remedies for existing troubles. The popular tide of medicine is always therapeutics, and the less one knows of anatomy and physiology the more sure he is to address himself exclusively to this department, and to rely upon empirical remedies. The same procedure is followed in social science, and it is accompanied by the same contempt for scientific doctrine and knowledge and remedies. To bring out the points which here seem to mè important, it will be necessary to go back for a moment to some facts which I have already described.

One of the chief characteristics of the great improvements in industry, which have been described, is that they bring about new distributions of population. If machinery displaces laborers engaged in manufactures, these laborers are driven to small shopkeeping, if they have a little capital; or to agricultural labor, if they have no capital. Improvements in commerce will destroy a local industry and force the laborers to find a new industry or to change their abode. When forces of this character coöperate on a grand scale, they may and do produce very important redistributions of population. In like manner legislation may, as tariff legislation does, draw population to certain places, and its repeal may force them to unwelcome change. We may state the fact in this way: let us suppose that, in 1850, out of every hundred laborers in the population, the economical distribution was such that fifty should be engaged in agriculture, thirty in manufacturing, and the other twenty in other pursuits. That is to say that, with the machinery and appliances then available, thirty manufacturing laborers could use the raw materials and food produced by fifty agricultural laborers so as to occupy all to the highest advantage. Now suppose that, by improvements in the arts, twenty men could, in 1880, use to the best advantage the raw materials and food produced by sixty in agriculture. It is evident that a redistribution would be necessary by which ten should be turned from manufacturing to land. That such a change has been produced within the last thirty years and that it has reached a point at which is setting in the counter movement to the former tendency from the land to the cities and towns, seems to me certain. There are even indications of great changes going on in the matter of distribution which will correct the loss and waste involved in the old methods of distribution long before any of the fancy plans for correcting them can be realized, and which are setting free both labor and capital in that department. Now if we can economize labor and capital in manufacturing, transportation, and distribution, and turn this labor and capital back upon the soil, we must vastly increase wealth, for that movement would enlarge the stream of wealth from its very source.

Right here, however, we need to make two observations.

1. The modern industrial system which I have described, with its high organization and fine division of labor, has one great drawback. The men, or groups of men, are dissevered from one another, their interests are often antagonistic, and the changes which occur take the form of conflicts of interest. I mean this: if a shoemaker worked alone, using a small capital of his own in tools and stock, and working for orders, he would have directly before him the facts of the market. He would find out without effort or reflection when "trade fell off," when there was risk of not replacing his capital, when the course of fashion or competition called upon him to find other occupation, and so on. When a journeyman shoemaker works for wages, he pays no heed to these things. The employer, feeling them, has no recourse but to lower wages. It is by this measure that, under the higher organization, the need of new energy, or of a change of industry, or of a change of place is brought home to the workman. To him, however, it seems an arbitrary and cruel act of the master. Hence follow trade wars and strikes as an especial phenomenon of the modern system. It is just because it is a system, or more properly still, an organism, that the readjustments which are necessary from time to time in order to keep its parts in harmonious activity, and to keep it in harmony with physical surroundings, are brought about through this play of the parts on each other.

2. A general movement of labor and capital towards land, throughout the civilized world, means a great migration towards the new countries. This does not by any means imply the abandonment or decay of older countries, as some have seemed to believe. On the contrary, it means new prosperity for them. When I read that the United

States are about to feed the world, not only with wheat and provisions, but with meat also, that they are to furnish coal and iron to mankind, that they are to displace all the older countries as exporters of manufactures, that they are to furnish the world's supply of the precious metals, and I know not what all besides, I am forced to ask what is the rest of the world going to do for us? What are they to give us besides tea, coffee, and sugar? Not ships, for we will not take them and are ambitious to carry away all our products ourselves. Certainly this is the most remarkable absurdity into which we have been led by forgetting that trade is an exchange. Neither can any one well expect that all mankind are to come and live here. The conditions of a large migration do, however, seem to exist. A migration of population is still a very unpopular idea in all the older states. The prejudice against it is apparent amongst Liberals and Tories, economists and sentimentalists. There is, however, a condition which is always suppressed in stating the social problem as it presents itself in hard times. That problem, as stated, is: "How are the population to find means of support?" and the suppressed condition is: "if they insist on staying and seeking support where they are and in pursuits to which they are accustomed." The hardships of change are not for one moment to be denied, but nothing is gained by sitting down to whine about them. The sentimental reasons for clinging to one's birthplace may be allowed full weight, but they cannot be allowed to counterbalance important advantages. I do not see that any but land owners are interested to hold population in certain places, unless possibly we add governing classes and those who want military power. When I read declamations about nationality and the importance of national divisions to political economy (observe that I do not say to political science), I never can find any sense in them, and I am very sure that the writers never put any sense into them.

We may now return to consider the remedies proposed for hard times. We shall see that although they are quack remedies, and although they set at defiance all the economic doctrines which have been so laboriously established during the last century, they are fitted to meet the difficulty as it presents itself to land owners, governments, military powers, socialists, and sentimentalists. The tendency is towards an industrial system controlled by a natural coöperation far grander than anybody has ever planned, towards a community of interest and welfare far more beneficent than any universal republic or fraternity of labor which the Internationalists hope for, and towards a free and peaceful rivalry amongst nations in the arts of civilization. It is necessary to stop this tendency. What are the means proposed?

1. The first is to put a limit to civil liberty. By civil liberty (for I feel at once the need of defining this much-abused word) I mean the status which is created for an individual by those institutions which guarantee him the use of his own powers for his own development. For three or four centuries now, the civilized world has been struggling towards the realization of this civil liberty. Progress towards it has been hindered by the notion that liberty was some vague abstraction, or an emancipation from some of the hard conditions of human life, from which men never can be emancipated while they live on this earth. Civil liberty has also been confused with political activity or share in civil government. Political activity itself, however, is only a means to an end, and is valuable because it is necessary to secure to the individual free exercise of his powers to produce and exchange according to his own choice and his own conception of happiness, and to secure him also that the products of his labor shall be applied to his satisfaction and not to that of any others. When we come to understand civil liberty for what it is, we shall probably

go forward to realize it more completely. It will then appear that it begins and ends with freedom of production, freedom of exchange, and security of property. It will then appear also that governments depart from their prime and essential function when they undertake to transfer property instead of securing it, and it may then be understood that legal tender laws, and protective tariffs as amongst the last and most ingenious devices for transferring one man's product to another man's use, are gross violations of civil liberty. At present the attempt is being made to decry liberty, to magnify the blunders and errors of men in the pursuit of happiness into facts which should be made the basis of generalizations about the functions of government, and to present the phenomena of the commercial crisis as reasons for putting industry once more in leading strings. It is only a new foe with an old face. Those who have held the leading strings of industry in time past have always taken rich pay for their services, and they will do it again.

2. The second form of remedy proposed is quite consistent with the last. It consists in rehabilitating the old and decaying superstition of government. It is called the state, and all kinds of poetical and fanciful attributes are ascribed to it. It is presented, of course, as a superior power, able and ready to get us out of trouble. If an individual is in trouble, he has to help himself or secure the help of friends as best he can, but if a group of persons are in trouble together, they constitute a party, a power, and begin to make themselves felt in the state. The state has no means of helping them except by enabling them to throw the risks and losses of their business upon other people who already have the burdens and losses of their own business to bear, but who are less well organized. The "state" assumes to judge what is for the public interest and imposes taxes or interferes with contracts to force individuals

to the course which will realize what it has set before itself. When, however, all the fine phrases are stripped away, it appears that the state is only a group of men with human interests, passions, and desires, or, worse yet, the state is, as somebody has said, only an obscure clerk hidden in some corner of a governmental bureau. In either case the assumption of superhuman wisdom and virtue is proved false. The state is only a part of the organization of society in and for itself. That organization secures certain interests and provides for certain functions which are important but which would otherwise be neglected. The task of society, however, has always been and is yet, to secure this organization, and yet to prevent the man in whose hands public power must at last be lodged from using it to plunder the governed—that is, to destroy liberty. This is what despots, oligarchs, aristocrats, and democrats always have done, and the latest development is only a new form of the old abuse. The abuses have always been perpetrated in the name of the public interest. It was for the public interest to support the throne and the altar. It was for the public interest to sustain privileged classes, to maintain an established church, standing armies, and the passport and police system. Now, it is for the public interest to have certain industries carried on, and the holders of the state power apportion their favor without rule or reason, without responsibility, and without any return service. In the end, therefore, the high function of the state to regulate the industrial organization in the public interest is simply that the governing group interferes to make some people give the products of their labor to other people to use and enjoy. Every one sees the evils of the state meddling with his own business and thinks that he ought to be let alone in it, but he sees great public interests which would be served if the state would interfere to make other people do what he wants to have them do.

Now if these two measures could be carried out — if liberty could be brought into misapprehension and contempt, and if the state-superstition could be saved from the decay to which it is doomed, the movements of population and the changes in industry, commerce, and finance, could be arrested. The condemnation of all such projects is, once and for all, that they would arrest the march of civilization. The joy and the fears which have been aroused on one side and on the other by the reactionary propositions which have been made during the last five years are both greatly exaggerated. Such reactionary propositions are in the nature of things at such a time. It must be expected that the pressure of distress and disappointed hopes will produce passionate reaction and senseless outcries. From such phenomena to actual practical measures is a long step. Every step towards practical realization of any reactionary measures will encounter new and multiplying obstacles. A war of tariffs at this time would so fly in the face of all the tendencies of commerce and industry that it would only hasten the downfall of all tariffs. Purely retaliatory tariffs are a case of what the children call "cutting off your nose to spite your face." Some follies have become physically impossible for great nations nowadays. Germany has been afflicted: first, by too eager hopes, second, by the great calamity of too many and too pedantic doctors, third, by a declining revenue, and fourth, by socialistic agitation amongst the new electors. It appears that she is about to abandon the free-trade policy although she does not embrace protection with much vigor. The project already comes in conflict with numerous and various difficulties which had not been foreseen, and, in its execution, it must meet with many more. The result remains to be studied. France finds that the expiration of each treaty of commerce produces consequences upon her industry which are unendurable, and while the task of adjusting rival and contending interests so as to create a new system drags along, she is compelled to ward off, by temporary arrangements, the revival of the general tariff which the treaties had superseded. In the meantime her economists, who are the most sober and the best trained in the world, are opening a a vigorous campaign on the general issue. If England should think of reviving protection, she would not know what to protect. If she wanted to retaliate, she could only tax raw materials and food. The proposition, as soon as it is reduced to practical form, has no footing. As for ourselves we know that our present protective system never could have been fastened upon us if it had not been concealed under the war legislation, and if its effects had not been confused with those of the war. It could not last now if the public mind could be freed from its absorption in sectional politics, so that it would be at liberty to turn to this subject.

In conclusion, let me refer again to another important subject on which I have touched in this paper — what we call the silver question. It would, no doubt, be in the power of civilized nations to take some steps which would alleviate the inconveniences connected with the transition of several important nations from a silver to a gold currency. For one nation, which has no share in the trouble at all, to come forward out of "magnanimity" or any other motive to save the world from the troubles incident to this step, is quixotic and ridiculous. It might properly leave those who are in the trouble to deal with it amongst themselves. Either they or all might, however, do much to modify the effects of the change. The effort to bring about an international union to establish a bimetallic currency at a fixed ratio is quite another thing. It will stand in the history of our time as the most singular folly which has gained any important adherence. As a practical measure the international union is simply impossible. As a scientific proposition, bimetallism is as absurd as perpetual motion. It proposes to establish perpetual rest in the fluctuations of value of two commodities, to do which it must extinguish the economic forces of supply and demand of those commodities upon which value depends. The movement of the great commercial nations towards a single gold currency is the most important event in the monetary history of our time, and one which nothing can possibly arrest. It produces temporary distress, and the means of alleviating that distress are a proper subject of consideration; but the advantages which will be obtained for all time to come immeasurably surpass the present loss and inconvenience.

I return, then, to the propositions with which I set out. Feebleness and vacillation in regard to economic doctrine are natural to a period of commercial crisis, on account of the distress, uncertainty, and disorder which then prevail in industry and trade; but that is just the time also when a tenacious grasp of scientific principles is of the highest importance. The human race must go forward to meet and conquer its problems and difficulties as they arise, to bear the penalties of its follies, and to pay the price of its acquisitions. To shrink from this is simply to go back and to abandon civilization. The path forward, as far as any human foresight can now reach, lies in a better understanding and a better realization of liberty, under which individuals and societies can work out their destiny, subject only to the incorruptible laws of nature.

PROSPERITY STRANGLED BY GOLD [1]

SOME of the silver fallacies were stated by Mr. St. John, in his address before the silver convention, with such precision that his speech offers a favorable opportunity for dealing with them.

He says that "it is amongst the first principles in finance that the value of each dollar, expressed in prices, depends upon the total number of dollars in circulation." There is no such principle of finance as the one here formulated. The "quantity doctrine" of currency is gravely abused by all bimetallists, from the least to the greatest, and it is at best open to great doubt. When the dollars in question are dollars of some money of account which can circulate beyond the territory of the State in which it is issued, the quantity doctrine cannot be true within that territory. It may be noted, in passing, that this is the reason why no scheme of the silver people for manipulating prices in the United States can possibly succeed. Silver and gold will be exported and imported until their values conform throughout the world, and prices fixed in one or the other of them will conform to the world's prices, after all the trouble and waste and loss of translating them two or three times over have been endured.

The quantity doctrine, however, means that the value of the currency is a question of supply and demand, and everybody knows that to double or halve the supply does not halve or double the value, or have any other effect which is simple and direct. If it did have such effect speculation would not be what it is.

[1] *Leslie's Weekly*, August 20, 1896.

Mr. St. John goes on to argue that our population increases two millions every year, on account of which we need more dollars; that the production of gold does not furnish enough to meet this need, and that, therefore, prices fall. This argumentation is very simple and very glib. Prosperity and adversity are put into a syllogism of three lines. But, if we can avert the fall in prices and adversity by coining silver, it must be by adding the silver to the gold which we now have. "High" and "low" prices are only relative terms. They mean higher and lower than at another time or place; higher and lower than we have been used to. If misery depends on ten-cent corn we are advised to cut the cents in two and we shall get twenty-cent corn and prosperity. Corn will not be altered in value in gold, or outside of the United States, and, as all other things will be marked up at the same time and in the same way, its value in other things will not be altered by this operation. When we get used to twenty-cent corn it will seem just as low and just as "hard for the debtor" as ten-cent corn is now. Then we can divide by ten and get two-dollar corn, by adding free coinage of copper. When we get used to that we shall be no better satisfied with it. We can then make paper dollars and coin them without limit. Million-dollar corn will then become as bitter a subject for complaint as ten-cent corn is now. The fact that people are discontented is no argument for anything.

The fact that prices are low is made the subject of social complaint and of political agitation in the United States. Prices have undergone a wave since 1850. They arose until about 1872. They have fallen again. They are lower than they were at the top of the wave all the world over. This fact, the explanation of which would furnish a very complicated task for trained statisticians and economists, is made a topic of easy interpretation and solution in political conventions and popular harangues, and it is proposed to

adopt violent and portentous measures upon the basis of
the flippant notions which are current about it.   But what
difference does it make whether the "plane" of prices is
high or low?   If corn is at forty cents a bushel and calico
at twenty cents a yard, a bushel buys two yards.   If corn
is at ten cents a bushel and calico at five cents a yard, a
bushel will buy two yards.   So of everything else.   If, then,
there has been a *general* fall, and that is the alleged grievance, neither farmers nor any other one class has suffered
by it.

It is undoubtedly true that a period of advancing prices
stimulates energy and enterprise.   It does so even when, if
all the facts were well known, it might be found that capital was really being consumed in successive periods of production.   Falling prices discourage enterprise, although, if
all facts were known to the bottom, it might be found
that capital was being accumulated in successive periods
of production.

It is also true that a depreciation of the money of account, *while it is going on*, stimulates exports and restrains
imports.

But who can tell how we are to make prices always go
up, unless by constant and unlimited inflation?   Who can
tell how we are to avoid fluctuations in prices or eliminate
the element of contingency, risk, foresight, and speculation?

It is also true that, although high prices and low prices
are immaterial at any one time, the change from one to the
other, from one period of time to another, affects the burden
of outstanding time contracts.   Men make contracts for
dollars, not for dollar's-worths.   Selling long or short is one
thing; lending is another.   Borrowers and lenders never
guarantee each other the purchasing power of dollars at a
future time.   If the contracts were thus complicated they
would become impossible. Between 1850 and 1872 the
debtors made no complaint and the creditors never thought

of getting up an agitation to have debts scaled up. The debtors now are demanding that they be allowed to play heads I win, tails you lose, and Mr. St. John and others tell us that they have the votes to carry it; as if that made any difference in the forum of discussion.

Increase in population does not prove an increased need of money. It may prove the contrary. If the population becomes more dense over a given area, a higher organization may make less money necessary. If railroads and other means of communication are extended, money is economized. If banks and other credit institutions are multiplied, and if credit operations are facilitated by public security, good administration of law, etc., less money is needed. If these changes are going on at the same time that population is increasing (and such is undoubtedly the case in the United States), who can tell whether the net result is to make more or less currency necessary? Nobody; and all assertions about the matter are wild and irresponsible.

If it was true that an increase of two millions in the population called for more dollars, how does anybody know whether the current gold production is adequate to meet the new requirement or not? The assertion is arithmetical. It says that two quantities are not equal to each other. The first quantity is the increase in the currency called for by two million more people. How much more is needed? Nobody knows, and there is no way to find out. The silver men have put figures for it from time to time, but the figures rested on nothing and were mere bald assertions. The second quantity is the amount of new gold annually available for coinage in the United States. How much is this? Nobody knows, because if an attempt is made to define what is meant it is found that there is no idea in the words. The people of the United States buy and coin just as much gold as they want at any time. Hence

two things are said to be unequal to each other, when nobody knows how big either one of them is. It may be
added that it makes no difference how big either one of
them is. How much additional tin is needed annually for
the increase of our population? Do the mines produce it?
Nobody knows or asks. The mines produce, and the people
buy, what they want. The case is the same as to gold.

We find, then, that Mr. St. John begins with a doctrine
which is untenable; then he asserts a relation between
population and the need of money which does not exist;
then he assumes that this need is greater than the amount
of new gold produced, although neither he nor anybody else
knows how big either one of these quantities is. This is
the argumentation by which he aims to show that prices
are reduced and misery produced by the single gold standard. It is the argumentation which is current among the
silver people. Not a step of it will bear examination. The
inference that we must restore the free coinage of silver, to
escape this strangulation of prosperity, falls to the ground.

CAUSE AND CURE OF HARD TIMES [1]

IT is an essential part of the case of the silver men that the country is having "hard times." The bolters from the Republican convention say, in their manifesto: "Discontent and distress prevail to an extent never before known in the history of the country." This is an historical assertion. It is distinctly untrue. There is no such discontent and distress as there was in 1819, or in 1840, or in 1875, to say nothing of other periods. The writers did not know the facts of the history, and they made use of what is nowadays a mere figure of speech. People who want to say that a social phenomenon is big, and who do not know what has been before, say that it is unparalleled in history.

There has been an advancing paralysis of enterprise and arrest of credit ever since the Sherman act of 1890 was passed. The bolters say that "No reason can be found for such an unhappy condition of things save in a vicious monetary system." The reason for it has been that the cumulative effect of the silver legislation was steadily advancing to a crisis. The efforts by which the effects of that legislation had been put off were no longer effective, and it was evident that the country was on the verge of a cataclysm in which the standard of value would be changed. What man can fail to see the effect of such a fear on credit and enterprise? And with such a fear in the market, how idle it is to try to represent the trouble as caused by the fact that the existing standard was of gold, or of silver, or of anything else! Men will make contracts and go on with business by the use of any medium, the terms of which can be defined, understood, and maintained until the contract is solved, but uncertainty as to the terms, or danger of change in them, makes credit and enterprise impossible. In the whole history of finance no crisis can be found which was so utterly unnecessary, and so distinctly caused by the measures of policy which had gone before it, as that of 1893.

So much being admitted as to "hard times," it remains true, however, that by far the greatest part of the current declamation about hard times is false. Prosperity and adversity of society are not capable of exact verification. At all times some people, classes, industries, are less prosperous than others. The fashion has grown up among politicians and stump orators of using assertions about prosperity and distress as arguments for their purpose, and parties come before the public with prosperity policies. They have programs for "making the country prosperous." If this country, with its population, its resources, and its chances, is not prosperous by the intelligence, industry, and thrift of its population, does any sane man suppose that politicians and stump orators have any devices at their control for making it so? The orators of the present day see prosperity where they need to see it for the purposes of their argument. They say that all gold-standard countries in Europe are in distress. Mr. St. John says that Mexico is prosperous. As to Canada, we have seen no statement. According to some discussions which are current, the bicycle rivals the gold standard as a calamity-producer. As the bicycle has certainly gravely affected the distribution of expenditure and the accumulation of capital, its efficiency as a crisis-maker, in its degree, whatever that may be, can be rationally discerned, but nobody has ever been able to show any rational grounds of belief that the gold standard is a crisis-maker.

A crisis will also be produced whenever capital has been invested on a large scale in any unproductive investment, whereby it is not reproduced, but is lost. The enterprises are always made the basis of engagements and contracts. When the enterprises fail, the engagements cannot be met; other engagements based on these also fail, and so on through the whole industrial organization.   Such crises are inevitable in a new country.   Enterprises run in fashions.   At any one time great groups of producers tend to one line of industry.   That industry is sure to be overdone and to come to a crisis.   In a free country, where every man is at liberty to direct his enterprise as he sees fit, what is the sense, when it turns out that he has made a mistake, of trying to throw the losses on other people? No one would propose it as to an individual or a number, but when there is a great interest it makes itself a political power and produces a platform for the same purpose, generally with inflated principles of humanity, justice, democracy, and Americanism as wind-attachments to make it float.

Mr. St. John says that the farmers are spending ten dollars an acre to get eight or nine dollars an acre.   What farmer in the United States can tell how many dollars he spends on an acre?   What is the sense of these pretendedly accurate figures?   But, if they had sense, what would be the gain of cutting the dollars in two?   If the farmer spent twenty silver dollars on an acre and got back sixteen or eighteen, how would he be benefited?   The dollars of outlay are of the same kind as the dollars of return in any case.   If it is true that the return does not equal the outlay, it must be on account of some facts of production, and it requires but a moment's reflection to see that changing the currency in which outlay and income are reckoned cannot change the relation between the two.

A dispassionate view of facts will go to prove that the world is reasonably and ordinarily prosperous at the present time, except where particular classes and industries are affected by special circumstances, as some classes and industries are being affected at all times.   The land-owners of western Europe are in distress on account of the competition of new land, with cheapened means of transportation, but now we are told that the holders of the other side of the competition, the land-owners of the new soil, are victims of distress. It must be, then, that too much labor and capital are being expended on the soil the world over, and that, too, in spite of all the protective tariffs drawing people to the textile and metal industries. Our silver men say that this is not the correct inference. They say that the people on the new land suffer because the prices are set in coins of gold and the debits and credits are kept in terms of those coins. The prices are fixed in the world's market in gold. They will be so fixed, whatever we may do with our coinage laws. If the proceeds, in being brought home, are converted into silver value, a new opportunity for brokerage and exchange gambling will be given to the hated bankers and brokers of Wall Street. That is the only difference which will be produced. It would be far more sensible to say that distress is produced by doing the business on the English system of weights and measures, in bushels and pecks, and that prosperity would be produced by doing it on the metric system, in litres and hectolitres, for that charge would at least be harmless. Our distress could all be dispelled in a week by an act of Congress making all contracts, beyond political peradventure, that which they are in law and fact, gold contracts.

There is, however, another cause of hard times for some people which is far more important in our present case than any other. That is the case of the boom which has collapsed. We hear a great deal about "Wall Street gambling." The gambling in Wall Street is insignificant compared with the gambling in land, buildings, town sites, and crops which goes on all over the country, and which is participated in chiefly by the men who declaim about Wall Street. For three hundred years our history has been marked by the alternations of "prosperity" and "distress" which are produced by the booms and their collapses. When the collapse comes the people who are left long of goods and land always make a great outcry and start a political agitation. Their favorite device always is to try to inflate the currency and raise prices again until they can unload.

It is a very popular thing to tell men that they have a grievance. That most of them find it hard to earn as much money as they need to spend goes without saying. Now comes the wily orator and tells them that this is somebody's fault. In old times, if a man was sick, it was always assumed that somebody had bewitched him. The witch was to be sought. The medicine-man had to name somebody, and then woe to the one who was named. Our medicine-men say that it is the gold-bugs, Wall Street, England, who are to blame for hard times. Whether there is any rational proof of connection is as immaterial as it always was in witchcraft. It is a case of pain and passion. The "gold standard" has done it! There is something to hate and denounce. All would be well if silver could be coined at four hundred and twelve and a half grains to the dollar. But the assumption is that while the farmers would sell their products for twice as many "dollars" as now, in silver, all the prices of things which they want to buy would remain at the same number of dollars and cents as now, in gold; that is, it is believed that wheat would be at, say, one dollar and fifty cents per bushel in silver, instead of seventy-five cents in gold, but that cloth would remain at fifty cents a yard in silver, if it is now fifty cents a yard in gold. When this assumption is brought out into clear words, every one knows that such can never be the result. The proposed cure is like a witch cure. It lacks rational basis, and cannot command the confidence of men of sense. If the times were ever so bad, such a cure could only make them worse.

SHALL AMERICANS OWN SHIPS?[1]

SINCE the war, public attention has been drawn more or less to the marked decline in American shipping. It has been generally assumed and conceded that this was a matter for regret, and some discussion has arisen as to remedies — what to do, in fact, in order to bring it about that Americans should own ships. In these discussions, there has generally been a confusion apparent in regard to three things which ought to be very carefully distinguished from each other: ship-building, the carrying trade, and foreign commerce.

1. As to ship-building — Americans began to build ships, as an industry, within fifteen years after the settlement at Massachusetts Bay. Before the Revolution they competed successfully as ship-builders with the Dutch and English, and they sold ships to be used by their rivals. Tonnage and navigation laws played an important part in the question of separation between the colonies and England, and the same laws took an important place in the formation of the Federal Constitution. One generation was required for the people of this country to get over the hard logical twist in the notion that laws which were pernicious when laid by Great Britain were beneficial when laid by ourselves. The vacillation which has marked the history of our laws about tonnage and navigation is such that it does not seem possible to trace the effects of legislation upon ship-building. In the decade 1850–1860 a very great decline in the number of ships built, especially for ocean traffic, began to be marked. Sails began to give

[1] *The North American Review*, June, 1881, CXXXII, 559–566.

way to steam, but the building of steamships required great advantages of every kind in the production of engines and other apparatus — that is, it required the presence, in a highly developed state, of a number of important auxiliary and coöperating industries. As iron was introduced into ship-building, of course the ship-building industry became dependent upon cheap supplies of iron as it had before been dependent on cheap supplies of wood. No doubt these changes in the conditions of the industry itself have been the chief cause of the decline in ship-building in this country, and legislation has had only incidental effects. It is a plain fact of history that the decline in ship-building began before the war and the high tariff. Of course the effects produced by changes in the conditions of an industry are inevitable; they are not to be avoided by any legislation. They are annoying because they break up acquired habits and established routine, and they involve loss in a change from one industry to another, but legislation can never do anything but cause that loss to fall on some other set of people instead of on those directly interested. Within the last few years it has become certain that steel is to be the material of ocean vessels — a new improvement which will not tend to bring the industry back to this country. On the whole, therefore, the decline in ship-building of the last twenty-five years seems to indicate that somebody else than ourselves must build the world's ships for the present. We have, by legislative devices, forced the production of a few ocean steamers, but these cases prove nothing to the contrary of our inference. If this nation has a hobby for owning some ships built in this country, and is willing to pay enough for the gratification of that hobby, no doubt it can secure the pleasure it seeks. A fisherman who has caught nothing sometimes buys fish at a fancy price; he saves himself mortification and gets a dinner, but the possession of the fish does not prove that he has profitably employed his time or that he has had sport.

2. The carrying trade differs from ship-building as carting differs from wagon-building. Carrying is the industry of men who own ships; their interests are more or less hostile to those of the ship-builders. Ship owners want to buy new ships at low prices; they want the number of competing ships kept small; they want freights high. In all these points the interest of the ship-builder is the opposite: the ship owner is indifferent where he gets his ships; he only wants them cheap and good. There is no sentiment in the matter any more than there is in the purchase of wagons by an express company, or carriages by a livery-stable keeper.

3. Foreign commerce is still another thing. It consists in the exchange of the products of one country for those of another. The merchant wants plenty of ships to carry all the goods at the lowest possible freights, but it is of no importance to him where the ships were built, or who owns and sails them.

A statement and definition of these three industries suffices to show what confusion must arise in any discussion in which they are not properly distinguished. It is plain that there are three different questions: (1) Can the farmer build a vehicle? (2) Can he get his crop carried to market? (3) Can he sell his crop? It is evident that a country which needs a protective tariff on iron and steel must give up all hopes of building ships for ocean traffic. For the country which, by the hypothesis, needs a protective tariff on iron and steel cannot produce those articles as cheaply as some other country. Its ships, however, must compete upon the ocean with those of the country which has cheap iron and steel. The former embody a larger capital than the latter, and they must be driven from the ocean. If, then, subsidies are given to protect the carrying trade, when prosecuted in ships built of protected iron, the loss is transferred from the ship owners to the people who pay taxes on shore. These taxes, however, add to the cost of production of all things produced in the country, and thereby lessen the power of the country to compete in foreign commerce. This lessens the amount of goods to be carried both out and in, lowers freights, throws ships out of use, and checks the building of ships; and the whole series of legislative aids and encouragements must be begun over again, with a repetition and intensification of the same results. As long as the system lasts it works down, and the statistics show, very naturally, that fewer and fewer ships are built in the country, and that less and less of the carrying trade is carried on under the national flag. In view of the three different and sometimes adverse interests which are connected by their relation to the shipping question, it is not strange that when the representatives of those interests meet to try to consider that question, there should simply be a scramble between them to see which can capture the convention. The last convention of this sort was captured by the owners of a lot of unsalable and unsailable old hulks, who had hit upon the brilliant idea of getting the nation to pay them an annual bounty for the use of their antiquated and dilapidated property. Strange to say, in a country which is charged with being too practical and hardheaded, this proposition received respectful attention and consideration. It is also strange that our people should believe that taxing farmers to force the production of iron, taxing farmers again to force the production of ships out of protected iron, and taxing farmers again to pay subsidies to enable protected ships to do business, is a way to make this country rich.

So soon as the three different industries, or departments of business, which I have described are distinguished from each other, it is apparent that the fundamental one of the three is foreign commerce. If we have no commerce we need no carrying, and it would be absurd to build ships; if we have foreign commerce its magnitude determines the amount of demand there is for freight and for ships. The circle of taxation which I have mentioned, and which is obviously only a kind of circuit, described from and upon the farmer as a center and fulcrum to bear the weight of the whole, is necessarily and constantly vicious, because it presses down on the foreign commerce, which is the proper source of support for carrying and ship-building. On the other hand, the emancipation of foreign commerce from all trammels of every sort is the only means of increasing the natural, normal, and spontaneous support of carrying and ship-building, assuming that the carrying trade and ship-building are ends in themselves.

It is, however, no object at all for a country to have either ship-building industry, or carrying trade, or foreign commerce; herein lies the fundamental fallacy of all the popular and Congressional discussions about ships and commerce. It is only important that the whole population should be engaged in those industries which will pay the best under the circumstances of the country. For the sake of exposing the true doctrine about the matter, we may suppose (what is not conceivable as a possible fact) that a country might not find greater profit in the exportation of any part of any of its products than in the home use of the same. If this could be true, and if it were realized, the proof of it would be that no foreign trade would exist. There would be no ground for regret since the people would be satisfied and better off than as if they had a foreign trade. Carrying trade and ship-building would not exist.

If a country had a foreign trade of any magnitude whatever, it would not be any object for that country to do its own carrying. The figures which show the amount paid by the people of the United States to non-American ship owners for freight, and the figures which show the small percentage of our foreign commerce which is carried under the American flag, in themselves prove nothing at all. The only question which is of importance is this: are the people of the United States better employed now than they would be if engaged in owning and sailing ships? If they were under no restraints or interferences, that question also would answer itself. If Americans owned no ships and sailed no ships, but hired the people of other countries to do their ocean transportation for them, it would simply prove that Americans had some better employment for their capital and labor. They would get their transportation accomplished as cheaply as possible. That is all they care for, and it would be as foolish for any nation to insist on doing its own ocean transportation, devoting to this use capital and labor which might be otherwise more profitably employed, as it would be for a merchant to insist on doing his own carting, when some person engaged in carting offered him a contract on more advantageous terms than those on which he could do the work.

Furthermore, the people of a country which had little foreign commerce might find it very advantageous to prosecute the carrying trade. In history, the great trading nations have been those which had a small or poor territory at home: the Dutch were the great carriers of the seventeenth and eighteenth centuries, when the foreign commerce of their own territory was insignificant; the New Englanders of the last century and of the first quarter of this century became the carriers of commodities to and fro between all parts of the world, especially between our middle and southern states and the rest of the world. They took to the sea because their land did not furnish them with products which could remunerate their capital and labor so well as the carrying trade did. They won a high reputation for the merchant service, which was in their hands, and they

earned fortunes by energy, enterprise, promptitude, and
fidelity. The carrying trade is an industry like any other;
it is neither more nor less desirable in itself than any other.
In any natural and rational state of things it would be
absurd to be writing essays about it. If any one thought
he could make more profit in that business than in some
other he would set about it. When the census was taken
he would be found busy at that business, would be so
reported, and that would be the end of the matter as a
phenomenon of public interest.

If a nation had foreign commerce, and some of its citizens
found the carrying trade an advantageous employment
for their labor and capital as compared with other possible
industries in the country, it would not follow that some
other citizens of that country ought to engage in ship-
building. It is no object to build ships, but only to get
such ships as are wanted, in the most advantageous manner.
If a man should refuse to carry on a carting business unless he could make his own wagons, it would be such a
reflection on his good sense that his business credit would
be very low. If some Americans could buy and sail ships so
as to make profits, what is the sense of saying that they
shall not do it because some other Americans cannot build
ships at a profit? Only one answer to this question has
ever been offered by anybody, and that is the prediction
that, some day, if we go without ships long enough, we shall,
by the mere process of going without, begin to get some
— a prediction for which the prophets give no guarantee,
in addition to their personal authority, save the fact that
we have fewer ships and worse ones every year.

I have said above that, if there were no restraints or
interferences, we should simply notice whether any Americans took to the carrying trade or not, and should thence
infer that they might or might not be better employed in
some other industry. It is impossible, now, to say whether,

if all restrictions were removed, the carrying trade or ship-building would be a profitable industry in the United States or not. Any opinion given by anybody on that point is purely speculative. The present state of the iron and steel industries, and of the manufacture of engines and machinery, is so artificial that no one can judge what would be the possibilities of those industries under an entirely different state of things. It is, however, just because the present state of things prevents a free trial that it is indefensible; we are working in the dark and on speculation all the time and have none of the natural and proper tests and guarantees for what we are doing. We are controlled by the predictions of prophets, the notions of dogmatizers, the crude errors of superficial students of history, the wrong-headed inferences of shallow observers, and the selfish machinations of interested persons. We can distinguish many forces which are at work on our ship-building and on our carrying trade, but none of them are genuine or respectable. We are submitting to restraints and losses, and we have no guarantee whatever that we shall ever win any compensation. The teaching of economic science is distinctly that we never shall win any. We are expending capital without any measurement or adjustment of the *quid pro quo;* we are spending without calculation, and receiving something or nothing — we do not know which. The wrong of all this is not in the assumption that we have not certain industries which we would have (for we cannot tell whether that is so or not), but the wrong is in the arbitrary interference which prevents us from having them, if any man wants to put his capital into them, and which prevents us from obtaining the proper facts on which to base a judgment about the state and relations of industries in the country.

Whenever the question of ships is raised, the clamor for subsidies and bounties is renewed, and we are told

again that England has established her commerce by
subsidies. It would be well if we could have an understanding, once for all, whether England's example is a good
argument or not. As she has tried, at some time or other,
nearly every conceivable economic folly, and has also
made experiment of some sound economic principles, all
disputants find in her history facts to suit them, and it
needs only a certain easily acquired skill in misunder-
standing things to fashion any required argument from the
economic history of England. Some of our writers and
speakers seem to be under a fascination which impels them
to accept as authoritative examples the follies of English
history, and to reject its sound lessons. In the present case,
however, the matter stands somewhat differently. England
is a great manufacturing area; it imports food and raw
materials, and exports finished products; it has, therefore,
a general and public interest in maintaining communication
with all parts of the world. The analogy in our case is
furnished by the subsidized railroads in our new states, or,
perhaps even better, by the mail routes which we sustain
all over our territory, from general considerations of public
advantage, although many such routes do not pay at all.
Subsidies to ships for the mere sake of having ships, or
ocean traffic, when there is no business occasion for the subsidized lines, would have no analogy with English subsidies.

If then the question is put: Shall Americans own ships?
I do not see how any one can avoid the simple answer:
Yes, if they want them. Universally, if an American wants
anything, he ought to have it if he can get it, and if he hurts
no one else by getting it. To enter on the question whether
he is going to make it or buy it, and whether he is going
to buy it of A or of B, is an impertinence. We boast a
great deal of having a free country; our orators shout
themselves hoarse about liberty and freedom. Stop one
of them, however, and ask him if he means free trade and

free ships, and he will demur. No; not that; that will not do. He is in favor of freedom for himself and his friends in those respects in which they want liberty against other people, but he is not in favor of freedom for other people against restraints which are advantageous to him and his political allies. He is in favor of freedom for those who are being oppressed — by somebody else; not for those who are being oppressed by himself. I heard it asserted not long ago that we have no monopolies in this country, *because* it is a free country. It is not a free country, because there are more artificial monopolies in it than in any other country in the world. The popular notion that it is free rises from the fact that there are fewer natural monopolies in it than in any other great civilized country. It is necessary, however, to go to Turkey or Russia to find instances of legislative and administrative abuses to equal the existing laws and regulations of the United States about ships, the carrying trade, and foreign commerce. These laws have been brought to public attention again and again, but apparently with little effect in awakening popular attention, while the newspapers carry all over the country details about abuses in Ireland, Russia, and South Africa. We should stop bragging about a free country and about the enlightened power of the people in a democratic republic to correct abuses, while laws remain which treat the buying, importing, owning, and sailing of ships as pernicious actions, or, at least, as doubtful and suspicious ones. I have no conception of a free man or a free country which can be satisfied if a citizen of that country may not own a ship, if he wants one, getting it in any legitimate manner in which he might acquire other property; or may not sail one, if he finds that a profitable industry suited to his taste and ability; or may not exchange the products of his labor with that person, whoever he may be, who offers the most advantageous terms.

THE CHALLENGE OF FACTS [1]

SOCIALISM is no new thing. In one form or another it is to be found throughout all history. It arises from an observation of certain harsh facts in the lot of man on earth, the concrete expression of which is poverty and misery. These facts challenge us. It is folly to try to shut our eyes to them. We have first to notice what they are, and then to face them squarely.

Man is born under the necessity of sustaining the existence he has received by an onerous struggle against nature, both to win what is essential to his life and to ward off what is prejudicial to it. He is born under a burden and a necessity. Nature holds what is essential to him, but she offers nothing gratuitously. He may win for his use what she holds, if he can. Only the most meager and inadequate supply for human needs can be obtained directly from nature. There are trees which may be used for fuel and for dwellings, but labor is required to fit them for this use. There are ores in the ground, but labor is necessary to get out the metals and make tools or weapons. For any real satisfaction, labor is necessary to fit the products of nature for human use. In this struggle every individual is under the pressure of the necessities for food, clothing, shelter, fuel, and every individual brings with him more or less energy for the conflict necessary to supply his needs. The relation, therefore, between each man's needs and each man's energy, or "individualism," is the first fact of human life.

[1] Written in the 1880's. Original title was Socialism.

It is not without reason, however, that we speak of a "man" as the individual in question, for women (mothers) and children have special disabilities for the struggle with nature, and these disabilities grow greater and last longer as civilization advances. The perpetuation of the race in health and vigor, and its success as a whole in its struggle to expand and develop human life on earth, therefore, require that the head of the family shall, by his energy, be able to supply not only his own needs, but those of the organisms which are dependent upon him. The history of the human race shows a great variety of experiments in the relation of the sexes and in the organization of the family. These experiments have been controlled by economic circumstances, but, as man has gained more and more control over economic circumstances, monogamy and the family education of children have been more and more sharply developed. If there is one thing in regard to which the student of history and sociology can affirm with confidence that social institutions have made "progress" or grown "better," it is in this arrangement of marriage and the family. All experience proves that monogamy, pure and strict, is the sex relation which conduces most to the vigor and intelligence of the race, and that the family education of children is the institution by which the race as a whole advances most rapidly, from generation to generation, in the struggle with nature. Love of man and wife, as we understand it, is a modern sentiment. The devotion and sacrifice of parents for children is a sentiment which has been developed steadily and is now more intense and far more widely practiced throughout society than in earlier times. The relation is also coming to be regarded in a light quite different from that in which it was formerly viewed. It used to be believed that the parent had unlimited claims on the child and rights over him. In a truer view of the matter, we are coming to see that the rights are on the side of the child and the duties on the side of the parent. Existence is not a boon for which the child owes all subjection to the parent. It is a responsibility assumed by the parent towards the child without the child's consent, and the consequence of it is that the parent owes all possible devotion to the child to enable him to make his existence happy and successful.

The value and importance of the family sentiments, from a social point of view, cannot be exaggerated. They impose self-control and prudence in their most important social bearings, and tend more than any other forces to hold the individual up to the virtues which make the sound man and the valuable member of society. The race is bound, from generation to generation, in an unbroken chain of vice and penalty, virtue and reward. The sins of the fathers are visited upon the children, while, on the other hand, health, vigor, talent, genius, and skill are, so far as we can discover, the results of high physical vigor and wise early training. The popular language bears witness to the universal observation of these facts, although general social and political dogmas have come into fashion which contradict or ignore them. There is no other such punishment for a life of vice and self-indulgence as to see children grow up cursed with the penalties of it, and no such reward for self-denial and virtue as to see children born and grow up vigorous in mind and body. It is time that the true import of these observations for moral and educational purposes was developed, and it may well be questioned whether we do not go too far in our reticence in regard to all these matters when we leave it to romances and poems to do almost all the educational work that is done in the way of spreading ideas about them. The defense of marriage and the family, if their sociological value were better understood, would be not only instinctive but rational. The struggle for existence with which we have to deal must be understood, then, to be that of a man for himself, his wife, and his children.

The next great fact we have to notice in regard to the struggle of human life is that labor which is spent in a direct struggle with nature is severe in the extreme and is but slightly productive. To subjugate nature, man needs weapons and tools. These, however, cannot be won unless the food and clothing and other prime and direct necessities are supplied in such amount that they can be consumed while tools and weapons are being made, for the tools and weapons themselves satisfy no needs directly. A man who tills the ground with his fingers or with a pointed stick picked up without labor will get a small crop. To fashion even the rudest spade or hoe will cost time, during which the laborer must still eat and drink and wear, but the tool, when obtained, will multiply immensely the power to produce. Such products of labor, used to assist production, have a function so peculiar in the nature of things that we need to distinguish them. We call them capital. A lever is capital, and the advantage of lifting a weight with a lever over lifting it by direct exertion is only a feeble illustration of the power of capital in production. The origin of capital lies in the darkness before history, and it is probably impossible for us to imagine the slow and painful steps by which the race began the formation of it. Since then it has gone on rising to higher and higher powers by a ceaseless involution, if I may use a mathematical expression. Capital is labor raised to a higher power by being constantly multiplied into itself. Nature has been more and more subjugated by the human race through the power of capital, and every human being now living shares the improved status of the race to a degree which neither he nor any one else can measure, and for which he pays nothing.

Let us understand this point, because our subject will require future reference to it. It is the most short-sighted ignorance not to see that, in a civilized community, all the advantage of capital except a small fraction is gratuitously enjoyed by the community. For instance, suppose the case of a man utterly destitute of tools, who is trying to till the ground with a pointed stick. He could get something out of it. If now he should obtain a spade with which to till the ground, let us suppose, for illustration, that he could get twenty times as great a product. Could, then, the owner of a spade in a civilized state demand, as its price, from the man who had no spade, nineteen-twentieths of the product which could be produced by the use of it? Certainly not. The price of a spade is fixed by the supply and demand of products in the community. A spade is bought for a dollar and the gain from the use of it is an inheritance of knowledge, experience, and skill which every man who lives in a civilized state gets for nothing. What we pay for steam transportation is no trifle, but imagine, if you can, eastern Massachusetts cut off from steam connection with the rest of the world, turnpikes and sailing vessels remaining. The cost of food would rise so high that a quarter of the population would starve to death and another quarter would have to emigrate. To-day every man here gets an enormous advantage from the status of a society on a level of steam transportation, telegraph, and machinery, for which he pays nothing.

So far as I have yet spoken, we have before us the struggle of man with nature, but the social problems, strictly speaking, arise at the next step. Each man carries on the struggle to win his support for himself, but there are others by his side engaged in the same struggle. If the stores of nature were unlimited, or if the last unit of the supply she offers could be won as easily as the first, there would be no social problem. If a square mile of land could support an indefinite number of human beings, or if it cost only twice as much labor to get forty bushels of wheat from an acre as to get twenty, we should have no social problem. If a square mile of land could support millions, no one would ever emigrate and there would be no trade or commerce. If it cost only twice as much labor to get forty bushels as twenty, there would be no advance in the arts. The fact is far otherwise. So long as the population is low in proportion to the amount of land, on a given stage of the arts, life is easy and the competition of man with man is weak. When more persons are trying to live on a square mile than it can support, on the existing stage of the arts, life is hard and the competition of man with man is intense. In the former case, industry and prudence may be on a low grade; the penalties are not severe, or certain, or speedy. In the latter case, each individual needs to exert on his own behalf every force, original or acquired, which he can command. In the former case, the average condition will be one of comfort and the population will be all nearly on the average. In the latter case, the average condition will not be one of comfort, but the population will cover wide extremes of comfort and misery. Each will find his place according to his ability and his effort. The former society will be democratic; the latter will be aristocratic.

The constant tendency of population to outstrip the means of subsistence is the force which has distributed population over the world, and produced all advance in civilization. To this day the two means of escape for an overpopulated country are emigration and an advance in the arts. The former wins more land for the same people; the latter makes the same land support more persons. If, however, either of these means opens a chance for an increase of population, it is evident that the advantage so won may be speedily exhausted if the increase takes place. The social difficulty has only undergone a temporary amelioration, and when the conditions of pressure and competition are renewed, misery and poverty reappear. The victims of them are those who have inherited disease and depraved appetites, or have been brought up in vice and ignorance, or have themselves yielded to vice, extravagance, idleness, and imprudence. In the last analysis, therefore, we come back to vice, in its original and hereditary forms, as the correlative of misery and poverty.

The condition for the complete and regular action of the force of competition is liberty. Liberty means the security given to each man that, if he employs his energies to sustain the struggle on behalf of himself and those he cares for, he shall dispose of the product exclusively as he chooses. It is impossible to know whence any definition or criterion of justice can be derived, if it is not deduced from this view of things; or if it is not the definition of justice that each shall enjoy the fruit of his own labor and self-denial, and of injustice that the idle and the industrious, the self-indulgent and the self-denying, shall share equally in the product. Aside from the *a priori* speculations of philosophers who have tried to make equality an essential element in justice, the human race has recognized, from the earliest times, the above conception of justice as the true one, and has founded upon it the right of property. The right of property, with marriage and the family, gives the right of bequest.

Monogamic marriage, however, is the most exclusive of social institutions. It contains, as essential principles, preference, superiority, selection, devotion. It would not be at all what it is if it were not for these characteristic traits, and it always degenerates when these traits are not present. For instance, if a man should not have a distinct preference for the woman he married, and if he did not select her as superior to others, the marriage would be an imperfect one according to the standard of true monogamic marriage. The family under monogamy, also, is a closed group, having special interests and estimating privacy and reserve as valuable advantages for family development. We grant high prerogatives, in our society, to parents, although our observation teaches us that thousands of human beings are unfit to be parents or to be entrusted with the care of children. It follows, therefore, from the organization of marriage and the family, under monogamy, that great inequalities must exist in a society based on those institutions. The son of wise parents cannot start on a level with the son of foolish ones, and the man who has had no home discipline cannot be equal to the man who has had home discipline. If the contrary were true, we could rid ourselves at once

of the wearing labor of inculcating sound morals and
manners in our children.

Private property, also, which we have seen to be a
feature of society organized in accordance with the
natural conditions of the struggle for existence produces
inequalities between men. The struggle for existence
is aimed against nature. It is from her niggardly hand
that we have to wrest the satisfactions for our needs,
but our fellow-men are our competitors for the meager
supply. Competition, therefore, is a law of nature.
Nature is entirely neutral; she submits to him who
most energetically and resolutely assails her. She
grants her rewards to the fittest, therefore, without
regard to other considerations of any kind. If, then,
there be liberty, men get from her just in proportion to
their works, and their having and enjoying are just in
proportion to their being and their doing. Such is the
system of nature. If we do not like it, and if we try to
amend it, there is only one way in which we can do it.
We can take from the better and give to the worse.
We can deflect the penalties of those who have done
ill and throw them on those who have done better.
We can take the rewards from those who have done
better and give them to those who have done worse.
We shall thus lessen the inequalities. We shall favor
the survival of the unfittest, and we shall accomplish
this by destroying liberty. Let it be understood that
we cannot go outside of this alternative: liberty, inequality, survival of the fittest; not-liberty, equality,
survival of the unfittest. The former carries society
forward and favors all its best members; the latter
carries society downwards and favors all its worst
members.

For three hundred years now men have been trying

to understand and realize liberty. Liberty is not the right or chance to do what we choose; there is no such liberty as that on earth. No man can do as he chooses: the autocrat of Russia or the King of Dahomey has limits to his arbitrary will; the savage in the wilderness, whom some people think free, is the slave of routine, tradition, and superstitious fears; the civilized man must earn his living, or take care of his property, or concede his own will to the rights and claims of his parents, his wife, his children, and all the persons with whom he is connected by the ties and contracts of civilized life.

What we mean by liberty is civil liberty, or liberty under law; and this means the guarantees of law that a man shall not be interfered with while using his own powers for his own welfare. It is, therefore, a civil and political status; and that nation has the freest institutions in which the guarantees of peace for the laborer and security for the capitalist are the highest. Liberty, therefore, does not by any means do away with the struggle for existence. We might as well try to do away with the need of eating, for that would, in effect, be the same thing. What civil liberty does is to turn the competition of man with man from violence and brute force into an industrial competition under which men vie with one another for the acquisition of material goods by industry, energy, skill, frugality, prudence, temperance, and other industrial virtues. Under this changed order of things the inequalities are not done away with. Nature still grants her rewards of having and enjoying, according to our being and doing, but it is now the man of the highest training and not the man of the heaviest fist who gains the highest reward. It is impossible that the man with capital and the man without capital should be equal. To affirm that they are equal would be to say that a man who has no tool can get as much food out of the ground as the man who has a spade or a plough; or that the man who has no weapon can defend himself as well against hostile beasts or hostile men as the man who has a weapon. If that were so, none of us would work any more. We work and deny ourselves to get capital just because, other things being equal, the man who has it is superior, for attaining all the ends of life, to the man who has it not. Considering the eagerness with which we all seek capital and the estimate we put upon it, either in cherishing it if we have it, or envying others who have it while we have it not, it is very strange what platitudes pass current about it in our society so soon as we begin to generalize about it. If our young people really believed some of the teachings they hear, it would not be amiss to preach them a sermon once in a while to reassure them, setting forth that it is not wicked to be rich, nay even, that it is not wicked to be richer than your neighbor.

It follows from what we have observed that it is the utmost folly to denounce capital. To do so is to undermine civilization, for capital is the first requisite of every social gain, educational, ecclesiastical, political, æsthetic, or other.

It must also be noticed that the popular antithesis between persons and capital is very fallacious. Every law or institution which protects persons at the expense of capital makes it easier for persons to live and to increase the number of consumers of capital while lowering all the motives to prudence and frugality by which capital is created. Hence every such law or institution tends to produce a large population, sunk in misery.

All poor laws and all eleemosynary institutions and expenditures have this tendency. On the contrary, all laws and institutions which give security to capital against the interests of other persons than its owners, restrict numbers while preserving the means of subsistence. Hence every such law or institution tends to produce a small society on a high stage of comfort and well-being. It follows that the antithesis commonly thought to exist between the protection of persons and the protection of property is in reality only an antithesis between numbers and quality.

I must stop to notice, in passing, one other fallacy which is rather scientific than popular. The notion is attributed to certain economists that economic forces are self-correcting. I do not know of any economists who hold this view, but what is intended probably is that many economists, of whom I venture to be one, hold that economic forces act compensatingly, and that whenever economic forces have so acted as to produce an unfavorable situation, other economic forces are brought into action which correct the evil and restore the equilibrium. For instance, in Ireland overpopulation and exclusive devotion to agriculture, both of which are plainly traceable to unwise statesmanship in the past, have produced a situation of distress. Steam navigation on the ocean has introduced the competition of cheaper land with Irish agriculture. The result is a social and industrial crisis. There are, however, millions of acres of fertile land on earth which are unoccupied and which are open to the Irish, and the economic forces are compelling the direct corrective of the old evils, in the way of emigration or recourse to urban occupations by unskilled labor. Any number of economic and legal nostrums have been proposed for this situation, all of which propose to leave the original causes untouched. We are told that economic causes do not correct themselves. That is true. We are told that when an economic situation becomes very grave it goes on from worse to worse and that there is no cycle through which it returns. That is not true, without further limitation. We are told that moral forces alone can elevate any such people again. But it is plain that a people which has sunk below the reach of the economic forces of self-interest has certainly sunk below the reach of moral forces, and that this objection is superficial and short-sighted. What is true is that economic forces always go before moral forces. Men feel self-interest long before they feel prudence, self-control, and temperance. They lose the moral forces long before they lose the economic forces. If they can be regenerated at all, it must be first by distress appealing to self-interest and forcing recourse to some expedient for relief. Emigration is certainly an economic force for the relief of Irish distress. It is a palliative only, when considered in itself, but the virtue of it is that it gives the non-emigrating population a chance to rise to a level on which the moral forces can act upon them. Now it is terribly true that only the better ones emigrate, and only the better ones among those who remain are capable of having their ambition and energy awakened, but for the rest the solution is famine and death, with a social regeneration through decay and the elimination of that part of the society which is not capable of being restored to health and life. As Mr. Huxley once said, the method of nature is not even a word and a blow, with the blow first. No explanation is vouchsafed. We are left to find out for ourselves why our ears are boxed. If we do not find out, and find out correctly, what the error is for which we are being punished, the blow is repeated and poverty, distress, disease, and death finally remove the incorrigible ones. It behooves us men to study these terrible illustrations of the penalties which follow on bad statesmanship, and of the sanctions by which social laws are enforced. The economic cycle does complete itself; it must do so, unless the social group is to sink in permanent barbarism. A law may be passed which shall force somebody to support the hopelessly degenerate members of a society, but such a law can only perpetuate the evil and entail it on future generations with new accumulations of distress.

The economic forces work with moral forces and are their handmaidens, but the economic forces are far more primitive, original, and universal. The glib generalities in which we sometimes hear people talk, as if you could set moral and economic forces separate from and in antithesis to each other, and discard the one to accept and work by the other, gravely misconstrue the realities of the social order.

We have now before us the facts of human life out of which the social problem springs. These facts are in many respects hard and stern. It is by strenuous exertion only that each one of us can sustain himself against the destructive forces and the ever recurring needs of life; and the higher the degree to which we seek to carry our development the greater is the proportionate cost of every step. For help in the struggle we can only look back to those in the previous generation who are responsible for our existence. In the competition of life the son of wise and prudent ancestors has immense advantages over the son of vicious and imprudent ones. The man who has capital possesses immeasurable advantages for the struggle of life over him who has none. The more we break down privileges of class, or industry, and establish liberty, the greater will be the inequalities and the more exclusively will the vicious bear the penalties. Poverty and misery will exist in society just so long as vice exists in human nature.

I now go on to notice some modes of trying to deal with this problem. There is a modern philosophy which has never been taught systematically, but which has won the faith of vast masses of people in the modern civilized world. For want of a better name it may be called the sentimental philosophy. It has colored all modern ideas and institutions in politics, religion, education, charity, and industry, and is widely taught in popular literature, novels, and poetry, and in the pulpit. The first proposition of this sentimental philosophy is that nothing is true which is disagreeable. If, therefore, any facts of observation show that life is grim or hard, the sentimental philosophy steps over such facts with a genial platitude, a consoling commonplace, or a gratifying dogma. The effect is to spread an easy optimism, under the influence of which people spare themselves labor and trouble, reflection and forethought, pains and caution — all of which are hard things, and to admit the necessity for which would be to admit that the world is not all made smooth and easy, for us to pass through it surrounded by love, music, and flowers.

Under this philosophy, "progress" has been represented as a steadily increasing and unmixed good; as if the good steadily encroached on the evil without involving any new and other forms of evil; and as if we could plan great steps in progress in our academies and lyceums, and then realize them by resolution. To

minds trained to this way of looking at things, any
evil which exists is a reproach. We have only to consider it, hold some discussions about it, pass resolutions,
and have done with it. Every moment of delay is,
therefore, a social crime. It is monstrous to say that
misery and poverty are as constant as vice and evil
passions of men! People suffer so under misery and
poverty! Assuming, therefore, that we can solve all
these problems and eradicate all these evils by expending our ingenuity upon them, of course we cannot
hasten too soon to do it.

A social philosophy, consonant with this, has also
been taught for a century. It could not fail to be
popular, for it teaches that ignorance is as good as
knowledge, vulgarity as good as refinement, shiftless-
ness as good as painstaking, shirking as good as faithful
striving, poverty as good as wealth, filth as good as
cleanliness — in short, that quality goes for nothing in
the measurement of men, but only numbers. Culture,
knowledge, refinement, skill, and taste cost labor, but
we have been taught that they have only individual,
not social value, and that socially they are rather drawbacks than otherwise. In public life we are taught to
admire roughness, illiteracy, and rowdyism. The ignorant, idle, and shiftless have been taught that they are
"the people," that the generalities inculcated at the
same time about the dignity, wisdom, and virtue of
"the people" are true of them, that they have nothing
to learn to be wise, but that, as they stand, they possess
a kind of infallibility, and that to their "opinion" the
wise must bow. It is not cause for wonder if whole
sections of these classes have begun to use the
powers and wisdom attributed to them for their
interests, as they construe them, and to trample on all

the excellence which marks civilization as on obsolete superstition.

Another development of the same philosophy is the doctrine that men come into the world endowed with "natural rights," or as joint inheritors of the "rights of man," which have been "declared" times without number during the last century. The divine rights of man have succeeded to the obsolete divine right of kings. If it is true, then, that a man is born with rights, he comes into the world with claims on somebody besides his parents. Against whom does he hold such rights? There can be no rights against nature or against God. A man may curse his fate because he is born of an inferior race, or with an hereditary disease, or blind, or, as some members of the race seem to do, because they are born females; but they get no answer to their imprecations. But, now, if men have rights by birth, these rights must hold against their fellow-men and must mean that somebody else is to spend his energy to sustain the existence of the persons so born. What then becomes of the natural rights of the one whose energies are to be diverted from his own interests? If it be said that we should all help each other, that means simply that the race as a whole should advance and expand as much and as fast as it can in its career on earth; and the experience on which we are now acting has shown that we shall do this best under liberty and under the organization which we are now developing, by leaving each to exert his energies for his own success. The notion of natural rights is destitute of sense, but it is captivating, and it is the more available on account of its vagueness. It lends itself to the most vicious kind of social dogmatism, for if a man has natural rights, then the reasoning is clear up to the finished socialistic doctrine that a man has a natural right to whatever he needs, and that the measure of his claims is the wishes which he wants fulfilled. If, then, he has a need, who is bound to satisfy it for him? Who holds the obligation corresponding to his right? It must be the one who possesses what will satisfy that need, or else the state which can take the possession from those who have earned and saved it, and give it to him who needs it and who, by the hypothesis, has not earned and saved it.

It is with the next step, however, that we come to the complete and ruinous absurdity of this view. If a man may demand from those who have a share of what he needs and has not, may he demand the same also for his wife and for his children, and for how many children? The industrious and prudent man who takes the course of labor and self-denial to secure capital, finds that he must defer marriage, both in order to save and to devote his life to the education of fewer children. The man who can claim a share in another's product has no such restraint. The consequence would be that the industrious and prudent would labor and save, without families, to support the idle and improvident who would increase and multiply, until universal destitution forced a return to the principles of liberty and property; and the man who started with the notion that the world owed him a living would once more find, as he does now, that the world pays him its debt in the state prison.

The most specious application of the dogma of rights is to labor. It is said that every man has a right to work. The world is full of work to be done. Those who are willing to work find that they have three days' work to do in every day that comes. Work is the necessity to which we are born. It is not a right, but an irksome necessity, and men escape it whenever they can get the fruits of labor without it. What they want is the fruits, or wages, not work. But wages are capital which some one has earned and saved. If he and the workman can agree on the terms on which he will part with his capital, there is no more to be said. If not, then the right must be set up in a new form. It is now not a right to work, nor even a right to wages, but a right to a certain rate of wages, and we have simply returned to the old doctrine of spoliation again. It is immaterial whether the demand for wages be addressed to an individual capitalist or to a civil body, for the latter can give no wages which it does not collect by taxes out of the capital of those who have labored and saved.

Another application is in the attempt to fix the hours of labor *per diem* by law. If a man is forbidden to labor over eight hours per day (and the law has no sense or utility for the purposes of those who want it until it takes this form), he is forbidden to exercise so much industry as he may be willing to expend in order to accumulate capital for the improvement of his circumstances.

A century ago there were very few wealthy men except owners of land. The extension of commerce, manufactures, and mining, the introduction of the factory system and machinery, the opening of new countries, and the great discoveries and inventions have created a new middle class, based on wealth, and developed out of the peasants, artisans, unskilled laborers, and small shop-keepers of a century ago. The consequence has been that the chance of acquiring capital and all which depends on capital has opened before classes which formerly passed their lives in a dull round of ignorance and drudgery. This chance has brought with it the same alternative which accompanies every other opportunity offered to mortals. Those who were wise and able to profit by the chance succeeded grandly; those who were negligent or unable to profit by it suffered proportionately. The result has been wide inequalities of wealth within the industrial classes. The net result, however, for all, has been the cheapening of luxuries and a vast extension of physical enjoyment. The appetite for enjoyment has been awakened and nourished in classes which formerly never missed what they never thought of, and it has produced eagerness for material good, discontent, and impatient ambition. This is the reverse side of that eager uprising of the industrial classes which is such a great force in modern life. The chance is opened to advance, by industry, prudence, economy, and emigration, to the possession of capital; but the way is long and tedious. The impatience for enjoyment and the thirst for luxury which we have mentioned are the greatest foes to the accumulation of capital; and there is a still darker side to the picture when we come to notice that those who yield to the impatience to enjoy, but who see others outstrip them, are led to malice and envy. Mobs arise which manifest the most savage and senseless disposition to burn and destroy what they cannot enjoy. We have already had evidence, in more than one country, that such a wild disposition exists and needs only opportunity to burst into activity.

The origin of socialism, which is the extreme development of the sentimental philosophy, lies in the undisputed facts which I described at the outset. The socialist regards this misery as the fault of society. He thinks that we can organize society as we like and that an organization can be devised in which poverty and misery shall disappear. He goes further even than this. He assumes that men have artificially organized society as it now exists. Hence if anything is disagreeable or hard in the present state of society it follows, on that view, that the task of organizing society has been imperfectly and badly performed, and that it needs to be done over again. These are the assumptions with which the socialist starts, and many socialists seem also to believe that if they can destroy belief in an Almighty God who is supposed to have made the world such as it is, they will then have overthrown the belief that there is a fixed order in human nature and human life which man can scarcely alter at all, and, if at all, only infinitesimally.

The truth is that the social order is fixed by laws of nature precisely analogous to those of the physical order. The most that man can do is by ignorance and self-conceit to mar the operation of social laws. The evils of society are to a great extent the result of the dogmatism and self-interest of statesmen, philosophers, and ecclesiastics who in past time have done just what the socialists now want to do. Instead of studying the natural laws of the social order, they assumed that they could organize society as they chose, they made up their minds what kind of a society they wanted to make, and they planned their little measures for the ends they had resolved upon. It will take centuries of scientific study of the facts of nature to eliminate from human society the mischievous institutions and traditions which the said statesmen, philosophers, and ecclesiastics have introduced into it. Let us not, however, even then delude ourselves with any impossible hopes. The hardships of life would not be eliminated if the laws of nature acted directly and without interference. The task of right living forever changes its form, but let us not imagine that that task will ever reach a final solution or that any race of men on this earth can ever be emancipated from the necessity of industry, prudence, continence, and temperance if they are to pass their lives prosperously. If you believe the contrary you must suppose that some men can come to exist who shall know nothing of old age, disease, and death.

The socialist enterprise of reorganizing society in order to change what is harsh and sad in it at present is therefore as impossible, from the outset, as a plan for changing the physical order. I read the other day a story in which a man dreamt that somebody had invented an application of electricity for eradicating certain facts from the memory. Just think of it! What an emancipation to the human race, if a man could so emancipate himself from all those incidents in his past life which he regrets! Let there no longer be such a thing as remorse or vain regret! It would be half as good as finding a fountain of eternal youth. Or invent us a world in which two and two could make five. Two two-dollar notes could then pay five dollars of debts. They say that political economy is a dismal science and that its doctrines are dark and cruel. I think the hardest fact in human life is that two and two cannot make five; but in sociology while people will agree that two and two cannot make five, yet they think that it might somehow be possible by adjusting two and two to one another in some way or other to make two and two equal to four and one-tenth.

I have shown how men emerge from barbarism only by the use of capital and why it is that, as soon as they begin to use capital, if there is liberty, there will be inequality. The socialist looking at these facts says that it is capital which produces the inequality. It is the inequality of men in what they get out of life which shocks the socialist. He finds enough to criticize in the products of past dogmatism and bad statesmanship to which I have alluded, and the program of reforms to be accomplished and abuses to be rectified which the socialists have set up have often been admirable. It is their analysis of the situation which is at fault. Their diagnosis of the social disease is founded on sectarian assumptions, not on the scientific study of the structure and functions of the social body. In attacking capital they are simply attacking the foundations of civilization, and every socialistic scheme which has ever been proposed, so far as it has lessened the motives to saving or the security of capital, is anti-social and anti-civilizing.

Rousseau, who is the great father of the modern socialism, laid accusation for the inequalities existing amongst men upon wheat and iron. What he meant was that wheat is a symbol of agriculture, and when men took to agriculture and wheat diet they broke up their old tribal relations, which were partly communistic, and developed individualism and private property. At the same time agriculture called for tools and machines, of which iron is a symbol; but these tools and machines are capital. Agriculture, individualism, tools, capital were, according to Rousseau's ideas, the causes of inequality. He was, in a certain way, correct, as we have already seen by our own analysis of the facts of the social order. When human society reached the agricultural stage machinery became necessary. Capital was far more important than on the hunting or pastoral stage, and the inequalities of men were devel-

oped with great rapidity, so that we have a Humboldt
a Newton, or a Shakespeare at one end of the scale and
a Digger Indian at the other.   The Humboldt or Newton
is one of the highest products produced by the constant
selection and advance of the best part of the human
race, *viz.*, those who have seized every chance of advancing; and the Digger Indian is a specimen of that
part of the race which withdrew from the competition
clear back at the beginning and has consequently never
made any advance beyond the first superiority of man
to beasts.   Rousseau, following the logic of his own
explanation of the facts, offered distinctly as the cure
for inequality a return to the hunting stage of life as
practiced by the American Indians.   In this he was
plainly and distinctly right.   If you want equality you
must not look forward for it on the path of advancing
civilization.   You may go back to the mode of life of
the American Indian, and, although you will not then
reach equality, you will escape those glaring inequalities
of wealth and poverty by coming down to a comparative
equality, that is, to a status in which all are equally
miserable.   Even this, however, you cannot do without
submitting to other conditions which are far more
appalling than any sad facts in the existing order of
society.   The population of Massachusetts is about
two hundred to the square mile; on the hunting stage
Massachusetts could not probably support, at the
utmost, five to the square mile; hence to get back to
the hunting stage would cost the reduction of the
population to two and a half where there are now
one hundred.   In Rousseau's day people did not even
know that this question of the power of land to support
population was to be taken into account.

Socialists find it necessary to alter the definition of

capital in order to maintain their attacks upon it.   Karl
Marx, for instance, regards capital as an accumulation
of the differences which a merchant makes between his
buying price and his selling price.   It is, according to
him, an accumulation of the differences which the
employer gains between what he pays to the employees
for making the thing and what he obtains for it from
the consumer.   In this view of the matter the capitalist
employer is a pure parasite, who has fastened on the
wage-receiving employee without need or reason and
is levying toll on industry. All socialistic writers
follow, in different degrees, this conception of capital.
If it is true, why do not I levy on some workers somewhere and steal this difference in the product of their
labor?   Is it because I am more honest or magnanimous
than those who are capitalist-employers?   I should
not trust myself to resist the chance if I had it.   Or
again, let us ask why, if this conception of the origin
of capital is correct, the workmen submit to a pure
and unnecessary imposition.   If this notion were true,
co-operation in production would not need any effort
to bring it about; it would take an army to keep it
down.   The reason why it is not possible for the first
comer to start out as an employer of labor is that capital
is a prerequisite to all industry.   So soon as men pass
beyond the stage of life in which they live, like beasts,
on the spontaneous fruits of the earth, capital must
precede every productive enterprise.   It would lead
me too far away from my present subject to elaborate
this statement as it deserves and perhaps as it needs,
but I may say that there is no sound political economy
and especially no correct conception of wages which is
not based on a complete recognition of the character
of capital as necessarily going before every industrial

operation. The reason why co-operation in produc
tion is exceedingly difficult, and indeed is not possibl
except in the highest and rarest conditions of educa
tion and culture amongst artisans, is that workmen can
not undertake an enterprise without capital, and tha
capital always means the fruits of prudence and self
denial already accomplished. The capitalist's profits
therefore, are only the reward for the contribution he
has made to a joint enterprise which could not go or
without him, and his share is as legitimate as that o
the hand-worker.

The socialist assails particularly the institution o
bequest or hereditary property, by which some mer
come into life with special protection and advantage
The right of bequest rests on no other grounds thar
those of expediency. The love of children is the
strongest motive to frugality and to the accumulatior
of capital. The state guarantees the power of beques
only because it thereby encourages the accumulatior
of capital on which the welfare of society depends. I
is true enough that inherited capital often proves ;
curse. Wealth is like health, physical strength, educa
tion, or anything else which enhances the power of the
individual; it is only a chance; its moral characte
depends entirely upon the use which is made of it
Any force which, when well used, is capable of elevating
a man, will, if abused, debase him in the same propor
tion. This is true of education, which is often and
incorrectly vaunted as a positive and purely beneficen
instrumentality. An education ill used makes a mar
only a more mischievous scoundrel, just as an educatior
well used makes him a more efficient, good citizen and
producer. So it is with wealth; it is a means to all the
higher developments of intellectual and moral culture

A man of inherited wealth can gain in youth all the advantages which are essential to high culture, and which a man who must first earn the capital cannot attain until he is almost past the time of life for profiting by them. If one should believe the newspapers, one would be driven to a philosophy something like this: it is extremely praiseworthy for a man born in poverty to accumulate a fortune; the reason why he wants to secure a fortune is that he wants to secure the position of his children and start them with better advantages than he enjoyed himself; this is a noble desire on his part, but he really ought to doubt and hesitate about so doing because the chances are that he would do far better for his children to leave them poor. The children who inherit his wealth are put under suspicion by it; it creates a presumption against them in all the activities of citizenship.

Now it is no doubt true that the struggle to win a fortune gives strength of character and a practical judgment and efficiency which a man who inherits wealth rarely gets, but hereditary wealth transmitted from generation to generation is the strongest instrument by which we keep up a steadily advancing civilization. In the absence of laws of entail and perpetuity it is inevitable that capital should speedily slip from the hold of the man who is not fit to possess it, back into the great stream of capital, and so find its way into the hands of those who can use it for the benefit of society.

The love of children is an instinct which, as I have said before, grows stronger with advancing civilization. All attacks on capital have, up to this time, been shipwrecked on this instinct. Consequently the most rigorous and logical socialists have always been led sooner or later to attack the family. For, if bequest should be abolished, parents would give their property to their children in their own life-time; and so it becomes a logical necessity to substitute some sort of communistic or socialistic life for family life, and to educate children in masses without the tie of parentage. Every socialistic theory which has been pursued energetically has led out to this consequence. I will not follow up this topic, but it is plain to see that the only equality which could be reached on this course would be that men should be all equal to each other when they were all equal to swine.

Socialists are filled with the enthusiasm of equality. Every scheme of theirs for securing equality has destroyed liberty. The student of political philosophy has the antagonism of equality and liberty constantly forced upon him. Equality of possession or of rights and equality before the law are diametrically opposed to each other. The object of equality before the law is to make the state entirely neutral. The state, under that theory, takes no cognizance of persons. It surrounds all, without distinctions, with the same conditions and guarantees. If it educates one, it educates all — black, white, red, or yellow; Jew or Gentile native or alien. If it taxes one, it taxes all, by the same system and under the same conditions. If it exempts one from police regulations in home, church and occupation, it exempts all. From this statement it is at once evident that pure equality before the law is impossible. Some occupations must be subjected to police regulation. Not all can be made subject to militia duty even for the same limited period. The exceptions and special cases furnish the chance for abuse. Equality before the law, however, is one of the cardinal principles of civil liberty, because it leaves each man to run the race of life for himself as best he can. The state stands neutral but benevolent. It does not undertake to aid some and handicap others at the outset in order to offset hereditary advantages and disadvantages, or to make them start equally. Such a notion would belong to the false and spurious theory of equality which is socialistic. If the state should attempt this it would make itself the servant of envy. I am entitled to make the most I can of myself without hindrance from anybody, but I am not entitled to any guarantee that I shall make as much of myself as somebody else makes of himself.

The modern thirst for equality of rights is explained by its historical origin. The mediaeval notion of rights was that rights were special privileges, exemptions, franchises, and powers given to individuals by the king; hence each man had just so many as he and his ancestors had been able to buy or beg by force or favor, and if a man had obtained no grants he had no rights. Hence no two persons were equal in rights and the mass of the population had none. The theory of natural rights and of equal rights was a revolt against the mediaeval theory. It was asserted that men did not have to wait for a king to grant them rights; they have them by nature, or in the nature of things, because they are men and members of civil society. If rights come from nature, it is inferred that they fall like air and light on all equally. It was an immense step in advance for the human race when this new doctrine was promulgated. Its own limitations and errors need not now be pointed out. Its significance is plain, and its limits are to some extent defined when we note its historical origin.

I have already shown that where these guarantees

exist and where there is liberty, the results cannot be equal, but with all liberty there must go responsibility. If I take my own way I must take my own consequences; if it proves that I have made a mistake, I cannot be allowed to throw the consequences on my neighbor. If my neighbor is a free man and resents interference from me he must not call on me to bear the consequences of his mistakes.   Hence it is plain that liberty, equality before the law, responsibility, individualism, monogamy, and private property all hold together as consistent parts of the same structure of society, and that an assault on one part must sooner or later involve an assault on all the others.

To all this must be added the political element in socialism.   The acquisition of some capital—the amount is of very subordinate importance — is the first and simplest proof that an individual possesses the industrial and civil virtues which make a good citizen and a useful member of society.   Political power, a century ago, was associated more or less, even in the United States, with the possession of land.   It has been gradually extended until the suffrage is to all intents and purposes universal in North and South America, in Australia, and in all Europe except Russia and Turkey.   On this system political control belongs to the numerical majority, limited only by institutions. It may be doubted, if the terms are taken strictly and correctly, whether the non-capitalists outnumber the capitalists in any civilized country, but in many cities where capital is most collected they certainly do.   The powers of government have been abused for ages by the classes who possessed them to enable kings, courtiers, nobles, politicians, demagogues, and their friends to live in exemption from labor and self-denial, that is, from the universal lot of man. It is only a continuation of the same abuse if the new possessors of power attempt to employ it to secure for themselves the selfish advantages which all possessors of power have taken. Such a course would, however, overthrow all that we think has been won in the way of making government an organ of justice, peace, order, and security, without respect of persons; and if those gains are not to be lost they will have to be defended, before this century closes, against popular majorities, especially in cities, just as they had to be wcn in a struggle with kings and nobles in the centuries past.

The newest socialism is, in its method, political. The essential feature of its latest phases is the attempt to use the power of the state to realize its plans and to secure its objects. These objects are to do away with poverty and misery, and there are no socialistic schemes yet proposed, of any sort, which do not, upon analysis, turn out to be projects for curing poverty and misery by making those who have share with those who have not. Whether they are paper-money schemes, tariff schemes, subsidy schemes, internal improvement schemes, or usury laws, they all have this in common with the most vulgar of the communistic projects, and the errors of this sort in the past which have been committed in the interest of the capitalist class now furnish precedents, illustration, and encouragement for the new category of demands. The latest socialism divides into two phases: one which aims at centralization and despotism — believing that political form more available for its purposes; the other, the anarchical, which prefers to split up the state into townships, or "communes," to the same end. The latter furnishes the true etymology and meaning of "communism" in its present use, but all socialism, in its second stage, merges into a division of property according to the old sense of communism.

It is impossible to notice socialism as it presents itself at the present moment without pointing out the immense mischief which has been done by sentimental economists and social philosophers who have thought it their professional duty, not to investigate and teach the truth, but to dabble in philanthropy. It is in Germany that this development has been most marked, and as a consequence of it the judgment and sense of the whole people in regard to political and social questions have been corrupted. It is remarkable that the country whose learned men have wrought so much for every other science, especially by virtue of their scientific method and rigorous critical processes, should have furnished a body of social philosophers without method, discipline, or severity of scholarship, who have led the nation in pursuit of whims and dreams and impossible desires. Amongst us there has been less of it, for our people still possess enough sterling sense to reject sentimental rubbish in its grosser forms, but we have had and still have abundance of the more subtle forms of socialistic doctrine, and these open the way to the others. We may already see the two developments forming a congenial alliance. We have also our writers and teachers who seem to think that "the weak" and "the poor" are terms of exact definition; that government exists, in some especial sense, for the sake of the classes so designated; and that the same classes (whoever they are) have some especial claim on the interest and attention of the economist and social philosopher. It may be believed that, in the opinion of these persons, the training of men is the only branch of human effort in which the labor and care should be spent, not on the best specimens but on the poorest.

It is a matter of course that a reactionary party should arise to declare that universal suffrage, popular education, machinery, free trade, and all the other innovations of the last hundred years are all a mistake. If any one ever believed that these innovations were so many clear strides towards the millennium, that they involve no evils or abuses of their own, that they tend to emancipate mankind from the need for prudence, caution, forethought, vigilance — in short, from the eternal struggle against evil — it is not strange that he should be disappointed. If any one ever believed that some "form of government" could be found which would run itself and turn out the pure results of abstract peace, justice, and righteousness without any trouble to anybody, he may well be dissatisfied. To talk of turning back, however, is only to enhance still further the confusion and danger of our position. The world cannot go back. Its destiny is to go forward and to meet the new problems which are continually arising. Under our so-called progress evil only alters its forms, and we must esteem it a grand advance if we can believe that, on the whole, and over a wide view of human affairs, good has gained a hair's breadth over evil in a century. Popular institutions have their own abuses and dangers just as much as monarchical or aristocratic institutions. We are only just finding out what they are. All the institutions which we have inherited were invented to guard liberty against the encroachments of a powerful monarch or aristocracy, when these classes possessed land and the possession of land was the greatest social power. Institutions must now be devised to guard civil liberty against popular majorities, and this necessity arises first in regard to the protection of property, the first and greatest function of government and element in civil liberty. There is no escape from any dangers involved in this or any other social struggle save in going forward and working out the development. It will cost a struggle and will demand the highest wisdom of this and the next generation. It is very probable that some nations — those, namely, which come up to this problem with the least preparation, with the least intelligent comprehension of the problem, and under the most inefficient leadership — will suffer a severe check in their development and prosperity; it is very probable that in some nations the development may lead through revolution and bloodshed; it is very probable that in some nations the consequence may be a reaction towards arbitrary power. In every view we take of it, it is clear that the general abolition of slavery has only cleared the way for a new social problem of far wider scope and far greater difficulty. It seems to me, in fact, that this must always be the case. The conquest of one difficulty will only open the way to another; the solution of one problem will only bring man face to face with another. Man wins by the fight, not by the victory, and therefore the possibilities of growth are unlimited, for the fight has no end.

The progress which men have made in developing the possibilities of human existence has never been made by jumps and strides. It has never resulted from the schemes of philosophers and reformers. It has never been guided through a set program by the wisdom of any sages, statesmen, or philanthropists. The progress which has been made has been won in minute stages by men who had a definite task before them, and who have dealt with it in detail, as it presented itself, without referring to general principles, or attempting to bring it into logical relations to an *a priori* system. In most cases the agents are unknown and cannot be found. New and better arrangements have grown up imperceptibly by the natural effort of all to make the best of actual circumstances. In this way, no doubt, the new problems arising in our modern society must be solved or must solve themselves. The chief safeguard and hope of such a development is in the sound instincts and strong sense of the people, which, although it may not reason closely, can reject instinctively. If there are laws — and there certainly are such — which permit the acquisition of property without industry, by cunning, force, gambling, swindling, favoritism, or corruption, such laws transfer property from those who have earned it to those who have not. Such laws contain the radical vice of socialism. They demand correction and offer an open field for reform because reform would lie in the direction of greater purity and security of the right of property. Whatever assails that right, or goes in the direction of making it still more uncertain whether the industrious man can dispose of the fruits of his industry for his own interests exclusively, tends directly towards violence, bloodshed, poverty, and misery. If any large section of modern society should rise against the rest for the purpose of attempting any such spoliation, either by violence or through the forms of law, it would destroy civilization as it was destroyed by the irruption of the barbarians into the Roman Empire.

The sound student of sociology can hold out to mankind, as individuals or as a race, only one hope of better and happier living. That hope lies in an enhancement of the industrial virtues and of the moral forces which thence arise. Industry, self-denial, and temperance are the laws of prosperity for men and states; without them advance in the arts and in wealth means only corruption and decay through luxury and vice. With them progress in the arts and increasing wealth are the prime conditions of an advancing civilization which is sound enough to endure. The power of the human race to-day over the conditions of prosperous and happy living are sufficient to banish poverty and misery if it were not for folly and vice. The earth does not begin to be populated up to its power to support population on the present stage of the arts; if the United States were as densely populated as the British Islands, we should have 1,000,000,000 people here. If, therefore, men were willing to set to work with energy and courage to subdue the outlying parts of the earth, all might live in plenty and prosperity. But if they insist on remaining in the slums of great cities or on the borders of an old society, and on a comparatively exhausted soil, there is no device of economist or statesman which can prevent them from falling victims to poverty and misery or from succumbing in the competition of life to those who have greater command of capital. The socialist or philanthropist who nourishes them in their situation and saves them from the distress of it is only cultivating the distress which he pretends to cure.

REPLY TO A SOCIALIST [1]

ALWAYS dig out the major premise!" said an experienced teacher of logic and rhetoric. The major premise of Mr. Sinclair is that everybody ought to be happy, and that, if anybody is not so, those who stand near him are under obligations to make him so. He nowhere expresses this. The major premise is always most fallacious when it is suppressed. The statement of the woes of the garment workers is made on the assumption that it carries upon its face some significance. He deduces from the facts two inferences for which he appeals to common consent: (1) that such a state of things ought not to be allowed to continue forever, and (2) that somehow, somewhere, another "system" must be found. The latter inference is one which the socialists always affirm, and they seem to be satisfied that it has some value, both in philosophy and in practical effort. They criticize the "system," by which they mean the social world as it is. They do not perceive that the world of human society is what has resulted from thousands of years of life. It is not a system any more than a man sixty years old is a system. It is a product. To talk of making another system is like talking of making a man of sixty into something else than what his life has made him. As for the inference that some other industrial system must be found, it is as idle as anything which words can express. It leads

[1] *Collier's Weekly*, October 29, 1904.

to nothing and has no significance. The industrial system has changed often and it will change again. Nobody invented former forms. No one can invent others. It will change according to conditions and interests, just as the gilds and manors changed into modern phases. It is frightful to know of the poverty which some people endure. It is also frightful to know of disease, of physical defects, of accidents which cripple the body and wreck life, and of other ills by which human life is encompassed. Such facts appeal to human sympathy, and call for such help and amelioration as human effort can give. It is senseless to enumerate such facts, simply in order to create a state of mind in the hearer, and then to try to make him assent that "the system ought to be changed." All the hospitals, asylums, almshouses, and other eleemosynary institutions prove that the world is not made right. They prove the existence of people who have not "equal chances" with others. The inmates can not be happy. Generally the institutions also prove the very limited extent to which, with the best intentions and greatest efforts, the more fortunate can do anything to help the matter — that is, to "change the system."

The notion that everybody ought to be happy, and equally happy with all the rest, is the fine flower of the philosophy which has been winning popularity for two hundred years. All the petty demands of natural rights, liberty, equality, etc., are only stepping-stones toward this philosophy, which is really what is wanted. All through human history some have had good fortune and some ill fortune. For some the ills of life have taken all the joy and strength out of existence, while the fortunate have always been there to show how glorious life might be and to furnish dreams of bliss to tantalize those who have failed and suffered. So men have constructed in philosophy theories of universal felicity. They tell us that every one has a natural right to be happy, to be comfortable, to have health, to succeed, to have knowledge, family, political power, and all the rest of the things which anybody can have. They put it all into the major premise. Then they say that we all ought to be equal. That proposition abolishes luck. In making propositions we can imply that all ought to have equally good luck, but, inasmuch as there is no way in which we can turn bad luck into good, or misfortune into good fortune, what the proposition means is that if we can not all have good luck no one shall have it. The unlucky will pull down the lucky. That is all that equality ever can mean. The worst becomes the standard. When we talk of "changing the system," we ought to understand that that means abolishing luck and all the ills of life. We might as well talk of abolishing storms, excessive heat and cold, tornadoes, pestilences, diseases, and other ills. Poverty belongs to the struggle for existence, and we are all born into that struggle. The human race began in utter destitution. It had no physical or metaphysical endowment whatever. The existing "system" is the outcome of the efforts of men for thousands of years to work together, so as to win in the struggle for existence. Probably socialists do not perceive what it means for any man now to turn about and pass his high judgment on the achievements of the human race in the way of civilization, and to propose to change it, by resolution, in about "six years." The result of the long effort has been that we all, in a measure, live above the grade of savages, and that some reach comfort and luxury and mental and moral welfare. Efforts to change the system have not been wanting. They have all led back to savagery. Mr. Sinclair thinks that the French Revolution issued out in liberty. The French Revolution is open to very many different interpretations and constructions; but, on the whole, it left essential interests just about where it found them. A million men lost their lives to get Louis de Bourbon off the throne and Napoleon Bonaparte on it, and by the spoils of Europe to make rich nobles of his generals. That is the most definite and indisputable result of the Revolution. Mr. Sinclair also repeats the familiar warning or threat that those who are not competent to win adequate success in the struggle for existence will "rise." They are going to "shoot," unless we let him and his associates redistribute property. It seems that it would be worth while for them to consider that, by their own hypothesis, those-who-have will possess advantages in "shooting": (1) they will have the guns; (2) they will have the talent on their side because they can pay for it; (3) they can hire an army out of the ranks of their adversaries.

In all this declamation we hear a great deal about votes and political power, "ballots or bullets." Of course this is another outcome of the political and social philosophy of the last two centuries. Mr. Sinclair says that "Democracy is an attitude of soul. It has its basis in the spiritual nature of man, from which it follows that all men are equal, or that, if they are not, they must become so." Then Democracy is a metaphysical religion or mythology. The age is not friendly to metaphysics or mythology, but it falls under the dominion of these old tyrants in its political philosophy. If anybody wants to put his soul in an attitude, he ought to do it. The "system" allows that liberty,

and it is far safer than shooting. It is also permitted
to believe that, if men are not equal, they will become
so. If we wait a while they will all die, and then they
will all be equal, although they certainly will not be so
before that.

There are plenty of customs and institutions among
us which produce evil results. They need reform; and
propositions to that end are reasonable and useful. A
few years ago we heard of persons who wanted to abolish
poverty. They had no plan or scheme by which to do it;
in the meantime, however, people were working day by
day to overcome poverty as well as they could, each for
himself. The talk about abolishing poverty by some
resolution or construction has died out. The "industrial system" is just the organized effort which we are
all making to overcome poverty. We do not want to
change the system unless we can be convinced that we
can make a shift which will accomplish that purpose
better. Then, be it observed, the system will be
changed without waiting for any philosophers to propose it. It is being changed every day, just as quickly
as any detail in it can be altered so as to defeat poverty better. This is a world in which the rule is, "Root,
hog, or die," and it is also a world in which "the longest
pole knocks down the most persimmons." It is the
popular experience which has formulated these sayings.
How can we make them untrue? They contain immense tragedies. Those who believe that the problems
of human pain and ill are waiting for a speculative
solution in philosophy or ethics can dream of changing
the system; but to everybody else it must seem worse
than a waste of time to wrangle about such a thing. It
is not a proposition; it does not furnish either a thesis
to be tested or a project to be considered.

I am by no means arguing that "everything is for the best in the best of worlds," even in that part of it where the Stars and Stripes still float.   I am, on the contrary, one of those who think that there is a great deal to be dissatisfied about.   I may be asked what I think would be a remedy for the distress of the garment workers. I answer candidly that I do not know — that is why I have come forward with no proposition.   My business now is to show how empty and false Mr. Sinclair's proposition is, and how harmful it would be to heed it. He only adds to our trouble and burden by putting forward erroneous ideas and helping to encourage bad thinking.   The plan to rise and shoot has no promise of welfare in it for anybody.

Neither is there any practical sense or tangible project behind the suggestion to redistribute property.   Some years ago I heard a socialist orator say[1] that he could get along with any audience except "these measly, mean-spirited workingmen, who have saved a few hundred dollars and built a cottage, with a savings bank mortgage, of which they rent the second story and live in the first.   They," said he, "will get up and go out, a benchful at a time, when I begin to talk about rent."   If he had been open to instruction from facts, he might have learned much from the conduct of those measly workingmen.   They will fight far more ferociously for their cottages than the millionaires for their palaces.   A redistribution of property means universal war.   The final collapse of the French Revolution was due to the proposition to redistribute property.   Property is the opposite of poverty; it is our bulwark against want and distress, but also against disease and

[1] This was one of Professor Sumner's pet anecdotes; we risk its repetition here and elsewhere. — THE EDITORS.

all other ills, which, if it can not prevent them, it still holds at a distance. If we weaken the security of property or deprive people of it, we plunge into distress those who now are above it.

Property is the condition of civilization. It is just as essential to the state, to religion, and to education as it is to food and clothing. In the form of capital it is essential to industry, but if capital were not property it would not do its work in industry. If we negative or destroy property we arrest the whole life of civilized society and put men back on the level of beasts. The family depends on property; the two institutions have been correlative throughout the history of civilization. Property is the first interest of man in time and in importance. We can conceive of no time when property was not, and we can conceive of no social growth in which property was not the prime condition. The property interest is also the one which moves all men, including the socialists, more quickly and deeply than any other. Property is that feature of the existing "industrial system" which would most stubbornly resist change if it was threatened in its essential character and meaning. There is a disposition now to apologize for property, even while resisting attack upon it. This is wrong. Property ought to be defended on account of its reality and importance, and on account of its rank among the interests of men.

What the socialists complain of is that we have not yet got the work of civilization all done and that what has been done does not produce ideal results. The task is a big one — it may even be believed that it is infinite, because what we accomplish often only opens new vistas of trouble. At present we are working on with all the wisdom we have been able to win, and we hope to gain more. If the socialists could help by reasonable and practical suggestions, their aid would be welcome. When they propose to redistribute property, or to change the industrial system, they only disturb the work and introduce confusion and destruction. When they talk about rising and shooting, as if such acts would not be unreasonable or beyond possibility, they put themselves at the limit of the law, and may, before they know it, become favorers of crime.

WHAT IS THE "PROLETARIAT"?[1]

THE latest social agitation is marked by a fondness for big words and high-sounding phrases. The words which are most in favor are not those which are especially sonorous but those which have a philosophical clink and are a little pedantic; and as for the phrases, it is interesting and remarkable to notice in what mouths one may find a forlorn tatter of Hegelian philosophy. The leaders of the movement have created a dialect all their own, which has a strange and foreign sound to the uninitiated, and which suggests far-reaching observations on social philosophy to those who can find the occult significance of the phraseology. It is certain that it becomes a fashion and an affectation among the adherents of the movement to use the terms and bandy the catch phrases of the sect. They are largely the victims of the "phrase."

The dialect of a movement, however, is never a matter to be treated with indifference; in its origin, and in the mouths of the leaders, it had a motive and a logical sense. No American artisan can understand what he means when he talks about the "bourgeoisie" or the "proletariat." The former word certainly is entirely exotic; if it be explained to mean the middle class, it has no application to American society, and it has lost all the side signification which gives it its importance in Europe, when it is so explained. Such words are a part of the foreign dress of a set of ideas which are not yet naturalized. The word, however, cannot be given

[1] *The Independent,* October 28, 1886.

up by the leaders because the essence of their cause is
in it with its acquired and historical side significations.

Proletariat should be a term of reproach. A proletarian at Rome was a man, who, having no property,
could serve the state only with his offspring (*proles*),
whom he gave to military service. No class in any
modern state could correspond to that class at Rome.
The only persons in a modern state to whom the name
might perhaps have been transferred with some convenience are tramps and vagabonds, men without
homes, family, calling, property, or reputation. The
name has, however, been adopted and accepted without
any dislike. It is a grand, foreign, classical, pedantic,
and mysterious term, into which it is easy to distil all
the side significations of class hatred and social rancor
which any one may wish to transmit. After all it
means nothing but what we used to call the masses, and
it has just the same lack of definition and the same
vagueness of limit in its social application. The new
term, however, already begins to give precision to the
social body which it specializes as a fighting faction.
Such is the purpose and the utility of it.

If we try to define the limits of the class so named
according to the present usage of language, it appears,
in the first place, that there is no exclusion at the bottom.
The term is most significant when used politically, and
there are none who have political standing who are not
available allies. Hence the proletariat includes all the
dependent and delinquent classes so far as they have
not lost political privileges.

It is the upper limit which is vague and undefined.
Not all wage-receivers are in the proletariat, for those
who get more than some vague limit or whose wages
are paid at longer intervals (highly skilled laborers and

salaried men) are not included. Not all the employed are in it, for high officials would not be recognized as belonging to it; not all laborers are in it, for we are all laborers except the little group of people of leisure. The President of the United States is an employee and a laborer. Not all capitalists are excluded from it, for many of its members have important savings. Here, however, we undoubtedly come nearest to a definition; for those who have savings would almost all break loose from the proletariat as soon as they recognized the sense of many of its propositions. This fact is so well known that those among the artisan and manual labor classes who have savings are regarded with peculiar dislike in the circles of proletarian agitation. The great millionaires are not denounced with such vigor as the "mean, sneaking workingman who has saved a few dollars which he has laid away in the savings bank, or who has built a little house and rents it for seven or eight dollars a month." "I have seen that class of men," said one orator, "march out by the bench-full as soon as I began to talk about interest and rent. I can talk to great capitalists and employers, but I can do nothing with those men." Still, on the other hand, not all who have not capital would be included; for there are plenty of people who have good incomes, all of which they spend, whose style of life would prevent them from being recognized as members of the proletariat. Peasants in Europe and farmers here do not belong to it; it is a city class quite as much as the bourgeoisie.

At the end of the last century a great revolution took place in which the bourgeoisie wrested political power from the nobles. The peasants and the town mob shared in the revolution and the latter finally got control of it. When the excesses had provoked reaction and order was restored, the bourgeoisie, as the most intelligent and capable section of the population, took control and secured, to some extent, their own ideal of civil liberty and economic prosperity. Their writers have generally agreed, therefore, in regarding the revolution as a great blessing, attended by some most lamentable, but perhaps inevitable excesses. It may yet be necessary to pay a heavy price for the revision of this opinion, for it is now claimed that revolution is a proper and, in fact, the only true and possible mode of social reform; that the bourgeoisie have arrogated to themselves all the gains of the last great revolution, and that another is needed to wrest from them, in turn, what they wrested from the nobles. The proletariat is, in fact, the faction which is formed for this assault. It finds its recruits where it can get them — among the discontented, the hot-headed, the ill-balanced, the ambitious, those who have nothing to lose, the flatterers of rising power, and other such persons who naturally gravitate toward a revolutionary party. It is plain that the thing to be struggled for is political power, not reform; in all great political struggles this is the real object, to gain political power and control of the force of the state.

The government of the bourgeoisie has been faulty enough, and there would be no reason to look with apprehension upon a transfer of the power of the state, if it were sought with the object of more thoroughly doing justice to all. The bourgeois government has threatened, and threatens now more than ever, to degenerate into a plutocracy. If sober and intelligent citizens could see some new power rising in the state, able and intelligently determined to correct and restrain this tendency, they could only welcome its coming.

So far, however, the proletariat has uttered nothing but truculent assertions about what it intends to do for itself against every other interest in the state. It seems to have noted all the sins and shortcomings of the bourgeoisie; but when we look to see what promise of reform it holds out, we find that it only cites the misdoings of the bourgeoisie as excuses and precedents for what it intends to do.

All the forces which gave the bourgeoisie the victory over the nobles are working in favor of the proletariat. The real question of moment is: What will they do with the state when they get control of it? That they will be utterly disappointed in the hopes which their leaders are now encouraging as to what they can do, is certain; but before they find it out society may go through a period of confusion and strife in which all the achievements of civilization will be put in jeopardy. Two parties are already taking shape for that contest. Mr. George recently called them, with the felicity which is his chief power, the House of Have and the House of Want; he defined them as those who are satisfied as things are and those who want to reform. Others have understood them to mean that the "land ought to belong, not to those who own it, but to those who want it." If it should appear upon due study that the latter is the more correct definition according to the facts, it will be another case in which Mr. George's felicity of expression far surpasses his power of analysis. We are indebted to him at least for an excellent terminology, which does away with the old clumsiness of "those-who-have" and "those-who-have-not."

STATE INTERFERENCE [1]

I DESIRE, in this paper, to give an explanation and justification of extreme prejudice against State interference, and I wish to begin with a statement from history of the effect upon the individual of various forms of the State.

It appears, from the best evidence we possess, according to the most reasonable interpretation which has been given to it, that the internal organization of society owes its cohesion and intensity to the necessity of meeting pressure from without. A band of persons, bound by ties of neighborhood or kin, clung together in order to maintain their common interests against a similar band of their neighbors. The social bond and the common interest were at war with individual interests. They exerted coercive power to crush individualism, to produce uniformity, to proscribe dissent, to make private judgment a social offense, and to exercise drill and discipline.

In the Roman State the internal discipline gave victory in contests with neighbors. Each member of the Roman community was carried up by the success of the body of which he was a member to the position of a world-conqueror. Then the Roman community split up into factions to quarrel for the spoils of the world, until the only escape from chronic civil war and anarchy was a one-man power, which, however, proved only a mode of disintegration and decay, not a cure for it. It has often

[1] *North American Review*, August, 1887, CXLV, 109–119.

been remarked with astonishment how lightly men and women of rank at Rome in the first century of our era held their lives. They seem to have been ready to open their veins at a moment's notice, and to quit life upon trivial occasion. If we can realize what life must have been in such a State we can, perhaps, understand this. The Emperor was the State. He was a mortal who had been freed from all care for the rights of others, and his own passions had all been set free. Any man or woman in the civilized world was at the mercy of his caprices. Anyone who was great enough to attract his attention, especially by the possession of anything which mortals covet, held his life at the utmost peril. Since the Empire was the world, there was no escape save to get out of the world. Many seemed to hold escape cheap at that price.

At first under the Empire the obscure people were safe. They probably had little to complain of, and found the Empire gay and beneficent; but it gradually and steadily absorbed every rank and interest into its pitiless organization. At last industry and commerce as well as all civil and social duties took the form of State functions. The ideal which some of our modern social philosophers are preaching was realized. The State was an ethical person, in the strictest sense of the word, when it was one man and when every duty and interest of life was construed towards him. All relations were regulated according to the ethics of the time, which is, of course, all that ethical regulation ever can amount to. Every duty of life took the form and name of an "obsequium"; that is, of a function in the State organism.

Now the most important relation of the citizen to the State is that of a soldier, and the next is that of a taxpayer, and when the former loses importance the latter becomes the chief. Accordingly the obsequia of the citizens in the later centuries were regulated in such a way that the citizen might contribute most to the fiscus. He was not only made part of a machine, but it was a tax-paying machine, and all his hopes, rights, interests, and human capabilities were merged in this purpose of his existence. Slavery, as we ordinarily understand the term, died out, but it gave way to a servitude of each to all, when each was locked tight in an immense and artificial organization of society. Such must ever be the effect of merging industry in the State. Every attempt of the Roman handicraftsmen to better themselves was a breach of the peace; disobedience was rebellion; resistance was treason; running away was desertion.

Here, then, we have a long history, in which the State power first served the national interest in contest with outside powers, and then itself became a burden and drew all the life out of the subject population.

In the Middle Ages a society which had been resolved into its simple elements had to re-form. The feudal form was imposed upon it by the conditions and elements of the case. It was as impossible for a man to stand alone as it had been on the hunting or pastoral stage of life or on the lower organizations of civilization. There was once more necessity to yield personal liberty in order to get protection against plunder from others, and in order to obtain this protection it was necessary to get into a group and to conform to its organization. Here again the same difficulty soon presented itself. Protection against outside aggression was won, but the protecting power itself became a plunderer.

This oppression brought about guild and other organizations for mutual defense. Sometimes these organizations themselves won civil power; sometimes they were under some political sovereign, but possessed its sanction. The system which grew up was one of complete regulation and control. The guilds were regulated in every function and right. The masters, journeymen, and apprentices were regulated in their relations and in all their rights and duties. The work of supplying a certain community with any of the necessaries of life was regarded as a privilege and was monopolized by a certain number. The mediæval system, however, did not allow this monopoly to be exploited at the expense of consumers, according to the good will of the holders of it. The sovereign interfered constantly, and at all points, wherever its intervention was asked for. It fixed prices, but it also fixed wages, regulated kinds and prices of raw materials, prescribed the relation of one trade to another, forbade touting, advertising, rivalry; regulated buying and selling by merchants; protected consumers by inspection; limited importations, but might force production and force sales.

Here was plainly a complete system, which had a rational motive and a logical method. The object was to keep all the organs of society in their accepted relations to each other and to preserve all in activity in the measure of the social needs. The plan failed entirely. It was an impossible undertaking, even on the narrow arena of a mediæval city. The ordinances of an authority which stood ready to interfere at any time and in any way were necessarily inconsistent and contradictory. Its effect upon those who could not get into the system — that is, upon the vagabondage of the period — has never, so far as I know, been studied carefully, although that is the place to look for its most distinct social effect. The most interesting fact about it, however, is that the privilege of one age became the bondage of the next and that the organization which had grown up for the mutual defense of the artisans lost its original purpose and became a barrier to the rise of the artisan class. The organization was a fetter on individual enterprise and success.

The fact should not be overlooked here that, if we are to have the mediæval system of regulation revived, we want it altogether. That system was not, in intention, unjust. According to its light it aimed at the welfare of all. It was not its motive to give privileges, but a system of partial interference is sure to be a system of favoritism and injustice. It is a system of charters to some to plunder others. A mediæval sovereign would never interfere with railroads on behalf of shippers and stop there. He would fix the interest on bonds and other fixed charges. He would, upon appeal, regulate the wages of employees. He would fix the price of coal and other supplies. He would never admit that he was the guardian of one interest more than another, and he would interfere over and over again as often as stockholders, bondholders, employees, shippers, etc., could persuade him that they had a grievance. He would do mischief over and over again, but he would not do intentional injustice.

After the mediæval system broke up and the great modern States formed, the royal power became the representative and champion of national interests in modern Europe, and it established itself in approximately absolute power by the fact that the interest of the nations to maintain themselves in the rivalry of States seemed the paramount interest. Within a few months we have seen modern Germany discard every other interest in order to respond to the supposed necessity of military defense. Not very long ago, in our Civil War, we refused to take account of anything else until the military task was accomplished.

In all these cases the fact appears that the interest of the individual and the social interest have been at war with each other, while, again, the interests of the individual in and through the society of which he is a member are inseparable from those of the society. Such are the two aspects of the relation of the unit and the whole which go to make the life of the race. The individual has an interest to develop all the personal elements there are in him. He wants to live himself out. He does not want to be planed down to a type or pattern. It is the interest of society that all the original powers it contains should be brought out to their full value. But the social movement is coercive and uniformitarian. Organization and discipline are essential to effective common action, and they crush out individual enterprise and personal variety. There is only one kind of cooperation which escapes this evil, and that is cooperation which is voluntary and automatic, under common impulses and natural laws. State control, however, is always necessary for national action in the family of nations and to prevent plunder by others, and men have never yet succeeded in getting it without falling under the necessity of submitting to plunder at home from those on whom they rely for defense abroad.

Now, at the height of our civilization and with the best light that we can bring to bear on our social relations, the problem is: Can we get from the State security for individuals to pursue happiness in and under it, and yet not have the State itself become a new burden and hindrance only a little better than the evil which it wards off?

It is only in the most recent times, and in such measure as the exigencies of external defense have been diminished by the partial abandonment of motives of plunder and conquest, that there has been a chance for individualism

to grow. In the latest times the struggle for a relaxation
of political bonds on behalf of individual liberty has
taken the form of breaking the royal power and forcing
the king to take his hands off. Liberty has hardly yet
come to be popularly understood as anything else but
republicanism or anti-royalty.

The United States, starting on a new continent, with
full chance to select the old-world traditions which they
would adopt, have become the representatives and cham-
pions in modern times of all the principles of individualism
and personal liberty. We have had no neighbors to fear.
We have had no necessity for stringent State discipline.
Each one of us has been able to pursue happiness in his
own way, unhindered by the demands of a State which
would have worn out our energies by expenditure simply
in order to maintain the State. The State has existed of
itself. The one great exception, the Civil War, only
illustrates the point more completely *per contra*. The
old Jeffersonian party rose to power and held it, because
it conformed to the genius of the country and bore along
the true destinies of a nation situated as this one was.
It is the glory of the United States, and its calling in
history, that it shows what the power of personal liberty
is — what self-reliance, energy, enterprise, hard sense
men can develop when they have room and liberty and
when they are emancipated from the burden of traditions
and faiths which are nothing but the accumulated follies
and blunders of a hundred generations of "statesmen."

It is, therefore, the highest product of political institutions so far that they have come to a point where,
under favorable circumstances, individualism is, under
their protection, to some extent possible. If political institutions can give security for the pursuit of happiness
by each individual, according to his own notion of it, in

his own way, and by his own means, they have reached their perfection. This fact, however, has two aspects. If no man can be held to serve another man's happiness, it follows that no man can call on another to serve his happiness. The different views of individualism depend on which of these aspects is under observation. What seems to be desired now is a combination of liberty for all with an obligation of each to all. That is one of the forms in which we are seeking a social philosopher's stone.

The reflex influence which American institutions have had on European institutions is well known. We have had to take as well as give. When the United States put upon their necks the yoke of a navigation and colonial system which they had just revolted against, they showed how little possible it is, after all, for men to rise above the current notions of their time, even when geographical and economic circumstances favor their emancipation. We have been borrowing old-world fashions and traditions all through our history, instead of standing firmly by the political and social philosophy of which we are the standard-bearers.

So long as a nation has not lost faith in itself it is possible for it to remodel its institutions to any extent. If it gives way to sentimentalism, or sensibility, or political mysticism, or adopts an affectation of radicalism, or any other *ism*, or molds its institutions so as to round out to a more complete fulfillment somebody's theory of the universe, it may fall into an era of revolution and political insecurity which will break off the continuity of its national life and make orderly and secure progress impossible. Now that the royal power is limited, and that the old military and police States are in the way of transition to jural States, we are promised a new advance to democracy. What is the disposition of the new State as regards the scope of its power? It unquestionably manifests a disposition to keep and use the whole arsenal of its predecessors. The great engine of political abuse has always been political mysticism. Formerly we were told of the divine origin of the State and the divine authority of rulers. The mystical contents of "sovereignty" have always provided an inexhaustible source of dogma and inference for any extension of State power. The new democracy having inherited the power so long used against it, now shows every disposition to use that power as ruthlessly as any other governing organ ever has used it.

We are told that the State is an ethical person. This is the latest form of political mysticism. Now, it is true that the State is an ethical person in just the same sense as a business firm, a joint stock corporation, or a debating society. It is not a physical person, but it may be a metaphysical or legal person, and as such it has an entity and is an independent subject of rights and duties. Like the other ethical persons, however, the State is just good for what it can do to serve the interests of man, and no more. Such is far from being the meaning and utility of the dogma that the State is an ethical person. The dogma is needed as a source from which can be spun out again contents of phrases and deductions previously stowed away in it. It is only the most modern form of dogmatism devised to sacrifice the man to the institution which is not good for anything except so far as it can serve the man.

One of the newest names for the coming power is the "omnicracy." Mankind has been trying for some thousands of years to find the right -ocracy. None of those which have yet been tried have proved satisfactory. We want a new name on which to pin new hopes, for mankind "never is, but always to be blessed." Omnicracy has this much sense in it, that no one of the great dogmas of the modern political creed is true if it is affirmed of anything less than the whole population, man, woman, child, and baby. When the propositions are enunciated in this sense they are philosophically grand and true. For instance, all the propositions about the "people" are grand and true if we mean by the people every soul in the community, with all the interests and powers which give them an aggregate will and power, with capacity to suffer or to work; but then, also, the propositions remain grand abstractions beyond the realm of practical utility. On the other hand, those propositions cannot be made practically available unless they are affirmed of some limited section of the population, for instance, a majority of the males over twenty-one; but then they are no longer true in philosophy or in fact.

Consequently, when the old-fashioned theories of State interference are applied to the new democratic State, they turn out to be simply a device for setting separate interests in a struggle against each other inside the society. It is plain on the face of all the great questions which are offered to us as political questions to-day, that they are simply struggles of interests for larger shares of the product of industry. One mode of dealing with this distribution would be to leave it to free contract under the play of natural laws. If we do not do this, and if the State interferes with the distribution, how can we stop short of the mediæval plan of reiterated and endless interference, with constant diminution of the total product to be divided?

We have seen above what the tyranny was in the decay of the Roman Empire, when each was in servitude to all; but there is one form of that tyranny which may be still worse. That tyranny will be realized when the same system of servitudes is established in a democratic state; when a man's neighbors are his masters; when the "ethical power of public opinion" bears down upon him at all hours and as to all matters; when his place is assigned to him and he is held in it, not by an emperor or his satellites, who cannot be everywhere all the time, but by the other members of the "village community" who can.

So long as the struggle for individual liberty took the form of a demand that the king or the privileged classes should take their hands off, it was popular and was believed to carry with it the cause of justice and civilization. Now that the governmental machine is brought within everyone's reach, the seduction of power is just as masterful over a democratic faction as ever it was over king or barons. No governing organ has yet abstained from any function because it acknowledged itself ignorant or incompetent. The new powers in the State show no disposition to do it. Nevertheless, the activity of the State, under the new democratic system, shows itself every year more at the mercy of clamorous factions, and legislators find themselves constantly under greater pressure to act, not by their deliberate judgment of what is expedient, but in such a way as to quell clamor, although against their judgment of public interests. It is rapidly becoming the chief art of the legislator to devise measures which shall sound as if they satisfied clamor while they only cheat it.

There are two things which are often treated as if they were identical, which are as far apart as any two things in the field of political philosophy can be: (1) That everyone should be left to do as he likes, so far as possible, without any other social restraints than such as are unavoidable for the peace and order of society.

(2) That "the people" should be allowed to carry out their will without any restraint from constitutional institutions. The former means that each should have his own way with his own interests; the latter, that any faction which for the time is uppermost should have its own way with all the rest.

One result of all the new State interference is that the State is being superseded in vast domains of its proper work. While it is reaching out on one side to fields of socialistic enterprise, interfering in the interests of parties in the industrial organism, assuming knowledge of economic laws which nobody possesses, taking ground as to dogmatic notions of justice which are absurd, and acting because it does not know what to do, it is losing its power to give peace, order, and security. The extralegal power and authority of leaders over voluntary organizations of men throughout a community who are banded together in order to press their interests at the expense of other interests, and who go to the utmost verge of the criminal law, if they do not claim immunity from it, while obeying an authority which acts in secret and without responsibility, is a phenomenon which shows the inadequacy of the existing State to guarantee rights and give security. The boycott and the plan of campaign are certainly not industrial instrumentalities, and it is not yet quite certain whether they are violent and criminal instrumentalities, by which some men coerce other men in matters of material interests. If we turn our minds to the victims of these devices, we see that they do not find in the modern State that security for their interests under the competition of life which it is the first and unquestioned duty of the State to provide. The boycotted man is deprived of the peaceful enjoyment of rights which the laws and institutions of his country allow him, and he has no redress. The State has forbidden all private war on the ground that it will give a remedy for wrongs, and that private redress would disturb the peaceful prosecution of their own interests by other members of the community who are not parties to the quarrel; but we have seen an industrial war paralyze a whole section for weeks, and it was treated almost as a right of the parties that they might fight it out, no matter at what cost to bystanders. We have seen representative bodies of various voluntary associations meet and organize by the side of the regular constitutional organs of the State, in order to deliberate on proposed measures and to transmit to the authorized representatives of the people their approval or disapproval of the propositions, and it scarcely caused a comment. The plutocracy invented the lobby, but the democracy here also seems determined to better the instruction. There are various opinions as to what the revolution is which is upon us, and as to what it is which is about to perish. I do not see anything else which is in as great peril as representative institutions or the constitutional State.

I therefore maintain that it is at the present time a matter of patriotism and civic duty to resist the extension of State interference. It is one of the proudest results of political growth that we have reached the point where individualism is possible. Nothing could better show the merit and value of the institutions which we have inherited than the fact that we can afford to play with all these socialistic and semi-socialistic absurdities. They have no great importance until the question arises: Will a generation which can be led away into this sort of frivolity be able to transmit intact institutions which were made only by men of sterling thought and power, and which can be maintained only by men of the same type? I am familiar with the irritation and impatience with which remonstrances on this matter are received. Those who know just how the world ought to be reconstructed are, of course, angry when they are pushed aside as busybodies. A group of people who assail the legislature with a plan for regulating their neighbor's mode of living are enraged at the "dogma" of non-interference. The publicist who has been struck by some of the superficial roughnesses in the collision of interests which must occur in any time of great industrial activity, and who has therefore determined to waive the objections to State interference, if he can see it brought to bear on his pet reform, will object to absolute principles. For my part, I have never seen that public or private principles were good for anything except when there seemed to be a motive for breaking them. Anyone who has studied a question as to which the solution is yet wanting may despair of the power of free contract to solve it. I have examined a great many cases of proposed interference with free contract, and the only alternative to free contract which I can find is "heads I win, tails you lose" in favor of one party or the other. I am familiar with the criticisms which some writers claim to make upon individualism, but the worst individualism I can find in history is that of the Jacobins, and I believe that it is logically sound that the anti-social vices should be most developed whenever the attempt is made to put socialistic theories in practice. The only question at this point is: Which may we better trust, the play of free social forces or legislative and administrative interference? This question is as pertinent for those who expect to win by interference as for others, for whenever we try to get paternalized we only succeed in getting policed.

WHAT MAKES THE RICH RICHER AND THE POOR POORER? [1]

KARL MARX says, "An accumulation of wealth at one pole of society indicates an accumulation of misery and overwork at the other." [2] In this assertion, Marx avoids the very common and mischievous fallacy of confusing causes, consequences, and symptoms. He suggests that what is found at one pole indicates, or is a symptom of what may be found at the other. In the development of his criticisms on political economy and the existing organization of society, however, Marx proceeds as if there were a relation of cause and effect in the proposition just quoted, and his followers and popularizers have assumed as an indisputable postulate that the wealth of some is a cause of the poverty of others. The question of priority or originality as between Marx, Rodbertus, and others is at best one of vanity between them and their disciples, [3] but it is of great interest and importance to notice that the doctrine that wealth at one pole makes misery at the other is the correct logical form of the notion that progress and poverty are correlative. This doctrine rests upon another and still more fundamental one, which is not often formulated,

[1] *Popular Science Monthly*, January, 1887, XXX, 289–296.

[2] "Das Capital," I, 671.

[3] On this question see Anton Menger, "Das Recht auf den vollen Arbeitsertrag," Stuttgart, 1886. This writer traces back for a century the fundamental socialistic notions. He aims to develop the jural as distinguished from the economic aspect of socialism.

but which can be detected in most of the current socialistic discussions, *viz.*, that all the capital which is here
now would be here under any laws or institutions about
property, as if it were due to some independent cause;
and that some have got ahead of others and seized upon
the most of it, so that those who came later have not been
able to get any.   If this notion about the source of capital is not true, then wealth at one pole cannot cause
poverty at the other.   If it is true, then we can make
any regulations we like about the distribution of wealth,
without fear lest the measures which we adopt may prevent any wealth from being produced.

In Rome, under the empire, wealth at one pole was a
symptom of misery at the other, because Rome was not
an industrial state.   Its income came from plunder.
The wealth had a source independent of the production
of the society of Rome.   That part of the booty which
some got, others could not have.   No such thing is true
of an industrial society.   The wealth of the commercial
cities of Italy and southern Germany, in the Middle
Ages, was largely in the hands of merchant-princes.   If
one were told that some of these merchants were very
rich, he would have no ground of inference that others
in those cities must have been poor.   The rich were
those who developed the opportunities of commerce
which were, in the first instance, open to all.   What they
gained came out of nothing which anybody else ever had
or would have had.   The fact that there are wealthy
men in England, France, and the United States to-day
is no evidence that there must be poor men here.   The
riches of the rich are perfectly consistent with the high
condition of wealth of all, down to the last.   In fact,
the aggregations of wealth, both while being made and
after realization, develop and sustain the prosperity

of all. The forward movement of a strong population, with abundance of land and highly developed command by machinery over the forces of nature, must produce a state of society in which, misfortune and vice being left out of account, average and minimum comfort are high, while special aggregations may be enormous.

Whatever nexus there is between wealth at one pole and poverty at the other can be found only by turning the proposition into its converse — misery at one pole makes wealth at the other. If the mass at one pole should, through any form of industrial vice, fall into misery, they would offer to the few wise an opportunity to become rich by taking advantage of them. They would offer a large supply of labor at low wages, a high demand for capital at high rates of interest, and a fierce demand for land at high rent.

It is often affirmed, and it is true, that competition tends to disperse society over a wide range of unequal conditions. Competition develops all powers that exist according to their measure and degree. The more intense competition is, the more thoroughly are all the forces developed. If, then, there is liberty, the results can not be equal; they must correspond to the forces. Liberty of development and equality of result are therefore diametrically opposed to each other. If a group of men start on equal conditions, and compete in a common enterprise, the results which they attain must differ according to inherited powers, early advantages of training, personal courage, energy, enterprise, perseverance, good sense, etc., etc. Since these things differ through a wide range, and since their combinations may vary through a wide range, it is possible that the results may vary through a wide scale of degrees. Moreover, the more intense the competition, the greater are the prizes of success and the heavier are the penalties of failure. This is illustrated in the competition of a large city as compared with that of a small one. Competition can no more be done away with than gravitation. Its incidence can be changed. We can adopt as a social policy, "Woe to the successful!" We can take the prizes away from the successful and give them to the unsuccessful. It seems clear that there would soon be no prizes at all, but that inference is not universally accepted. In any event, it is plain that we have not got rid of competition — i.e., of the struggle for existence and the competition of life. We have only decided that, if we cannot all have equally, we will all have nothing.

Competition does not guarantee results corresponding with merit, because hereditary conditions and good and bad fortune are always intermingled with merit, but competition secures to merit all the chances it can enjoy under circumstances for which none of one's fellowmen are to blame.

Now it seems to be believed that although competition produces wide grades of inequality, yet almsgiving, or forcible repartition of wealth, would not do so. Here we come to the real, great, and mischievous fallacy of the social philosophy which is in vogue. Whether there are great extremes of rich and poor in a society is a matter of very little significance; there is no ground for the importance which is attached to that fact in current discussion. It is constantly affirmed in one form or another that, although one man has in half a lifetime greatly improved his own position, and can put his children in a far better condition than that in which he started, nevertheless he has not got his fair share in the gains of civilization, because his neighbor, who started where he did, has become a millionaire. John, who is eating a beefsteak off iron-stone china, finds that the taste of it is spoiled because he knows that James is eating pheasants off gold. William, who would have to walk anyway, finds that his feet ache a great deal worse because he learns that Peter has got a horse. Henry, whose yacht is twenty feet long, is sure that there is something wrong in society because Jacob has one a hundred feet long. These are weaknesses of human nature which have always been the fair game of the satirists, but in our day they are made the basis of a new philosophy and of a redistribution of rights and of property. If the laws and institutions of the society hinder any one from fighting out the battle of life on his or her own behalf to the best of one's ability, especially if they so hinder one to the advantage of another, the field of effort for intelligent and fruitful reform is at once marked out; but if examination should reveal no such operation of laws and institutions, then the inequality of achievements is no indication of any social disease, but the contrary.

The indication of social health or disease is to be sought in quite another fact. The question whether the society is formed of only two classes, the rich and the poor, the strong and the weak, or whether all the intervening grades are represented in a sound and healthy proportion, is a question which has importance because it furnishes indications of the state and prospects of the society. No society which consists of the two extreme classes only is in a sound and healthy condition.

If we regard the society of a new country, with little government regulation, free institutions, low taxes, and insignificant military duty, as furnishing us with the nearest example of a normal development of human society under civilization, then we must infer that such a society would not consist of two well-defined classes widely separated from each other, but that there would be no well-defined classes at all, although its members might, in their extremest range, be far apart in wealth, education, talent, and virtue. Such a society might, as it grew older, and its population became more dense, develop, under high competition, great extremes of economic power and social condition, but there is no reason to suppose that the whole middle range would not be filled up by the great mass of the population.

I have now cleared the ground for the proposition which it is my special purpose, in this paper, to offer:

It is the tendency of all social burdens to crush out the middle class, and to force the society into an organization of only two classes, one at each social extreme.

It is in the nature of the case impracticable to adjust social burdens proportionately to the power of individuals to support them. If this could be done, it is possible that the burdens might become great, even excessive, without producing the effect which I have stated. Since, however, it is impossible to so adjust them, and they must be laid on "equally" with reference to the unit of service, and not with reference to some unit of capacity to endure them, it follows that the effect must be as stated. So soon as the burden becomes so great that it surpasses the power of some part of the society, a division takes place between those who can and those who cannot endure it. At first, those who are close to this line, but just above it, are not far removed from those who are close to it, but just below it; but, as time goes on, and the pressure continues to operate, they are constantly separated from each other by a wider and wider interval.

Let us look at some of the historical facts which

show us this law. If we take early Roman history as
Mommsen relates it to us, we observe the constant re-
currence of the difficulty which arose from the tendency of the society toward two extreme classes. It was
plainly the pressure of military duty and taxes which
was constantly developing two classes, debtors and
creditors. The demands of the state fell upon different
men in very different severity according to circumstances.[1] One found himself just so well established
that he could endure without being crushed. Another
found that the time demanded, or the wound received,
or the loss sustained by an inroad, or by being on an
unsuccessful expedition, threw him back so that he fell
into debt. The former, securing a foothold and gaining
a little, bought a slave and established himself with a
greater margin of security. Slavery, of course, mightily
helped on the tendency. Twenty years later the second
man was the bankrupt debtor and bondman of the first.

All insecurity of property has the same effect, above
all, however, when the insecurity is produced by abuse
of state power. In the later history of Rome, the Roman
power, having conquered the world and dragged thousands born elsewhere into Italy as slaves, set to work to
plunder its conquest. The booty taken by emperors,
proconsuls, and freedmen-favorites, and by the sovereign
city, was shared, through the largesses, with the proletariat of the city. The largesses and slavery worked
together to divide the Romans into two classes. The
plunder of the provinces intensified the wealth of the
wealthy. The largesses pauperized and proletarianized
the populace of the great city.[2] They drew away citi-

---

[1] As to the heavy burdens of Roman citizenship, see Merivale, VIII, 284.

[2] See Mommsen, book III, chapters XI, XII; book V, chapter XI; Pöhlmann,
"Die Uebervölkerung der antiken Gross-Städte," Leipzig, 1884.

zens from the country and from honest industry, to swell the mob of the city. If a band of robbers should split into patricians and plebeians and divide the plunder unequally, it is plain that, as time went on, they must separate into two great factions, one immensely rich, the other miserably poor.[1] As for the victims, although at first the severity and security of Roman law and order were not too dear even at the price which they cost, nevertheless the inevitable effect of robbery came out at last, and the whole Roman world was impoverished.[2] Those only among the provincials could get or retain wealth who could gain favor with, or get on the side of the rulers. No satisfactory exposition of the political economy of the Roman commonwealth has yet been written. The effect of the Roman system on population, on the development of capital in the provinces, on the arts and sciences, on the distribution of the precious metals, on city population at Rome and Constantinople, on the development of talent and genius, offers lessons of profound importance, touching in many points on questions which now occupy us. The Roman Empire was a gigantic experiment in the way of a state which took from some to give to others. "At the beginning of the third century already the signs of a fatal loss of vitality manifested themselves with frightful distinctness, and spread with such rapidity that no sagacious observer

---

[1] See especially Friedländer, "Sittengeschichte," I, 22: "In the enjoyment of the extravagant abundance of advantages, excitements, and spectacles, which the metropolis offered, the highest and lowest classes were best off. The great majority of the free male inhabitants were fed partly or entirely at public expense. The great found there an opportunity and means for a royal existence as nowhere else on earth. The middle classes were most exposed to the disadvantages of life at Rome."

[2] See Merivale, VIII, 351; Gibbon, chapter XXXVI, at the end.

could deceive himself any longer as to the beginning dissolution of the gigantic body." [1]

All violence has the same effect.   In the fifth and sixth centuries of our era, the general disorder and violence which prevailed gradually brought about a division of society on a line which, of course, wavered for a long time. A man who was strong enough in his circumstances to just maintain himself in such times became a lord; another, who could not maintain himself, sought safety by becoming the lord's man.   As time went on, every retainer whom the former obtained made him seem a better man to be selected as lord; and, as time went on, any man who was weak but independent found his position more and more untenable.[2]

Taine's history shows distinctly that the middle class were the great sufferers by the French Revolution.   Attention has always been arrested by the nobles who were robbed and guillotined.   When, however, we get closer to the life of the period, we see that, taking the nation over for the years of the revolutionary disorder, the victims were those who had anything, from the peasant or small tradesman up to the well-to-do citizen.[3]   The rich bought their way through, and the nobles were replaced by a new gang of social parasites enriched by plunder and extortion.   These last come nearer than any others whom history presents to the type of what the

[1] Friedländer, I, preface.   While reading the proof of this article, I have read Professor Boccardo's "Manuale di Storia del Comercio, delle Industrie e dell' Economia Politica" (Torino-Napoli, 1886), in which, pp. 74, 75, he expresses the same view as is above given more nearly than I have ever seen it elsewhere.

[2] See Gibbon, chapter XXXVIII; Duruy, "Histoire du Moyen Age," pp. 233, 234; Hallam's "Middle Ages," chapter I, part II; Seebohm, "The English Village Community," chapter VIII.

[3] See Taine, vol. III, book V, chapter I.

"committee" in a socialistic state may be expected to be.[1]

All almsgiving has the same effect, especially if it is forced by state authority. The Christian Church of the fourth and fifth centuries, by its indiscriminate almsgiving on a large scale, helped on the degeneration of the Roman state.[2] A poor-law is only another case. The poor-rates, as they become heavier, at last drive into the workhouses the poorest of those who have hitherto maintained independence and paid poor-rates. With this new burden the chance of the next section upward to maintain themselves is imperiled, and so on indefinitely.

All taxation has the same effect. It presses hardest on those who, under the conditions of their position in life and the demands which are made upon them, are trying to save capital and improve their circumstances. The heavier it becomes, the faster it crushes out this class of persons — that is, all the great middle class — and the greater the barrier it sets up against any efforts of persons of that class to begin accumulation. If the taxes have for their object to take from some and give to others, as is the case with all protective taxes, we have only a more intense and obvious action in the same direction, and one whose effects must be far greater and sooner realized. The effect of protective taxes in this country, to drive out the small men and to throw special lines of industry into the hands of a few large capitalists, has been noted often. It is only a case of the law which I am defining.

My generalization might even be made broader. It is the tendency of all the hardships of life to destroy the middle class. Capital, as it grows larger, takes on new

[1] See Taine, vol. III, book III, chapter III.   [2] Pöhlmann, p. 62.

increments with greater and greater ease. It acquires a kind of momentum. The rich man, therefore, can endure the shocks of material calamity and misfortune with less distress the richer he is. A bad season may throw a small farmer into debt from which he can never recover. It may not do more to a large farmer than lessen one year's income. A few years of hard times may drive into bankruptcy a great number of men of small capital, while a man of large capital may tide over the distress and put himself in a position to make great gains when prosperity comes again.

The hardships and calamities which are strictly social are such as come from disorder, violence, insecurity, covetousness, envy, etc. The state has for its function to repress all these. It appears from what I have said that it is hard to maintain a middle class on a high stage of civilization. If the state does not do its work properly, such classes, representing the wide distribution of comfort and well-being, will die out. If the state itself gives license to robbery and spoliation, or enforces almsgiving, it is working to destroy the whole middle class, and to divide society into two great classes, the rich who are growing richer, not by industry but by spoliation, and the poor who are growing poorer, not by industrial weakness but by oppression.

Now, a state which is in any degree socialistic is in that degree on the line of policy whose disastrous effects have here been described. The state, it cannot too often be repeated, has nothing, and can give nothing, which it does not take from somebody. Its victims must be those who have earned and saved, and they must be the broad, strong, middle classes, from whom alone any important contributions can be drawn. They must be impoverished. Its pets, whoever they may be, must

be pauperized and proletarianized. Its agents alone —
that is, those who, in the name of the state, perform the
operation of taking from some to give to others — can
become rich, and if ever such a state should be organized they may realize wealth beyond the dreams of a
proconsul.

To people untrained in the study of social forces it
may appear the most obvious thing in the world that,
if we should confiscate the property of those who have
more than a determined amount, and divide the proceeds among those who have less than a certain amount,
we should strengthen the middle class, and do away with
the two extremes. The effect would be exactly the
opposite. We should diminish the middle classes and
strengthen the extremes. The more we helped at the
bottom, the more we should have to help, not only on
account of the increase of the population and the influx
of eager members of "the house of want," but also on
account of the demoralization of the lowest sections of
the middle class who were excluded. The more we
confiscated at the top, the more craft and fraud would
be brought into play to escape confiscation, and the wider
must be the scope of taxation over the upper middle
classes to obtain the necessary means.

The modern middle class has been developed with,
and in, an industrial civilization. In turn they have
taken control of this civilization and developed social
and civil institutions to accord with it. The organization which they have made is now called, in the cant of
a certain school, "capitalism" and a "capitalistic system." It is the first organization of human society that
ever has existed based on rights. By virtue of its own
institutions, it now puts itself on trial and stands open
to revision and correction whenever, on sober and ra-

tional grounds, revision can be shown to be necessary to guarantee the rights of any one. It is the first organization of human society that has ever tolerated dissent or criticism of itself. Nobles and peasants have never made anything but Poland and Russia. The proletariat has never made anything but revolution. The socialistic state holds out no promise that it will ever tolerate dissent. It will never consider the question of reform. It stands already on the same footing as all the old states. It knows that it is right, and *all* right. Of course, therefore, there is no place in it for reform. With extreme reconstructions of society, however, it may not be worth while to trouble ourselves; what we need to perceive is, that all socialistic measures, whatever their degree, have the same tendency and effect. It is they which may be always described as tending to make the rich richer and the poor poorer, and to extinguish the intervening classes.

THE CONCENTRATION OF WEALTH: ITS ECONOMIC JUSTIFICATION [1]

THE concentration of wealth I understand to include the aggregation of wealth into large masses and its concentration under the control of a few. In this sense the concentration of wealth is indispensable to the successful execution of the tasks which devolve upon society in our time. Every task of society requires the employment of capital, and involves an economic problem in the form of the most expedient application of material means to ends. Two features most prominently distinguish the present age from all which have preceded it: first, the great scale on which all societal undertakings must be carried out; and second, the transcendent importance of competent management, that is, of the personal element in direction and control.

I speak of "societal undertakings" because it is important to notice that the prevalent modes and forms are not confined to industrial undertakings, but are universal in all the institutions and devices which have for their purpose the satisfaction of any wants of society. A modern church is a congeries of institutions which seeks to nourish good things and repress evil ones; it has buildings, apparatus, a store of supplies, a staff of employees, and a treasury. A modern church (parish) will soon be as complex a system of institutions as a mediæval monastery was. Contrast such an establishment with the corresponding one of fifty years ago.

[1] *The Independent*, April–June, 1902.

A university now needs an immense "concentration of wealth" for its outfit and work. It is as restricted in its work as the corresponding institution of fifty years ago was, although it may command twenty times as much capital and revenue. Furthermore, when we see that all these and other societal institutions pay far higher salaries to executive officers than to workers, we must recognize the fact that the element of personal executive ability is in command of the market, and that means that it is the element which decides success. To a correct understanding of our subject it is essential to recognize the concentration of wealth and control as a universal societal phenomenon, not merely as a matter of industrial power, or social sentiment, or political policy.

Stated in the concisest terms, the phenomenon is that of a more perfect integration of all societal functions. The concentration of power (wealth), more dominant control, intenser discipline, and stricter methods are but modes of securing more perfect integration. When we perceive this we see that the concentration of wealth is but one feature of a grand step in societal evolution.

Some may admit that the concentration of wealth is indispensable, but may desire to distinguish between joint-stock aggregations on the one side and individual fortunes on the other. This distinction is a product of the current social prejudice and is not valid. The predominance of the individual and personal element in control is seen in the tendency of all joint-stock enterprises to come under the control of very few persons. Every age is befooled by the notions which are in fashion in it. Our age is befooled by "democracy"; we hear arguments about the industrial organization which are deductions from democratic dogmas or which appeal to prejudice by using analogies drawn from democracy to affect sentiment about industrial relations. Industry may be republican; it never can be democratic, so long as men differ in productive power and in industrial virtue. In our time joint-stock companies, which are in form republican, are drifting over into oligarchies or monarchies because one or a few get greater efficiency of control and greater vigor of administration. They direct the enterprise in a way which produces more, or more economically. This is the purpose for which the organization exists and success in it outweighs everything else. We see the competent men refuse to join in the enterprise, unless they can control it, and we see the stockholders willingly put their property into the hands of those who are, as they think, competent to manage it successfully. The strongest and most effective organizations for industrial purposes which are formed nowadays are those of a few great capitalists, who have great personal confidence in each other and who can bring together adequate means for whatever they desire to do. Some such nucleus of individuals controls all the great joint-stock companies.

It is obvious that "concentration of wealth" can never be anything but a relative term. Between 1820 and 1830 Stephen Girard was a proverb for great wealth; to-day a man equally rich would not be noticed in New York for his wealth. In 1848 John Jacob Astor stood alone in point of wealth; to-day a great number surpass him. A fortune of $300,000 was then regarded as constituting wealth; it was taken as a minimum above which men were "rich." It is certain that before long some man will have a billion. It is impossible to criticize such a moving notion. The concentration of capital is also necessarily relative to the task to be performed; we wondered lately to see a corporation formed which had a capital of a billion. No one will wonder at such a corporation twenty-five years hence.

There seems to be a great readiness in the public mind to take alarm at these phenomena of growth — there might rather seem to be reason for public congratulation. We want to be provided with things abundantly and cheaply; that means that we want increased economic power. All these enterprises are efforts to satisfy that want, and they promise to do it. The public seems to turn especially to the politician to preserve it from the captain of industry; but when has anybody ever seen a politician who was a match for a captain of industry? One of the latest phenomena is a competition of the legislatures of several states for the profit of granting acts of incorporation; this competition consists, of course, in granting greater and greater powers and exacting less and less responsibility.

It is not my duty in this place to make a judicial statement of the good and ill of the facts I mention — I leave to others to suggest the limitations and safeguards which are required. It is enough to say here that of course all power is liable to abuse; if anybody is dreaming about a millennial state of society in which all energy will be free, yet fully controlled by paradisaic virtue, argument with him is vain. If we want results we must get control of adequate power, and we must learn to use it with safeguards. If we want to make tunnels, and to make them rapidly, we have to concentrate supplies of dynamite; danger results; we minimize it, but we never get rid of it. In late years our streets have been filled with power-driven cars and vehicles; the risk and danger of going on the streets has been very greatly increased; the danger is licensed by law, and it is inseparable from the satisfaction of our desire to move about rapidly. It is in this light that we should view the evils (if there are any) from the concentration of wealth. I do not say that "he who desires the end desires the means," because I do not believe that that dictum is true; but he who will not forego the end must be patient with the incidental ills which attend the means. It is ridiculous to attempt to reach the end while making war on the means. In matters of societal policy the problem always is to use the means and reach the end as well as possible under the conditions. It is proper to propose checks and safeguards, but an onslaught on the concentration of wealth is absurd and a recapitulation of its "dangers" is idle.

In fact, there is a true correlation between (a) the great productiveness of modern industry and the consequent rapid accumulation of capital from one period of production to another and (b) the larger and larger aggregations of capital which are required by modern industry from one period of production to another. We see that the movement is constantly accelerated, that its scope is all the time widening, and that the masses of material with which it deals are greater and greater. The dominant cause of all this is the application of steam and electricity to transportation, and the communication of intelligence — things which we boast about as great triumphs of the nineteenth century. They have made it possible to extend efficient control, from a given central point, over operations which may be carried on at a great number of widely separated points, and to keep up a close, direct, and intimate action and reaction between the central control and the distributed agents. That means that it has become possible for the organization to be extended in its scope and complexity, and at the same time intensified in its activity.   Now whenever such a change in the societal organization becomes possible it also becomes *inevitable*, because there is economy in it.   If we confine our attention to industrial undertakings (although states, churches, universities, and other associations and institutions are subject to the same force and sooner or later will have to obey it) we see that the highest degree of organization which is possible is the one that offers the maximum of profit; in it the economic advantage is greatest.   There is therefore a gravitation toward this degree of organization.   To make an artificial opposition to this tendency from political or alleged moral, or religious, or other motives would be to have no longer any real rule of action; it would amount to submission to the control of warring motives without any real standards or tests.

It is a consequence of the principle just stated that at every point in the history of civilization it has always been necessary to concentrate capital in amounts large relatively to existing facts.   In low civilization chiefs control what capital there is, and direct industry; they may be the full owners of all the wealth or only the representatives of a collective theory of ownership. This organization of industry was, at the time, the most efficient, and the tribes which had it prospered better than others.   In the classical states with slavery and in the mediaeval states with serfdom, the great achievements which realized the utmost that the system was capable of were attained only where wealth was concentrated in productive enterprises in amounts, and under management, which were at the maximum of what the system and the possibilities of the time called for. If we could get rid of some of our notions about liberty and equality, and could lay aside this eighteenth century philosophy according to which human society is to be brought into a state of blessedness, we should get some insight into the might of the societal organization: what it does for us, and what it makes us do. Every day that passes brings us new phenomena of struggle and effort between parts of the societal organization. What do they all mean? They mean that all the individuals and groups are forced against each other in a ceaseless war of interests, by their selfish and mutual efforts to fulfill their career on earth within the conditions set for them by the state of the arts, the facts of the societal organization, and the current dogmas of world philosophy. As each must win his living, or his fortune, or keep his fortune, under these conditions, it is difficult to see what can be meant in the sphere of industrial or economic effort by a "free man." It is no wonder that we so often hear angry outcries about being "slaves" from persons who have had a little experience of the contrast between the current notions and the actual facts.

In fact, what we all need to do is to be taught by the facts in regard to the notions which we ought to adopt, instead of looking at the facts only in order to pass judgment on them and make up our minds how we will change them. If we are willing to be taught by the facts, then the phenomena of the concentration of wealth which we see about us will convince us that they are just what the situation calls for. They ought to be because they are, and because nothing else would serve the interests of society.

I am quite well aware that, in what I have said, I have not met the thoughts and feelings of people who are most troubled about the "concentration of wealth." I have tried to set forth the economic necessity for the concentration of wealth; and I maintain that this is the controlling consideration. Those who care most about the concentration of wealth are indifferent to this consideration; what strikes them most is the fact that there are some rich men. I will, therefore, try to show that this fact also is only another economic justification of the concentration of wealth.

I often see statements published, in which the objectors lay stress upon the great *inequalities* of fortune, and, having set forth the contrast between rich and poor, they rest their case. What law of nature, religion, ethics, or the state is violated by inequalities of fortune? The inequalities prove nothing. Others argue that great fortunes are won by privileges created by law and not by legitimate enterprise and ability. This statement is true, but it is entirely irrelevant; we have to discuss the concentration of wealth within the facts of the institutions, laws, usages, and customs which our ancestors have bequeathed to us and which we allow to stand. If it is proposed to change any of these parts of the societal order, that is a proper subject of discussion, but it is aside from the concentration of wealth. So long as tariffs, patents, etc., are part of the system in which we live, how can it be expected that people will not take advantage of them; what else are they for? As for franchises, a franchise is only an x until it has been developed. It never develops itself; it requires capital and skill to develop it. When the enterprise is in the full bloom of prosperity the objectors complain of it, as if the franchise, which never was anything but an empty place where something might be created, had been the completed enterprise. It is interesting to compare the exploitation of the telephone with that of the telegraph fifty years earlier. The latter was, in its day, a far more wonderful invention, but the time and labor required to render it generally available were far greater than what has been required for the telephone, and the fortunes which were won from the former were insignificant in comparison with those which have been won from the latter. Both the public and the promoters acted very differently in the two cases. In these later times promoters seize with avidity upon an enterprise which contains promise, and they push it with energy and ingenuity, while the public is receptive to "improvements"; hence the modern methods offer very great opportunities, and the rewards of those men who can "size up" a situation and develop its controlling elements with sagacity and good judgment, are very great. It is well that they are so, because these rewards stimulate to the utmost all the ambitious and able men, and they make it certain that great and useful inventions will not long remain unexploited as they did formerly. Here comes, then, a new reaction on the economic system; new energy is infused into it, with hope and confidence. We could not spare it and keep up the air of contentment and enthusiastic cheerfulness which characterizes our society. No man can acquire a million without helping a million men to increase their little fortunes all the way down through all the social grades. In some points of view it is an error that we fix our attention so much upon the very rich and overlook the prosperous mass, but the compensating advantage is that the great successes stimulate emulation the most powerfully.

What matters it then that some millionaires are idle, or silly, or vulgar; that their ideas are sometimes futile and their plans grotesque, when they turn aside from money-making? How do they differ in this from any other class? The millionaires are a product of natural selection, acting on the whole body of men to pick out those who can meet the requirement of certain work to be done. In this respect they are just like the great statesmen, or scientific men, or military men. It is because they are thus selected that wealth — both their own and that intrusted to them — aggregates under their hands. Let one of them make a mistake and see how quickly the concentration gives way to dispersion. They may fairly be regarded as the naturally selected agents of society for certain work. They get high wages and live in luxury, but the bargain is a good one for society. There is the intensest competition for their place and occupation. This assures us that all who are competent for this function will be employed in it, so that the cost of it will be reduced to the lowest terms; and furthermore that the competitors will study the proper conduct to be observed in their occupation. This will bring discipline and the correction of arrogance and masterfulness.

THE COÖPERATIVE COMMONWEALTH

Note by A. G. Keller

AMONG Professor Sumner's papers there turned up a curiosity which I do not like to pass over altogether, although it is more appropriate, perhaps, to the purposes of the biographer. Apparently Sumner amused himself, along in the seventies or early eighties, in figuring to himself the state of the world under a socialistic régime of the sort which he was always ridiculing and opposing. He did this by imagining the contents of a socialist newspaper, the *New Era*, of the date July 4, 1950, consisting of editorials, news notes, public announcements, criminal cases, and even a book review. The whole caricatures in high colors the phenomena attending such a régime in its period of exuberance. "The following," he writes, "is a complete and verbatim copy of a [New York City] newspaper of the date given. It is printed on a small quarter sheet of coarse paper. The printing is so bad that it is hard to read, and the typographical errors, all of which have been corrected, are inexcusable."

The motto of the paper is: "Let the Rich Pay! Let the Poor Enjoy!" The responsible editor is Lasalle Smith, and the proprietors Marx Jones, Chairman of the New York City Board of Ethical Control, Cabet Johnson, Chairman of the Board of Arbitration for Wages and Prices, Babœuf Brown, Chairman of the Board of Control for Rents and Loans, and Rousseau Peters, President of the Coöperative Bank. A notice warns readers that "This paper is published strictly under the coöperative rules established by the Typographical Union in our office and under the direction of the council of the same. The Committee of Grievances gives its assent and approval to each number before it is published. All subscriptions are payable monthly in advance to the Treasurer of the Typographical Union. The Typographical Union, being a member of the organized Coöperative Commonwealth, has police powers for the collection of all sums due to it."

A special notice reads as follows:

We send copies of this edition of our paper to a large number of persons who have not hitherto coöperated in our enterprise but whom we have enrolled until they signify their refusal. We call especial attention to the names and standing in the Coöperative Commonwealth of the proprietors of this journal. We believe that many of those whom we now invite to coöperate, and who have been under suspicion of being monopolists, capitalists, recalcitrants, and reactionists, will see that they cannot better establish their credit for civism than by accepting our invitation.

The following extracts are from the editorials:

Our reports of the Ethical Tribunal show that our noble Board of Ethical Control needs to guard diligently our interests. Another pestilent preacher has been condemned to the chain gang. At least we make sure that our streets will be cleaned, a task which no coöperators could be asked to perform, since all the ancient lawyers, professors, and preachers are now condemned to this business. The stubbornness and incorrigibility of these classes towards the Commonwealth is astonishing.

The Board of Ethical Control announce as the result of the plébiscite which was taken on April 1 last, that, by a vote of 5319 to 782, the Commonwealth voted to retain the present Board of Ethical Control for ten years, instead of reëlecting them annually as heretofore. This is as it should be. Why disturb the tranquillity of our happy state by constant elections when our affairs are entrusted to such competent hands?

The agents of the Board of Ethical Control reported 213 persons found dead in the streets at the dawn of day, 174 bearing marks of violence; the rest, not having coöperators' tickets, were ancient monopolists who had apparently perished of want. The Grand Coöperator said that he should submit to the Board of Ethical Control the question whether it is edifying to continue these reports.

There follow extracts from the inaugural of G. P. M. C.[1] Lasalle Brown, which begin with the sentiment:

Of old ye were enslaved by those who said: Work! Save! Study! We emancipate you by saying: Enjoy! Enjoy! Enjoy!

The first right of everyone born on this earth is the right to enjoy. The Coöperative Commonwealth assures this right to all its members.

We have not abolished private property. We only hold that every man is considered to have devoted his property to public use. We have not abolished landlords, capitalists, employers, or captains of industry. We retain and use them. Such members of a society are useful and necessary if only they be held firmly in check and forced to contribute to the public good.

We need "history" and "statistics" to batter down all the old system, but we should be the dupes of our own

---

[1] These initials, as will be seen below, mean Grand Passed Master Coöperator, while G. C. indicates the lower grade of Grand Coöperator.

processes if we used them against ourselves. All sensible coöperators should know that history and statistics are far greater swindles than science.

There are dangers in the Coöperative Commonwealth which demand vigilance. There is danger of jealousy and division amongst coöperators. Harmony is essential to the Coöperative Commonwealth and we must have it at any price.

Some say that our Commonwealth is weak. It is the strongest state that ever existed. No one before our time ever knew the power of a "mob," as it used to be called. At a tap of the bell, every coöperator is at hand. Our only danger is factious division of this power. Let every coöperator have rewards for harmony and penalties for faction — strict, sure, and heavy!

There is danger from science. The evolution heresy is a worse foe to coöperation than the old Christian dogma. Stamp it out!

There is danger from the virus of the old anarchism — worst of all because it is often enough like the truth to deceive the elect. It means liberty and individualism. Stamp it out!

Under the heading "Domestic News" occurs the following:

The Commissioners of Emigration have detected several persons striving to leave the city for Long Island, carrying gold with them. It is well known that many rich persons, animated by selfishness and disregarding their duties as trustees of their wealth for the public, have escaped to the wilds of Long Island beyond the Commune of Brooklyn, carrying with them all the gold which they could obtain. Hence the Commissioners of Emigration have arranged to patrol the East River by the Commonwealth galleys and have limited the ferry transits to the Fulton ferry between 8 and 9 A.M. and 5 and 6 P.M. Any persons found carrying away gold will be sent to the galleys and the gold confiscated. Gold is needed to buy supplies for the Commonwealth.

No dispatches from Philadelphia have been received for a fortnight. A steamboat of 100 tons burden is cruising in the Hudson River, taking toll of all goods in transit across the river. Reports disagree as to the character of the persons on this boat. By some it is asserted to be manned by coöperators who, being poor, are putting into effect ethical claims against material goods. By others it is said to be manned by a gang of monopolist scoundrels and vagabonds, who, driven to desperation by the boycott and plan of campaign, seek this means to perpetuate their existence. It behooves the Board of Ethical Control to learn which of these reports is correct before taking action.

A report comes from the West that the Indians have seized Illinois, killing the whites and taking possession of the improvements. They have imbibed the ancient capitalistic notions and are impervious to ethical and coöperative doctrines. They are rapidly increasing in numbers, strange as it may seem, for we have read in ancient books that they were dying out a century ago. It is suggested that they now increase because they are conquering, and that they will go on doing so until they exterminate all whites from the continent. In the absence of private mails, we humbly suggest that our Board of Ethical Control should communicate with similar boards of the communes to the westward.

Under the heading "Industrial":

The Board of Equalization of Production have set the amounts of various commodities which may be produced during the coming fall season. Those whom it concerns are to call at the office of the Board at once, pay the fees, and obtain their instructions. The penalty of over-production is fixed at 100 coöperative units per unit of product, half to the informer.

The Board of Arbitration for Contracts will sit daily at their office in Coöperative Hall from 10 to 12 A.M. to approve of contracts. The fee is 1000 coöperative units from each party. Notice is called to the ordinance of the Board of Ethical Control: "If two or more persons make a contract without the presence and approval of the Board of Arbitration or otherwise than in conformity with the regulations of said Board, they may be fined according to the circumstances of the case."

The Coöperative Railroad Commission, having found a mechanic to repair the locomotive, announce that they will recommence regular weekly trips to Yonkers on next Monday. A train will start at 9 A.M., or as soon thereafter as convenient. Accommodation for twenty-five passengers. Passports may be obtained until noon on Saturday. They must be viséd by the Railroad Commission and by the Coöperative Guardians of Public Morals at their office in the Coöperative Workhouse not later than two o'clock on the same time. The fare to Yonkers will be 10,000 coöperative units. On account of the inter-county commerce law, all freight and passengers will be trans-shipped at Yonkers. To prevent vexatious inquiries, the Commission hereby announce that they are not informed whether or when trains will be dispatched to points beyond.

Since the Commonwealth was founded, as our readers know, coöperators have refused to work in coal mines. No great harm has come of this since the factories and machinery have been abolished and railroads and steamers have almost gone out of use. Some coal, however, is a convenience, and our readers will see with pleasure that delinquents in considerable numbers are being sent to these mines under an agreement with our Board of Ethical Control with the similar authority of the Lehigh Commune in the ancient state of Pennsylvania.

We are informed that a number of ancient capitalists and monopolists, being in a starving condition, recently applied to the Board of the said Commune for leave to go into an abandoned coal mine and work it for their own support.

A week ago yesterday, Coöperative Association 2391, A. P. D., bricklayers, 7824, M. X. H., plasterers, 4823 N. K. J., hodcarriers, F. L. M. 8296, joiners, met to consider the state of the building trades. On account of the decrease in the population, by which great numbers of houses are vacant, building has ceased for years past and these once great associations have dwindled down. The Board of Ethical Control has caused public buildings to be constructed in order to give them work and has ordered landlords to make repairs to the same end. The conference on Friday, a week ago, was to consider further measures of relief. It was decided that no vacant house ought to be allowed to stand. Some maintained that no repairs ought to be allowed at all, in order that new houses might become necessary, but others thought that this would take away what little work is now obtained. G. C. Marx Rogers, former professor of political economy, made a speech in which he proposed that all houses now vacant and all ruins now standing which give shelter to unregistered vagabonds and boycotted persons should be destroyed; also that a committee be appointed to inspect all existing dwellings, mark those which are out of repair and unfit for coöperative residences, and that these latter should then be razed to the ground. This would cause an immediate demand for new houses. This proposition was unanimously adopted.

On Wednesday last the coöperative associations aforesaid met to hear the report of the committee. Twelve hundred and forty-seven houses had been noted so far as unfit for residences. The joint associations passed a decree against said houses, as a beginning, and ordered the committee of the whole to proceed to execute it.

They marched in a body to Bleecker Street, the northernmost limit of the ruined houses and demolished them entirely. They then moved southerly, destroying all vacant houses. Gradually, a number of persons gathered to look on. The agents of Ethical Supervision kept this crowd at a distance and secured the joint Coöperative Associations full independence in the execution of their decree.

In East Canal Street, Nonconformist Jonathan Merritt, lessee of a block of tenements, tried to dissuade or prevent the destruction of his buildings. He was roughly handled, his skull split open and his arm broken by the coöperators. The agents of Ethical Supervision took him in on a charge of disturbing the public peace.

When it came to the destruction of occupied buildings, the tenants objected. By the ordinance of the Board of Lodgings and Rents, each had been allotted to his domicile and was, of course, bound to keep it until allowed to change. It was also feared that no lodgings could be found. The Board of Lodgings and Rents immediately convened and issued new allotments of domicile. Suspects, nonconformists, recalcitrants, and reactionists were sent to lodge in the ancient churches and the coöperators were assigned to their tenements.

The revival and prosperity of the building trades is now assured.

Under the heading "Misdemeanors":

Of all forms of incivism, the most reprehensible is hoarding gold. All good coöperators who know of cases of this criminal selfishness are bound to report it at the Bureau of Ethical Supervision under penalty of incivism on the one hand and a reward of ten per cent of the sum on the other. All gold must be exchanged at the bank of G. C. Cabet Rogers for coöperative units.

An audacious lampoon has been printed at some secret press, the authors of which must be discovered at all cost. It is a blasphemous parody of the Coöperative Catechism. The Commission of Ethical Inquiry has directed all its powerful machinery to detect the authors of this outrage. Let every coöperator oppoint himself a detective to help. Search every house in your neighborhood! Trust nobody! Every person found in possession of a copy of this pamphlet will be summarily removed from the Commonwealth.

The supply of potatoes which forms the staple food of the mass of our population is obtained from the northern part of the commune, in what was formerly Westchester County. The great fields there are tilled by the delinquents under taxes and fines, incorrigible monopolists, survival capitalists and others under judicial sentence, under the direction of the Board of Ethical Control. The convicts work from sunrise to sunset, in order to mark the distinction between them and honorable coöperators, who work but five hours per day. The product of the fields on its way to the town is subjected to toll by the free coöperative associations of the suburbs. Hence it always threatens to be inadequate. Good coöperators cannot better serve the Commonwealth than by ferreting out violators of the ordinances and other persons guilty of incivism.

Karl Marx Jones, agent of the Board of Equalization of Distribution, has disappeared. It is thought that he has gone towards Boston. He reported to the Board, it will be remembered, two weeks ago, a case of hoarding of gold. He was sent to collect it and was made custodian of it. It has disappeared. The Board count upon the aid of communes to the eastward to recover the gold, but not very confidently. He left all his coöperative units behind him.

_____

Ordinances of the Committee of Inquiry appears as follows :

Boycotts are declared against Robert Dorr, for saying that the Coöperative Commonwealth is only a scheme to let a few exploit all the rest; Matthew Brown, for saying that it is all a woman's honor is worth to appear on the street of the Coöperative Commonwealth, even thickly veiled, for she runs the risk of attracting the attention of someone against whom no one can defend her; James Rowe, for refusing to aid the agents of the society in taking from her home without public scandal a woman charged with incivism; John White, for hiding gold coin; William Peck, for saying that Grand Coöperator Lasalle Brown secured the boycott of Elihu Snow to get his property away from him; Edward Grant, for saying that the Coöperative Commonwealth is only slavery in disguise and the treatment of persons convicted of incivism is slavery without disguise; Peter Moon, for saying that the Plan of Campaign is only a scheme to allow a man's debtors to rob him of a small fraction of their debts if they will let some of the Grand Coöperators rob him of all the remainder.

_____

A considerable number of minor offences are tried before Grand Coöperator Rodbertus Pease, Member of the Board of Ethical Control:

George Wood, aged sixty, was arraigned for carrying a pistol at night, not being a member of any coöperative club and therefore not entitled so to do. He declared that the streets were unsafe at night and that he never went out after dark if he could help it, but that he was compelled to go for a doctor for his sick grandchild and took the pistol for security. He was met by two coöperators who asked him to contribute to the Aged Coöperators' Retreat. On his declaring that he had nothing, they searched him and found the pistol. They then demanded his coöperator's ticket. As he had none, they took him to the Bureau of Ethical Supervision, where he was detained until morning. The two complainants appeared against him. They declared that they were poor men. On examination it appeared that he was an incorrigible adherent of the ancient monopolism. He was fined 10,000 coöperative units, half to the informers. He began to lament at this, saying that he was very poor — poorer than the complainants; but the Grand Coöperator declared that no man could be a poor man who was not a coöperator.

The Emigration Commissioners whose sole duty is to prevent any immigrants from coming into our commune put at the bar Fritz Meyer, charged with immigrating. He pretended to be a sailor on the *Ferdinand Lasalle*, but did not return on board of her before she sailed. In defence he pleaded that he was left by accident. He was condemned to serve on the yacht of the Board of Ethical Control at the pleasure of said Board.

Ulysses Perkins and others, some of whom were coöperators and some not, complained that their neighborhood was annoyed by the Coöperative Brotherhood who hold their evening festivals at Coöperative Hall. They declared that there was shouting and singing and that windows were broken in spite of the heavy shutters. Their complaint was dismissed as an attempt to oppress organized labor,

and the coöperators amongst them were especially repri-
manded. The Grand Coöperator remarked that the
prejudice against beer which was manifested in ancient
prohibitory and license laws was not respected by the
ethical judgment of our time.

On Monday last, several persons appeared to complain
that the roads outside of the city are infested by robbers.
They were detained and the Board of Ethical Control sent
out delegates to inquire. They reported yesterday, when
the complainants were brought before the tribunal to hear
their report. They denied that there was any robbery,
since robbery means undue exaction of rent or of work for
wages. The word was used by the complainants in the
ancient capitalistic sense. The delegates found many
coöperators enjoying holiday in the fields and by the way-
side. Some of them were playful and resented the exclusive
manner of passers-by who did not engage in sport. They
asked for treats, and they had appointed a committee to
solicit funds for their games. Some bands of banished
monopolists were reported to be infesting the woods, living by chance or by tilling some small fields which have
not been allotted to them, and plotting against the Commonwealth. The Grand Coöperator said that such persons would be promptly dealt with and dispatched a force
of guardians of Ethical Order against them. The complainants were discharged with a reprimand for misrepre-
senting the innocent enjoyment of the coöperators in the
suburb.

William Johnson, employer, was arraigned for contumacy.
The Board of Arbitration ordered him to pay 1000 coöperative units per day of six hours. He closed his works. The
Grand Coöperator ordered a second charge for malicious
lockout and fined him 10,000 coöperative units per day
until he should reopen his works.

Eliza Marcy, cook, actress, 26, was charged with defamation of Emily Wilson, coöperative seamstress. The accused presented a certificate of patronage from G. M. C. Brissot Robinson and was discharged from custody, a rescript of the charge being transmitted to G. M. C. Robinson for such action as he should deem proper.

Maria Waters, arraigned for working at type-setting below man's rates, pleaded poverty and distress as an excuse. She is the daughter of an ancient monopolist from whom she inherited $100,000 before the abolition of inheritance. She had therefore been denied admittance to any coöperative society. She was fined 1000 coöperative units and sent to the Ethical Workhouse to work it out.

Patrick Boyle, coöperative bricklayer, for mending his own table, he not being a member of the furniture-makers' union, was arraigned as a scab and sentenced to forfeit his coöperative ticket, be graded as a non-conformist, and pay 1000 coöperative units fine. Being unable to pay, he was put under G. M. C. Scroggs to work it out.

Under "Benefits and Amusements" :

In addition to the three regular Labor Days of July, the 10th, 20th, and 30th, the Board of Ethical Control has decreed an extra one on the 18th, with full wages. Commonwealth galleys will be ready to convey coöperators and their families to Blackwell's Island, where the dancing and dining rooms in the ancient prisons of despotism will be arranged for their entertainment. There will be a free circus at 3 P.M. and a free variety entertainment in the evening. The two latter have been provided by the liberality of G. P. M. C. Lasalle Brown.

Rents remitted for June and all arrears before January 1.

All coöperators in good standing are entitled to pensions of 100 coöperative units per week, with rations of coöperative bread and beer.

The agents of the Board of Equalization of Distribution will begin next Monday the distribution of July pensions to all coöperators in good and regular standing. The agents will call at the residences of coöperators. There has been some delay which has occasioned just murmurs. It has been due to delinquencies of tax-payers, amongst whom not a little old capitalistic virus remains.

Masked Ball on every Sunday evening in the ancient Trinity Church. Coöperative Enjoyment Association. Admission 100 c. u. All persons must wear coöperative medals displayed.

———

"Foreign News" reports the following débâcle:

It will be remembered that about three years ago the last remnant of English landlords was exiled to Guiana. The Commune of London granted them a ship, of which an immense number blocked the Thames, not having occupation, and they were allowed to navigate it if they could. Their children were taken away from them, to be educated in the principles of coöperation. From this mistaken complaisance a series of evil consequences have flowed.

Some of the exiles have had yachting experience and most of them, being trained in the ancient athletic sports, were able to navigate the ship. Instead of obeying the law, they sailed to Gibraltar and captured the ancient fortress. There they obtained arms and cannons, of which they put a number on board their ship and returned to London. Their first step was to seize the *Columbus*, a fine steamer of 1000 tons burden, one of the newest and in best repair of those lying in the river. They then filled her bunkers with

coal and wood which they took by force from the Commonwealth barges in the river. They next seized the arsenals
at Greenwich and Norwich, carried off a great number of
repeating rifles and ammunition, and destroyed all the rest.
The coöperators of London, being taken unawares and
being prepared only to cope with the city monopolists, who
had been disarmed, were unable to interfere.

The pirates moored their vessel opposite the city and
sent a message of the G. P. M. C. by a captured coöperator that they would bombard the city if their children
were not all delivered to them. A hundred of them landed
with repeating rifles and revolvers and marched to the
coöperative factories, where they set free all who chose
to join them. In short, they departed after securing their
children, a vast quantity of tools and machinery, arms,
supplies, and ammunition. A large number of flunkies
and snobs joined them, sufficient to man one or two other
vessels.

It now appears that they have taken possession of the
Island of Sicily and made it a base of concentration for a
grand political reaction. They have proclaimed as far as
possible that their island is a refuge for landlords, monopolists, and capitalists, and the roads of Europe are crowded
with vagabonds seeking to reach this nest of pirates. The
pirate state is growing. It is a republic like one of our
ancient states. It has an army of 5000 men who boast that
with the arms which they possess they can march from one
end of Europe to another. They control the Mediterranean
and all its coasts. They have served notice on the communal commonwealths of the Continent that they will
avenge any coercion exercised against any persons who
seek to join them, and six months ago they sent a force
of 6000 men to Lyons to set free a band of aristocrats who
were imprisoned there and were threatened with the
guillotine.

It is said that there are no artisans now who are able to manufacture repeating rifles like those which these robbers possess, except amongst themselves — they having hired mechanics to recover the art. Even the guns yet remaining on the Continent cannot be used because the art of making the ammunition is lost. It was a great mistake to let these pestilent scoundrels loose. Their state threatens the whole coöperative movement. Its existence has greatly strengthened the collectivists among coöperators, for it is said that the big empires must be restored (on coöperative principles) to cope with them.

* * *

"Personal Items" record the following:

G. P. M. C. Lasalle Brown last evening gave a grand ball and house-warming in his new house on Fifth Avenue. By demolishing and removing the unsightly ruined houses in the neighborhood, a beautiful park and garden have been added to this fine tenement. It was illuminated last evening by thousands of lamps and torches carried by the convicts who are under discipline in the household of the G. P. M. C. The guests were members of the Board of Ethical Control and their families, some of whom, remembering their own antecedents, observed with interest amongst the convicts sons and daughters of ancient monopolists, and in some cases white-haired survivals from the age of bankers, railroad kings, and merchant princes. Such are the revenges of history!

One hundred new carriages for the Board of Ethical Control have just arrived. They are of the most superb workmanship and cost $5000 in gold each. They belong, of course, to the Commonwealth and can only be used under permission of the Board of Ethical Control. They have been put, one each, under the care of separate members of

the Board, as no private individual is allowed to violate
equality by owning a carriage. We noticed with pleasure
yesterday the families of Grand Coöperators in these carriages in the park.

Non-conformists and others like them outside the pale of
the Commonwealth have, of late years, when they found
their position disagreeable, adopted the plan of attaching
themselves voluntarily as retainers or vassals to coöperators, especially to the leading members of the Board of
Ethical Control. In this way they secure some of the
advantages of coöperation. In order to show their position and relationship, they wear special tokens or marks.
The clients of the newly inaugurated G. P. M. C. have
just been put into uniform or livery. They attended him
in a body on his recent visit to his country seat at River-
dale, where they did guard duty. Added to his personal
bodyguard of coöperators and friends, they made an imposing body. This country-seat, by the way, has just been
surrounded by a high stone wall.

There occurs an obituary of one of the community's
leading lights :

G. C. Brissot Cunningham died at 01 Fifth Avenue on
Wednesday last. He was born May 16, 1905 and was educated for a lawyer. In 1930, putting himself in the fore-
most rank of the coöperative movement and identifying
himself with the most radical section, he was admitted to
the bar. By the abolition of inheritance, he found himself,
on the death of his father in the following year, thrown
entirely on his own resources. He then passed through
some years of obscurity and great poverty, which taught
him to feel for the poor.

Allying himself with the noble band which supported
our present G. P. M. C., he helped to bring about the foun-

dation of the coöperation in 1940 and was elected member of the Board of Ethical Control. In the Board he filled many of the most important and responsible positions on the several committees and was regularly reëlected. He devoted himself to securing the Commonwealth, flinching from no measure to establish it. He believed thoroughly in the motto "Enjoy." After he became a member of the Board of Ethical Control, the former mansion of the ——s on Fifth Avenue was allotted to him and furnished from the Commonwealth storehouse of forfeited property. He there kept up a munificent hospitality on the most altruistic principles. He neither cared to know whence his income came nor whither it went. In the spirit of a true coöperator, whatever belonged to the Commonwealth was his and whatever was his was free to any coöperator. His popularity with the masses was shown yesterday when they turned out in a body for his funeral. The non-coöperators who had felt his scourge were naturally absent. A few of them who could not conceal their joy at his death were summarily corrected by the coöperators. By his death at the early age of forty-five, our Commonwealth has lost a valuable supporter.

[According to the ordinance adopted by the Board of Ethical Control, February 10, 1945, since he died a member of the Board, his family will have a pension of $15,000 per annum in gold for twenty-five years and the use of his house for the same time. The Board will fill the vacancy next week. — Editor of this paper.]

The *Text-book of Coöperation*, ordained by the Board of Ethical Control for schools, is reviewed as follows:

This book is an authoritative exposition of the Coöperative Commonwealth in the commune form. It is to supersede all other books except the primer, writing-book, and elementary arithmetic. We have done with all the ancient rubbish. All the books which have not been destroyed are under the control of the Board of Ethical Control. Especially we are now rid of all pernicious trash about history, law, and political economy. The present book contains all that a good coöperator needs to know. Its tone is strictly ethical. By separating all children of incorrigibles and survivals from their parents and educating them on this book, we may soon hope to bring all capitalistic tradition to an end.

It is plainly proved here that the first right of every man and woman is the right to capital. This right is valid up to the time when he or she gets capital, when it becomes ethically subject to the similar right of someone else, who has no capital as yet, to have some. This principle carried out is the guarantee of justice and equality and is the fundamental principle of the Coöperative Commonwealth in the middle of the twentieth century.

The text-book describes the organization of our Commonwealth, with the duties of coöperators, and gives a list of the ordinances of the Board of Control.

There are now 1000 members of the Board of Ethical Control and 10,000 agents in their employ, chosen by lot monthly from all coöperators. The Board is divided into ten Boards of 100 each for various branches of duty. The members receive no salary but are remunerated by fees. They enjoy no privileges or rights in the Commonwealth, but have the duty of regulating all coöperative affairs according to their conscientious convictions of justice. The ten chairmen of Boards form an exclusive commission which decrees boycotts and plans of campaign. There are no laws or lawyers in the system and no courts or juries of the ancient type, now happily almost forgotten. There are no police, no detectives, no army, no militia, and no prisons. The ancient prison at Sing Sing, which is now within the limits of this commune, is turned into a Coöperators' Retreat.   Under this happy régime no coöperator can do wrong.   Our only culprits are recalcitrants, suspects, incorrigibles, survivals, and other would-be perpetuators of the old régime of monoply and capitalistic extortion.   Such persons are compelled to expiate their selfishness and incivism by hard labor, but they are taken for this purpose into the households or factories of the members of the Board of Ethical Control, where they are subject to ethical discipline and produce those things which are essential to the community and which the Board of Ethical Control contracts to provide.   The employments are such as free coöperators consider disagreeable, unhealthy, or degrading.

The Committee of Inquiry into Incivism is a committee of the Board of Ethical Control and has the high and important duty of watching over coöperative duties.   Its number and members are unknown, lest they should be objects of malice.   Its sessions and procedure are secret. It employs 100 agents but has a right to command the services at any time of all coöperators.   Complaints of incivism may be lodged night or day by any coöperator in the lion's mouth in the court of the Coöperative Hall (ancient United States postoffice).

The Committee proceeds against persons guilty of incivism by boycotts chiefly.   This measure puts the culprit outside the pale of the Commonwealth which he has maligned or in which he has refused to take his share.   Such persons become vagabonds, and disappear or perish.

The chapter on coöperative religion is in the form of a catechism and is to be thoroughly learned by heart by all pupils.   It inculcates the doctrines of our social creed by which each one is bound to serve the health, wealth, and happiness of every other.   Those who have the means of material enjoyment shall put them at the disposition and use of those who have them not.   It impresses above all the great duty of civism, or conformity to coöperative organization and obedience to the Board of Ethical Control.

There is complete equality and no distinction of class in the Coöperative Commonwealth. Every man, woman, and child is eligible to the Board of Ethical Control. The only distinction is of merit and service to the Commonwealth. In this the members of the Board of Ethical Control stand first. There is no second. Outside of the Coöperative Committee are, in order of demerit and detestation, probationers (coöperators who have forfeited their coöperative tickets for fault but who may be restored to membership), survivals (employers, capitalists, landlords, usurers, subject to the Commonwealth and continuing the ancient functions of such persons), nonconformists (stubborn persons who refuse to conform to the new order), recalcitrants (any of the former who have been subject to discipline five times), incorrigibles (after twenty cases of discipline), suspects (so decreed if charged but not convicted of incivism), reactionists (once coöperators but convicted of disorganization) and convicts (under boycott or plan of compaign). Every person must be registered and have always on his person a brass medal hung by a chain about his neck, bearing his designation and number, with the letters designating his group, domicile, also district, ward, and arrondissement. This constitutes his social designation. These medals are given out by the Board of Ethical Supervision. The fee is 1000 coöperative units, repeated each time that the person is re-classified and a new medal issued.

Advertisements are included, as, for example:

John Moon, licensed to sell pistols and ammunition. A few revolvers newly imported from the commune of Hartford at great difficulty and expense. Bliss Bldg.

Henry Black, pistols and bowie-knives. Sales strictly

within the ordinances. Every purchaser required to show coöperator's ticket, and sales registered. 268 Felicity Boulevard.

Elias Israel, pawn broker, loans at 10 % per month on coöperative private property only. Sales of forfeited goods every Sunday. 618 Joy Avenue.

The editor has no compunction about publishing these extracts, though it may be objected that they can be at most of historical or personal interest. Perhaps, in the light of the antics of the Bolsheviki, even such a parody as the foregoing may seem less wide of the potentialities of the socialistic system. In any case, if modern socialism has renounced some of the wild dreams of its past, that is largely owing to the criticism and ridicule poured upon them by vigorous opponents of the Sumner type. Says a prominent American, writing to the editor subsequently to the publication of one of the foregoing volumes of this series: "I have for many years publicly and privately urged socialists to read — *really* read — Sumner — as the most doughty and competent foe with whom they have to reckon."

REPUBLICAN GOVERNMENT [1]

THE best definition of a republican form of government I know of is one given by Hamilton. It is government in which power is conferred by a temporary and defeasible tenure. Every state must have and exert authority; the state gathers together and enforces in concrete form the will of the governing body as to what ought to be done. I may leave aside here those cases in which the governing body is an autocrat or an oligarchy or an aristocracy, because these forms of the state are dead or dying, and take into account only the states in which the people rule and in which, therefore, the governing body is so wide as to embrace at least all who contribute to the active duties and burdens of the state. You observe that, even in the widest democracies, their body is not commensurate with the population. The "people," for political purposes, does not include women, or minors, or felons, or idiots, even though it may include tramps and paupers. The word "people," therefore, when we talk of the people ruling, must be understood to refer to such persons as the state

[1] The *Chicago Tribune*, January 1, 1877, stated in reference to this essay: "William G. Sumner, professor of political economy in Yale College, delivered a lecture entitled 'A Republican Form of Government,' in the Sunday course, at McCormick hall, on yesterday afternoon. It was an effort of rather more grave and timely interest than experience would have led the average lecture patron to expect. The professor is still a young man; his appearance does not indicate a greater age than thirty-five. His clear and pleasant delivery added considerably to the power of his discourse in enabling his hearers to follow his line of argument, without any effort to concentrate attention upon each word."

itself has seen fit to endow with political privileges. The true rule which every state which is to be sound and enduring must set for itself in deciding to whom political functions may be entrusted, is that political rights and political duties, political burdens and political privileges, political power and political responsibility must go together and, as far as may be, in equal measure. The great danger of all wide democracies comes from the violation of this rule. The chief doctrine of democracy is equality, that is, equality of rights without respect to duties, and its theory of power is that the majority has the power without responsibility. If, then, it so happens that the rights and the powers fall to a numerical majority, while the duties and burdens are borne by a minority, we have an unstable political equilibrium, and dishonesty must follow.

In a state, however, in which the limits of co-ordinate rights and duties are observed in determining who shall be the people to rule, whether the limit includes a greater or smaller number of the inhabitants, we see the modern state which is capable of self-government and realizes self-government. Those who pay taxes, do jury duty, militia duty, police duty on the sheriff's posse, or are otherwise liable to bear the burdens of carrying out what the nation may attempt, are those who may claim of right to have a voice in determining what it shall attempt. They therefore make the national will, and out of the nation they form a state. The nation is an organism like a man; the state is like the man clothed and in armor, with tools and weapons in his hand. When, therefore, the will of the state is formed, the state must act with authority in the line of its determination and must control absolutely the powers at its disposal.

Right here, however, we pass over from the abstract to the concrete, from plain and easy reasoning on principles to practical contact with human nature. Power and authority in exercise must be in the hands of individuals. When wielded by boards and committees we find that they are divided and dispersed, and especially we find that, when divided, they escape responsibility. Thence arises irresponsible power, the worst abomination known to the modern constitutional or jural state. The most important practical questions are, therefore: Who shall be endowed with the authority of the state? How shall he be designated? How shall the authority be conferred? How shall the organs of authority be held to responsibility?

In constitutional monarchies these questions are answered by reducing the monarch to an emblem of stability, unity, and permanence, and surrounding him with ministers appointed by him, but under conditions which make them organs of the public will and which hold them to continual responsibility for all the acts of the state. The end is accomplished by indirect means which, nevertheless, secure the result with satisfactory certainty. In republics the organs of authority are designated by the express selection of the people; the people directly signify whom they choose to have as their organs or agents; they express their confidence distinctly either by word of mouth or by other convenient process; they show their will as to the policy of the state by choosing between advocates of different policies submitted to their selection. They do this either by the spoken word or the lifted hand, or by the ballot; they decide by majority vote or by such other combination as they may themselves think wisest; they confer authority for such time as they may determine; and they prescribe methods of responsibility such as they think adapted to the end.   These general prescriptions and limitations they lay down beforehand in the organic law of the state.

It follows that elections are the central and essential institution of republics, and that the cardinal feature in a republican form of government is the elective system. We may therefore expand Hamilton's definition as follows: A republican government is a form of self-government in which the authority of the state is conferred for limited terms upon officers designated by election.

I beg leave here to emphasize the distinction between a democracy and a republic because the people of the United States, living in a democratic republic, almost universally confuse the two elements of their system. Each, however, must stand or fall by itself.   Louis Napoleon gave the French democracy, under his own despotism; France is now called a republic although MacMahon was never voted for on a popular vote.   If the principle of equality is what we aim at we can probably get it — we can all be equally slaves together. If we want majority rule, we can have it — the majority can pass a *plébiscite* conferring permanent power on a despot.   A republic is quite another thing.   It is a form of self-government, and its first aim is not equality but civil liberty.   It keeps the people active in public functions and public duties; it requires their activity at stated periods when the power of the state has to be re-conferred on new agents.   It breaks the continuity of power to guard against its abuse, and it abhors as much the irresponsible power of the many as of the one. It surrounds the individual with safeguards by its permanent constitutional provisions, and by no means leaves the individual or the state a prey to the determination of a numerical majority. In our system the guarantees to liberty and the practical machinery of self-government all come from the constitutional republic; the dangers chiefly from democracy. Democracy teaches dogmas of absolute and sweeping application, while, in truth, there are no absolute doctrines in politics. Its spirit is fierce, intolerant, and despotic. It frets and chafes at constitutional restraints which seem to balk the people of its will and it threatens all institutions, precedents, and traditions which, for the moment, stand in the way. When the future historian comes to critizise our time, he will probably say that it was marked by a great tendency toward democratic equality. He will perhaps have to mention more than one nation which, in chasing this chimaera, lost liberty.

If now a republican form of government be such as I have described it, we must observe first of all that it makes some very important assumptions. It assumes, or takes for granted, a high state of intelligence, political sense, and public virtue on the part of the nation which employs this form of self-government. It is impossible to exaggerate the necessity that these assumptions should be calmly observed and soberly taken to heart. Look at the facts. A people who live under a republican form of government take back into their own hands, from time to time, the whole power of the state; every election brings with it the chances of a peaceful revolution, but one which may involve a shock to the state itself in a sudden and violent change of policy. The citizen, in casting his vote, joins one phalanx which is coming into collision with another inside the state. The people divide themselves to struggle for the power of the state. The occasion is one which seems fitted to arouse the deadliest passions — those which are especially threatening to civil order.

The opinion of the people is almost always informal and indefinite. A small group, therefore, who know what they want and how they propose to accomplish it, are able by energetic action to lead the whole body. Hence the danger which arises for us, in this country, from incorporated or combined interests; it is and always has been our greatest danger. An organized interest forms a compact body, with strong wishes and motives, ready to spend money, time, and labor; it has to deal with a large mass, but it is a mass of people who are ill-informed, unorganized, and more or less indifferent. There is no wonder that victory remains with the interests. Government by interests produces no statesmen, but only attorneys. Then again we see the value of organization in a democratic republic. Organization gives interest, motive, and purpose; hence the preliminaries of all elections consist in public parades, meetings, and excitement, which win few voters. They rather consolidate party ranks, but they stimulate interest; they awaken the whole mass to a participation which will not otherwise be obtained. So far, then, it is evident that the republican system, especially in a democratic republic, demands on the part of the citizen extraordinary independence, power to resist false appeals and fallacies, sound and original judgment, far-sighted patriotism, and patient reflection.

We may, however, go farther than this. The assumption which underlies the republican system is that the voter has his mind made up, or is capable of making up his mind, as to all great questions of public policy; but this is plainly impossible unless he is well informed as to some great principles of political science, knows something of history and of experiments made elsewhere, and also understands the great principles of civil liberty. It is assumed that he will act independently of party if party clashes with patriotism. He is assumed to be looking at the public good with independent power to discern it and to act for it. Thus it follows, in general, that the citizen of a republic is animated by patriotism, that he is intelligent enough to see what patriotism demands, that he can throw off prejudice and passion and the mysterious influence of the public opinion of the social group to which he belongs, that he has education enough to form an opinion on questions of public policy, that he has courage enough to stand by his opinion in the face of contumely and misrepresentation and local or class unpopularity, that he will exercise his political power conscientiously and faithfully in spite of social and pecuniary allurements against his opinion, and that he is intelligent enough to guard himself against fraud. Finally it is assumed that the citizen will sacrifice time, interest, and attention, in no slight degree, to his public duty. In short, it comes to this: the franchise is a prerogative act; it is the act of a sovereign; it is performed without any responsibility whatever except responsibility to one's judgment and one's own conscience. And furthermore, although we are fond of boasting that every citizen is a sovereign, let us not forget that if every one is a sovereign every one is also a subject. The citizen must know how to obey before he is fit to command, and the only man who is fit to help govern the community is the man who can govern himself.

With these assumptions and requirements of republican self-government before us, you are ready to ask: "Where are there any men who fulfill the requirements?"

If we apply the standards vigorously no men satisfy them; it is only a question of less or more, for the assumptions of republican self-government are superhuman. They demand more of human nature than it can yet give, even in the purest and most enlightened communities which yet exist. Hence republican self-government does not produce anything like its pure, theoretical results. The requirements, however, must be satisfied up to a reasonable limit or republican self-government is impossible. No statesman would propose to apply the republican system to Russia or Turkey to-day; our American Indians could not be turned into civilized states under republican forms; the South American republics present us standing examples of states in which the conditions of republican government are not sufficiently well fulfilled for the system to be practicable. In our own experience faults and imperfections present themselves which continually arouse our fears, and the present condition of some of our southern states raises the inquiry, with terrible force and pertinency, whether the assumptions of republican self-government are sufficiently realized there for the system to succeed. I may add, in passing, that the current discussion of questions pending in those states is marked by a constant confusion between democracy and the republican form of government.

I go on, however, to discuss the theory of elections, since this is the essential feature of the republic. Recent events have forced us to re-examine the whole plan and idea of elections, although the institution is one in familiarity with which we have all grown up. When an election is held in a town meeting by *viva voce* vote, or by a show of hands, the process is simple and direct. When the town grows to such a size that the body of voters cannot be brought within the sound of one voice, the physical difficulties become so great that this method is no longer available. It becomes necessary to adopt some system or method, aside from those previously employed, by which the question can be put and the vote taken. We are so familiar with the ballot as hardly to appreciate the fact that it is a distinct invention to accomplish a purpose and meet a new necessity. Right here, however, lies the birth of the political "machine"; for in the next step it is found that organization and previous concert are necessary. With this comes the necessity for nomination, and it is then found that the center of gravity of the system lies rather in the nomination than in the election. The nomination takes the form of a previous and informal election; it offers an opportunity for the majority to exert controlling power. The machinery is multiplied at every step, and with every increase of machinery comes new opportunity for manipulation and new demand for work. The election is to be popular throughout the state, but, for the purpose of nominating, the constituency is broken up into districts which send nominating delegates. Thus this subdivision enables labor to be concentrated upon small bodies in which chicanery, bargaining, and improper influence can be brought to bear. By ward-primaries, caucuses, nominating committees, pledged delegations, and so on, the ultimate power is concentrated in the hands of a few who, by concerted action, are able to control the result. At the same time the body of voters, finding political labor increased and political duty made more burdensome, abandon this entire department of political effort, while the few who persist in it have the continual consciousness of being duped. Upon the larger constituency of voters it is impossible to act, save by public methods, by public writing and speaking, which, although they often deal with base and unworthy motives, are nevertheless generally bound in decency to handle proper arguments. With every increase of machinery come new technicalities, new and arbitrary notions of regularity, fresh means of coercing the better judgment of delegates, and new opportunities for private and unworthy influences to operate. I do not hesitate to say that the path of political reform lies directly in the line of more independent and simple methods of nomination.

To return, however, to the election proper, the theory is that the body of voters shall cast ballots with the name of one or the other candidate. The votes are to be secret in the interest of independence; they are to be impersonal or anonymous, no man's vote being distinguishable from that of any other man after it is cast; they are to be equal, that is, every voter is to cast but one. The law can provide guarantees for all these limitations. Can the law go any further? Having endowed certain persons with certain qualifications to cast ballots, under the assumption that they are fit and qualified to discharge the duty, can it go any further? I think not. I do not see how the law can even confer upon the voter a power to do his duty, if he does not possess that power. If the people think that a man who cannot read his ballot is not fit to cast it, they can by the law of the state exclude all persons who cannot read from the franchise; but if they do not judge that such a qualification is essential, while in fact it is, they cannot possibly eliminate from the ballot-boxes the error or mischief which has come into them by the votes of illiterate or incompetent persons. They can provide for universal education and in time they can thus eliminate this element of harm, but that cannot operate for the time being. Again, if the state by its laws has given a share in political power to men who cannot form an opinion, or can be cheated, or can be frightened out of an opinion, or can be induced to use their power, not as they think best, but as others wish, then the ballot-boxes will not contain a true expression of the will of the voters, or it will be a corrupt and so, probably, a mischievous and ruinous will; but I do not see how a law can possibly be framed to correct that wrong, and make foolish men give a wise judgment or corrupt men give an honest judgment which shall redound to the public welfare. There is no alchemy in the ballot-box. It transmutes no base metal into gold. It gives out just what was put in, and all the impersonality and other safeguards may obscure but they never alter this fact. If the things which the elective system assumes to be true are not true, then the results which are expected will not follow; you will not get any more honor, honesty, intelligence, wisdom, or patriotism out of the ballot-box than the body of voters possess, and there may not be enough for self-government. You have to understand that you will certainly meet with fraud, corruption, ignorance, selfishness, and all the other vices of human nature, here as well as elsewhere. These vices will work toward their own ends and against the ends of honest citizens; they will have to be fought against and it will take the earnest endeavor of honest citizens to overcome them. The man who will never give time and attention to public duty, who always votes with his party, who wants to find a ballot already printed for him, so that he can cast it in a moment or two on his way to business on election day, has no right to complain of bad government. The greatest test of the republican form of government is the kind of men whom it puts in office as a matter of fact, and in any republic the indolence of the public and its disposition to trust to machinery will steadily detract from so much virtue, honesty, wisdom, and patriotism as there may be in the community.

Here I say again, I do not see how the law can help in the matter. All the machinery of nominating conventions and primaries lies outside of the law. It is supported only by public acquiescence and it is the strongest tyranny among us. The fact is that everything connected with an election is political, not legal; that is to say, it is the domain of discretion, judgment, sovereign action. It is a participation in government; it presupposes the power and the will to act rightly and wisely for the ends of government. Where that power and will exist the ends of government will be served; where they do not exist those ends will not be served, — and it is plain that no one can create them. Law prescribes only methods of action; action itself comes from human thought, feeling, and will, and government is action. The autocrat of Russia governs Russia; suppose that he were corrupt or perverse, or ignorant, or otherwise incompetent, and it must follow that the purposes of government would be lost in Russia — no law could give the autocrat of Russia a better mind or heart for his duties. Just so if the sovereign people in any state taken as a whole have not the mind or heart to govern themselves, no law can give them these. We can never surround an incompetent voter by any legal restraint, or protection, or stimulus, or guarantee, which shall enable him to exercise his prerogative, if he is not able to do so as an antecedent matter of fact. His motives lie in his own mind, beyond the reach of all human laws and institutions; the conflicting arguments, prejudices, passions, fears, and hopes which move him meet in an arena where we cannot follow them. If a body of voters in the commonwealth, so large as to control it, are below the grade of intelligence and independence which are necessary to make the election process practicable, then you cannot apply the republican form of government there; it is a hopeless task to take any such community, and by any ingenious device of legal machinery try to make the republican form of government work there so as to produce good government.

It follows, then, that the law can only mark out the precautions necessary to be observed to secure the true expression of the people's will, provided there be a people present who are capable of forming a will and expressing it by this method. The domain of these precautions is in the period anterior to the election — the law must define beforehand who are people fit, on general principles, to share in the government of the state. It will necessarily define these persons by classes and will leave out some who are fit if examined rationally and individually, and it will include many others who are unfit if examined in the same way. It must aim at a practical working system; it must then provide by registration or other appropriate means for finding out who among the population come within the defined qualifications; it must then surround the actual act of voting with such safeguards as seem necessary to secure to each voter a single impersonal vote. When the votes are cast, however, and the polls are closed, the public will is expressed as well as it is possible to have it expressed by an election in that community at that time. It might have been possible to get an expression of the will of that community in some other way, and perhaps in some better way, but that would not have been a republican form of government. The republican way to find out what the people want is to hold an election. If anybody proposes an improved method it may be worth while to consider it as a matter of political speculation, for every one knows by ample observation and experience that the process of elections is open to serious imperfections; it is liable to many abuses, and scarcely ever does an election take place anywhere in which there is not more or less abuse practiced. We know that it is really an imperfect makeshift and practical expedient for accomplishing the end in view. It only accomplishes it better than any other plan yet devised, but if any one can propose a better plan we are ready to give it attention. One thing, however, we never can allow to be consistent with a republican form of government, and that is, that we should hold an election and then correct the result as thus reached by some other result, reached in some other way by guess, estimate, magic, census, clairvoyance, or revelation.

If we pursue the republican system, we must accept the fact that we have in the boxes an arithmetical product which represents the will of the people, expressed as accurately as our precautions have been able to secure. If there was a qualified voter who had no opinion, or was afraid to express it, we have not got his will there, but we have got all that the republican system could get. To secure the truth, now, as to what the will of the people is, we have before us a simple process of counting the ballots. The truth will be presented as an arithmetical fact; it will not be open to any doubt or guess, but will be as positive as anything on earth. Simple as this matter of counting mere units may appear, we all know that the greatest dangers of the election system lie in this very process. The question of who shall count has become quite as important as who shall vote. The whole republican plan or system runs its greatest risk in the manipulation of the ballots after they are cast, and the question of its practicability comes down to this: Can we secure simple fidelity to the arithmetical facts in the count? This we certainly cannot do unless it is understood that absolute fidelity to the facts is the highest and only function of all officers and persons who are allowed to handle the ballots after they are cast. Every man who has grown up in familiarity with the election process knows that when we abandon the count of the votes as cast we go off into arbitrary manipulations and decisions for which we have no guarantee whatever, and that the political power of the state, if we allow any such manipulation, is transferred from those who vote to those who manipulate. If it is charged that frauds have been perpetrated in the election, that is to say that any of the laws which limit and define the exercise of the elective franchise have been broken, such charges raise questions of fact. If the charges are proved true, each charge affects the result by a given arithmetical quantity, and these effects can be added or subtracted as the case may be. Here we are dealing with facts, not opinions; we have solid ground under our feet. We do not work backward from the results, we work forward from the evidence; and so long as we use tribunals which seek only facts and remain steadfast to the truth as proved, the republican system suffers no shock. If, however, legislative committees or any other tribunals decide, in cases of contested elections, not by the truth but by party interest, we are face to face with the greatest treason against republican institutions which can possibly exist.

I believe that the American people love republican institutions. I have no doubt whatever that if we keep our records clean in regard to what republican institutions are, so that we recognize and repel the first inroads upon them, we can adapt our institutions to any exigencies that may arise. I think that the country has, to a certain extent, outgrown some of its institutions in their present form. I believe it has given its faith to some false and pernicious doctrines about equality and the rights of man. I believe that the astonishing social and economic developments of the last few years, together with some of the heavy problems which are legacies of the war, have thrown upon us difficulties whose magnitude we hardly yet appreciate and which we cannot cope with unless we set to work at them with greater energy and sobriety than we have yet employed. Some of these things involve or threaten the republic in its essence. We can deal with them all under its forms and methods if we have the political sense which the system requires. Here, however, lies the difficulty. Political institutions do not admit of sharp definition or rigid application; they need broad comprehension, gentle and conciliatory application; they require the highest statesmanship in public men. Self-government could not be established by all the political machinery which the wit of man could invent; on the contrary, the more machinery we have the greater is the danger to self-government. Civil liberty could not be defined by constitutions and treatises which might fill libraries; civil liberty cannot even be guaranteed by constitutions — I doubt if it can be stated in propositions at all. Yet civil liberty is the great end for which modern states

exist. It is the careful adjustment by which the rights
of individuals and the state are reconciled with one
another to allow the greatest possible development of
all and of each in harmony and peace. It is the triumph
of the effort to substitute right for might, and the
repression of law for the wild struggles of barbarism.
Civil liberty, as now known, is not a logical or rational
deduction at all; it is the result of centuries of experience
which have cost the human race an untold expenditure
of blood and labor. As the result we have a series of
institutions, traditions, and positive restraints upon the
governing power. These things, however, would not
in themselves suffice. We have also large communities
which have inherited the love of civil liberty and the
experience of it—communities which have imperceptibly
imbibed the conception of civil liberty from family life
and from the whole social and political life of the nation.
Civil liberty has thus become a popular instinct. Let
us guard well these prejudices and these instincts, for
we may be well assured that in them lies the only real
guarantee of civil liberty. Whenever they become so
blunted that an infringement of one of the old traditions
of civil liberty is viewed with neglect and indifference
then we must take the alarm for civil liberty. It seems
to me a physical impossibility that we should have a
Caesar here until after we have run through a long
course of degeneration. That is not our danger, and
while we look for it in that direction we overlook it on
the side from which it may come. There are numberless ways beside the usurpation of a dictator in which
civil liberty may be lost; there are numberless forms of
degeneration for a constitutional republic besides monarchy and despotism. We can keep the names and
forms of republican self-government long after their

power to secure civil liberty is lost. The degeneration may go on so slowly that only after a generation or two will the people realize that the old tradition is lost and that the fresh, spontaneous power of the people, which we call political sense, is dead. Such is the danger which continually menaces the republic, and the only safeguard against it is the jealous instinct of the people, which is quick to take the alarm and which will not, at any time or under any excuse, allow even a slight or temporary infringement upon civil liberty. Such infringements when made are always made under specious pretexts. Kings who set aside civil liberty always do it for "higher reasons of state"; in a republic likewise you will find, especially at great public crises, that men and parties are promptly ready to take the same course and assume the rôle of "saviors of society," for the sake of something which they easily persuade themselves to be a transcendent public interest. The constitutional republic, however, does not call upon men to play the hero; it only calls upon them to do their duty under the laws and the constitution, in any position in which they may be placed, and no more.

DEMOCRACY AND PLUTOCRACY [1]

ONE of the most difficult things to learn in social science is that every action inside of the social organism is attended by a reaction, and that this reaction may be spread far through the organism, affecting organs and modifying functions which are, at the first view of the matter, apparently so remote that they could not be affected at all. It is a more simple statement of the same fact to say that everything in the social organism displaces everything else. Therefore, if we set to work to interfere in .the operation of the organism, with our attention all absorbed in one set of phenomena, and regulate our policy with a view to those phenomena only, we are very sure to do mischief. The current speculations about social policy and social reform suffer very largely from this error.

The organization of a modern civilized society is intensely high; its parts are extremely complicated. Their relations with each other are close, and all the tendencies of our time are making them closer; and the closer they are, the more surely and immediately are interferences distributed through them. The bonds of connection between them are constantly becoming more delicate and subtle; and they are sublimated, as it were, so that they escape the observation of the senses. In a simple society, even though it be on the height of the best civilization, all the parts of the organization lie bare to view, and every one can see the relations of agriculturist, transporter, banker, merchant, professional

[1] *The Independent*, November 15, 1888.

man, debtor, creditor, employer, and employee, in their visible operation. In a highly organized society as, for instance, in a big city, those same relations have all become automatic and impersonal. They have escaped from control; they are regulated by assumptions and understandings that every one is to do so and so; that certain uniform and constant motives, aims, and desires will present themselves as long as human society endures; and that men will, therefore, continue to exert themselves in a certain manner for the satisfaction of their wants. This is what we mean by natural law, and by the field of a science of society. If any one will look over his dinner table the next time he sits down to dinner, he can see the proofs that thousands of producers, transporters, merchants, bankers, policemen, and mechanics, through the whole organization of society and all over the globe, have been at work for the last year or more to put that dinner within his reach, on the assumption that he, too, would do his work in the organization, whatever it is, and be prepared to pay for the dinner when it reaches him. All these thousands and millions of people, therefore, have co-operated with each other for the common good of all, without acquaintance or conventional agreement, and without any personal interest in each other, under the play of forces which lie in human nature and in the conditions of human existence on this earth.

Now, the organs of society do not impinge upon each other with hard and grating friction, like blocks of granite wedged together. If they did the case would be easier, for then we should have only a mechanical contact, and the relations would be of a simple order. Neither are the relations those of an orchestra, which produces harmony by voluntary co-operation under training, according to a predetermined scheme, yet subject to the laws of harmony in sound. Nor are the relations like those of an army, where the co-operation is arbitrary, and enforced by discipline, although controlled by expediency for the attainment of an end under set conditions. The organs are elastic and they are plastic. They suffer both temporary and permanent modifications in form and function by their interaction on each other, and by the arbitrary interferences to which they are subjected by legislation or artifice of any kind. Thus, for instance, it is impossible to say how taxes will diffuse themselves; they may force a change in the immediate organ on which they fall — transporters, merchants, bankers — or they may be transmitted more or less through the organization.

It is this elasticity and plasticity of the organs of society which give the social tinker his chance, and make him think that there are no laws of the social order, no science of society; no limits, in fact, to the possibilities of manipulation by "The State."

He is always operating on the limit of give and take between the organs; he regards all the displacement which he can accomplish as positively new creation; he does not notice at all, and probably is not trained to perceive, the reaction — the other side of the change; he does not understand that he must endure a change on one side for all the change which he affects on the other. Since it is so hard to learn that exchange means exchange, and therefore has two sides to it, a giving and a taking — since, I say it is so hard to learn this, and people talk even about buying and selling as if they were independent operations, a fallacy which is itself the outcome of a high organization with a money system — then it is not strange that it should be so hard to learn that all social change is change, has two sides to it — the cost and the gain, the price and the product, the sacrifice and the obtainment.

Hence we see one fallacy of nearly all the popular propositions of "reform": they would not be amiss, perhaps, if the change which they propose could be made and everything else remain the same.

In the proposition it is assumed that everything else is to remain the same. But it is inevitable that other things will not remain the same; they will all of them adjust themselves to the new elements which are introduced. If we make a change involving expense, taxes must be increased, and every taxed interest must undergo a change to fit it to the new conditions. I know of no reform by state agency which does not involve increased taxation.

Let us note another fact. In the advancing organization of society, the tendency is all the time to subdivide the functions, and each one is assumed by a different set of persons; thus the interests of living men and women become enlisted in all the play of the organs, and are at stake in all the legislative and other interferences. What I have called the elasticity and plasticity of the organs means in fact the rights, interest, happiness, and prosperity of the one set of human beings versus the same interests of another set of human beings. It is men who strive, and suffer, and plan, and fight, and steal, and kill, when the great impersonal and automatic forces push them up against each other, or push group against group. The tendency is all the time to go back from the industrial struggle to the military struggle. Every strike illustrates it. Better educated people, while talking about respect for law, seize upon legislation as the modern mode of pursuing the military struggle under the forms of peace and order — that is to say, they turn from industrial competition and industrial effort to legislative compulsion, and to arbitrary advantages won and secured through the direction and the power of the state. When the strikers and Knights of Labor declare that they are going to reach after this power, they have simply determined to contend for the latest form of force by which to supersede the industrial struggle for existence by a struggle of craft and physical force. Yet there are those who tell us that this is really a supersession of the struggle for existence by intelligence and "ethical" forces, as if every page of the Congressional Record did not reveal the sordidness of the plans and motives by which it is all controlled.

Here comes in another fallacy in the philosophy of state interference. Let the reader note for himself with what *naïveté* the advocate of interference takes it for granted that he and his associates will have the administration of their legislative device in their own hands and will be sure of guiding it for their purposes only. They never appear to remember that the device, when once set up, will itself become the prize of a struggle; that it will serve one set of purposes as well as another, so that after all the only serious question is: who will get it? Here is another ground for a general and sweeping policy of non-interference. Although you may be in possession of the power of the state to-day, and it might suit you very well, either to triumph over your business rivals and competitors; or to bend to your will the social organ which stands next to you, and with which you have the most friction (as, for instance, shippers with transporters); or to see your pet reform (temperance, for instance) marching on, you would far better consent to forego your satisfaction, lest presently your rivals, or the railroads, or the liquor-sellers, should beat you in a political struggle; and then you must suffer wrong and in the end be forced to give up industrial and persuasive methods altogether and devote your whole energy to the political struggle, as that on which all the rest depends.

Of all that I have here said, the Interstate Commerce Law is the instance which stands out in point with the greatest distinctness. The shippers and transporters, the competing railroads, the people who can extort passes and those who do not want to give them, the people at way-stations and those at competing points, and other interests also which cluster about the transportation, which is the most important element in the opening up of this great and rich continent, all clash and struggle for shares in the wealth which the people of the United States produce. The contest has phases and vicissitudes of every description. The politicians, editors, economists, *littérateurs*, lawyers, labor agitators, and countless others who, in one way or another, have something to make out of it, join in the struggle, taking sides with the principal parties, or hovering around the strife for what may turn up in it. When once the fatal step is taken of invoking legislation, the contest is changed in its character and in its arena. That is all that is accomplished; from that time on the questions are: who will get this legislative power? Which interest or coalition of interests (such as passed the bill) will get this, the decisive position in the battle, under its control? Already, in some of the Western States, the next phase has developed itself. The majority interest, by numbers, seizes the power of the state and proceeds to realize its own interest against all others in the most ruthless fashion. That capital has means of defense is unquestionable; that it will defend itself is certain; that it cannot defend itself without resorting to all the vices of plutocracy seems inevitable. Thus the issue of democracy and plutocracy, numbers against capital, is made up. It is the issue which menaces modern society, and which is destined to dispel the dreams which have been cherished, that we were on the eve of a millennium. On the contrary, it will probably appear that the advance of civilization constantly brings new necessity for a still more elevated activity of reason and conscience, and does not tend at all to a condition of stability, in which the social and political problems of the race would reach a definitive solution.

DEFINITIONS OF DEMOCRACY AND PLUTOCRACY [1]

ALL the words in -ocracy properly describe political forms according to the chief spring of political power in them: an autocracy is a political form in which the predominant force is the will of the monarch himself; an aristocracy is a form in which the predominant and controlling force is the will of a limited body, having the possession of the qualities which are most esteemed and envied in that society; a theocracy is a form in which the predominant force is some conception of God and his will, and, inasmuch as the will of God can come to men only through some finite channel, a theocracy easily passes into a hierocracy, in which the predominant force is possessed and wielded by a priesthood; a bureaucracy is a form in which the ultimate control of things political lies in the hands of a body of office-holders. In each case the name designates that organ which, upon ultimate analysis, is found to have the power to say what shall be and what shall not be.

A democracy, then, is a political form in which the ultimate power lies with the *demos*, the people. This mass, however, while unorganized, could not express its will or administer the affairs of the state; there has never been any state organized on such a plan. The *demos*, for political purposes, has always excluded women, minors, resident aliens, slaves, paupers, felons, etc., according to the constitution in each case; the "people," therefore, has always meant some defined section of the

[1] *The Independent,* December 20, 1888.

population, not the whole of it. Furthermore, in any modern state, even a superficial study of the current phrases and accepted formulæ will show that the word "people" is used in a technical sense to mean, not even the whole body of legal voters, but a limited number of them. A writer who rages at the idea that there are any "classes" will, in the next paragraph, reiterate all the current formulæ about the "people," and reveal by the context that he means to distinguish the people as peasants, artisans, and uneducated persons, from the rich, the educated, and the banking, mercantile, and professional classes.

Yet the current dogmas about the rights and wisdom of the people have no truth whatever, and no moral beauty, except when they are affirmed of the whole population, without any exception whatever. The dogmas in question are not really maxims or principles of actual political life and administration; they are sublime conceptions of the undeveloped power of growth and civilization in human society. As inspiring ideals, as educational motives, as moral incentives, they have incalculable value; but then they are philosophical and academical generalities, not every-day rules of action for specific exigencies. When they are once dragged down into the mud of practical politics, and are cut to the measure of party tactics, they are most pernicious falsehoods.

For instance, the notion that a human society, acting as a whole, bringing its reason and conscience to bear on its problems, traditions, and institutions, constantly reviewing its inherited faiths, examining its experiments, profiting by its own blunders, reaching out after better judgment and correcting its prejudices, can, in the sweep of time, arrive at the best conclusions as to what is socially true and wise and just, that man can get on earth, is a grand conception, and it is true. If the doctrine that the people ought to rule, and that the people know what is wise and right means this, it is true and fruitful. It will be noticed, however, that this doctrine implies that the people are to embrace every element in the society, including all the women and children, for in no sense could this grand consensus be true unless it was universal. It is of its very essence that the whole voice should be in it; it is its catholicity which constitutes its guarantee. If the feminine element is left out of it, its guarantee is gone; it is one-sided and imperfect; it is no longer human and social; it has sunk from the grade of a grand and inspiring conception to that of the party cry of a dominant interest. Neither is it true if the children are left out of it, for it is only in the sweep of time, after long and patient revision, that the judgments have authority. It must therefore be the work of generations to make those judgments; it is only the undying society, in its continuity and undistinguished generations, which can make them, and if they are to be true, the fire and hope of youth are as essential components as the inertness and conservatism of age.

Now, however, turn this same dogma into a maxim that peasants and artisans are the "people," that they are the depositaries of social and political wisdom, as distinguished from the sages and philosophers. Tell the young man not to worry about learning, to sneer at culture, to spend his nights on the street and his Sundays reading dime novels and the *Police Gazette*, and, when election day comes, to throw his vote so as to make a political job for himself or his friend; tell him that this is what is meant by the doctrine that the people ought to rule, and that in doing all this he will be uttering the oracles of political wisdom — then the great doctrine has turned into one of the most grotesque and mischievous falsehoods ever imagined.

In practise, therefore, democracy means that all those who are once admitted to political power are equal and that the power lies with the numerical majority of these equal units. If then the political divisions form themselves class-wise, then the most numerous class becomes the *demos* and is the depositary of political power. For this reason if we establish a democracy and then set the classes and the masses against each other, it is the utmost treason against democracy, because it ingrafts upon it from the start the worst vices of social discord and social greed which have disgraced the older political forms.

A plutocracy is a political form in which the real controlling force is wealth. This is the thing which seems to me to be really new and really threatening; there have been states in which there have been large plutocratic elements, but none in which wealth seemed to have such absorbing and controlling power as it threatens us. The most recent history of the civilized states of Western Europe has shown constant and rapid advance of plutocracy. The popular doctrines of the last hundred years have spread the notion that everybody ought to enjoy comfort and luxury — that luxury is a sort of right. Therefore if anybody has luxury while others have it not, this is held to prove that men have not equally shared in the fruits of civilization, and that the state in which such a condition of things exists has failed to perform its function; the next thing to do is to get hold of the state and make it perform its function of guaranteeing comfort and physical well-being to all. In the mean time, with the increasing thirst for luxury and the habit of thinking of it as within the scope of every man's rights, the temptations of dishonest gain increase, and especially are all those forms of gain which come, not from defalcation and theft, but from the ingenious use of political opportunities, put under a special code by themselves. A man who is "on the make," to use a slang phrase produced from the very phenomena to which I refer, does not think of himself as dishonest, but only as a man of the world. He is only utilizing the chances which he can get or make to win gain from the conjuncture of political and social circumstances, without intentional crime such as the statute has forbidden. This runs all the way from the man who sells his vote to the statesman who abuses official power, and it produces a class of men who have their price.

The principle of plutocracy is that money buys whatever the owner of money wants, and the class just described are made to be its instruments. At the same time the entire industrial development of the modern world has been such as to connect industry with political power in the matter of joint-stock companies, corporations, franchises, concessions, public contracts, and so on, in new ways and in great magnitude. It is also to be noted that the impersonal and automatic methods of modern industry, and the fact that the actual superintendent is often a representative and quasi-trustee for others, has created the corporate conscience. An ambitious Roman used to buy and bribe his way through all the inferior magistracies up to the consulship, counting upon getting a province at last out of which he could extort enough to recoup himself, pay all his debts, and have a fortune besides. Modern plutocrats buy their way through elections and legislatures, in the confidence of being able to get powers which will recoup them for all the outlay and yield an ample surplus besides.

What I have said here about the venality of the

humbler sets of people, and about the greed and arrogance of plutocrats, must not be taken to apply any further than it does apply, and the facts are to be taken only as one's knowledge will warrant. I am discussing forces and tendencies, and the magnitude attained as yet by those forces and tendencies ought not to be exaggerated. I regard plutocracy, however, as the most sordid and debasing form of politicial energy known to us. In its motive, its processes, its code, and its sanctions it is infinitely corrupting to all the institutions which ought to preserve and protect society. The time to recognize it for what it is, in its spirit and tendency, is when it is in its germ, not when it is full grown.

Here, then, in order to analyze plutocracy further, we must make some important distinctions. Plutocracy ought to be carefully distinguished from "the power of capital." The effect of the uncritical denunciations of capital, and monopoly, and trust, of which we hear so much, is, as I shall try to show further on, to help forward plutocracy.

THE CONFLICT OF PLUTOCRACY AND DEMOCRACY [1]

NOT every rich man is a plutocrat. In the classical nations it was held that the pursuits of commerce and industry were degrading to the free man; and as for commerce, it was believed that every merchant was necessarily a cheat, that he must practise tricks from the necessity of the case, and that a certain ever-active craftiness and petty deceit were the traits of character in which his occupation educated him. As for the handicrafts, it was argued that they distorted a man's body and absorbed his mind and time, so that he was broken in spirit, ignorant, and sordid. The same ideas as to commerce and, in part, as to handicrafts, prevailed through the Middle Ages.

The classical civilization was built upon human slave power. For that reason it exhausted itself — consumed itself. It reached a climax of organization and development, and then began to waste capital and use up its materials and processes. It is, however, clear that any high civilization must be produced and sustained by an adequate force. In the case just mentioned it was human nerve and muscle. Now, modern civilization is based on capital, that is, on tools and machines, which subjugate natural forces and make them do the drudgery. It is this fact which has emancipated slaves and serfs, set the mass of mankind free from the drudgery which distorts the body and wears out the mind, at the same time producing a high civilization and avoiding the wear and tear on men.

[1] *The Independent*, January 10, 1889.

The "dignity of labor" and the "power of capital" are therefore both products of the same modern movement. They go together; it is the power of capital which has made labor cease to be servile; it is the power of capital which has set women free from the drudgery of the grain-mill and the spinning-room; it is the power of capital which has enabled modern men to carry on mining and quarrying without misery, although in the classical times those forms of labor were so crushing that only the worst criminals or the lowest order of slaves were condemned to them. Every high civilization is unnatural, inasmuch as it is the product of art and effort. It is, therefore, unstable — ready to fall again to the original level, if the force and intelligence by which it is produced and maintained should fail. Our civilization is supported by capital and by modern science; if either of these fail — if we exhaust our capital, or if our science is not adequate to the tasks which fall upon it, our civilization will decline.

The dignity of capital is correlative with the dignity of labor. The capitalist has not simply fallen under the ban from which the laborer has escaped; the modern times have produced classes of men, masters of industry and accumulators of capital, who are among the most distinct and peculiar products of modern times. At what other epoch in history has any such class of men existed? There have, in earlier times, been great merchants, who have shown that the notion of a merchant as a man who cheats in weights and bets on differences, is a contemptible and ignorant calumny; the great masters of industry, however, are something entirely modern, and the vituperation of such a class as parasites, plunderers, speculators, and monopolists, is as ignorant and inexcusable as the older misconceptions of laborers which have gone out of fashion. A great capitalist is no more necessarily a plutocrat than a great general is a tyrant.

A plutocrat is a man who, having the possession of capital, and having the power of it at his disposal, uses it, not industrially, but politically; instead of employing laborers, he enlists lobbyists. Instead of applying capital to land, he operates upon the market by legislation, by artificial monopoly, by legislative privileges; he creates jobs, and erects combinations, which are half political and half industrial; he practises upon the industrial vices, makes an engine of venality, expends his ingenuity, not on processes of production, but on "knowledge of men," and on the tactics of the lobby. The modern industrial system gives him a magnificent field, one far more profitable, very often, than that of legitimate industry.

I submit, then, that it is of the utmost importance that we should recognize the truth about capital and capitalists, so as to reject the flood of nonsense and abuse which is afloat about both; that we should distinguish between the false and the true, the good and the bad, and should especially form a clear idea of the social political enemy as distinguished from everybody else. The recent history of every civilized state in the world shows the advance of plutocracy, and its injurious effects upon political institutions. The abuse and the vice, as usual, lie close beside the necessary and legitimate institution. Combinations of capital are indispensable, because we have purposes to accomplish which can be attained in no other way; monopolies exist in nature, and, however much modified by art, never cease to have their effect. Speculation is a legitimate function in the organization, and not an abuse or a public wrong. Trusts, although the name is a mistake, are evidently increasing in number all over the world, and are in great measure a result of the modern means of communication, which have made it possible for persons having a common interest, although scattered over the earth, if their number is not too great, to form combinations for the exploitation of a natural monopoly. What is gained by uncritical denunciation of these phenomena, or by indiscriminate confusion of definitions? The only effect of such procedure will be to nourish the abuses and destroy the utilities.

The first impulse is, when a social or industrial phenomenon presents itself, which is not considered good or pleasant, to say that we must pass a law against it. If plutocracy is an abuse of legislation and of political institutions, how can legislation do away with it? The trouble is that the political institutions are not strong enough to resist plutocracy; how then can they conquer plutocracy? Democracy especially dreads plutocracy, and with good reason.

There is no form of political power which is so ill-fitted to cope with plutocracy as democracy. Democracy has a whole set of institutions which are extra-legal, but are the most powerful elements in it; they are the party organization, the primary, the convention, etc. All this apparatus is well adapted to the purposes of plutocracy: it has to do with the formative stage of political activity; it is very largely operated in secret; it has a large but undefined field of legitimate, or quasi-legitimate, expenditure, for which there is no audit. As the operations of this apparatus are extra-legal they are irresponsible, yet they reach out to, and control, the public and civil functions. Even on the field of constitutional institutions, plutocracy always comes into the contest with a small body, a strong organization, a powerful motive, a definite purpose, and a strict discipline, while on the other side is a large and unorganized body, without discipline, with its ideas undefined, its interests illy understood, with an indefinite good intention.

If legislation is applied to the control of interests, especially when the latter are favored by the facts of the situation, the only effect is to impose on the interests more crafty and secret modes of action. Mr. Adams says that, since the Interstate Commerce Law was passed, the methods of railroad men have become more base and more secret than ever before. The legislator, in further efforts to succeed in his undertaking, can only sacrifice more of the open and honest rights which are within his reach, just as the Russian Government, in trying to reach the discontented elements in its society, and crush them by severity, only puts honest people to unlimited inconvenience and loss, but does not catch the Nihilists. Under a democracy, when the last comes to the last, the contest between numbers and wealth is nothing but a contest between two sets of lawyers, one drawing Acts in behalf of the state, and the other devising means of defeating those Acts in behalf of their clients. The latter set is far better paid in consideration, in security, and in money.

I therefore maintain that this is a lamentable contest, in which all that we hold dear, speaking of public interests, is at stake, and that the wise policy in regard to it is to minimize to the utmost the relations of the state to industry. As long as there are such relations, every industrial interest is forced more or less to employ plutocratic methods. The corruption is greater, perhaps, on those who exercise them than on the objects of them. *Laissez-faire*, instead of being what it appears to be in most of the current discussions, cuts to the very bottom of the morals, the politics, and the political economy of the most important public questions of our time.

DEMOCRACY AND MODERN PROBLEMS [1]

RENUNCIATION is not agreeable to any body or person, but I have expressed the opinion that democracy ought to renounce; that its prosperity and success depend upon renunciation. This needs some explanation and illustration.

In another form the same idea has often been enunciated. If we want a free government we must be content to forego a great many fine things which other civil forms might get for us. A "free government," under the democratic republican form, first of all renounces all the ceremonial and pageantry of the aristocratic or monarchical form; that is of little importance, although perhaps we assume too easily that the poetic and imaginative element is absent from a democratic community. But a democratic republic will never be neat, trim, and regular in its methods, or in the external appearance which it presents; it will certainly lack severity and promptitude of operation. A great many things are sure to be left at loose ends; in a word, there is sure to be little discipline. There is a lounging air, a lack of formality, an exaggerated horror of red tape, a neglect of regularity.

Beyond this, however, and more important, is the fact that there are important functions which older forms of the state have been accustomed to perform, which the democratic republic cannot well perform: it cannot make war without great waste and expense, both of life and money; it cannot do any work which requires high

[1] *The Independent*, March 28, 1889.

and strict organization, and do it well — if it tries to do work of that kind, it does it only at great expense, and under great waste. Germany is the best drilled and disciplined state of modern times, while the United States is the leading example of a democratic republic. The judgments of these two countries about each other, and their influence on each other, are among the most remarkable facts in modern life. The judgments of Germans generally on the United States are those of men accustomed to an administrative system which works accurately and promptly, also pedantically and cheaply, on a system which is inaccurate and unprompt, and is not cheap; they are accustomed to respect state action, to believe in it, and to rely upon it; with a population trained to respond at the tap of the drum, uneducated to individual initiative, and with a bureaucracy of long tradition and intense training, the state may present itself as an entity of a different sort, and an agent of different power from the American State. The question then is, whether we can draw any inferences as to state functions from Germany, or whether we should be willing to see the American State undergo those changes which it would have to undergo in order to fit it to undertake all the functions which are undertaken by the German State.

This question needs only to be stated to answer itself. The especial changes which the American State would have to undergo would be to weaken democracy and to strengthen bureaucracy. These are the two changes which would be the most impossible of all which could be attempted. It is much more probable that democracy will sweep away all the bulrushes in the shape of "monarchical institutions" which are being built up against it, and, seizing upon the military organization and the state socialistic institutions as at once its prey and its instrumentalities, will triumph over everything else, in Germany as well as elsewhere.

If we turn back, then, to the free democratic state as the state of the present and future, the one which is alone possible for us and which must go on to meet and work out its destiny, then I think it will appear that its civil service is its weakest point. The recent history of the French Republic, joined with our own, has gone far to show that a republican system with party government is drawn toward the abuse of the civil service by forces which it is folly to underestimate. One must shut one's eyes to facts if one would deny that the sentiments "I am a Democrat," "this is a Republican Administration," strike a responsive chord in the hearts of the masses, where denunciations of the corruption of the civil service, or of wasteful expenditures of public money, fall on dull ears. These watchwords, however, are only the doctrines: "To the victor belong the spoils," and "Woe to the vanquished," in a little less cynical and shocking form, and they mean that, in the modern democratic state, parties fight each other for control of the state, which they rule, having won it, like a conquered territory. If this state, then, has state-socialistic functions, it is sure to produce the worst exploitation of man by man which has ever existed; to live under it, and not be in it, would be to suffer a tyranny such as no one has experienced yet.

I should not like to be understood to speak lightly of preaching as a means of awakening the reason and conscience of men to convictions which are universally right and true. Anything which can be gained in this direction is sure to produce manifold fruit in politics and economic policy; but hitherto we have not done much against the abuse of the civil service except by preaching. The statesman has to accomplish his purposes by adopting measures, and by founding institutions which can set social forces in operation, or prevent their operation. He must have an adequate means or must make the best of a case as he finds it.

In the present case, therefore, I maintain that the way to minimize the dangers to democracy, and from it, is to reduce to the utmost its functions, the number of its officials, the range of its taxing power, the variety of its modes of impinging on the individual, the amount and range of its expenditures, and, in short, its total weight; for among the other vices and errors of the prevailing tendency, this is one of the worst, that we do not see that whatever extends the functions of the state increases its weight. Against this view nothing has ever yet been brought forward but the pure assumption which has all experience against it, that, if the state should not do things they would not be done at all.

And there is another course of thought which seems to me to run in the same direction.

We often boast that this is an age of deliberation, and it is, of course, true that, as compared with any earlier period, men of the most civilized states do act by deliberation where formerly they acted by instinct. It is, however, still true of even the most enlightened community which could be found, that the mass of the people in it live by instinct. The torments of always giving one's self a reason, satisfactory to reason and conscience, for everything one does, are a privilege of high culture. The ancient philosophers never got further than the question: what is the highest good in life? The modern thinking world reached so high as to spend a year, perhaps, in debating whether life is worth living. That was certainly a proud triumph; the mass of mankind, however, are contented and eager to live without deliberating about it.

Now democracy calls for a great amount of deliberation and reflection from the mass of mankind; and especially, if we are determined not to follow the policy of letting things work themselves out, but are determined to exert ourselves upon them, according to ideals which we have formed, then the democratic state is destined to make bigger and bigger demands upon the reflective power of its citizens. If it does so, it will fail to get the response which it expects. Once more the path of wisdom seems to lie in making the demands of the state as few and simple as possible, and in widening the scope of the automatic organs of society which are non-political, in order to see whether they will not prove capable, if trusted.

When we are told that the state would do all things better, if we would give it more things to do, the answer is that there is nothing which the state has not tried to do, and that it has only exceptionally performed anything well, even war or royal marriages, and that, on the contrary, here in the United States, where the other policy has had more trial than anywhere else — favored, it is true, by circumstances — it has proved beneficent in the extreme. Therefore, if, after all, it is only a question of whether to put faith in the state or to put faith in liberty, an educated American ought not to hesitate long which to do.

SEPARATION OF STATE AND MARKET [1]

I CANNOT find an example of a state which has not been, in a great measure, subject to the power of capital. It is impossible to live and to carry on any enterprises of utility or pleasure, without capital; those who denounce capital most earnestly bear plainest testimony to this; they are squirming about in an effort to escape from, or to turn their backs on, this fact. Hence men have always struggled to get possession of this power. Those who had state power found capital indispensable; they made alliances with those who had it. The latter made terms under which they accomplished their own ends, and satisfied their own tastes. If any examples can be found to the contrary, they are great and powerful despotisms, which were strong enough to disregard all but a military caste, or a priesthood, but even in these cases the power of capital made itself felt indirectly through its influence on the oligarchy which maintained the throne.

I cannot find a case of any state in which the ruling element really practised abnegation of power, or showed a disposition to deprive itself of functions. If democracy contains any great hope for mankind, it lies in the belief that democracy is to distinguish itself from all other forms of the state in this respect. Jeffersonian democracy, by its most important dogmas and maxims, seemed to justify this hope, and if it has won any triumphs, it has won them by this policy. It was not afraid to be

[1] *The Independent*, February 14, 1889.

called non-government or "atomistic." The old *Congressional Globe* bore the motto: "The world is governed too much." Jeffersonian democracy, however, in its best estate, was able only partly to fulfil its own ideal, for it found that a state power which undertook to live by the principles of self-abnegation could not simply rest at ease or be quietly neutral. It had to defend itself against the forces which tried to direct it, and to push back against the organizations which were trying to drive it on to the undertakings which it disavowed. In the latest developments of democracy, the world over, there is very little of this reluctance to assume functions.

By *imperium* the Romans meant the concept of military and civil power combined in a supreme authority. Every government aims to develop and maintain this conception in its chief organ as a realized fact, and democracy is no exception. The "people" — that is the ruling majority for the time being — instead of divesting itself of any part of the traditional functions of the civil authority, is notably tenacious of everything which it imagines to be "sovereignty"; and it resents any curtailment, as if such curtailment would contain an imputation upon the equality of democracy with the other -ocracies which have had the powers. So we are gravely told that "the state is the depository of the coercive power of society"; as if that was an intelligible proposition, or one embodying a distinct notion applicable to any question of theory or any problem of practise. It is upon such turgid and empty dicta that all absolutism has been built up in the past; and such are now being fabricated with a zeal hitherto unequaled for the purposes of democratic absolutism. Indeed, we seem destined speedily to discover that democracy, instead of being a single and homogeneous system, is a thing of such various phases and forms that it is scarcely possible to compare two cases of it, or that such a definition can be made that two commentators can understand each other.

Democracy is atomistic. It breaks the society up into individuals who are political units. The peril of such a system is that it is at the mercy of any organization formed inside of it which gives coherence and order to its disintegrated elements. Such an organization will begin to move the whole. To understand the significance of this, let us here bring another set of observations into the scope of our study.

Status holds down individual energy and power. If a black man is told that the only status allowed by social institutions to him is that of a slave, no black man can work out into realization the powers which he may possess. If the status of women is fixed by custom and law, no woman can show her power to do anything outside of the limits. The social arrangement which sets free individual energy is liberty; for under this each one may prove what he is by what he does, and the society profits by the expansion and evolution of all the power there is in it. Now democracy and liberty are not the same thing by any means; but, in the latest history, they have been closely allied with each other, and democracy as a political form has helped and been helped by liberty in the social order. The product of liberty and democracy is individualism. Under it men have been emancipated from tradition, authority, caste, superstition, and to a certain extent from prejudices and delusions; if we could maintain liberty and democracy long enough, we might perhaps produce individualistic results so great that men would be emancipated from delusions and from phrases.

This movement, however, like every other, has its perils and abuses. If individualism destroys institutions, and if democracy, with its dream of equality, simply works disintegration, the society is at the sport of the new elements which combine and organize on new centers, for actual disintegration and atomization of society is impossible.

What then are the centers on which the new organizations form, and what is the character of the new organizations? In our modern society they are sure to be interests, meaning by that, groups of persons united by a desire for the success of the same enterprises and seeking pecuniary gain from that success. Here is where the plutocratic element finds entrance into the democratic system, and here lies the weakness of democracy, in the face of the plutocratic forces with which it has to cope in modern society.

What, in the face of such an antagonism, is the significance of this new notion that "the state is an ethical person" — a triviality in the guise of an apothegm? If the state is an ethical person, and is rent by interests which may be sordid, and are at best commercial, what becomes of its ethical authority, and how can its ethical character abide? In order to save its own existence — not its ethical character, but its purely brute existence — it has to take sides with some interests against others, which is just what all modern civilized states are doing.

And yet, as I said at the outset of this essay, it has seemed not impossible that democracy might contain within itself the form and potency of better things. It has seemed that it might be simple-minded enough to throw off all the big dogmas of state-olatry, might be so open and visible, and might feel itself so well known of all men, that it should laugh down all inflated theories of itself; might be so hard-headed as to treat all political mysticism with contempt; might be so practical that it would know better than to try to do too much, or to busy itself with schemes of universal happiness.

The first condition of its fulfilling any such hope is that it shall renounce. It is the strongest system that has ever existed when it is achieving peace, order, and security; it is the weakest system that ever existed when it attempts to turn its force to industrial or social objects, and it forfeits strength in the former field by all its attempts in the latter. The state is the greatest monopoly of all; it can brook no rival or colleague in its domain; it is necessarily sole and supreme. If the state is purely a civil organization this monopoly character of it is beneficial; if, however, the state enters as an agent into the industrial or social relations of its own subjects, it becomes the greatest and worst of all monopolies, the one best worth having under one's control, the best prize of base struggles, and the most powerful engine by which some men may exploit others.

The most notable product of democracy, especially of American democracy, up to this time, is the maxim of the separation of church and state. There have been strong efforts at times in this country to formulate a maxim of the separation of the state and the market. It is to that policy that democracy ought to come, if it can command the wisdom and the will to attain to it; it would thereby cut the ground from under plutocracy. Plutocracy, as we have seen, consists in the political power of capital. If capital were excluded from all interest in state action, and thrown upon the laws of the market, there would remain only that power of capital which is rooted in the industrial and social order, which nothing can set aside or overcome. If there were no longer any legislative monopolies nor any legislative guarantee of natural monopolies, the only monopolies which would remain would be such as no one can abolish.

SOCIAL WAR IN DEMOCRACY [1]

IT is one of those popular assumptions of our time which, although never distinctly formulated, have such an important part in all our accepted faiths, that social forces change in the progress of civilization, so that, for example, slavery and feudalism pass away completely. The students of social history, however, find that social forces are ever the same; only the phenomena present themselves under new combinations. It is when this fact forces itself upon the observation of men in spite of their pet dogmas, that we hear about the "labor problem," or "wage slavery." Men toss and heave and squirm, changing their position from generation to generation; they have always just got, or are about just to get, the final and completely satisfactory solution, and they find that the hardships of life, the difficulty of getting a living, the task of rearing children, pain, disease, and death, remain about the same. The new discovery, instead of annihilating ills and closing the account of earthly hardship, proves only the point of departure for new ills unknown before; and the old ills brighten as they take their flight, for their unappreciated advantages come to light.

Let us notice how class struggles have run through modern history and see what the position of democracy is in respect to class struggles and social war.

The feudal system properly had only two classes, nobles and peasants; kings were differentiated from nobles and they made a breach in the system. In Russia

[1] *The Independent*, April 11, 1889.

and Poland these three classes fought it out, and the difference in the results has a value for the student of political class struggles which no one has yet, to my knowledge, developed. In Russia the crown won; the nobles never became "nobles" in the Western sense; the peasants were reduced to serfdom as mere pawns in the game. They always maintained a tradition that the Czar had subjected them to servitude under the nobles that the latter might fight for the fatherland — a capital instance of what comes of sacrificing private rights to "the greater good of the state." In Poland the crown was subjugated to the nobles, and then the latter developed a tyranny over the peasants far worse than that of Russia, and reduced their country first to anarchy and then to foreign conquest.

In Western Europe another class was differentiated from the two classes of feudalism — the middle class, the *bourgeoisie* of the cities. This made four classes, and political history has been moulded by their alliances and conflicts. The middle class was at war with feudalism; while the lords were strong the monarchs and cities combined against them. In Germany the crown could not win a real victory, while in France and Spain it did do so. In England the four classes came to a compromise and adjustment under the Constitution, but their rubbing against each other has marked the history of that country for five hundred years.

Now, if we have a democratic republic, the crown disappears out of it. If the economic situation is that of a new country, with sparse population and an abundance of land, there are no nobles, and in an older country, under the democratic republican form, there cease to be any nobles. Titles are a mere matter of courtesy and have only social value. There remain then only two classes, the *bourgeoisie* and the peasantry, and these undergo very important modifications. The high *bourgeoisie* develops into a class of wealth and luxury, supplanting, imitating, reproducing with variations, the old baronage; it struggles to form out of itself a patriciate — a body of selected families defined by its own sympathies and voluntary recognition, or a body of locupletes or optimates, or a timocracy of those who have enjoyed the honors of the state. The process has been repeated so often in the classical states, in the Italian republics, and in the rich cities of the Middle Ages that it ought to be sufficiently familiar to us. The force at work is plainly the trait of human nature which leads men to gratify their vanity, to seek to excel, to try to guarantee the future of their children, and to secure the fruits of their own efforts. Like all other traits of human nature, it has its good side and its bad side.

On the other hand the modern representatives of the ancient peasantry are very different from their predecessors. The middle class is constantly fed from them at the bottom. A class of yeomen farmers or peasant proprietors has little in common in its status, its fund of ideas, or its outlook, with mediæval peasants. There are no peasants in the modern Western world with whom the other classes can play, or whom they can afford to disregard.

In this matter also the modern statesman is all ready to act. The chip which floated on the current thought that it made the river go; so statesmen and political philosophers think that they make institutions and mould history. The thing which makes and breaks institutions is economic forces, acting on the interests of men, and, through them, on human nature. The statesman who goes along with these forces, wins great "triumphs"; but he is like the chip on the current, after all; the most that he does is to show in which direction it is going. Now the cheapening of transportation between the great centers of population and the great outlying masses of unoccupied land is the greatest fact of our time, and it is the greatest economic and social revolution which has ever taken place. We, of this generation, are the first ones to see the real effects of the discovery of America beginning to operate on the whole social system of the Old World. Through the reduction in the rent of land there, the present forces are undermining and will presently sweep away the whole class system built upon the competition of a dense population for a limited area of land. The fall in rent, the obliteration of social distinctions, the decline of aristocracy, the rise of democracy, the subdivision of great estates, the rise of peasant proprietors, are all consequences of the economic revolution — consequences which no statesman or philosopher has made or can prevent; but there will, no doubt, be a great number of conventions held and innumerable "resolutions" will be passed "approving" of the change, and thereby claiming to have caused it; and the world will be enriched by a number of great statesmen who will be credited with having made it all.

A land-owning peasant class and a property-owning middle class do not appear likely to go to war with each other. On the contrary, the social combinations which must arise under the new order of things are already discernible: it is plainly the antagonism of those-who-have and those-who-have-not which is to rise out of the social residuum, when kings and nobles and old-fashioned peasants are gone; and the middle class, covering a wider compass between its extremes, is left alone. It is then that the test of democracy and of the current political

philosophy must come. With a proud and powerful
plutocracy on one side, and a hungry proletariat on the
other, can democracy find resources anywhere for controlling the elements of human greed and passion? A
plutocracy wants to obtain free swing for its powers
through and over the social organization. It wants,
above all, security and guarantees for what-is, for
what-has-been-accomplished for capital and accumulated
wealth. The proletariat wants free swing for the forces
of new creation, for what-is-to-be,for the unaccomplished.
The former wants quiet enjoyment, the latter wants
free chance for enterprise.

It is an easy thing, now, to get a majority to vote that
the capital-which-is belongs to the chances of the new
effort for what-is-to-be, and to resolve accordingly that
those-who-have-not, belonging to the party of enterprise
and of the future, ought to, and of right must take possession of the capital now "detained" by the party of
the past and of the thing-accomplished, in order to go
on with progress. We have already had an abundance
of philosophers profound enough to prophesy this unto
us; but when these notions turn from the precepts of
philosophers into the program of parties under a democracy, we see that the old social war is not over. It is
not settled: the old evils are not abolished; the passions
are not stifled — they are all here under new forms. The
robbery of a merchant by a robber baron, the robbery
of an investor by a railroad wrecker, and the robbery of
a capitalist by a collectivist, are all one. Democracy
as a political form, instead of settling anything, has set
them all loose; what, now, should be and can be its policy toward them? If it stands away from them, only
insisting on peace and order and upon submission by
everybody to the administration of rights according to

contract, then the landlord who finds that his rents fall, or the railroad investor who gets no dividends, or the producer who is dissatisfied with the price which his product brings, will have no recourse except each against himself. He will have to learn more, and to become wiser. Inasmuch as this would call reason and conscience into play, there might really be some hope that we might gain something toward doing away with social war; but that democracy can solve the antagonisms in the newest order of things, can adjust the rights of the contending interests by a series of "ethical" decisions, or that it can, by siding with one party, give it a victory over the other, and thereby found a stable social order, it is folly to believe.

LEGISLATION BY CLAMOR [1]

IT is already evident that one feature of the "new time" into which we are hastening will be the subjection of legislatures to the pressure of groups of persons who are capable of controlling newspapers or combining votes. Under the old notions of legislation, the duty of legislators was to study carefully the details of proposed legislation, to debate and discuss measures, and so, by deliberation, to arrive at decisions as to what should be enacted. The notion was that the statesman should know what he intended to do and should consider the proper means of reaching the desired result. This theory of legislation never has been very thoroughly put into practice anywhere, but now the idea seems to be that it is antiquated, that we do not intend to seek a more complete realization of it as a reform in legislation, but that we abandon it altogether. At the same time, therefore, that there is a vast extension of the field of legislation, we abandon all sound traditions as to the method of legislative activity. Legislative bodies not only lay themselves open to be acted upon by outside influences, but they submit to clamor more than to any other influence. The tendency can be traced through the legislation of France, England, and the United States, during the last twenty years. If a faction of any kind assails the legislature with sufficient determination, they carry their point although the sincere opinion of nearly all who vote for the measure may be that it is foolish, or idle, or mischievous, or

[1] *The Independent*, February 24, 1887.

crude, or irrational, or extravagant, or otherwise improper.

Opinions differ greatly as to what it is that is "falling" or "going to decay" just at present. These phenomena support the notion that it is "the state" which is passing away. On the one hand, the highest wisdom of those who want anything now is to practice terrorism, to make themselves as disagreeable as possible, so that it shall be necessary to conciliate them, and those who appeal to reason find themselves disregarded. On the other hand, the public men seek peace and quiet by sacrificing any one who cannot or does not know enough to make a great clamor in order to appease a clamorous faction. It is thought to be the triumph of practical statesmanship to give the clamorers something which will quiet them, and a new and special kind of legislative finesse has been developed, *viz.*, to devise projects which shall seem to the clamorous petitioners to meet their demands, yet shall not really do it.

The most important case of legislation of this kind which has been passed in this country is the Bland Silver Bill. It contains no rational plan for accomplishing any purpose whatever. It never had any purpose which could be stated intelligibly. It does not introduce the double standard, does not help debtors, and if it favors silver-miners at all, does so in an insignificant degree. It satisfies the vanity of a few public men, quiets the clamor of a very noisy faction who did not know what they wanted and do not know whether they have got it or not, complicates the monetary system of the country, and contains possibilities of great mischief or great loss. It was passed as a patched-up compromise under the most rhythmical and best sustained clamor ever brought to bear on a public question. Those who raised the clamor went off content because they thought that they had obtained *something*, and they now resist the repeal of the law because they would feel that they had lost *something*.

The oleomargarine law is another case. The scientific evidence submitted to the committee of Congress was clear and uniform, that oleomargarine is a substitute for butter, just as maple sugar is a substitute for cane sugar; that it is not adulterated and not unwholesome. If it had been regarded as unwholesome, in spite of this evidence, or if it had been the purpose to make it recognizable, measures having these purposes in view, however ridiculous (like Senator Blair's proposition to color it red or blue), or however mischievous, would at least have been rational. The law to tax it two cents a pound was not rational, even with the object of practicing protectionism in favor of the dairymen. If the assertions made about the profits of the manufacture, and about the supply and demand of butter in the market, are even approximately true, then the tax comes out of the manufacturers, and is simply a toll levied by the state on the manufacture of a new commodity. It cannot avail to limit the production; the state simply mulcts the producers of a part of their profits. The enactment was a case of sacrificing to a clamorous faction the rights and interests of others who were absent.

The doctors of the Koran, at Mecca and Medina, were told that coffee, when the plant was yet new to them, was deleterious. They straightway forbade the faithful to drink it, and obedience or disobedience to this law embittered the strife of sects. History is full of similar prejudice against what is new and similar state interposition against improvement. If anybody

who finds butter beyond his means wants to use oleomargarine, it is an improvement to give him the chance
to do so.

The laws about convict labor are other instances.
The Illinois Bureau of Labor Statistics says that the
clamor is a proof that something is wrong, and that the
clamorers are not bound to solve the problem or propose a remedy; that they need only present their objections to what is and demand that the powers that be
find a remedy. The labor bureaus themselves might be
offered as a case of legislation by clamor; the necessity
of justifying their own existence, and of conciliating the
laborers, makes labor bureau literature one of the trials
of the day. The doctrine that clamor is a proof of a
grievance is so easy and summary that it is sure to be
popular, and its broad availability for the purposes of
the world-betterers need not be pointed out. It is also
characteristic of this school of thought that the legislature is commanded to find a remedy for the alleged
grievance. A legislature, if it acts rightly, has to recon-
cile interests and adjust rights. In so doing it can
rarely give to any one interest a clear and prompt remedy
for what that interest chooses to consider a grievance.
Are convicts to be idle? Are the tax-payers to be indefinitely burdened? These are parts of the problem
of convict labor; but, so far from having made a comprehensive solution of the convict labor question, including
these elements of it, the people who have assumed to
direct legislation show that they have not even mastered
the comparison of the three plans proposed for using
prison labor.

The Illinois Commissioner says that a wrong ought
not to be overlooked because it is a little wrong. That
is a thoroughly sound doctrine, and it would be easy

to bring from labor bureau literature illustrations of the wrong of neglecting it; but business competition is not a wrong at all, and convict labor legislation is not based on any established grievance of free laborers, nor is it adapted to remedy any grievance, if one existed.

The latest case of legislation by clamor is the Inter-State Railroad Act. Clamor has forced through a crude measure. What does it aim at? What are the means by which it attempts to attain its object? These are the questions which should go before legislation. No one can answer them in regard to this bill. *Something* has been done, and the clamor subsides. To act in this way is to set all reason and common sense at defiance. Thousands of voters would no doubt have been incensed at Congress if it had done nothing. They will not read the bill, and could not understand it if they did; but they are satisfied that something has been done. To do a bad thing in legislation is far worse than to do nothing.

People who study the railroad law, and who cannot understand it, say that it will be all right if the President only appoints a good commission, and that the law will mean whatever the commission interprets it to mean. We have come very far away from old and sound traditions of good government if we pin our faith for the adjustment of rights on the wisdom and integrity of men, and not on impersonal institutions. Where has the President this reserve of wise, good, and competent men? Where did he get them? Where does he keep them? The railroads, banks, insurance companies, and factory owners of the country are all eagerly looking for just that kind of men, and are ready to pay them from ten to thirty thousand dollars a year. The President must keep them close, therefore, for the state only pays from three to eight or ten thousand. To read the cur-

rent discussion of this law one would think that our railroad system only needed to be put into the hands of five
men whom the President can pick out in a few weeks and
who will be able to solve all the problems, when the fact
is that the railroads have expended energy and money
without stint for years to do just that very thing, and
have themselves employed commissioners at high salaries to try to solve their problems for them. It is true
that they did not look for their commissioners among
ex-members of Congress.

In all these cases it is immaterial what opinion one may
hold as to the subject matter of the legislation or what
view one may think correct about the questions involved.
The point is that this legislation by clamor fits no consistent idea of the matter, proceeds on no rational plan,
settles no question, but only produces new confusion
and new evils, carrying the difficulties forward in constantly increasing magnitude as the consequences of
legislative blunders are added to the original ills.

FEDERAL LEGISLATION ON RAILROADS [1]

DANIEL WEBSTER once said: "A strong conviction that something must be done is the parent of many bad measures." He made the observation early in his career; but it was a sign of his statesmanlike power to detect the common element in heterogeneous incidents of public life that he should have made it; scarcely a year passes which does not give us a new illustration of its truth. The next instance of headlong legislation with which this country is threatened is an act regulating railroads.

Two fallacies are of constant repetition in propositions for more government regulation. The first and widest is to argue that competition is not perfect in its action and does not satisfactorily solve the problem; it is inferred that we must have some form of government regulation. Plainly this inference is a *non sequitur*, unless it can be shown that government regulation will produce perfect and satisfactory results; or that regulation, although imperfect, will just complement and make up for the imperfections of competition. The second fallacy is illustrated when, after trying for a long time to solve a problem of the social order without success, we declare, in despair, that the state will have to take it in hand and legislate about it. This is a worse *non sequitur* than the other.

Both these fallacies are involved in the current arguments for the proposed legislation about railroads. Railroads are still new and still in their infancy. It seems reasonable to believe that they are capable of

[1] *The Independent*, January 20, 1887.

great development beyond what any one can now foresee; new inventions are reasonably sure to cause trans-
formations in railroad business and methods. We have
only just reached the point where a few men are competent to manage great lines of railroad on their technical
side; we have only just begun to educate men for the
railroad business as a profession. Railroad men do not
seem yet to have any code of right behavior or right
management between themselves — people often deride
the professional code of lawyers or doctors, but the
value of such a code is seen if we take a case like the one
before us, where a new profession has not yet developed
a code. The social and economic questions raised by
railroads and about railroads are extremely difficult and
complicated; we have not, so far, accomplished much
of anything toward solving them by experience or theory.
The discussion, so far as it has yet gone, has shown only
that we have the task yet before us and that, so far, all
has been a struggle of various interests to use railroads
for their own advantage. The true solution of the only
proper legislative problem, viz., how to adjust all the interests so that no one of them can encroach upon the
others, has scarcely been furthered at all. It is only
necessary to take up a volume of the evidence taken by
one of the Congressional committees on this subject, or
any debate about it which has arisen in Congress, to see
how true it is that conflicting interests are struggling
for advantage over each other.

The railroad question is far wider than the scope of
any proposed legislation with regard to it; it is so wide
that in any period of five or ten years new phases of it
come to the front and occupy public attention. Just
now the prominent phase is the effect of competition on
a weak market; for the time being, the means of trans-

portation seem to have been multiplied in excess of the demand. The railroad monopoly is in the position of any monopoly which has overproduced its market. Pooling would be the mode of applying combination and restriction of production to this business; that pooling would suit the condition of things just at this moment, and would be a corrective for the evils which just now command public attention, is very probable. But the country is undoubtedly destined to enter on a new period of expanding a hitherto unknown prosperity, and what would be the effects of pooling on a strong and rising market under great demand for transportation? If a law is passed it becomes a rigid and unavoidable constraint. It is not, however, my purpose to argue that pooling is a good thing or a bad thing; the arguments upon that point are so strong upon either side that a case is made out for neither. Under such circumstances, to legislate is to decide, and to commit the interests at stake to a decision which is immature and is founded on nothing but the notion that something must be done. Competition has borne not only upon the rates but also upon the quality of cars and stations, upon speed and punctuality, upon parlor car and other conveniences. What would be the effect of strict pooling upon these?

The second point which seems now to occupy attention is the effect of railroads upon natural distances; it is assumed that it must be wrong that railroads should make a place which is near further off than one which is remote. It is a matter of familiar experience that railroads do invert relations of distance and make places which are two hundred miles off economically nearer than places one hundred miles off; and in doing this they also invert the interests of a great many people. It is a rash and mischievous undertaking to try to offset or correct this by arbitrary legislation. It is not possible to draft an intelligible and workable regulation to do it. The short-haul clause in the bill now before the Senate is already a subject of disputed interpretation, and whenever the courts come to act upon it they will interpret it as its language seems to require, not as anybody now says that it is intended to mean. The interests of the extreme West constantly demand that the full power of railroads to annihilate distance and time shall be exerted in their favor; during the last summer, Senator Edmunds pointed out to his Vermont constituents their grievance, in the fact that railroads pour into the Eastern market, in competition with them, all the products of the West — *i.e.*, do just what the West demands. Cheap freights westward benefit Eastern manufacturers and Western consumers while they injure Western manufacturers; cheap freights eastward favor Western farmers and cattle raisers and Eastern consumers while they injure Eastern farmers. How can the legislator meddle in this great complex of interests without doing harm to everybody, especially when he goes about it without any theoretical or practical principles to guide him, with nothing but the conviction that many things in the existing order are not as we should like them to be and that something must be done?

The railroad question, properly speaking, I repeat, goes far beyond the points which are now attracting attention. The railroad company has relations to its employees, to the state which taxes its property, to the municipalities whose streets its line crosses, to adjoining real-estate owners, to the legislators and editors who want free passes, etc., etc. In all these relations there are two parties, for even a railroad company has rights. Competing lines have relations to each other, and these often raise questions in which there is no simple "justice" — the competing lines may not be subject to the same legislative regulations.   A country three thousand miles in extent is not much troubled by the extra prejudice which is imported into the question of long and short haul when it seems to include favor to foreigners at the expense of citizens; but if there is anything real in the latter grievance it is difficult to see why it should not also exist in a concealed form here.   Finally, it cannot be forgotten that the railroad issue includes the question as to how those who have contributed the capital to build the road are to obtain their remuneration.   If the state undertakes to regulate all the rest, it will see itself forced at last to regulate this also.   Hitherto the stockholders have been left to get their remuneration out of their own enterprise if they could; if they could not, they have been left to make the best of it.   If, however, the state interferes with the whole management of their enterprise, how will it at last escape the justice of the demand that it compensate them or secure them a return on their investment?

In the present state of the case it behooves us to remember that, in the varying phases of the industrial world of our time, first one interest gets a chance and then another; it is not in human wit to stand over this system and correct or adjust it so as to offset all the special combinations of industrial advantage and disadvantage. It is no question whether we like living in an age of steam or not; the steam-engine was invented in the course of time, just when all the antecedents which were necessary for it had been provided; it has come to stay and we must learn to live with it.   We have sung a great many paeans over it, but it may be doubted whether we have found out yet what an uncomfortable social comrade it may prove to be when it is full grown. Many of its workings are very capricious in the chances which they throw in the way of one man or which they take away from another. Can we do anything wiser than to take the good chances and the ill chances over a period of years and make the best of them?

What we need most in regard to all social problems, if we want to solve them either by voluntary action or by legislation, is knowledge. If we could have a commission to study railroads, if its powers were only such as are required to enable it to get information and to investigate cases, and if its *personnel* were such as to inspire confidence that it was capable of conducting the investigation and that it would conduct it disinterestedly from the standpoint of justice to all interests, the commission might be very useful. It is very probable that legislation might ultimately prove necessary or expedient, but it would not then be an embodiment of anybody's whim or view of the matter but would be guided by experience and observation. Blundering experiments in legislation cannot be simply abandoned if they do not work well; even if they are set aside, they leave their effects behind; and they create vested interests which make it difficult to set them aside.

THE SHIFTING OF RESPONSIBILITY [1]

IF there are any ethical propositions which may be accepted as reasonably established, the following are among the number: to every one his own; that responsibility should be equal to liberty; that rights and duties are correlative; and that those should reap the consequences who have set in action the causes. The socialistic and semi-socialistic propositions which are before the public are immoral in that they all sin against these ethical principles.

We are using, at the same time, two weights and measures. We have at the same time two sets of dogmas, one for politics and the other for social matters. We affirm that all men are equal. If they are so, and if a state can be founded on the assumption that they are so, then each one of them must take his share in the burdens of the society; especially must each one take the responsibility for himself. No sooner, however, is this inference drawn than we are told that there are some people who are not equal to others and who cannot be held to the same duties or responsibilities. They are weak, ignorant, undisciplined, poor, vicious, or otherwise unfit. It is asserted that the strong, learned, well-trained, rich, and virtuous are bound to take care of the aforesaid persons. The democratic doctrine in politics is that wisdom resides in the masses; that it is a false and aristocratic doctrine to maintain that the educated or trained men are better fitted to direct common public interests than the uneducated; that, in fact, the educated men fail conspicuously whenever they undertake to

[1] *The Independent*, March 24, 1887.

lead, and that there is a resource of strong, untrained common sense in the masses on which a state may be built in complete security.

No sooner, however, have we accepted this doctrine as orthodox and indisputable matter of political faith, than we are told that educated men and others who have enjoyed exceptional advantages, or who have acquired any of those forms of training which make men better — not than other men, but than they would themselves have been without the expenditure of capital and labor — have a duty to perform: to lead, guide, and instruct the real rulers. It is asserted that when the masses go astray it is the fault of the educated classes who did not instruct them. Therefore we arrive at this doctrine: if a young man desires to fit himself to discharge the duties of life well, he needs to spend his youth in study and work, he needs to accumulate capital and to subject himself to discipline. This is a duty which is incumbent on all and is enjoined on all, without exception. If, however, some conform to it and some do not, let it not be maintained that the former shall have wealth and honor and power in the society. On the contrary, only the latter shall have those things; for, since all the things which improve men are hard and irksome, and the mass of mankind shirk them, and the power rests with the mass, the "minority" receive as their share the function of persuading the "majority" to do right, if they can, and if they do not succeed, they bear the responsibility for whatever goes wrong. Such a doctrine is profoundly immoral, for there is a dislocation involved in it between work and reward.

We encourage our children to earn and save and we stimulate them to look forward to the accumulation of wealth. We explain to them the advantages of capital.

We point out to them the woes of poverty, the consequences of improvidence, the penalties of idleness;
the better parents we are the more we do this.   We
try to make them understand the world in which they
live, so that they may hold sound principles and direct
their energies wisely.   The motive and purpose is to
avoid the penalties which they see unwise men suffer, and
to attain to the material prosperity and comfort which
all men need and desire.   Some obey;   some do not.
Those who obey might think that they are justified,
then, in having, holding, and enjoying what they have
earned.   They might say that wealth is a reward for
duty done, and that the faithful workman is entitled
to sit down and enjoy the fruits of his labor.

If one of them draws any such inference he will be
immediately corrected by the new philosophy.   He will
be told that wealth is a duty and a responsibility;   that
he holds it not for himself, but for others;   and if he asks
for whom, he will be told that he is only a trustee for
those who did not obey the teachings of boyhood about
industry, temperance, prudence, and frugality.   He
tried to take his own course and let others take theirs;
he tried to do right and prosper and let others do ill and
suffer if they preferred;   but he finds, as a result of his
course, that he has made himself responsible for those
who took the other course, while they are not responsible
for anybody, not even for themselves.   This new kind of
trustee also is not allowed to administer his trust for the
benefit of the beneficiaries, according to his own judgment;   that is done for him by the doctors of the new
philosophy.   His function is limited to producing and
saving.

If a man, in the organization of labor, employs other
men to assist in an industrial enterprise, it was formerly

thought that the rights and duties of the parties were defined by the contract which they made with each other. The new doctrine is that the employer becomes responsible for the welfare of the employees in a number of respects. They do not each remain what they were before this contract, independent members of society, each pursuing happiness in his own way according to his own ideas of it. The employee is not held to any new responsibility for the welfare of the employer; the duties are all held to lie on the other side. The employer must assure the employed against the risks of his calling, and even against his own negligence; the employee is not held to assure himself, as a free man with all his own responsibilities, although the scheme may be so devised that the assurance is paid for out of his wages; he is released from responsibility for himself. The common law recognizes the only true and rational liability of employers, *viz.*, that which is deducible from the responsibilities which the employer has assumed in the relation. The new doctrines which are preached and which have been embodied in the legislation of some countries, are not based on any rational responsibility of the employer but on the fact that the employee may sometimes find himself in a very hard case, either through his own negligence or through unavoidable mischances of life, and that there is nobody else who can be made to take care of him but his employer.

In the advance of the industrial organization it has come about that interests have been subdivided and rights have been created in the various interests. The most important of these divisions is that between a specific interest, like that of the mortgagees or bond-holders, and a contingent interest, like that of the title-holder or the stock-holder. The tendency to separate

these interests, and to define the rights corresponding
to them, is rich in advantage to different classes in the
community and in advantage to the industrial development. The specific interest in the gains of the enterprise is that of the landlord, mortgagee, bondholder,
or employee; the contingent interest in the gains is
that of the title-holder, stock-holder, tenant, or employer.
The specific interest is always free from risk and excluded
from control. The maintenance of this separation of
interests is not possible unless there is the most firm
enforcement of contracts. In some of the cases the difficulty is that the specific interest tries to get a share in
the contingent gains, when it is found out that there are
such. In other cases, the contingent gain not having
been realized, those who own it try to encroach upon the
specific or guaranteed interest. If it is possible for either
to succeed, then a contract relation is transformed into
a relation of "heads I win, tails you lose." The responsibilities of the parties are made to vary from the engagements into which they have entered. The current attacks
on landlords and creditors are, therefore, radically unjust, and the insecurity for the more refined relations
and interests which arises from the weakening of the
contract relation is injurious to the whole industrial
organization.

In short, the policy which we are invited to accept
is one in which every duty which a man accomplishes is
made the basis, not for rights and rewards, but for new
duties and subjection to new demands. Every duty
which is neglected becomes a ground for new rights and
claims. The well-to-do man is to do without things
which his means might buy for himself in order that he
may pay taxes to provide those same things in a public
way for people who have not earned them. The man who

by toil has tried to get the knowledge which alone
enables men to judge, is not to have the deciding voice,
but is to stand behind the man who has neglected to get
knowledge while the latter gives the deciding voice,
and to take or avert the consequences. All this is
preached to us on the ground that it is public-spirited,
unselfish, and altruistic. It is immoral to the very last
degree and opposed to the simplest common sense. It
cannot fail to avenge itself in social consequences of the
most serious character.

THE CONQUEST OF THE UNITED STATES BY SPAIN [1]

DURING the last year the public has been familiarized with descriptions of Spain and of Spanish methods of doing things until the name of Spain has become a symbol for a certain well-defined set of notions and policies. On the other hand, the name of the United States has always been, for all of us, a symbol for a state of things, a set of ideas and traditions, a group of views about social and political affairs. Spain was the first, for a long time the greatest, of the modern imperialistic states. The United States, by its historical origin, its traditions, and its principles, is the chief representative of the revolt and reaction against that kind of a state. I intend to show that, by the line of action now proposed to us, which we call expansion and imperialism, we are throwing away some of the most important elements of the American symbol and are adopting some of the most important elements of the Spanish symbol. We have beaten Spain in a military conflict, but we are submitting to be conquered by her on the field of ideas and policies. Expansionism and imperialism are nothing but the old philosophies of national prosperity which have brought Spain to where she now is. Those philosophies appeal to national vanity and national cupidity. They are seductive, especially upon the first view and the most superficial judgment, and therefore it cannot be denied

[1] *Yale Law Journal*, January, 1899, VIII, 168–193.

that they are very strong for popular effect. They are delusions, and they will lead us to ruin unless we are hard-headed enough to resist them. In any case the year 1898 is a great landmark in the history of the United States. The consequences will not be all good or all bad, for such is not the nature of societal influences. They are always mixed of good and ill, and so it will be in this case. Fifty years from now the historian, looking back to 1898, will no doubt see, in the course which things will have taken, consequences of the proceedings of that year and of this present one which will not all be bad, but you will observe that that is not a justification for a happy-go-lucky policy; that does not affect our duty to-day in all that we do to seek wisdom and prudence and to determine our actions by the best judgment which we can form.

War, expansion, and imperialism are questions of statesmanship and of nothing else. I disregard all other aspects of them and all extraneous elements which have been intermingled with them. I received the other day a circular of a new educational enterprise in which it was urged that, on account of our new possessions, we ought now to devote especial study to history, political economy, and what is called political science. I asked myself, Why? What more reason is there for pursuing these studies now on behalf of our dependencies than there was before to pursue them on behalf of ourselves? In our proceedings of 1898 we made no use of whatever knowledge we had of any of these lines of study. The original and prime cause of the war was that it was a move of partisan tactics in the strife of parties at Washington. As soon as it seemed resolved upon, a number of interests began to see their advantage in it and hastened to further it. It was necessary to make appeals to the public which would bring quite other motives to the support of the enterprise and win the consent of classes who would never consent to either financial or political jobbery. Such appeals were found in sensational assertions which we had no means to verify, in phrases of alleged patriotism, in statements about Cuba and the Cubans which we now know to have been entirely untrue.

Where was the statesmanship of all this? If it is not an established rule of statecraft that a statesman should never impose any sacrifices on his people for anything but their own interests, then it is useless to study political philosophy any more, for this is the alphabet of it. It is contrary to honest statesmanship to imperil the political welfare of the state for party interests. It was unstatesmanlike to publish a solemn declaration that we would not seize any territory, and especially to characterize such action in advance as "criminal aggression," for it was morally certain that we should come out of any war with Spain with conquered territory on our hands, and the people who wanted the war, or who consented to it, hoped that we should do so.

We talk about "liberty" all the time in a big and easy way, as if liberty was a thing that men could have if they want it, and to any extent to which they want it. It is certain that a very large part of human liberty consists simply in the choice either to do a thing or to let it alone. If we decide to do it, a whole series of consequences is entailed upon us in regard to which it is exceedingly difficult, or impossible, for us to exercise any liberty at all. The proof of this from the case before us is so clear and easy that I need spend no words upon it. Here, then, you have the reason why it is a rule of sound statesmanship not to embark on an adventurous policy. A statesman could not be expected to know in advance

that we should come out of the war with the Philippines
on our hands, but it belongs to his education to warn
him that a policy of adventure and of gratuitous enterprise would be sure to entail embarrassments of some
kind. What comes to us in the evolution of our own
life and interests, that we must meet; what we go to
seek which lies beyond that domain is a waste of our
energy and a compromise of our liberty and welfare.
If this is not sound doctrine, then the historical and
social sciences have nothing to teach us which is worth
any trouble.

There is another observation, however, about the war
which is of far greater importance: that is, that it was a
gross violation of self-government. We boast that we
are a self-governing people, and in this respect, particularly, we compare ourselves with pride with older nations.
What is the difference after all? The Russians, whom
we always think of as standing at the opposite pole of
political institutions, have self-government, if you mean
by it acquiescence in what a little group of people at the
head of the government agree to do. The war with
Spain was precipitated upon us headlong, without reflection or deliberation, and without any due formulation of
public opinion. Whenever a voice was raised in behalf
of deliberation and the recognized maxims of statesmanship, it was howled down in a storm of vituperation and
cant. Everything was done to make us throw away
sobriety of thought and calmness of judgment and to
inflate all expressions with sensational epithets and
turgid phrases. It cannot be denied that everything in
regard to the war has been treated in an exalted strain
of sentiment and rhetoric very unfavorable to the truth.
At present the whole periodical press of the country
seems to be occupied in tickling the national vanity to

the utmost by representations about the war which are extravagant and fantastic. There will be a penalty to be paid for all this. Nervous and sensational newspapers are just as corrupting, especially to young people, as nervous and sensational novels. The habit of expecting that all mental pabulum shall be highly spiced, and the corresponding loathing for whatever is soberly truthful, undermines character as much as any other vice. Patriotism is being prostituted into a nervous intoxication which is fatal to an apprehension of truth. It builds around us a fool's paradise, and it will lead us into errors about our position and relations just like those which we have been ridiculing in the case of Spain.

There are some now who think that it is the perfection of statesmanship to say that expansion is a fact and that it is useless to discuss it. We are told that we must not cross any bridges until we come to them; that is, that we must discuss nothing in advance, and that we must not discuss anything which is past because it is irretrievable. No doubt this would be a very acceptable doctrine to the powers that be, for it would mean that they were relieved from responsibility, but it would be a marvelous doctrine to be accepted by a self-governing people. Senator Foraker has told us that we are not to keep the Philippines longer than is necessary to teach the people self-government. How one man can tell what we are to do before the constitutional authorities have decided it, I do not know. Perhaps it is a detail in our new method of self-government. If his assurances are to be trusted, we are paying $20,000,000 for the privilege of tutoring the Tagals up to liberty and self-government. I do not believe that, if the United States undertakes to govern the islands, it will ever give them up except to superior force, but the weakening of imperialism shown by this gentleman's assurances, after a few days of mild debate in the senate, shows that agitation of the subject is not yet in vain.   Then again, if we have done anything, especially if we have acted precipitately, it is a well-recognized course of prudent behavior to find out where we are, what we have done, and what the new situation is into which we have come.   Then, too, we must remember that when the statesman lays a thing down the historian takes it up, and he will group it with historical parallels and contrasts.   There is a set of men who have always been referred to, in our Northern states, for the last thirty years, with especial disapproval.   They are those Southerners who, in 1861, did not believe in secession, but, as they said, "went with their states."   They have been condemned for moral cowardice.   Yet within a year it has become almost a doctrine with us that patriotism requires that we should hold our tongues while our interests, our institutions, our most sacred traditions, and our best established maxims have been trampled underfoot.   There is no doubt that moral courage is the virtue which is more needed than any other in the modern democratic state, and that truckling to popularity is the worst political vice.   The press, the platform, and the pulpit have all fallen under this vice, and there is evidence that the university also, which ought to be the last citadel of truth, is succumbing to it likewise. I have no doubt that the conservative classes of this country will yet look back with great regret to their acquiescence in the events of 1898 and the doctrines and precedents which have been silently established. Let us be well assured that self-government is not a matter of flags and Fourth of July orations, nor yet of strife to get offices.   Eternal vigilance is the price of that as of every other political good.   The perpetuity of self-government depends on the sound political sense of the people, and sound political sense is a matter of habit and practice. We can give it up and we can take instead pomp and glory. That is what Spain did. She had as much self-government as any country in Europe at the beginning of the sixteenth century. The union of the smaller states into one big one gave an impulse to her national feeling and national development. The discovery of America put into her hands the control of immense territories. National pride and ambition were stimulated. Then came the struggle with France for world-dominion, which resulted in absolute monarchy and bankruptcy for Spain. She lost self-government and saw her resources spent on interests which were foreign to her, but she could talk about an empire on which the sun never set and boast of her colonies, her gold-mines, her fleets and armies and debts. She had glory and pride, mixed, of course, with defeat and disaster, such as must be experienced by any nation on that course of policy; and she grew weaker in her industry and commerce and poorer in the status of the population all the time. She has never been able to recover real self-government yet. If we Americans believe in self-government, why do we let it slip away from us? Why do we barter it away for military glory as Spain did?

There is not a civilized nation which does not talk about its civilizing mission just as grandly as we do. The English, who really have more to boast of in this respect than anybody else, talk least about it, but the Phariseeism with which they correct and instruct other people has made them hated all over the globe. The French believe themselves the guardians of the highest and purest culture, and that the eyes of all mankind are fixed on Paris, whence they expect oracles of thought and taste. The Germans regard themselves as charged with a mission, especially to us Americans, to save us from egoism and materialism. The Russians, in their books and newspapers, talk about the civilizing mission of Russia in language that might be translated from some of the finest paragraphs in our imperialistic newspapers. The first principle of Mohammedanism is that we Christians are dogs and infidels, fit only to be enslaved or butchered by Moslems. It is a corollary that wherever Mohammedanism extends it carries, in the belief of its votaries, the highest blessings, and that the whole human race would be enormously elevated if Mohammedanism should supplant Christianity everywhere. To come, last, to Spain, the Spaniards have, for centuries, considered themselves the most zealous and self-sacrificing Christians, especially charged by the Almighty, on this account, to spread true religion and civilization over the globe. They think themselves free and noble, leaders in refinement and the sentiments of personal honor, and they despise us as sordid money-grabbers and heretics. I could bring you passages from peninsular authors of the first rank about the grand rôle of Spain and Portugal in spreading freedom and truth. Now each nation laughs at all the others when it observes these manifestations of national vanity. You may rely upon it that they are all ridiculous by virtue of these pretensions, including ourselves. The point is that each of them repudiates the standards of the others, and the outlying nations, which are to be civilized, hate all the standards of civilized men. We assume that what we like and practice, and what we think better, must come as a welcome blessing to Spanish-Americans and Filipinos. This is grossly and obviously untrue. They hate our ways. They are hostile to our ideas. Our religion, language,

institutions, and manners offend them. They like their
own ways, and if we appear amongst them as rulers,
there will be social discord in all the great departments
of social interest. The most important thing which we
shall inherit from the Spaniards will be the task of sup-
pressing rebellions. If the United States takes out of
the hands of Spain her mission, on the ground that Spain
is not executing it well, and if this nation in its turn
attempts to be school-mistress to others, it will shrivel
up into the same vanity and self-conceit of which Spain
now presents an example. To read our current literature one would think that we were already well on the
way to it. Now, the great reason why all these enterprises which begin by saying to somebody else, We know
what is good for you better than you know yourself
and we are going to make you do it, are false and
wrong is that they violate liberty; or, to turn the same
statement into other words, the reason why liberty, of
which we Americans talk so much, is a good thing is
that it means leaving people to live out their own lives
in their own way, while we do the same. If we believe
in liberty, as an American principle, why do we not
stand by it? Why are we going to throw it away to enter
upon a Spanish policy of dominion and regulation?

The United States cannot be a colonizing nation for a
long time yet. We have only twenty-three persons to
the square mile in the United States without Alaska.
The country can multiply its population by thirteen;
that is, the population could rise above a billion before
the whole country would be as densely populated as
Rhode Island is now. There is, therefore, no pressure of
population, which is the first condition of rational expansion, unless we could buy another territory like the Mississippi Valley with no civilized population in it. If we

could do that it would postpone the day of over-population still further, and make easier conditions for our people in the next generations. In the second place, the islands which we have taken from Spain never can be the residence of American families, removing and settling to make their homes there. The climatic conditions forbid it. Although Spaniards have established themselves in Spanish America, even in the tropics, the evils of Spanish rule have largely arisen from the fact that Spaniards have gone to the colonies as adventurers, eager to make fortunes as quickly as possible, that they might return to Spain to enjoy them. That the relation of our people to these possessions will have that character is already apparent. It is, therefore, inaccurate to speak of a colonial system in describing our relation to these dependencies, but as we have no other term, let us use this one and inquire *what kind of a colonial system we are to establish.*

I. Spain stands, in modern history, as the first state to develop and apply a colonial system to her outlying possessions. Her policy was to exclude absolutely all non-Spaniards from her subject territories and to exploit them for the benefit of Spain, without much regard for the aborigines or the colonists. The cold and unnecessary cruelty of the Spaniards to the aborigines is appalling, even when compared with the treatment of the aborigines by other Europeans. A modern economist stands aghast at the economic measures adopted by Spain, as well in regard to her domestic policy as to her colonies. It seems as if those measures could only have been inspired by some demon of folly, they were so destructive to her prosperity. She possesses a large literature from the last three centuries, in which her publicists discuss with amazement the question whether it was a

blessing or a curse to get the Indies, and why, with all
the supposed conditions of prosperity in her hands, she
was declining all the time. We now hear it argued that
she is well rid of her colonies, and that, if she will devote
her energies to her internal development and rid her
politics of the corruption of colonial officials and interests,
she may be regenerated. That is a rational opinion. It
is the best diagnosis of her condition and the best pre-
scription of a remedy which the occasion has called forth.
But what, then, will happen to the state which has taken
over her colonies? I can see no answer except that that
nation, with them, has taken over the disease and that
it now is to be corrupted by exploiting dependent communities just as she has been. That it stands exposed
to this danger is undeniable.

It would not be becoming to try, in a paragraph, to set
forth the causes of the decadence of Spain, and although
the economic history of that country has commanded
such attention from me as I could give to it consistently
with other obligations, yet I could not feel prepared to
do any justice to that subject; but one or two features
of the history can be defined with confidence, and they
are such as are especially instructive for us.

In the first place Spain never intended, of set purpose,
to ruin the material prosperity of herself or her colonies.
Her economic history is one long lesson to prove that
any prosperity policy is a delusion and a path to ruin.
There is no economic lesson which the people of the
United States need to take to heart more than that.
In the second place the Spanish mistakes arose, in part,
from confusing the public treasury with the national
wealth. They thought that, when gold flowed into the
public treasury, that was the same as an increase of
wealth of the people. It really meant that the people

were bearing the burdens of the imperial system and that the profits of it went into the public treasury; that is, into the hands of the king. It was no wonder, then, that as the burdens grew greater the people grew poorer. The king spent the revenues in extending the imperial system in Germany, Italy, and the Netherlands, so that the revenues really became a new cause of corruption and decay. The only people who were well off, in the midst of the increasing distress, were the ecclesiastics and nobles, who were protected by entails and charters, which, in their turn, were a new cause of restriction and destruction to the industries of the country. As to the treatment of the aborigines in the outlying possessions of Spain, the orders from the home government were as good as could possibly be desired. No other European government issued any which were nearly so enlightened or testified to such care about that matter. Spanish America is still covered with institutions founded by Spain for the benefit of the aborigines, so far as they have not been confiscated or diverted to other uses. Nevertheless the Spanish rule nearly exterminated the aborigines in one hundred and fifty years. The Pope gave them into servitude to the Spaniards. The Spaniards regarded them as savages, heretics, beasts, not entitled to human consideration. Here you have the great explanation of man's inhumanity to man. When Spaniards tortured and burned Protestants and Jews it was because, in their minds, Protestants and Jews were heretics; that is to say, were beyond the pale, were abominable, were not entitled to human consideration. Humane men and pious women felt no more compunctions at the sufferings of Protestants and Jews than we would at the execution of mad dogs or rattlesnakes. There are plenty of people in the United States to-day who regard negroes as human beings, perhaps, but of a different order from white men, so that the ideas and social arrangements of white men cannot be applied to them with propriety. Others feel the same way about Indians. This attitude of mind, wherever you meet with it, is what causes tyranny and cruelty. It is this disposition to decide off-hand that some people are not fit for liberty and self-government which gives relative truth to the doctrine that all men are equal, and inasmuch as the history of mankind has been one long story of the abuse of some by others, who, of course, smoothed over their tyranny by some beautiful doctrines of religion, or ethics, or political philosophy, which proved that it was all for the best good of the oppressed, therefore the doctrine that all men are equal has come to stand as one of the corner-stones of the temple of justice and truth. It was set up as a bar to just this notion that we are so much better than others that it is liberty for them to be governed by us.

The Americans have been committed from the outset to the doctrine that all men are equal. We have elevated it into an absolute doctrine as a part of the theory of our social and political fabric. It has always been a domestic dogma in spite of its absolute form, and as a domestic dogma it has always stood in glaring contradiction to the facts about Indians and negroes and to our legislation about Chinamen. In its absolute form it must, of course, apply to Kanakas, Malays, Tagals, and Chinese just as much as to Yankees, Germans, and Irish. It is an astonishing event that we have lived to see American arms carry this domestic dogma out where it must be tested in its application to uncivilized and half-civilized peoples. At the first touch of the test we throw the doctrine away and adopt the Spanish doctrine. We are told by all the imperialists that these people are not fit for liberty and self-government; that it is rebellion for them to resist our beneficence; that we must send fleets and armies to kill them if they do it; that we must devise a government for them and administer it ourselves; that we may buy them or sell them as we please, and dispose of their "trade" for our own advantage. What is that but the policy of Spain to her dependencies? What can we expect as a consequence of it? Nothing but that it will bring us where Spain is now.

But then, if it is not right for us to hold these islands as dependencies, you may ask me whether I think that we ought to take them into our Union, at least some of them, and let them help to govern us. Certainly not. If *that* question is raised, then the question whether they are, in our judgment, fit for self-government or not is in order. The American people, since the Civil War, have to a great extent lost sight of the fact that this state of ours, the United States of America, is a confederated state of a very peculiar and artificial form. It is not a state like the states of Europe, with the exception of Switzerland. The field for dogmatism in our day is not theology, it is political philosophy. "Sovereignty" is the most abstract and metaphysical term in political philosophy. Nobody can define it. For this reason it exactly suits the purposes of the curbstone statesman. He puts into it whatever he wants to get out of it again, and he has set to work lately to spin out a proof that the United States is a great imperialistic state, although the Constitution, which tells us just what it is and what it is not, is there to prove the contrary.

The thirteen colonies, as we all know, were independent commonwealths with respect to each other. They had little sympathy and a great deal of jealousy. They came into a union with each other upon terms which were stipulated and defined in the Constitution, but they united only unwillingly and under the pressure of necessity. What was at first only a loose combination or alliance has been welded together into a great state by the history of a century. Nothing, however, has altered that which was the first condition of the Union; *viz.*, that all the states members of it should be on the same plane of civilization and political development; that they should all hold the same ideas, traditions, and political creed; that their social standards and ideals should be such as to maintain cordial sympathy between them. The Civil War arose out of the fact that this condition was imperfectly fulfilled. At other times actual differences in standpoint and principle, or in ideals and opinion, have produced discord within the confederation. Such crises are inevitable in any confederated state. It is the highest statesmanship in such a system to avoid them, or smooth them over, and above all, never to take in voluntarily any heterogeneous elements. The prosperity of such a state depends on closer and closer sympathy between the parts in order that differences which arise may be easily harmonized. What we need is more intension, not more extension.

It follows, then, that it is unwisdom to take into a State like this any foreign element which is not congenial to it. Any such element will act as a solvent upon it. Consequently we are brought by our new conquests face to face with this dilemma: we must either hold them as inferior possessions, to be ruled and exploited by us after the fashion of the old colonial system, or we must take them in on an equality with ourselves, where they will help to govern us and to corrupt a political system which they do not understand and in which they cannot participate. From that dilemma there is no escape except to give them independence and to let them work out their own salvation or go without it. Hayti has been independent for a century and has been a theater of revolution, tyranny, and bloodshed all the time. There is not a Spanish-American state which has proved its capacity for self-government as yet. It is a fair question whether any one of them would have been worse off than it is to-day if Spanish rule had been maintained in it. The chief exception is Mexico. Mr. Lummis, an American, has recently published a book on Mexico, in which he tells us that we would do well to go to school to Mexico for a number of important public interests, but Mexico has been, for ten or fifteen years, under a dictator, and the republican forms have been in abeyance. What will happen there when the dictator dies nobody knows. The doctrine that we are to take away from other nations any possessions of theirs which we think that we could manage better than they are managing them, or that we are to take in hand any countries which we do not think capable of self-government, is one which will lead us very far. With that doctrine in the background, our politicians will have no trouble to find a war ready for us the next time that they come around to the point where they think that it is time for us to have another. We are told that we must have a big army hereafter. What for; unless we propose to do again by and by what we have just done? In that case our neighbors have reason to ask themselves whom we will attack next. They must begin to arm, too, and by our act the whole western world is plunged into the distress under which the eastern world is groaning. Here is another point in regard to which the conservative elements in the country are making a great mistake to allow all this militarism and imperialism to go on without protest. It will be established as a rule that, whenever political ascendency is threatened, it can be established again by a little war, filling the minds of the people with glory and diverting their attention from their own interests. Hard-headed old Benjamin Franklin hit the point when, referring back to the days of Marlborough, he talked about the "pest of glory." The thirst for glory is an epidemic which robs a people of their judgment, seduces their vanity, cheats them of their interests, and corrupts their consciences.

This country owes its existence to a revolt against the colonial and navigation system which, as I have said, Spain first put in practice. The English colonial system never was even approximately so harsh and tyrannical as that of Spain. The first great question which arose about colonies in England was whether they were parts of the possessions of the king of England or part of the dominion of the crown. The constitutional difference was great. In the one case they were subject to the king and were not under the constitutional guarantees; in the other case they were subject to the Parliament and were under the constitutional guarantees. This is exactly the same question which arose in the middle of this century in this country about territories, and which helped to bring on the Civil War. It is already arising again. It is the question whether the Constitution of the United States extends over all men and territory owned by the United States, or whether there are to be grades and planes of rights for different parts of the dominions over which our flag waves. This question already promises to introduce dissensions amongst us which will touch the most vital elements in our national existence.

The constitutional question, however, goes even deeper than this. Of the interpretation of clauses in the Constitution I am not competent to speak, but the Constitution is the organic law of this confederated state in which we live, and therefore it is the description of it as it was planned and as it is. The question at stake is nothing less than the integrity of this state in its most essential elements. The expansionists have recognized this fact by already casting the Constitution aside. The military men, of course, have been the first to do this. It is of the essence of militarism that under it military men learn to despise constitutions, to sneer at parliaments, and to look with contempt on civilians. Some of the imperialists are not ready to go quite so fast as yet. They have remonstrated against the military doctrine, but that only proves that the military men see the point at issue better than the others do. Others say that if the legs of the Constitution are too short to straddle the gulf between the old policy and the new, they can be stretched a little, a view of the matter which is as flippant as it is in bad taste. It would require too much time to notice the various contemptuous and jaunty references to the Constitution which every day brings to our notice, and from the same class, at least, who, two years ago, were so shocked at a criticism of the *interpretation* of the Constitution which was inserted in the Chicago platform.

The question of imperialism, then, is the question whether we are going to give the lie to the origin of our own national existence by establishing a colonial system of the old Spanish type, even if we have to sacrifice our existing civil and political system to do it. I submit that it is a strange incongruity to utter grand platitudes about the blessings of liberty, etc., which we are going to impart to these people, and to begin by refusing to extend the Constitution over them, and still more, by throwing the Constitution into the gutter here at home. If you take away the Constitution, what is American liberty and all the rest? Nothing but a lot of phrases.

Some will answer me that they do not intend to adopt any Spanish colonial system; that they intend to imitate the modern English policy with respect to colonies. The proudest fact in the history of England is that, since the Napoleonic wars, she has steadily corrected abuses, amended her institutions, redressed grievances, and so has made her recent history a story of amelioration of all her institutions, social, political, and civil. To do this she has had to overcome old traditions, established customs, vested rights, and all the other obstacles which retard or prevent social improvement. The consequence is that the traditions of her public service, in all its branches, have been purified, and that a body of men has grown up who have a noble spirit, high motives, honorable methods, and excellent standards. At the same time the policy of the country has been steadily growing more and more enlightened in regard to all the great interests of society. These triumphs of peace are far greater than any triumphs of war. It takes more national grit to correct abuses than to win battles. England has shown herself very willing indeed to learn from us whatever we could teach, and we might learn a great deal from her on matters far more important than colonial policy. Her reform of her colonial policy is only a part, and perhaps a consequence, of the improvements made elsewhere in her political system.

We have had some experience this last summer in the attempt to improvise an army. We may be very sure that it is equally impossible to improvise a colonial system. The present English colonial system is aristocratic.

It depends upon a large body of specially trained men, acting under traditions which have become well established, and with a firm *esprit de corps*. Nobody can get into it without training. The system is foreign to our ideas, tastes, and methods. It would require a long time and radical changes in our political methods, which we are not as yet at all disposed to make, to establish any such thing here, and then it would be an imitation. Moreover, England has three different colonial systems, according to the development of the resident population in each colony or dependency, and the selection of the one of these three systems which we will adopt and apply involves all the difficulties which I have been discussing.

There is, however, another objection to the English system. A great many people talk about the revenue which we are to get from these possessions. If we attempt to get any revenues from them we shall repeat the conduct of England towards her colonies against which they revolted. England claimed that it was reasonable that the colonies should pay their share of imperial expenses which were incurred for the benefit of all. I have never been able to see why that was not a fair demand. As you know, the colonies spurned it with indignation, on the ground that the taxation, being at the discretion of a foreign power, *might* be made unjust. Our historians and publicists have taught us that the position of the colonists was right and heroic, and the only one worthy of freemen. The revolt was made on the *principle* of no taxation, not on the size of the tax. The colonists would not pay a penny. Since that is so, we cannot get a penny of revenue from the dependencies, even for their fair share of imperial expenditures, without burning up all our histories, revising all the great principles of our heroic period, repudiating our great men of that period,

and going over to the Spanish doctrine of taxing dependencies at the discretion of the governing State.   Already
one of these dependencies is in arms struggling for liberty
against us.   Read the threats of the imperialists against
these people, who dare to rebel against us, and see whether
I am misstating or exaggerating the corruption of imperialism on ourselves.   The question is once more,
whether we are prepared to repudiate the principles
which we have been insisting on for one hundred and
fifty years, and to embrace those of which Spain is the
oldest and most conspicuous representative, or not.

In regard to this matter of taxation and revenue, the
present English colonial system is as unjust to the mother-
country as the old system was to the colonies, or more
so.   The colonies now tax the mother-country.   She
pays large expenses for their advantage, for which they
return nothing.   They set up tax barriers against her
trade with them.   I do not believe that the United States
will ever consent to any such system, and I am clear in
the opinion that they never ought to.   If the colonies
ought not to be made tributary to the mother-country,
neither ought the mother-country to be made tributary
to them.   The proposition to imitate England's colonial
policy is evidently made without the necessary knowledge
of what it means, and it proves that those who thrust
aside prudent objections by declaring off-hand that we
will imitate England have not any serious comprehension
of what it is that they propose to us to do.

The conclusion of this branch of the subject is that it
is fundamentally antagonistic to our domestic system to
hold dependencies which are unfit to enter into the Union.
Our system cannot be extended to take them in or adjusted to them to keep them out without sacrificing its
integrity.   If we take in dependencies which, as we now

agree, are not fit to come in as states, there will be constant political agitation to admit them as states, for such agitation will be fomented by any party which thinks that it can win votes in that way. It was an enormous blunder in statecraft to engage in a war which was sure to bring us into this predicament.

II. It seems as if this new policy was destined to thrust a sword into every joint in our historical and philosophical system. Our ancestors revolted against the colonial and navigation system, but as soon as they got their independence, they fastened a navigation system on themselves. The consequence is that our industry and commerce are to-day organized under a restrictive system which is the direct offspring of the old Spanish restrictive system, and is based on the same ideas of economic policy; viz., that statesmen can devise a prosperity policy for a country which will do more for it than a spontaneous development of the energy of the people and the resources of the territory would do. On the other hand, inside of the Union we have established the grandest experiment in absolute free trade that has ever existed. The combination of the two is not new, because it is just what Colbert tried in France, but it is original here and is an interesting result of the presence in men's minds of two opposite philosophies, the adjustment of which has never yet been fought out. The extension of our authority over these new territories forces the inconsistency between our internal and our external policy out of the field of philosophy into that of practical politics. Wherever the boundary line of the national system falls we have one rule inside of it and another outside of it. Are the new territories to be taken inside or to be treated as outside? If we develop this dilemma, we shall see that it is of the first importance.

If we treat the dependencies as inside the national system, we must have absolute free trade with them. Then if, on the policy of the "open door," we allow all others to go to them on the same terms as ourselves, the dependencies will have free trade with all the world, while we are under the restrictive system ourselves. Then, too, the dependencies can obtain no revenues by import duties.

If we take the other branch of the dilemma and treat the dependencies as outside of our national policy, then we must shut out their products from our market by taxes. If we do this on the policy of the "open door," then any taxes which the islands lay upon imports from elsewhere they must also lay upon imports from us. Then they and we will be taxing each other. If we go upon the protectionist policy, we shall determine our taxes against them and theirs against other nations, and we shall let them lay none against us. That is exactly the Spanish system. Under it the colonies will be crushed between the upper and the nether millstone. They will revolt against us for just the same reason for which they revolted against Spain.

I have watched the newspapers with great interest for six months, to see what indications were presented of the probable currents of opinion on the dilemma which I have described. There have been but few. A few extreme protectionist newspapers have truculently declared that our protective system was to be extended around our possessions, and that everybody else was to be excluded from them. From a number of interviews and letters, by private individuals, I select the following as expressing well what is sure to be the view of the unregenerate man, especially if he has an interest to be protected as this writer had.

"I am opposed to the 'open door' policy, as I understand it. To open the ports of our new territories free
to the world would have the effect of cheapening or
destroying many of the benefits of territorial acquisition,
which has cost us blood and money. As a nation we are
well qualified to develop and handle the trade of our new
possessions, and by permitting others to come in and
divide the advantages and profits of this trade we not
only wrong our own citizens, who should be given preference, but exhibit a weakness that ill becomes a nation of
our prominence."

This is exactly the view which was held in Spain,
France, Holland, and England in the eighteenth century,
and upon which the navigation system, against which
our fathers revolted, was founded. If we adopt this
view we may count upon it that we shall be embroiled
in constant wars with other nations, which will not consent that we should shut them out of parts of the earth's
surface until we prove that we can do it by force. Then
we shall be parties to a renewal of all the eighteenth
century wars for colonies, for supremacy on the sea, for
"trade," as the term is used, for world supremacy, and
for all the rest of the heavy follies from which our fathers
fought to free themselves. That is the policy of Russia
and France at the present time, and we have before our
eyes proofs of its effect on the peace and welfare of mankind.

Our modern protectionists have always told us that
the object of their policy is to secure the home market.
They have pushed their system to an extravagant excess.
The free traders used to tell them that they were con-
structing a Chinese wall. They answered that they
wished we were separated from other nations by a gulf
of fire. Now it is they who are crying out that they are

shut in by a Chinese wall. When we have shut all the world out, we find that we have shut ourselves in. The protective system is applied especially to certain selected lines of production. Of course these are stimulated out of proportion to the requirements of the community, and so are exposed to sharp fluctuations of high profits and over-production. At great expense and loss we have carried out the policy of the home market, and now we are called upon at great expense and loss to go out and conquer territory in order to widen the market. In order to have trade with another community the first condition is that we must produce what they want and they must produce what we want. That is the economic condition. The second condition is that there must be peace and security and freedom from arbitrary obstacles interposed by government. This is the political condition. If these conditions are fulfilled, there will be trade, no matter whether the two communities are in one body politic or not. If these conditions are not fulfilled, there will be no trade, no matter what flag floats. If we want more trade we can get it any day by a reciprocity treaty with Canada, and it will be larger and more profitable than that of all the Spanish possessions. It will cost us nothing to get it. Yet while we were fighting for Puerto Rico and Manila, and spending three or four hundred millions to get them, negotiations with Canada failed through the narrow-mindedness and bigotry which we brought to the negotiation. Conquest can do nothing for trade except to remove the political obstacles which the conquered could not, or would not, remove. From this it follows that the only justification for territorial extension is the extension of free and enlightened policies in regard to commerce. Even then extension is an irksome necessity. The question always is, whether you are taking an asset or a liability. Land grabbing means properly taking territory and shutting all the rest of the world out of it, so as to exploit it ourselves. It is not land grabbing to take it and police it and throw it open to all. This is the policy of the "open door." Our external commercial policy is, in all its principles, the same as that of Spain. We had no justification, on that ground, in taking anything away from her. If we now seek to justify ourselves, it must be by going over to the free policy; but, as I have shown, that forces to a crisis the contradiction between our domestic and our external policy as to trade. It is very probable, indeed, that the destruction of our restrictive system will be the first good result of expansion, but my object here has been to show what a network of difficulties environ us in the attempt to establish a commercial policy for these dependencies. We have certainly to go through years of turmoil and political bitterness, with all the consequent chances of internal dissension, before these difficulties can be overcome.

III. Another phenomenon which deserves earnest attention from the student of contemporaneous history and of the trend of political institutions is the failure of the masses of our people to perceive *the inevitable effect of imperialism on democracy*. On the twenty-ninth of last November [1898] the Prime Minister of France was quoted in a cable dispatch as follows: "For twenty-eight years we have lived under a contradiction. The army and democracy subsist side by side. The maintenance of the traditions of the army is a menace to liberty, yet they assure the safety of the country and its most sacred duties."

That antagonism of democracy and militarism is now coming to a crisis in France, and militarism is sure to win, because the French people would make any other sacrifice rather than diminish their military strength. In Germany the attempt has been going on for thirty years to establish constitutional government with parliamentary institutions. The parts of the German system are at war with each other. The Emperor constantly interferes with the operation of the system and utters declarations which are entirely personal. He is not responsible and cannot be answered or criticised. The situation is not so delicate as in France, but it is exceedingly unstable. All the desire of Germans for self-government and civil liberty runs out into socialism, and socialism is repressed by force or by trickery. The conservative classes of the country acquiesce in the situation while they deplore it. The reason is because the Emperor is the war lord. His power and authority are essential to the military strength of the State in face of its neighbors. That is the preponderating consideration to which everything else has to yield, and the consequence of it is that there is to-day scarcely an institution in Germany except the army.

Everywhere you go on the continent of Europe at this hour you see the conflict between militarism and industrialism. You see the expansion of industrial power pushed forward by the energy, hope, and thrift of men, and you see the development arrested, diverted, crippled, and defeated by measures which are dictated by military considerations. At the same time the press is loaded down with discussions about political economy, political philosophy, and social policy. They are discussing poverty, labor, socialism, charity, reform, and social ideals, and are boasting of enlightenment and progress, at the same time that the things which are done are dictated by none of these considerations, but only by military interests. It is militarism which is eating up all the products of science and art, defeating the energy of the population and wasting its savings. It is militarism which forbids the people to give their attention to the problems of their own welfare and to give their strength to the education and comfort of their children. It is militarism which is combating the grand efforts of science and art to ameliorate the struggle for existence.

The American people believe that they have a free country, and we are treated to grandiloquent speeches about our flag and our reputation for freedom and enlightenment. The common opinion is that we have these things because we have chosen and adopted them, because they are in the Declaration of Independence and the Constitution. We suppose, therefore, that we are sure to keep them and that the follies of other people are things which we can hear about with complacency. People say that this country is like no other; that its prosperity proves its exceptionality, and so on. These are popular errors which in time will meet with harsh correction. The United States is in a protected situation. It is easy to have equality where land is abundant and where the population is small. It is easy to have prosperity where a few men have a great continent to exploit. It is easy to have liberty when you have no dangerous neighbors and when the struggle for existence is easy. There are no severe penalties, under such circumstances, for political mistakes. Democracy is not then a thing to be nursed and defended, as it is in an old country like France. It is rooted and founded in the economic circumstances of the country. The orators and constitution-makers do not make democracy. They are made by it. This protected position, however, is sure to pass away. As the country fills up with popu-

lation, and the task of getting a living out of the ground
becomes more difficult, the struggle for existence will
become harder and the competition of life more severe.
Then liberty and democracy will cost something, if they
are to be maintained.

Now what will hasten the day when our present advantages will wear out and when we shall come down to the
conditions of the older and densely populated nations?
The answer is: war, debt, taxation, diplomacy, a grand
governmental system, pomp, glory, a big army and navy,
lavish expenditures, political jobbery — in a word, imperialism. In the old days the democratic masses of
this country, who knew little about our modern doctrines
of social philosophy, had a sound instinct on these matters, and it is no small ground of political disquietude to
see it decline. They resisted every appeal to their vanity
in the way of pomp and glory which they knew must be
paid for. They dreaded a public debt and a standing
army. They were narrow-minded and went too far with
these notions, but they were, at least, right, if they wanted
to strengthen democracy.

The great foe of democracy now and in the near future
is plutocracy. Every year that passes brings out this
antagonism more distinctly. It is to be the social war
of the twentieth century. In that war militarism, expansion and imperialism will all favor plutocracy. In
the first place, war and expansion will favor jobbery,
both in the dependencies and at home. In the second
place, they will take away the attention of the people
from what the plutocrats are doing. In the third place,
they will cause large expenditures of the people's money,
the return for which will not go into the treasury, but
into the hands of a few schemers. In the fourth place,
they will call for a large public debt and taxes, and these

things especially tend to make men unequal, because any
social burdens bear more heavily on the weak than on
the strong, and so make the weak weaker and the strong
stronger.   Therefore expansion and imperialism are a
grand onslaught on democracy.

The point which I have tried to make in this lecture is
that expansion and imperialism are at war with the best
traditions, principles, and interests of the American people,
and that they will plunge us into a network of difficult
problems and political perils, which we might have
avoided, while they offer us no corresponding advantage
in return.

Of course "principles," phrases, and catch-words are
always invented to bolster up any policy which anybody
wants to recommend.   So in this case.   The people who
have led us on to shut ourselves in, and who now want
us to break out, warn us against the terrors of "isolation."   Our ancestors all came here to isolate themselves
from the social burdens and inherited errors of the old
world.   When the others are all over ears in trouble,
who would not be isolated in freedom from care?   When
the others are crushed under the burden of militarism,
who would not be isolated in peace and industry?   When
the others are all struggling under debt and taxes, who
would not be isolated in the enjoyment of his own earnings for the benefit of his own family?   When the rest
are all in a quiver of anxiety, lest at a day's notice they
may be involved in a social cataclysm, who would not
be isolated out of reach of the disaster?   What we are
doing is that we are abandoning this blessed isolation to
run after a share in the trouble.

The expansionists answer our remonstrances on behalf
of the great American principles by saying that times
have changed and that we have outlived the fathers of

the republic and their doctrines.   As far as the authority
of the great men is concerned, that may well be sacrificed
without regret.   Authority of persons and names is a
dangerous thing.   Let us get at the truth and the right.
I, for my part, am also afraid of the great principles,
and I would make no fight on their behalf.   In the ten
years before the Revolution our ancestors invented a fine
lot of "principles" which they thought would help their
case.   They repudiated many of them as soon as they
got their independence, and the rest of them have since
made us a great deal of trouble.   I have examined them
all critically, and there is not one of them which I consider
sound, as it is popularly understood.   I have been denounced as a heretic on this account by people who now
repudiate them all in a sentence.   But this only clears
the ground for the real point.   There is a consistency of
character for a nation as well as for a man.   A man
who changes his principles from week to week is destitute
of character and deserves no confidence.   The great men
of this nation were such because they embodied and
expressed the opinion and sentiments of the nation in
their time.   Their names are something more than clubs
with which to knock an opponent down when it suits
one's purpose, but to be thrown away with contempt
when they happen to be on the other side.   So of the
great principles; whether some of us are skeptical about
their entire validity and want to define and limit them
somewhat is of little importance.   If the nation has
accepted them, sworn by them, founded its legislation
on them, imbedded them in the decisions of its courts,
and then if it throws them away at six months' warning,
you may depend upon it that that nation will suffer in
its moral and political rectitude a shock of the severest
kind.   Three years ago we were ready to fight Great

Britain to make her arbitrate a quarrel which she had with Venezuela. The question about the Maine was one of the fittest subjects for arbitration that ever arose between two nations, and we refused to listen to such a proposition. Three years ago, if you had said that any proposition put forth by anybody was "English," he might have been mobbed in the streets. Now the English are our beloved friends, and we are going to try to imitate them and adopt their way of doing things. They are encouraging us to go into difficulties, first because our hands will be full and we shall be unable to interfere elsewhere, and secondly, because if we are in difficulties we shall need allies, and they think that they will be our first choice as such. Some of our public journals have been pouring out sentimental drivel for years about arbitration, but last summer they turned around and began to pour out sentimental drivel about the benefits of war. We congratulate ourselves all the time on the increased means of producing wealth, and then we take the opposite fit and commit some great folly in order to prove that there is something grander than the pursuit of wealth. Three years ago we were on the verge of a law to keep immigrants out who were not good enough to be in with us. Now we are going to take in eight million barbarians and semi-barbarians, and we are paying twenty million dollars to get them. For thirty years the negro has been in fashion. He has had political value and has been petted. Now we have made friends with the Southerners. They and we are hugging each other. We are all united. The negro's day is over. He is out of fashion. We cannot treat him one way and the Malays, Tagals, and Kanakas another way. A Southern senator two or three days ago thanked an expansionist senator from Connecticut for enunciating doctrines which proved that, for the last thirty years, the Southerners have been right all the time, and his inference was incontrovertible. So the "great principles" change all the time; or, what is far more important, the phrases change. Some go out of fashion, others come in; but the phrase-makers are with us all the time. So when our friends the expansionists tell us that times have changed, what it means is that they have a whole set of new phrases which they want to force into the place of the old ones. The new ones are certainly no more valid than the old ones. All the validity that the great principles ever had they have now. Anybody who ever candidly studied them and accepted them for no more than they were really worth can stand by them now as well as ever. The time when a maxim or principle is worth something is when you are tempted to violate it.

Another answer which the imperialists make is that Americans can do anything. They say that they do not shrink from responsibilities. They are willing to run into a hole, trusting to luck and cleverness to get out. There are some things that Americans cannot do. Americans cannot make $2 + 2 = 5$. You may answer that that is an arithmetical impossibility and is not in the range of our subject. Very well; Americans cannot collect two dollars a gallon tax on whisky. They tried it for many years and failed. That is an economic or political impossibility, the roots of which are in human nature. It is as absolute an impossibility on this domain as the former on the domain of mathematics. So far as yet appears, Americans cannot govern a city of one hundred thousand inhabitants so as to get comfort and convenience in it at a low cost and without jobbery. The fire department of this city is now demoralized by political jobbery — and Spain and all her possessions are not worth as much to you and me as the efficiency of the fire department of New Haven.   The Americans in Connecticut cannot abolish the rotten borough system.   The English abolished their rotten borough system seventy years ago, in spite of nobles and landlords.   We cannot abolish ours in spite of the small towns.   Americans cannot reform the pension list.   Its abuses are rooted in the methods of democratic self-government, and no one dares to touch them.   It is very doubtful indeed if Americans can keep up an army of one hundred thousand men in time of peace.   Where can one hundred thousand men be found in this country who are willing to spend their lives as soldiers; or if they are found, what pay will it require to induce them to take this career?   Americans cannot disentangle their currency from the confusion into which it was thrown by the Civil War, and they cannot put it on a simple, sure, and sound basis which would give stability to the business of the country.   This is a political impossibility.   Americans cannot assure the suffrage to negroes throughout the United States; they have tried it for thirty years and now, contemporaneously with this war with Spain, it has been finally demonstrated that it is a failure.   Inasmuch as the negro is now out of fashion, no further attempt to accomplish this purpose will be made.   It is an impossibility on account of the complexity of our system of State and Federal government.   If I had time to do so, I could go back over the history of negro suffrage and show you how curbstone arguments, exactly analogous to the arguments about expansion, were used to favor it, and how objections were thrust aside in this same blustering and senseless manner in which objections to imperialism are met.   The ballot, we were told, was an educator and would solve all difficulties in its own path as by magic. Worse still, Americans cannot assure life, liberty, and the pursuit of happiness to negroes inside of the United States. When the negro postmaster's house was set on fire in the night in South Carolina, and not only he, but his wife and children, were murdered as they came out, and when, moreover, this incident passed without legal investigation or punishment, it was a bad omen for the extension of liberty, etc., to Malays and Tagals by simply setting over them the American flag. Upon a little serious examination the off-hand disposal of an important question of policy by the declaration that Americans can do anything proves to be only a silly piece of bombast, and upon a little reflection we find that our hands are quite full at home of problems by the solution of which the peace and happiness of the American people could be greatly increased. The laws of nature and of human nature are just as valid for Americans as for anybody else, and if we commit acts we shall have to take consequences, just like other people. Therefore prudence demands that we look ahead to see what we are about to do, and that we gauge the means at our disposal, if we do not want to bring calamity on ourselves and our children. We see that the peculiarities of our system of government set limitations on us. We cannot do things which a great centralized monarchy could do. The very blessings and special advantages which we enjoy, as compared with others, bring disabilities with them. That is the great fundamental cause of what I have tried to show throughout this lecture, that we cannot govern dependencies consistently with our political system, and that, if we try it, the State which our fathers founded will suffer a reaction which will transform it into another empire just after the fashion of all the old ones. That is what imperialism means. That is what it will be; and the democratic republic, which has been, will stand in history, like the colonial organization of earlier days, as a mere transition form.

And yet this scheme of a republic which our fathers formed was a glorious dream which demands more than a word of respect and affection before it passes away. Indeed, it is not fair to call it a dream or even an ideal; it was a possibility which was within our reach if we had been wise enough to grasp and hold it. It was favored by our comparative isolation, or, at least, by our distance from other strong states. The men who came here were able to throw off all the trammels of tradition and established doctrine. They went out into a wilderness, it is true, but they took with them all the art, science, and literature which, up to that time, civilization had produced. They could not, it is true, strip their minds of the ideas which they had inherited, but in time, as they lived on in the new world, they sifted and selected these ideas, retaining what they chose. Of the old-world institutions also they selected and adopted what they chose and threw aside the rest. It was a grand opportunity to be thus able to strip off all the follies and errors which they had inherited, so far as they chose to do so. They had unlimited land with no feudal restrictions to hinder them in the use of it. Their idea was that they would never allow any of the social and political abuses of the old world to grow up here. There should be no manors, no barons, no ranks, no prelates, no idle classes, no paupers, no disinherited ones except the vicious. There were to be no armies except a militia, which would have no functions but those of police. They would have no court and no pomp; no orders, or ribbons, or decorations, or titles. They would have no public debt. They repudiated with scorn the notion that a public debt is a public blessing; if debt was incurred in war it was to be paid in peace and not entailed on posterity. There was to be no grand diplomacy, because they intended to mind their own business and not be involved in any of the intrigues to which European statesmen were accustomed. There was to be no balance of power and no "reason of state" to cost the life and happiness of citizens. The only part of the Monroe doctrine which is valid was their determination that the social and political systems of Europe should not be extended over any part of the American continent, lest people who were weaker than we should lose the opportunity which the new continent gave them to escape from those systems if they wanted to. Our fathers would have an economical government, even if grand people called it a parsimonious one, and taxes should be no greater than were absolutely necessary to pay for such a government. The citizen was to keep all the rest of his earnings and use them as he thought best for the happiness of himself and his family; he was, above all, to be insured peace and quiet while he pursued his honest industry and obeyed the laws. No adventurous policies of conquest or ambition, such as, in the belief of our fathers, kings and nobles had forced, for their own advantage, on European states, would ever be undertaken by a free democratic republic. Therefore the citizen here would never be forced to leave his family or to give his sons to shed blood for glory and to leave widows and orphans in misery for nothing. Justice and law were to reign in the midst of simplicity, and a government which had little to do was to offer little field for ambition. In a society where industry, frugality, and prudence were honored, it was believed that the vices of wealth would never flourish.

We know that these beliefs, hopes, and intentions have been only partially fulfilled. We know that, as time has gone on and we have grown numerous and rich, some of these things have proved impossible ideals, incompatible with a large and flourishing society, but it is by virtue of this conception of a commonwealth that the United States has stood for something unique and grand in the history of mankind and that its people have been happy. It is by virtue of these ideals that we have been "isolated," isolated in a position which the other nations of the earth have observed in silent envy; and yet there are people who are boasting of their patriotism, because they say that we have taken our place now amongst the nations of the earth by virtue of this war. My patriotism is of the kind which is outraged by the notion that the United States never was a great nation until in a petty three months' campaign it knocked to pieces a poor, decrepit, bankrupt old state like Spain. To hold such an opinion as that is to abandon all American standards, to put shame and scorn on all that our ancestors tried to build up here, and to go over to the standards of which Spain is a representative.

ADVANCING SOCIAL AND POLITICAL OR-GANIZATION IN THE UNITED STATES [1]

Colonial society; embryonic society. — American history disproves the notion of the "Boon of Nature, etc." — Movement of American history away from anarchistic liberty. — Colonial industrial organization the slightest possible. — No employer and employee or other classes. — Social organization was characterized by equality and democracy. — But there were modifications of democracy: 1. Aristocratic distinctions, so far as possible; 2. Distinctions by talent and industry; 3. Slavery. — Summary of points about democracy and classes.— Colonial society furnishes a test of the village community notion. — No society of free and independent tillers only. — Analysis of democracy; definition of its varieties. — Aristocracy of slavery. — Jacobinism and sansculottism. — The Constitution-makers and democracy. — Sense of radical and conservative in America. — Upper classes and political duty. — Significance of organization. — Advantages of a new country. — The escape from tradition. — No manors. — Agriculture and land tenure in the colonies. — The town and township. — Extension of loyalty from town to province, then to Union. — The advancing civil organization. — Disruptive forces. — Anarchistic liberty; it is limited in towns by unpopularity and gossip. — Character produced by anarchistic liberty. — Character produced by great chances of wealth. — Liberty due to freedom from powerful neighbors. — Merits of the quarrel with England, 1763–1775. — Effects of disorganization in the Revolution. — Effects of disorganization under the Confederation. — Constitution unwelcome; why? — Grand extension of discipline and reign of law. — How the federal government took the place of Great Britain. — It had to deal with the same anarchistic elements. — Necessity that these should be overcome. — The work of the Federal party. — The course of the Jeffersonians. — The Supreme Court has helped the integration. — Police were needed in cities to uphold the authority of law. — Survival of Revolutionary delusions in the Civil War. — Latest phenomena of those delusions. — Combination of the different stages of organization in the United States now. — Inevitableness of struggle for mastery in the Union. — The future will see condensation of the organization. — Advantage of rapidity of growth. — Institutions in the Constitution. — War between democracy and institu-

[1] Written probably in 1896 or 1897.

tions. — Compromise between them. — The contemporaneous transfer of power to the masses with civil liberty, in the place of anarchistic liberty. — Reasons for the power of democracy. — Economic causes of the present social and political revolution. — This has given power and chances to the masses. — Decline of representative institutions. — Risks of high organization. — Prophets are either optimists or alarmists. — Error of optimists. — Error of alarmists.

THE fact which gives chief value to the study of the early history of the United States is that in it we can see a society begin from its earliest germ and can follow its growth. It is a case of an embryo society, not however of savages but of civilized men. They came armed with the best knowledge and ability which men, up to the time of their migration, had won. They began with the laws, customs, institutions, arts, and sciences of their mother-country at the time, and of course they tried to imitate the social organization in which they had been brought up. This they did not do, however, without some variations, for they had notions of their own about government, religion, and social order. The emigrants were, in many cases, the radicals of their time and in coming to America they seized the opportunity to try to realize some of their pet ideas.

Very soon also it became apparent that transplanted institutions and customs must undergo change. Under changed physical and social circumstances the social relations alter and the social organization is forced to adapt itself. That is what happened here; and it is the perception and appreciation of such changes, in their causes and nature, which is one of the chief objects to be sought in the study of our colonial history. It is often said that this colonial history is dull and insipid, and so it is if you look only at the magnitude and complication of the events or the grade of the passions at play and the interests at stake. It is from the point of view which I have just indicated and in the study of the facts which I have described that that history wins very high philosophical importance and presents elements to the student of society which he can find nowhere else; for later colonial enterprises have been undertaken with the help of steam and constant communication between the colony and the mother-country, and so under conditions of less complete isolation. Our colonies consisted of little groups, thrown on the coast of this continent and left to find out how to carry on the struggle for existence here, in ignorance of the geography, the climate, and other most essential facts, with very little capital, and with only the most imperfect connection with the mother-country from which they must expect help and reinforcements. It is, however, just this isolation, with the necessity of self-adjustment to the conditions, which gives interest and value to the story of the colonies as social experiments. It is a fact of more importance than the story of dynasties and wars that not a single permanent settlement could be made on the territory now occupied by the United States until more than a hundred years after Columbus discovered America; for it is a fact which at once proves the folly of the notion that there is such a thing as a "boon of nature," or that "land" is a free gift from nature of a thing useful to man. Why did a hundred men perish miserably when trying, in the sixteenth century, to found a settlement on territory where now seventy million live in prosperity? It was because nature offers, not a boon but a battle; not a gift but a task; and those men, with the means they possessed, were not competent for the task or able to win the battle. Although the settlements at Jamestown, Plymouth, and Massachusetts Bay did not perish, the story of their first years shows with what toil, pain, and risk a foothold could be won for beginning the struggle for existence here. It is anything but a picture of men quietly walking in to take their places at the "banquet of life," bounteously and gratuitously offered by nature.

But from the social germ planted by these colonists all that we have and are has grown up by expansion, adaptation, absorption of new elements, death or abolition of old ones — in short, by all the working and fighting, suffering and erring which go into the life of a big, ambitious, and vigorous society.

In following out this conception of American history we shall find that it presents a very remarkable contrast to the history of modern Europe. In the latter the movement which runs through the history is one of advancing organization, attended by an extension socially, industrially, and politically, of individual liberty; in the United States, however, while the social organization has advanced with gigantic strides, it has been attended by restrictions of individual liberty. Here I use the word "liberty" in its anarchistic sense of exemption from restraint, and not in its legal and institutional sense. While the progress of time has brought in Europe the abolition of minute and vexatious restrictions upon individual self-determination, in the United States it has increased the number of laws, customs, and usages which, extending over all departments of social activity except religion, interfere with the freedom of individual action. This is one of the penalties of high organization. If as a member of a great and strong organization you win advantages, you must pay for them by conformity and co-operation within the organization; but these will limit your individual liberty. If we bear in mind this contrast between American and

European history, it will help to explain many apparent contradictions in their philosophy which may perplex us when studying them side by side. All that I have yet to say will further expound and develop this contrast.

We shall also find another and most remarkable fact of American social history in this: that, while the lines of the social organization have been more strictly drawn and the social discipline has been steadily made more stringent, there have been new and other developments of individual activity which have far more than offset the loss of the earlier rude and, in truth, barbaric liberty.

A very amusing incident is mentioned in Winthrop's history of New England.[1] A land-owner hired a man to work for him, but, not being able to pay the stipulated wages, he gave the man a pair of oxen and discharged him. The laborer asked to go on with their relation. "How shall I pay you?" said the employer. "With more oxen," replied the man. "But when the oxen are all gone?" "Then you can work for me and earn them back again." There is in this story a whole volume of demonstration of the social relations of that time and that society. We can see that the relation of employer and employee was, under then-existing circumstances, impossible; when land was available in unlimited amount, how could one man be land-owner and another laborer? Why should not the latter go on a little further and become another land-owner? The two would then be alike and equal.[2] If, however, one of them worked for the other, what wages would he

---

[1] II, 220; compare Coxe's Carolina emigrants who became herdsmen because poor; their servants became rich.

[2] Franklin's Works, IV, 19, 24, 171; II, 475.

demand? Evidently as much as he could gain by taking up land and working for himself. But this would equal all that he could produce as a laborer for another or all that his employer's land could produce, so far as it occupied one man's labor. Hence the laborer and the employer could only exchange places and impoverish each other alternately; and so no wages system was possible. For the same reason no complete wages system exists yet. Where increased human power was required in the colonies, it must be got by free co-operation, as in log-rolling and barn-raising. But this means that there was no industrial organization. All were farmers; ministers, teachers, merchants, mechanics, sailors carried on other occupations only incidentally; all owned land and drew their subsistence in a large proportion directly from land. It was far down in the eighteenth century before mechanics, sailors, merchants, lawyers, and doctors were differentiated as distinct and independent classes of persons. Thus in a century and a half or two centuries there has grown up here all this vast and complicated industrial organization which we now see, with its hundreds of occupations, its enormous plant and apparatus of all kinds, connected throughout by mutual relations of dependence, kept in order by punctuality and trustworthiness in the fulfillment of engagements, dependent upon assumptions that men will act in a certain way and want certain things, and, in spite of its intricacy and complication, working to supply our wants with such smoothness and harmony that most people are unaware of its existence. They live in it as they do in the atmosphere.

I shall return to this point in a moment and try to show the commanding significance of this fact that we all earn our living in and as parts of a great industrial organization; and indeed the purpose of this entire essay will be to try to get some due appreciation of the whole social and political organization, especially in its advancing phases, and of its dominion over us and our interests. But we have not yet quite exhausted all the significance of the incident which I mentioned at the outset. We see from it that not even the simplest class distinctions, those of employer and employee, were possible here at that time. No man could gain anything by owning more land than he could till; the people who got grants of land made disagreeable experience of the truth of this. Because land was the best property a man could own in England, and ten thousand acres was a great estate there, they supposed that a man who got a grant of ten thousand acres in America got a great fortune, whereas in reality he got only a chance to sink a fortune without hope of return. As there could be no landlord, there could be no tenant; no man would hire another's land when he could get land of his own for the labor of reducing it to tillage. Now landlords, tenant-farmers, and laborers are the three groups which form the fundamental framework of a class-divided society; but if they are all merged in a class of peasant-proprietors or yeomen-farmers, there is absolutely no class organization. All are equal, by the facts of the case, as nearly as human beings can be equal.[1] A farmer tilling as much land as his own labor will suffice to cultivate never can accumulate a fortune in the midst of a society of others just like himself. Neither need any one of them lack subsistence for himself and family. His children are not a burden but a

[1] St. Jean de Crèvecœur, Lettres d'un Cultivateur Américain, Paris, 1787, I, 267.

help; they offer the only aid which he can hope for, since the relation of hire is impossible. If his sons, as they grow up, go off and take up land of their own, it is an advantage to him to have many sons, that the series may last as long as his own working years. If the minister and schoolmaster, as the only representatives of the professional classes, live amongst these farmers in the same way and on the same scale, and if the merchants of the commercial towns are few and their gains are slow and small,[1] there result just such commonwealths as existed in the northern colonies. The people of a town all club together to support a school for their children and a "common school system" is born unawares. It is plain that *equality* is the prevailing characteristic of this society; its members are equal in fortune, in education, in descent (at least after a generation or two), in mode of life, in social standing, in range of ideas, in political importance, and in everything else which is social, and *nobody made them so.* Such a society was what we call democratic, using the word in reference to the institutions, ideas, customs, and mores existing in it, and without reference to politics. It was made so, not by any resolutions or constitutions, but by the existing economic circumstances, of which the most important was the ratio of the population to the land. Nobody could have made the communities otherwise than democratic under the existing circumstances under which the struggle for existence was carried on.

The picture of colonial society which I have just

---

[1] The West India trade was a great source of wealth at Hartford. Three persons there, in 1775, were said to be worth about $80,000 each. Hinman, R. R., A Historical Collection . . . of the Part sustained by Conn. during the War of the Revolution, Hartford, 1842, p. 15.

drawn is the one which is generally presented and it may be familiar to the reader. In order to render it truthful, however, it is necessary at once to add some very important modifications.

In the first place, the English traditions and prejudices which had been inherited were distinctly aristocratic and the pet notions and doctrines of the colonists were not those of equality. If any man had anything to pride himself on as a distinction, he made the most of it, as nearly all men everywhere have done; and if the distinction was one of relationship to people of social importance in England, it was quite tenaciously nourished. Social distinction, however, if we may trust some reports, cost a man political ostracism. St. Jean de Crèvecœur[1] says that the richest man in Connecticut in 1770 was worth about $60,000; but he could not be elected to any office, and with difficulty obtained for his son a position as teacher in a Latin school in order to keep him in and of the people.

Then again, the innate and utterly inevitable inequality of men in industry, energy, enterprise, shrewdness, and so on, quickly differentiated these yeomen-farmers. Some families kept up the industrial virtues for generations; others manifested a lack of them. There were social failures then as there are always. Most of them "went West," choosing an avenue of escape whose immense importance in the whole social history of this country must not for a moment be lost sight of; but we hear also of shiftless, lawless, and vagabond people who lived on the mountains or on the outskirts of the town, given to drink, quarreling, and petty thieving. This phenomenon warns us that the pleasing picture of an Arcadian simplicity, equality,

[1] *L. c.*, I, 242.

and uniformity, such as has often been applied to our colonial society, is unreal. It is impossible in human nature. Put a group of men in equal circumstances, under wide and easy conditions, and instead of getting equal, uniform, and purely happy results, you will get a differentiation in which some will sink to misery, vice, and pauperism.

Yet again, when considering inequality, we must remember the existence of slavery in this society; of that I will speak presently in another connection.

We must, therefore, understand that the notion of our colonies as pure and ideal democracies is unhistorical. While broad features might seem to justify it, the details, in which lie all the truth and reality, greatly modify the picture.

But there is a wider aspect of this matter and one which, so far as I know, has never been noticed at all. I cannot find anywhere in history any case of a society of free and equal men consisting exclusively of independent tillers of the soil. We are forced to ask whether such a thing is a social impossibility. A notion has had wide currency within the last thirty years that "village communities" are a stage of primitive democratic organization through which most modern civilized societies have passed. That there have been villages which were organized for industrial and social purposes is as certain as that there have been states; but the "village community" has been personified and elevated to the rank, not of a social organization expedient for a purpose, but of an independent organism, something more than a society although less than an intelligent being. Hence it has been made to appear that the breaking up of village communities was not the abandoning of an organization which was no longer useful, but was the killing of something of an exalted and ideal character. This is all mythology. It is impossible to find any village community which was ever anything more than a group of people who were trying to get their living out of the ground as well as they could under the circumstances in which they found themselves. That is just what we are doing now. The most peculiar features of the village community were dictated by envy and jealousy, lest one man should be better off than another, and the chief lesson the study of them enforces is that when laws and customs are made with a view to equality they crush out progress.

But the point to which I wish now to call attention especially is even stronger if we assume that village communities were once such ideal societies, with vigorous and healthy forces inside of them; if they ever consisted of free and equal men, standing sturdily together, working industriously, sharing fairly, maintaining rights and justice of which they had a clear and natural apprehension, making every man do his duty, letting no man encroach upon another, and resisting all oppression from without. For the question then is: If any territory ever was occupied by such units, why did they sink into serfdom? The things which are strong vindicate their strength by their resistance and their achievements; it will not do, therefore, to say that the village communities were overridden by force; what is claimed for them is that they contained the most powerful and persistent social forces which can be called into play. All western Europe was feudalized and its cultivators of the soil were reduced to serfdom. Scandinavia was only partially feudalized, but it illustrates the point even better, because we can follow the reduction of free peasants as far down as they went towards serfdom, and we know that it was not their own energy of resistance which kept them from going lower. Furthermore, all over Europe among the peasant-tillers of the soil, while they were free yeomen (if they ever were so), there were slaves. These were owned by the freeholders. But if the yeomen were themselves slaveholders, their society is excluded from my proposition, for the society does not then consist of free and equal tillers of the soil alone.

I wish to bring into connection with this another fact which may seem at first to lie far removed from it. In stages of half-civilization where tillage is just beginning we find that the tillers are ruled by warlike nomads. This relation has been found all over the globe; especially where the tillers occupy a fertile plain below steppes or mountain slopes, the latter are inhabited by wild and wandering tribes which periodically descend into the plains to rob and plunder or levy tribute. A large part of Africa has long presented this state of things. It is evident that the settled tillers unlearn the arts of war, for they want peace, order, regularity. They must spend great labor on permanent works of construction and irrigation which are, however, at the mercy of an invader. The nomads are warlike and have greater physical power; they either make periodical raids or they compromise for a regular tribute. Great states have grown in the course of time out of this latter relation, the ruling nomads becoming the nobles and the tillers the peasantry or serfs. The first of these stages shows us militarism and industrialism in conflict; the second shows us the two combined and adjusted in a great state. This antagonism of militarism and industrialism is the most important thread of philosophy which can be run through history.

Here, then, is a startling phenomenon and a problem for the sociologist to elucidate. Does the tiller of the soil gravitate to servitude by some inherent necessity? There are no peasant-proprietors now in Europe who are not maintained by arbitrary operation of law. Whole schools of social philosophy have taken up the notion that peasant-proprietors are fine things to have and that they must be got or produced at any price in the old countries. It is not my intention now to discuss the problem thus raised, but I hasten to bring what I have said to bear on the subject before us. We see why it is interesting and important to ask whether the American colonies do present an exceptional case of what we are looking for, *viz.*, a society consisting exclusively of free and equal tillers of the soil. To this the answer is that they do not. They used slaves; the great need of an organization of labor by which combined effort could be brought to bear was what caused the introduction of slavery. We have positive testimony from the colonial period that the practical reason for slavery was that without it laborers could not be induced to go and stay where the work was to be done, especially in remote districts. Slavery, of course, became developed and established more and more to the southward, as those districts were reached whose products — tobacco, rice, and indigo — could be cultivated only on a large scale by a great organization of labor, many laborers being combined under one overseer. In the northern states, when slavery was abolished, towns had grown up, professional classes had begun to be formed, artisans and merchants constituted distinct classes, and the whole social organization had become so complex that the simple society consisting exclusively of tillers of the soil was not to be sought there. It is true that our new states have, within a hundred years, come nearer to presenting us that phenomenon than any other communities ever have; but then again it is to be remembered that they are parts in a world-wide organization of industry and commerce and are not any longer distinct communities.

In the course of my remarks on the last point, I have touched upon the case of slavery in the South. It has often been said that slavery in the South was an aristocratic institution. Aristocratic and democratic are indeed currently used as distinctly antagonistic to each other, but whether they are so or not depends upon the sense in which each of them is taken, for they are words of very shifting and uncertain definition. It is aristocratic to measure men and scale off their social relations by birth; it is democratic to deny the validity of such distinctions and to weigh men by their merits and achievements without regard to other standards. In this sense, however, democracy will not have anything to do with equality, for if you measure men by what they are and do, you will find them anything but equal. This form of democracy, therefore, is equivalent to aristocracy in the next sense. For, second, aristocracy means inequality and the social and political superiority of some to others, while democracy means social and political equality in value and power. But no man ever yet asserted that "all men are equal," meaning what he said. Although he said, "all men," he had in mind some limitation of the group he was talking about. Thus, if you had asked Thomas Jefferson, when he was writing the first paragraph of the Declaration of Independence, whether in "all men" he meant to include negroes, he would have said that he was not talking about negroes. Ask anybody who says it now whether he means to include foreigners — Russian Jews, Hungarians, Italians — and he will draw his line somewhere. The law of the United States draws it at Chinamen. If you should meet with a man who should say, as I would, although I do not believe that all men are equal in any sense, that such laws are unjust and that all men ought to have an equal chance to do the best they can for themselves on earth, then you might ask him whether he thought that Bushmen, Hottentots, or Australians were equal to the best-educated and most cultivated white men. He would have to admit that he was not thinking of them at all. Now, if we draw any line at all, the dogma is ruined. If you say: "All men are equal except some who are not," you must admit tests and standards and you are like the aristocrats, only that they may have other standards than yours and may draw the line around a smaller group. Furthermore if you define a group and then say that all are equal within it, that is pure aristocracy; all peers are equal — that is what their name denotes. School-boys learn from their Greek books enthusiasm for Greek democracy, but in the height of Athenian glory there were four slaves for every Athenian freeman and "democracy" meant the equality of these latter in exploiting the emoluments of the Athenian state. This brings us to the case of our Southern slaveholders. It was not a paradox that the great Virginians were slaveholders and great democrats too; the paradox is in the use of the words, for we see that the terms dissolve into each other. Before you know which you are talking about, it is the other. The Southern democrats drew their line between white and black, but they affirmed the equality of all whites, that is, of all who were in the ring. This made them great popular leaders — of whites. If we should repeal our naturalization laws, admit no more immigrants to citizenship, restricting political power to those now here and letting them and their descendants possess it by universal manhood suffrage, we should create a democratic-aristocracy in a generation or two. Hence it is clear that a democratic-aristocracy is not a contradiction in terms.

So far then, we see, I think, that democracy in the sense of political equality for the members of the ruling race was produced in the colonies out of the necessities and circumstances of the case. No convention ever decreed it or chose it. It existed in the sense of social equality long before it was recognized and employed as a guiding principle in institutions and laws; its strength in the latter is due to the fact that it is rooted and grounded in economic facts. The current popular notion that we have democratic institutions because the men of the eighteenth century were wise enough to choose and create them is entirely erroneous. We have not made America; America has made us. There is, indeed, a constant reaction between the environment and the ideas of the people; the ideas turn into dogmas and pet notions, which in their turn are applied to the environment. What effect they have, however, except to produce confusion, error, mischief, and loss is a very serious question. The current of our age has been entirely in favor of the notion that a convention to amend the Constitution can make any kind of a state or society which we may choose as an ideal. That is a great delusion, but it is one of the leading social faiths of the present time.

I turned aside from the second sense of aristocracy

and democracy to show how the distinction applied to the case of our southern colonies. It will be an economy of time if I now return to that analysis before going further. Aristocracy means etymologically the rule of the best. Cicero [1] says: "*Certe in optimorum consiliis posita est civitatum salus.*" If there were any way of finding out who are the best and of keeping them such in spite of the temptations of power, we might accept this dictum. In practice aristocracy always means the rule of the few. Democracy means the rule of the many; in practice it always means the rule of a numerical majority. A dogma has been made out of this and it has been affirmed that the majority has a right to rule in a sense as absolute as that in which the divine right of kings was formerly laid down. It has been asserted that the majority had a right to misrule, to waste money, to perpetrate injustice, and so on, if such was its good pleasure. This doctrine is democratic absolutism and it is as slavish and false as any doctrine of royal absolutism. In the working of majority rule it always degenerates into oligarchy; a majority of a majority is endowed with power, in one sub-division after another, until at last a few control. On the other hand, many cases can be found in history where an aristocracy has applied majority rule inside of itself with a dogmatic absoluteness surpassing that of democracy itself.

The degenerate form of democracy, when it runs out into an oligarchy or when it is entirely unregulated by constitutional provisions, is often designated as jacobinism. It is the rule of a clique, arrogating to itself the name of the people or the right to act for the people. It is the inevitable outcome of any form of

[1] De Republica, I, 34.

democracy which is not restrained and regulated by institutions. A still more excessive degeneration of democracy is sansculottism. As a political form this is the rule of a street mob; as a philosophy it is hatred of all which is elegant, elevated, cultured, and refined. It stamps with rage and contempt on everything which is traditionally regarded as noble, praiseworthy, and admirable and it embraces with eagerness whatever is regarded by tradition as foul, base, and vulgar.

Returning now from this more philosophical analysis, which seemed necessary to a full understanding of terms, let us come back to the historical aspect of our subject. It does not appear that anybody paid any attention to the first paragraph of the Declaration of Independence when it was written or that anybody except Thomas Paine then held to the dogmas of democracy. The men of that generation were all afraid of what they always called unbridled democracy. The disturbances of public order between 1783 and 1787 greatly intensified this fear, so that the Constitution-makers were not in a mood for any pure democracy. A few of them held to the system of political maxims which simply expressed the satisfaction of the great mass of the people with the loose political and social organization which had existed up to that time; but these men had very little influence on the result. The Constitution of 1787 is also remarkable, considering the time at which it was framed, for containing no dogmatic utterances about liberty and equality and no enunciation of great principles. Indeed this was made a ground of complaint against it by the leaders of the popular party; they missed the dogmatic utterances to which they had become accustomed during the war and they forced the passage of the first ten amendments. Even then, however, the Constitution contained no declaration of rights, but was simply a working system of government which was constituted out of institutions and laws already operating and familiar. In the one or two points in which the Constitution-makers endeavored to devise something new and clever with which to avert an apprehended danger, as for instance in the case of the Electoral College, their wisdom has all been set at naught. It is noticeable that this was a safeguard against democracy. In another case, when they set no limit to the number of re-elections which a president might obtain, the democratic temper of the country has forced an unwritten law limiting the terms to two. Here I should like to point out a confirmation of one thing which I said at the outset, that the direction of political movement in this country and in Europe has been opposite. According to European usage, which has become current here also, we should want to call the Anti-federalists radicals, and we should call Hamilton, Madison, and the other advocates of the new Constitution conservatives. But if conservative means clinging to the old and if radical means favoring change and innovation, then the Anti-federalists were the conservatives and the Federalists were radicals.

There are people amongst us who are thrown into a flutter of indignation by the suggestion that there are any classes in our American society, yet from time to time we hear blame cast upon the educated and property classes for not taking a due share in politics. The existence of some class differentiation is then recognized. Democracy is in general and by its principles jealous of the interference of any who are distinguished from the mass by anything whatever; as soon as anybody is distinguished in any way he ceases to be one of the people. We hear the word "people" used in this way all the time and we know that it means, not the population but some part of the population which is hard to define but which, I think, means the mass with all the distinguished ones taken out. This is another recognition of class. Now it is part of the system of theoretical or dogmatic democracy to hold that wisdom is with the people in the sense just defined. They are said to know; they judge rightly; they perceive the truth; if we trust them, they will govern aright. Incidentally scorn is often cast on the sages and philosophers, the theorists and bookworms — and it is probably for the most part well-deserved; but the implication is that the mass of men have by nature and common sense the wisdom which the sages and philosophers lack. In any democratic system, therefore, the distinguished classes are kept aloof from the active control. There is nothing which the stump-orator, ambitious for influence and position, more energetically disclaims than the assumption that he is any better qualified to teach than any of his audience; he anxiously insists that he is only a common man and one of the people. This is the great reason why civil service reform has never won wide popular support — that it is considered undemocratic. It is so because it assumes that some men are more fit and capable for public office than other men are. Most of the time we give office to people whose vanity will be gratified by it, not to those who can serve us in the position. Those who have special ability, skill, capital, or knowledge are called upon in emergencies to help us out of difficulties, but they are watched with great jealousy lest they get a notion that they are essential and begin to assume that they must be retained and rewarded. They are therefore dismissed again as soon as possible and without reward. So far we have not got many of them to accept the rôle which is thus allotted to them, and although we scold them and tell them that they ought to carry the burdens, do the work, and take the blows while somebody else gets the glory and the pay, we do not seem to make much impression on them. As a class they turn to money-making as a far more pleasant and profitable occupation.

We began with an employer and an employee face to face with each other and we have been brought to notice the lack of industrial organization and the incongruity of class distinctions in the colonial days on account of industrial facts. Already, then, we begin to see that the conditions of the existing social organization are controlling facts for the welfare and interests of men. Let us try to realize the full significance of this obser- vation. We can perhaps understand it better now, having begun with the interpretation of a concrete case. Every one of us is born into society, that is to say, into some form and kind of society — the one which is existing at the time and place; we must live our lives in that society under the conditions which its constitu- tion and modes of action set for us. We can imagine the same human infant taken either to the United States, to Russia, to Turkey, to China, or to Central Africa, and it is plain that his career and existence would be determined in its direction, modes, and possibilities by the one of those societies which should become his social environment. It is equally true, although not so obvious because the contrast is less strong, that a man could not be and become in Massachusetts in the seventeenth or the eighteenth century what he can be and become there in the nineteenth. The social organi-

zation is produced by the reaction between the environment and the society, in the process of time. At any
point of time the existing social organization determines
the character of the great mass of the people; only the
élite amongst them react against it and slowly mold it
from generation to generation. The social organization existing at any time also determines the character,
range, and vitality of political institutions; it determines
what ideas can take root and grow and what ones fall
unnoticed; and it determines the ethical doctrines
which are accepted and acted upon. You need only
compare mediaeval and modern society to see how
profoundly true this is at every point.

The social organization of these colonies was that of a
new country and a young society. Its first advantage
was that it could throw off all the traditions of the
old countries which it did not like and retain all the
knowledge, arts, and sciences which it wanted. It is
one of the commanding facts in the history of the globe
that one part of it was hidden and unknown until a
very late day. Men living on the part which they did
know developed civilization, but their civilization was
mixed up with all the errors and calamities of thousands
of years. Then they found a new world to which they
could go, carrying what they wanted out of all which
they had inherited and rejecting what they did not
want. They undoubtedly made mistakes in their selection, because human error is ever present and is as
enduring as humanity; but some things which they
brought and should have left at home died out here
under the influence of the environment. The most
remarkable case of this is the manor system. A European of the seventeenth century could not think of
society outside of the manor system and we see manor

ideas and institutions imported here in more or less definite form; but they all shriveled up and became obsolete because they were totally unfit for a society in which land was unlimited and civil authority adequate to maintain peace. The only element of manor-making which was at work here was the lack of laborers. Serfdom and villainage were in large measure due to the necessity of holding the laborer to the spot in order that tillage might be carried on. In this country, at least in the northern states, slavery was due to the necessity of holding the laborer to the spot in order that tillage might go on.[1] Slavery, therefore, must be regarded as a product of some of the same conditions which in Europe made serfdom. Plantations took the place of manors in the South and yeoman farms with a small amount of slavery took the place of them in the North. This difference in land tenure and agricultural system between America and the old countries, which was foreseen and devised by no man but was imposed upon the colonists by the facts they had to deal with, became, of course, the cause of the greatest differences through the whole social organization. The development here was new, fresh, and original. Slavery appears as an incongruous element at first; as the population increased and the organization became more developed, that institution was dropped in the northern states. There its incongruity with the whole social system and the ethical ideas of a body of yeomen tilling their own soil first became apparent. At a later time, by the progress of the arts, slavery became dispensable and it has disappeared entirely. With its cessation it seemed that every vestige of a manor system or analogy to it had vanished

[1] Franklin's Works, II, 314.

from the land, but among the tentative organizations of labor in the southern states at the present time, out of which some new and suitable system for the conditions of industry there existing will be developed, there is a kind of manor system with labor rents. The problem of land tenure and of the agricultural system upon which a great free state can be built contains difficulties and mysteries which have not yet even been defined; but if one gets near enough to them to even guess at their magnitude and difficulty, he sees in a very grotesque light the propositions of the "single tax" and of state assumption of land. In our colonies, where these things shaped themselves with the greatest freedom to suit the welfare of the settlers themselves, all the principles of the English common law were overridden, so that this did not determine the result. The land of a town was originally divided equally between the settlers because all shared equally in the risk and trouble of settlement. Small estates existed because, as we have seen, there was no object in owning big ones. Equal division of estates in case of intestacy was introduced because, if primogeniture had been retained, younger sons would not have lived and worked on the father's land. Finally, land tenures gradually became allodial.[1] But an allodial tenure is the utmost private property in land conceivable; it makes of every freeholder a petty sovereign on his domain. We can plainly see that no other tenure would attract and hold settlers on raw land. The so-called unearned increment is the reward of the first settler who meets the first and greatest hardships incident to the peopling of new land. Thus we see that the land tenure and the agricultural system were

[1] Originally the tenures were in free and common soccage. These are so now in Pennsylvania. In every other state they are allodial.

fully consonant with the loose industrial organization and the democratic social organization which we have already noticed.

The settlements were made in little groups or towns. No civilized people have ever had so little civil organization as the colonial towns early in their settlement; there was little division of labor, scarcely any civil organization at all, and very little common action. Each town was at the same time a land company and an ecclesiastical body, and its organization under each of these heads was more developed than in its civil or political aspect. The methods of managing the affairs of a land company or a congregation were those of the town as a civil body also and the different forms of organization were not kept distinct. The administration of justice shows the confusion most distinctly: all common interests were dealt with by the one common body without distinction or classification; and as committees for executing the decisions of the body were the most obvious and convenient device for executive and administrative purposes, we find that device repeated with only slight variations.

Attempts have been made to endow this primitive system with some peculiar dignity and value. People have talked of "townships" instead of towns. Whenever the abstract is thus put for the concrete, our suspicions of myth-making should always be aroused. A town was a number of people living in a neighborhood and co-operating for common interests as convenience required; a township could be endowed with life and functions and could be made, by myth, into a force or sort of ruling providence. This township has been connected with so-called village-communities which we have seen to be another case of myth. The utility of

the study of the New England towns is, in part, in the
critical light which is thrown on the whole notion of
village-communities as it has become current in our
literature. The New England towns certainly lacked
the communal element; religious sympathy was the
strongest associative principle there was in them, but
otherwise the sentiment was strongly individualistic.
They were also so utterly loose in their ties, and the
internal cohesion was so slight, that they never exercised that educating and formative influence which
peasant villages in Europe, having through centuries
retained the same institutions and customs, undoubtedly did exercise. In the South, where the plantation
system existed, not even these nuclei of social organization were formed. Thus the whole of this country,
until the beginning of the eighteenth century, presented
the picture of the loosest and most scattered human
society which is consistent with civilization at all, and
there were not lacking phenomena of a positive decline
of civilization and gravitation towards the life of the
Indians. Political organization scarcely existed and
civil organization was but slight. Later generations
have condemned and ridiculed the religious bigotry of
the colonists with its attendant religious persecution
and the political ostracism of all but the ruling sect;
but if this strong religious sympathy had not existed,
what associative principle would they have had to hold
them together and build up a civil society?

I have said that the picture presented by the settlements in this country until the beginning of the eighteenth century was that of little groups of farmers
scattered along the coast and rivers, forming towns
under the loosest possible organization. Names such
as Massachusetts, Connecticut, were used then to cover

areas very great as compared with the amount of land under cultivation. Those names had very little meaning to the people of that time, for life and its interests were bounded by the town. Only in the eighteenth century can we see the horizon extend so that the province grows to be the real civil unit and grows into a real commonwealth; the process was slow, however, and for the most part unwilling. In the nineteenth century the conception of the national and civil unit has expanded so that our sense of nationality cleaves to the Union as a great confederated state. This advance in the feeling of the people as to what the country to which they belong is, and what that is which is the object of patriotism, is one of the interesting developments of our history. The merging of the town into the state and of the state into the United States has been brought about by the increase of population, the filling up of the country, the multiplication of interests reaching out all over it and grappling the people together. The bonds are those of kin, of industry and commerce, of religion through the various denominations and churches, of common pursuits in education, science, and art, and of associations for various purposes of culture or pleasure. This is what we mean by the advancing social organization. It unites us into a whole; it forms us into a society; it gives us sentiments of association and co-operation. Our states, instead of being separate bodies united only by neighborhood and alliance, are formed into one body with nerves running through it; and it is by virtue of these nerves, that is, of the lines of common feeling and interest which I have mentioned, that a touch at one point brings out a reaction from the whole.

There are other causes which are always at work in

the contrary direction. They are the forces of discord and divergent interest. In a state of seventy million people scattered over a continent the forces of disruption are always at work. The great social organization all the time tends to promote a great political organization; as the interests multiply and become complex, there is a call for federal legislation in order to get uniformity, *e.g.*, as to marriage, divorce, bankruptcy. The laws also get extensions from use and new application, the effects of which in a few years amaze us by their magnitude and importance, as, for example, the Interstate Commerce Law. Now all this extension, systematization, and uniformity-making produces symmetry, order, and elegance, but it goes with the old terror of our statesmen — consolidation. It is making of us a great empire. Few people, even of those who have lived through it, seem to notice the great change which has come over our federal system since the Civil War. The most important alteration is that in the feeling of the people about what sort of a government there is at Washington — what it is and what it can do. Young people should understand that the indescribable sense and feeling about that question, which we carry with us now, is totally different from the sentiments of our fathers between 1850 and 1860. Now there is a danger in centralization. A big system never can fit exactly at more than a few places, if at any; elsewhere it strains a little in its adaptation and it may strain very much. If it does, we shall hear an outcry of distress and it may be of anger and revolt, for the movement to higher organization means a movement away from liberty, and is always attended by irritation until men become habituated to the constraint of the organization and realize its benefits. In the course of our history this has been fully illustrated. Every step of the way up to the present system which, I think, we regard almost unanimously as an advance and a gain, as we look back upon it, has been contested. The advancing organization draws together and consolidates, provided its action is not so abrupt and harsh as to provoke rebellion and disruption. In every case it produces a more prompt civil reaction. By this we mean that there is a more prompt obedience to authority, greater punctuality in the performance of legal duties, and greater exactitude in the co-operation of institutions and persons who are called upon by the civil authority to perform civil functions for the good of the state. This means greater discipline and less liberty.

Here I use the word "liberty" in its primary sense: a status in which there are no restraints on the self-determination of the individual. That liberty is, of course, never more than relative, for there are restraints wherever there are any institutions, customs, or laws at all. Therefore this kind of liberty, if an attempt is made to realize it against laws and institutions, is anarchistic. I shall refer to it sometimes in speaking of the later history as anarchistic liberty.

No men on earth have ever been as free to do as they pleased as these American colonists were. Savage men are not free to do as they please and may be dismissed from comparison; civilized men in the Old World were born into a society already old; here, however, were civilized men who, after they had secured a footing, were limited by the very least restraint of any kind which can exist in human life. The fetters which they laid on themselves in accordance with their religious dogmas were no doubt a good thing, for otherwise there would have been no discipline at all, and for human welfare liberty and discipline need to be duly combined. In fact, the colonists, after two or three generations, threw off the puritanical restraints only too much.

Liberty had its cause and its enduring guarantee in the circumstances of the case. If a man lives alone in the middle of a farm of one hundred acres, what he does there will make little difference to his neighbors, each living in the same way. But if he and his family live in a tenement house, with a score of other families, separated only by thin partitions and floors, everything that he does or neglects will make a great difference to others. Therefore there are few laws made by the community as to how a man shall behave on a farm, whereas there are strict regulations by the state, the city, and the landlord as to how people shall behave in tenement houses. The latter regulations are no proof of meddlesomeness and officialism — they are a necessity of the case. On the other hand, the "liberty" of colonial farmers was no choice of theirs, no creation of law, no proof of clearer wisdom than that of Old-World statesmen — it was a necessity of the case.

In one respect, indeed, the townsmen of a colony lacked liberty — for in no case and in no sense can you find absolute liberty on this earth; that is an anarchistic dream. The public opinion of a town was an imperious mistress; Mrs. Grundy held powerful sway and Gossip was her prime minister. This accounts for the remarkable subserviency, in the early days of this country, of public men to popularity. Unpopularity in a town or petty neighborhood where everybody knows everybody else intimately is an extreme social penalty; it reaches a man through his wife and children and it affects him in all his important interests and relations. It was a powerful coercive force here and was, as far as it went, a restraint on liberty. It was not, however, an organizing force, and its influence does not contradict the observation that the organization was loose and slight.

The effect of this great liberty on both the virtues and the vices of colonial character was clearly marked. The people were very bold, enterprising, and self-reliant; they were even imprudent in their enterprises; they took great risks because the trouble and cost of precautions were great. They were not painstaking because there was so much to be done in subduing a continent that they could not stop to be careful; they had to be contented with expedients and to sacrifice the long future interest to the immediate one. It would have been unwise and wasteful to do otherwise. They were also very versatile; a man had to be a jack-of-all-trades because there was no elaborate industrial organization. They also took things very easily. They were not energetic; they could with ease get enough and they were not willing to work very hard to get a little more. They were optimistic; they went on, never fearing but what they could conquer any difficulties they might meet and borrowing very little trouble. Most of these traits, as we know, have become fixed in the national character. As a consequence, the colonists were divided into two well-marked types: one industrious and steady, the other shiftless and lazy. There were very few avenues to wealth and so there were few rewards for great exertion. The love of trading was due to the fact that it offered quicker and larger gains than could be got from tilling the ground. It is the opening of grand chances of exceptional success in the nineteenth century which has wrought a great transformation in the national character, for it has offered rewards for exceptional ability and exceptional achievement which have stimulated the whole population. Here is a fact — and it is one of the most salient and incontrovertible facts in our own history — which shows the shallowness and folly of a great deal of current lamentation or denunciation of the accumulation of wealth. If you will turn to European history, you will find that the moment when land would produce, not merely a subsistence for those who tilled it but also a profit, that is, the moment when it would bear rent, is the moment when the modern world began to spring into energetic life. Here land has never yet borne rent, but transportation rates have taken the place of rent and, together with manufacturing on a large scale and the application of capital to develop the continent, have opened far broader avenues of profit and have offered greater prizes than land-rent in the Old World. It is these chances which have filled the population with a fever of energy and enterprise and enthused them with hope, and in the might of such driving forces they have done marvellous things. It is true, as the French proverb says, that they have not made omelettes without smashing some eggs; and we have many social philosophers who are crying over the eggs.

What I have said thus far of liberty has referred to individual liberty. Political liberty inside of any country depends very largely upon its external relations. The great force for forging a society into a solid mass has always been war. So long as there were Indians to be fought, and so long as the Dutch were in New York or the French in Canada, the colonies had a foreign policy; they had enemies at the gates. Such a state of things forces some attention to military preparations. The state must make calls on its citizens for money and for military services and this state-pressure limits political liberty. After the French were driven out of Canada there was a great change in this respect: there was nothing more to fear, and all military exercises, being regarded as irksome, were almost entirely neglected. Internal liberty took a new expansion. In the prevailing dullness of colonial life one of the chief sports had been to bait the colonial governor; and the colonists now gave themselves up to this diversion with greater freedom than ever. Internal discord involved no risk of weakness in the presence of a neighboring enemy. Note well that those people are easily free who have no powerful neighbor to fear. Imagine, if you can, that the boundary of Russia had been at the Mississippi River and that she had been meddling with us in the eighteenth century as she did with Sweden and Poland — do you suppose that we could have got this liberty which our historians and orators talk about? If not, then you may be sure that no human shrewdness or wisdom entailed it on us as it is, but that it was born of a happy conjuncture of circumstances.

The absence of powerful neighbors has been an important fact in all our later history. It has freed us from the militarism which now weighs so heavily upon Europe and it has made it possible for us to develop to its highest limit a purely industrial social organization. It is true that the Civil War with its debt, taxation, bad currency, and pension burdens has made us acquainted with some of the burdens of militarism, but that is all our own fault; by virtue of the lack of strong neighbors we had a right to be free from it if we had been wise enough to profit by the advantages of our situation.

But an industrial society brings to bear upon its members an education widely different from that of a military civilization; the codes of citizenship, the conception of what is heroic, the standards of honor, the selection of things best worth working for, the types to which admiration is due, all differ in the two systems. Militarism is produced by a constant preoccupation with the chances of war and the necessity of being prepared for it, and this preoccupation bars the way when people want to think about the reform of institutions or the extension of popular education or any other useful social enterprise. From all that preoccupation the people of this country have been free; they have been able to give their attention without reserve to what would increase the happiness and welfare of the people.

Let us sum up what we have thus far gathered from our review of the colonial period. We have seen that the division of labor was slight; that there was scarcely any industrial organization; that, if slavery be left out of account, there was but little differentiation of classes; that the social ties, even before religious enthusiasm died out, were very few and narrow and strictly local; that, after that enthusiasm died out, such ties scarcely existed at all; that the horizon of life was the town and only at second stage the province. We have also seen that the most peculiar characteristics of the colonial society were the equality of its members and the large liberty of self-will enjoyed by individuals. We know that the separate provinces had very little sympathy or even acquaintance with each other; at one time and another, under the influence of a common danger from the Indians or the French, a feeble thrill of common interest ran through some of them, but it never proved strong enough to unite them. These social and political elements were the inheritance of the Union from the colonial period.

I by no means agree with the current histories about the facts and merits of the quarrel with England between 1763 and 1775. They are all tinctured with alleged patriotism and the serious facts of the case are sometimes passed over in silence. The behavior of the colonists was turbulent, lawless, and in many cases indefensible; and the grounds on which they based their case were often untenable in law and history and often inconsistent with each other. They sought these grounds as a lawyer seeks grounds on which to argue his case, choosing them, that is, on the basis of whether they will make more for him than against him, not whether they are true or not. The principles of 1774 were distinctly anarchical because they were put forward as a basis of continued relation to Great Britain but were inconsistent with that relation. Another cause of rebellion which was very strong in the South, although little stress is laid upon it in history, was the accumulated debt to British merchants which it was hoped would be cancelled by war. It is true that the English colonial policy of the eighteenth century did not rise above the eighteenth-century English level, which from our standpoint was base; but that it was not very shocking to eighteenth-century Americans is shown by the fact that they never fully, clearly, and in principle revolted against the Navigation Act, which was their greatest grievance. Even as to taxation the Americans never put their case on a clear and intelligible ground; they talked of various *abuses* of taxation, but they showed that they would not consent to any taxation. Adam Smith, taught no doubt by study of the case of our colonies, said: "Plenty of good land and liberty to manage their own affairs in their own way seem to be the two great causes of the prosperity of all new colonies." [1] The American colonies had the land but not the liberty. If they wanted to do anything which they thought expedient for their own interest they had to send to England for permission. Even if the reply was reasonably prompt, this cost a year; but inasmuch as applications were bandied about, neglected, and forgotten, in spite of the zeal of agents, there were fetters laid upon colonial development. As soon, therefore, as the colonists were able to be independent and dared be independent, it was necessary that they should be so. That is the cause and the justification of the Revolution. The rest is all the wrangling about rights, dogmas, laws, and precedents which accompanies every revolution. I see no use at all in the study of history unless the historian is absolutely faithful to the truth of the matter; but when, in a moment, my reason for introducing these remarks here appears, the case will then serve to prove, I think, how much more the truth is worth than anything else is worth in history.

All the laxness of the social organization, all the mischief of what has been called church-steeple patriotism, and all the weakness of anarchistic liberty appeared most distinctly in the Revolutionary War. In Congress, in the army administration, in the finances, in the medical department, the faults of lack of organization were conspicuous and their consequences were humiliating. The effects of lack of organization may be summed up in a word: such a lack makes it impossible to bring the power and resources of the community to bear on the task in hand. That is what was proved

[1] Wealth of Nations, II, 152.

in the history of the War. In the meantime the bonds of social order were relaxed on every side: the "committees" accustomed the people to arbitrary and tyrannical action; the cruel and wicked persecution of the Tories demoralized the Whigs; the corruption of the paper money produced bitter heart-burnings and discontent; the sudden enrichment of a few by privateering and speculation presented an irritating phenomenon which had not been seen before. The heated declamation about liberty had produced vague expectations and hopes which were, of course, disappointed; and all this culminated in the period of the Confederation, when it seemed to some that the whole social and political fabric was falling to pieces. There was, however, a great deal of jacobinism, to use a later term, the adherents of which were perfectly satisfied that things were going in the right direction.

Now if we do not know these facts and give them their due weight, how are we to appreciate the work of the Constitution-makers? How can we understand what their task was, what difficulties they had to overcome, what the grounds were of the opposition which they had to meet? Everyone knows nowadays that the people by no means leaped forward to grasp this Constitution, which is now so much admired and loved, as the blessing which they had been praying for. Why did they not? To put it in the briefest compass, the reason why not was this: that Constitution was an immense advance in the political organization at a single step. It made a real union; it reduced the independent (I avoid the word "sovereign") states to a status of some limitation; it created a competent executive — one who could *govern*, not influence or persuade; it created a treasury which could reach the property of the citizen by taxes, not by begging; it created a power which could enforce treaties. Considering the anarchical condition of things and the waywardness and irritation of the public temper, it is amazing that such a step could have been accomplished.

Its opponents declared that the new Union was simply taking the place which Great Britain had occupied; that its dominion was as intolerable as hers had been; that they had only changed masters by the War. Here is the point at which we need to recall what has been said about the attitude and behavior of the colonists between 1763 and 1774. If this is done it will be seen that the allegation about the Union having come to occupy the position which Great Britain had occupied was true; it had to claim what she had claimed and to meet with the same insubordination which she had met with. One cause of quarrel with England had been the regulation of commerce; but the Constitution had given Congress the power to regulate commerce — and we are still quarrelling about what this power means and how to use it. Another cause of quarrel had been over the legal-tender paper money, which Great Britain had tried to forbid; but the Constitution forbade legal-tender paper money to the states and, as was then believed, to the Union too. It forbade the states to impair the obligation of contracts, which went farther and was more explicit than anything Great Britain had done. Where England had been very careful about coming into direct contact with the individual citizen in the colonies, the Constitution distinctly and avowedly brought the Union into contact with the individual through the judiciary and through indirect internal taxes. The necessity had been experienced during the War of frowning down any partial confederations between less than the whole number of states, but precisely by so doing was the disapproval of England against the Stamp Act Congress and other congresses justified. The state governments had already found it necessary to use measures against smuggling like those which had given so much offence when used by Great Britain. In the treaty of peace, again, which the federal government was now authorized to enforce, British creditors were ensured the use of the courts to enforce payment. Finally in the matter of taxation the Union inherited all the embarrassments of Great Britain. The states had shown that they would not freely consent to any import duties in their ports for the federal treasury; but now the federal government had power to lay and collect them by its own officers. It also proceeded at once to use its power to lay excise taxes, and when this produced a rebellion, it put down the rebellion by armed force with a vigor and promptitude far surpassing anything which the English did, even during the War. In the trials which ensued to punish the violators of law, to which there is no parallel whatever in anything done by the English during the colonial period, the doctrine was laid down that it was high treason to go with arms to the house of an administrative officer of the law with intent to injure his property or otherwise intimidate him from the performance of his duty. But according to that ruling very many of those who took part in the Stamp Act riots were guilty of high treason. Therefore, to sum it up, the doctrines of the radical Whigs were now the doctrines of the radical Antifederalists. The latter claimed with truth that they were consistent, that they had all the same reason to oppose and dread the Union which they had had to oppose Great Britain, and that the Union had inherited and was perpetuating the position of Great Britain. It became a current expression of discontent with the federal system, of which you hear occasional echoes even now, that it was an imitation of the English system invented and fastened on the country by Alexander Hamilton — and this was rather a distortion of the true facts than an utter falsehood.

What, then, shall we infer from all these facts? Plainly this: that the Revolutionary doctrines were anarchistic, and inconsistent with peace and civil order; that they were riotous and extravagant; and that there could be no success and prosperity here until a constitutional civil government existed which could put down the lawless and turbulent spirit and discipline the people to liberty under law. This is the position which was taken by the Federal party; this is why New England, although it had been intensely Whig, became intensely Federal. The people knew the difference between war measures and peace measures and they realized the necessity of tightening again the bonds of social order. This is also why the Federal party was so unpopular; it was doing a most useful and essential work, but it is never popular to insist upon self-control, discipline, and healthful regulation. On the other hand Jefferson and his friends always prophesied smooth things, assuring "the people" that it was showing the highest political wisdom when it was doing as it had a mind to. Their doctrine was that "the people," that is, all the population except the educated and property classes, knew everything without finding it out or being aware of it, and distilled from votes infallible wisdom for the solution of political problems, although the individuals that made up "the people" might have no wisdom in their individual heads. Of course this was popular; men are delighted to hear that they have all rights without trouble and expense, that they are wise without hard experience or study, and that they shall have power without being put to any trouble to win it. The Jeffersonians, therefore, preached relaxation, negligence, and ease, while the Federalists were working for security, order, constitutional guarantees, and institutions. However, when the Jeffersonians got into power, the conservatism of authority got possession of them and they, in their turn, increased the federal power and developed and intensified the political organization. Perhaps they did it more prudently, wisely, and successfully than the Federalists did, just because they advocated it in phrases borrowed from the old pet doctrines of relaxation and undiscipline.

I shall no more than mention the development of the power of the Supreme Court in the interpretation of the Constitution; this began after the second war with England and was a powerful influence in carrying on the development and integration of our political institutions. I might also mention the introduction of police into our large cities, a measure which, when it was done, was viewed with great disfavor by the friends of liberty, although our large cities had been disgraced by frequent riots, and the dangerous classes in them had become organized and were almost independent of the law.

In the Civil War the delusion of the Southerners was, in large part, a survival of the old anarchism of the Revolutionary period. All the jargon of Secession is perpetuated from the period before the Revolution; the genealogy of it, down through the resolutions of '98 and Nullification, is clear and indisputable. It is pitiful to see with what sublime good faith the Southerners repeated the old phrases and maxims; they thought that they were enunciating accepted and indisputable truths and evoking, on their own behalf, the memories of our heroic age. But the defeat of the South in the War has not meant the definitive extrusion of those maxims and notions from our political system. If we do not wish another generation to grow up with another set of delusions to be cured by bloodshed, it would be well to correct the stories in our popular histories about the Boston Massacre and the Boston Tea Party and the doctrine about "no taxation without representation," as well as those about natural rights and the equality of all men. It is by no means true that what our young people need is an uncritical patriotic inflation. The principles of '76 were: (1) revolution, because there was a revolution on hand — but this principle can have no utility or applicability until there is another revolution on hand; (2) rebellion against the crown of England and secession from the British empire — but this principle, as we have found by experience, was good for once only, when the causes were serious enough to justify it; (3) independence — but independence is not a general principle; if it were, it would require a series of revolts until every town stood by itself. The commonwealers of last summer built their whole platform on delusive constructions of the popular dogmas of liberty and on phrases of historical reference to the Revolution. In these great strike riots you hear echoes of all the Fourth of July sentiments and corollaries of all the great Revolutionary principles. They are all delusions as to what this world is, what human society is, what we can do here. The uneducated and half-educated men who utter them are not half to blame for them. They have been taught so; they have caught

up catchwords and phrases; and now they are con-
verting these into maxims of action. Such delusions
are never cured without much pain and many tears.

When we gather together the observations we have
made, showing the advance of the entire social organization from the colonial settlement up to the present
time, in all its branches — the industrial system, the
relations of classes, the land system, the civil organization, and the organization of political institutions and
liberty — we see that it has been a life-process, a growth-
process, which our society had to go through just as
inevitably as an infant after birth must go on to the
stages of growth and experience which belong to all
human beings as such. This evolution in our case has
not been homogeneous. The constant extension or
settlement into the open territory to the west has kept
us in connection with forms of society representing the
stages through which the older parts of the country
have already passed. We could find to-day vast tracts
of territory in which society is on the stage of organization which existed along the Atlantic coast in the
seventeenth century; and between those places and the
densest centers of population in the East we could find
represented every intervening stage through which our
society has passed in two hundred years. This combination of heterogeneous stages of social and political
organization in one state is a delicate experiment; they
are sure to contend for the mastery in it, and that
strife threatens disruption. As I believe that this view
has rarely received any attention, it is one of the
chief points I have wished to make in surveying the
advance of social and political organization in this
country.

The Federalists opposed the creation of frontier states which should share, on an equal footing in some respects, with the old ones in the federal Union. They thought that the wishes, tastes, interests, and methods of the two classes of states would be inconsistent, that they would clash, and that the things which the old states held dear would be imperilled. This view afterwards became a subject of ridicule. New states were not new very long before they became old; they filled up with population, acquired capital, multiplied their interests, and became conservative. It seemed an idle and pedantic notion that there could be any political difficulty in the combination of new and old states; the more we got in, the bigger we grew — and that was the main point. Then again all political struggle centered in the struggle of North and South for supremacy in the Union; the other elements which were included in the struggle have blinded us to the fact that that was the real character of it — a struggle for supremacy in the Union. Just as certainly as you have a unit-group inside of which different elements can be differentiated, just so certainly will those elements strive for the mastery; it is a law of nature and is inevitable. In the Constitutional Convention of 1787 the one great question was: If we have a union, who will rule in it? It was not until equal representation in the Senate was agreed upon that union became possible. Then the great division was between large states and small ones. The resolutions of '98, by Virginia and her daughter, Kentucky, were aimed at a Yankee President and his supporters, by whom Virginia would not be ruled. As soon as the system was in full operation, the alliance of Virginia and New York attempted to control it; they threw the Federal party and the East out of power,

upon which you find New England going over forthwith
to secession and disunion. Then, as the new states
came in, the divisions of the old ones sought their
alliance. The coalition of the South and West in the
'20's could not be consolidated because the new states
came in so fast. The slave states and the non-slave
states then became the most clear, important, and positive differentiation there was. With the census of 1840,
however, it became clear that the slave states could
not retain the proportional power and influence which
they had had in the confederation; and it was their
turn to become disunionists. Fifty years of our history
have gone into that struggle, for it is not more than
well over now. Meanwhile other great interests have
been neglected and great abuses have grown up unnoticed: war taxation and war currency are still here
to plague us. Our people have come out of that struggle
with a great confidence that nothing can ever again put
the Union at stake. Let us not make that error. The
Union is always at stake. Instead of being a system
which can stand alone and bear any amount of abuse,
it is one of great delicacy and artificiality which requires the highest civic virtues and the wisest statesmanship to preserve it. It will be threatened again
whenever there is a well-defined group which believes
its interests jeopardized inside the Union and under the
dominion of those who control the Union.

At the point which we have now reached the whole continent has received a first occupation and settlement;
and from now on the process will be one of consolidation and condensation. This will raise the organization over the whole country. That process cannot go
on too rapidly at the present stage, for the more rapidly
it goes on the quicker it will tide us over the dangers

in which we find ourselves — dangers due to the great differences in the social and political organization which now exist. In all the past the *rapidity* of our growth has been one of our best safeguards; no state of things has existed long enough to allow people to understand it, to base plans upon it, and to carry them out, before the facts have all changed and frustrated all the plans. There have been plenty of presidential aspirants in the United States who have found that four years was a long time to bridge over with combinations based upon the assumption that circumstances in states and sections would remain that long unchanged.

There has been, however, another and apparently contradictory evolution side by side with the one already mentioned, and it is the combination of the two which has given to our history its unique character. The public men of the Revolutionary period were not democrats — they feared democracy. The Constitution-makers were under an especial dread of democracy, which they identified with the anarchism of the period of 1783–1787. They therefore established by the Constitution a set of institutions which are restrictions of democracy. They did not invent any of these institutions, for all of them were already familiar in the colonies, being of English origin and developed and adapted to the circumstances here. Their general character is that while they ensure the rule of the majority of legal voters, they yet insist upon it that the will of that majority shall be constitutionally expressed and that it shall be a sober, mature, and well-considered will. This constitutes a guarantee against jacobinism. Now the whole genius of this country has been democratic. I have tried to show that its inherited dogmas and its environment made it so inevitably. Down through our history, therefore, the democratic temper of the people has been at war with the Constitutional institutions. When the Constitution was established there was no such thing as universal manhood suffrage here; the suffrage was connected with freehold in land. This restriction, measured by the number of people it excluded, was a very important one. It was not until after the second war with England that a movement towards universal suffrage began in the old states; then it ran on with great rapidity until universal suffrage was established in them all. The democratic temper also seized upon that device in the Constitution which was the most positive new invention in it and which was developed as a safeguard against democracy, viz., the electoral college, and turned it into a mere form through which the voters should directly elect their own President. The same sentiments called forth an unwritten law that the President should serve only two terms and has always loudly favored one term. Perhaps, since the great precedent was the purchase of Louisiana by Jefferson, democracy ought also to be credited with forcing an unwritten addendum on the Constitution that the federal government could buy land. Democracy has chafed, at one time and another, against the veto of the President, the power of the Senate, and, above all, against the prerogatives of the judiciary — all of which are institutional checks on democracy. The most recent effort in the same direction is the plan to nominate senators by party convention and to compel the legislators to vote for the candidates thus set before them. No one will deny, moreover, that a democratic spirit has been breathed through all our institutions, has modified their action and determined their character. Opinions would differ as to whether its effect has always been good, but I doubt if anyone would deny that it has sometimes been good.

We see then, in our history, that neither have the Constitutional institutions and guarantees proved a cast-iron jacket in which to enclose our society and prevent its changes, nor, on the other hand, has democracy been able to override the institutions and render them nugatory. On the contrary, our institutions as they are to-day are the resultant of a struggle between the two — a struggle accompanying that expansion and intensification of the organization which I have aimed to describe.

Here, then, is an extraordinary phenomenon: an advance of the organization and an advance of liberty too, or, to speak more accurately, an advance in the organization with a transformation in the conception of liberty and the widest possible expansion of that liberty. While the discipline and constraint of the institutions have been exerted to reduce anarchistic liberty, they have enlarged and created civil liberty, or liberty under law. These two notions of liberty are totally different from one another. We are suffering from the fact that in our current philosophy, even amongst educated people, the notion of liberty is not sufficiently analyzed and this distinction is not sufficiently understood. Here has been a society advancing with the greatest rapidity in the number, variety, complication, and delicacy of its interests; yet it has at the same time opened the suffrage on gratuitous terms to all adult males, and granted them access to every public office, with corresponding control over all societal interests. Where else in history have all adult males in a society actually possessed political power, honors, and emoluments and at the same time been subject to no responsibilities, risks, charges, expenses, or burdens of any kind — these being all left to the educated and property classes? Where else has it ever been possible for a numerical majority to entail upon a society burdens which the minority must bear, while the aforesaid majority may scatter and leave the society and trouble themselves no further about it? The men of the Revolution never could have imagined any such state of things. In 1775 the convention of Worcester County, Massachusetts, petitioned the Provincial Congress "that no man may be allowed to have a seat therein who does not vote away his own money for public purposes in common with the other members' and with his constituents'." [1] That was the prevailing doctrine everywhere at the time, and yet within fifty years the evolution of civil institutions, instead of realizing that doctrine, produced the state of things which I have just described — and that state of things was produced contemporaneously with an integration of civil institutions, an elevation of the authority of law, and a sharpening of social discipline.

Now the current opinion amongst us undoubtedly is that the extension of the suffrage and the virtual transfer of the powers of government to the uneducated and non-property classes, compelling the educated and property classes, if they want to influence the government, to do so by persuading or perhaps corrupting the former, is a piece of political wisdom to which our fathers were led by philosophy and by the conviction that the doctrine of it was true and just. There were causes for it, however, which were far more powerful than preaching, argument, and philosophy; and besides, if you will notice how hopeless it is by any argument

[1] Massachusetts Journals, p. 651.

to make headway against any current of belief which has obtained momentum in a society, you will put your faith in the current of belief and not in the power of logic or exhortation. You will then look at the causes of the current of belief, and you will find them in the economic conditions which are controlling, at the time, the struggle for existence and the competition of life. At the beginning of this century it would have been just exactly as impossible to put aristocratic restrictions on democracy here as it would have been at the same time to put democratic restrictions on aristocracy in England. Now the economic circumstances of our century which have modified the struggle for existence and the competition of life have been, first, the opening of a vast extent of new land to the use and advantage of the people who had no social power of any kind; and, second, the advance in the arts. Of the arts, those of transportation have been the most important because they have made the new land accessible; but all the other applications of the arts have been increasing man's power in the struggle for existence, and they have been most in favor of the classes which otherwise had nothing but their hands with which to carry on that struggle. This has lessened the advantage of owning land and it has lessened the comparative advantage of having capital over that of having only labor. An education has not now as great value to give its possessor a special advantage — a share, that is, in a limited monopoly — as it had a century ago. This is true in a still greater degree of higher education, until we come up to those cases where exceptional talent, armed with the highest training, once more wins the advantages of a natural monopoly.

Hence it is that the great economic changes I have

mentioned have produced the greatest social revolution that has ever occurred. It has raised the masses to power, has set slaves free, has given a charter of social and political power to the people who have nothing, and has forced those-who-have to get power, if they want it, by persuading and influencing those-who-have-not. All the demagogues, philosophers, and principle-brokers are trying to lead the triumphal procession and crying: "We got it for you." "We are your friends." "It is to us that you owe it all." On the other hand the same social revolution has undermined all social institutions and prescriptions of an aristocratic character and they are rapidly crumbling away, even in the Old World, under the reaction from the New.

If now we put this result together with what we had reached before, we find that the advance of the social and political organization which should have been attended, according to all former philosophy, by greater social pressure and diminishing prosperity for the masses, although it has indeed been attended by lessening of the old anarchistic liberty, has also been accompanied by the far more important fact of enormously enlarged social and political power and chances for the masses. The world has passed into hands of new masters, and the all-absorbing questions for mankind and civilization now are: What will they do with it? How will they behave? Already in this country, and in all others which have adopted democratic forms, successive elections show a steady movement towards throwing out men of well-defined convictions and positive strength on either side, so that parliamentary institutions seem to be clearly on the decline. In every great civilized country, also, political parties are breaking up and are losing their character as groups of persons holding common convictions on questions of general policy. Their place is being taken by petty groups of representatives of certain interests. The more we enlarge the sphere of government, the more true it is that every act of legislation enriches or ruins those who are interested in some branch of industry; such persons say, therefore, that they cannot afford to neglect legislative proceedings. The consequence is the immense power of the lobby, and legislation comes to be an affair of coalition between interests to make up a majority. If that goes on, its logical and institutional outcome must be that the non-possessors, if united, must form the largest interest-group, and that they will then find that the easiest way ever yet devised to get wealth is to hold a parliament and, by a majority vote, order that the possessors of wealth shall give it to the non-possessors. This program has already been proposed and adopted and strong efforts are on foot to organize the parliamentary groups on this basis so as to put it into action.

We have abundant facts at hand to show us, also, that the higher the social organization is the more delicate it is and the more it is exposed to harm upon all sides and from slight influences. A great, complicated, and delicate social organization presents a vast array of phenomena of all kinds, many of which are paradoxical and contradictory in their relation to each other. The analysis of these phenomena and the interpretation of them is the easiest thing in the world if we go about it with a few so-called "ethical" principles; but if we approach it with any due conception of what it is that we are trying to do, we find it the hardest mental task ever yet cast upon mankind. We boast of our successes in science and art; but those successes have brought about a social organization and produced social problems which we cannot evade, and if we do not solve them aright, we may ruin all our other achievements and go down to barbarism again.

Here I find myself on the verge of prophecy and so here I arrest myself. The political prophets of our country have always been either optimists or alarmists. I should not be willing to be either. The optimists scoff at all warnings and misgivings; they think we need not trouble ourselves to think or take care, and they exhort us to go ahead, encouraging us with familiar phrases and commonplaces. I have suggested that we need to be prudent, to listen to reason, to use forethought and care. Social and political crises are sure to arise among us as they must in any human society — we have had enough of them to convince us that they will come again. I have suggested also that our political system calls for more political sense, sober judgment, and ever-active prudence than any other political system does. It also forbids us to do many things which states of other forms may undertake. It is especially incompatible with our form of democratic republic to charge the state with many and various functions, for our state should be simple to the last possible degree. It should handle as little money as possible; it should encourage the constant individual activity of its citizens and never do anything to weaken individual initiative. But the tendency to-day is all the other way. Our state should have as few office-holders as possible. The stubborn dogmatism of the old Jeffersonians on these points showed that they had stronger sense of the maxims necessary to maintain the kind of state they liked than anybody has nowadays; to suppose that these maxims are inconsistent with strength of government, in the distinct and exclusive field of government, is to give proof of a very shallow political philosophy. They are the conditions of strong government in purely civil affairs, for the more outside functions a state assumes the more it is hampered in its proper business. Furthermore, our federal state cannot enter on a great many enterprises which imperial states under the monarchical or aristocratic form have been wont to undertake; it cannot embark on an enterprising foreign policy or on conquest or on annexation without putting its internal equilibrium at stake. This is because of its peculiar structure and principles. We may see, how- ever, strong symptoms amongst us of all the old ambi- tions, the thirst for bigness and glory which have cost the people of Europe so dearly, and we hear all the dogmas of militarism once more brought to the front as rules of our policy. Here are things which call for something very different from heedless optimism.

The alarmists, on the other hand, have against them the immense vigor of this society, its power to react against calamity and to recover from errors. Alarmist predictions of the past have all been proved utterly mistaken. You can find such predictions scattered all the way along: in 1800, when the Federalists gave way to Jefferson; at the Second War; all through Jackson's time; at the Mexican War; at the Civil War — and it may be some encouragement to the timid to ask whether, at those crises, there did not seem to be as good cause for alarm, albeit a different one, as seems to exist now. It is evident that if George Washington and his contemporaries had tried to anticipate our problems and to solve them for us in advance they would have made ridiculous blunders, for they could not possibly have foreseen our case or understood the ele- ments which enter into it. Let us be very sure that if we try to look forward a century we are making just the same kind of ridiculous blunders. We cannot make anything else. One of the chief results of our historical studies is to show us the repeated and accumulated faults and errors of men in the past. You will observe that the common inference is that we, since we see the errors of the past, are perpetrating none in our own schemes and projects; but this is the greatest fallacy there is (and there are a great many) in our historical method of social study. The correct inference would be that we too, if we plot schemes of social action which reach beyond the immediate facts and the nearest interests, are only committing new errors, the effects of which will be entailed upon posterity. The reason for this is that the future contains new and unknown elements, incalculable combinations, unforeseeable changes in the moods, tastes, standards, and desires of the people. If we look back to Washington's time and see what changes have taken place in all these respects, then we may look to the future in full confidence that such changes will go on in the next hundred years.

These changes are what have turned the terrors of the alarmist to scorn. Certain it is that the Americans of the nineteenth century have been far happier, as a society, than any other society of human beings ever has been. They have been shielded from the commonest and heaviest calamities and have been free from the most vexatious burdens of human society; except at certain periods, taxation has been light and military duty an amusement; they have inherited a great untouched continent, with powers of science and art, for taking and using it, incomparably superior to anything ever possessed before by men. Very few of them apparently have understood or understand their own good fortune and its exceptional character. If all conditions should remain the same and the population go on increasing, the exceptional conditions would pass away and our posterity would have to contend sometime or other with all the old social problems again. The conditions, however, will not remain the same; they will change, no doubt in the direction of still greater and better chances. This fact is what gives the optimist his justification and makes his reckless blindness appear to be the shrewdest foresight. Furthermore, the problems which sometimes appal us nowadays are not peculiar to America; they are quite as heavy and as knotty in England, France, and Germany as they are here. In many points we are further on towards a solution than those countries are: we have better social defences from behind which to meet the dangers; and they do not come upon us, as they do upon the nations of Europe, mixed up with militarism, with the relics of feudal institutions, and with the traditions of absolute monarchy.

And now my task is done if, by a discussion of the teachings of our history, I have contributed to a better understanding of present facts and forces; for the highest wisdom and the most patriotic devotion to our country which we can manifest lie in the faithful performance of present civic duties and in diligent efforts to accomplish the tasks which lie immediately before us. We may be very sure that a succeeding century will take care of itself; also that it will not be able to take care of us. All the energy we spend, therefore, in preparing for it is worse than thrown away. It will be useless for its purpose and it will be abstracted from what we can spend on our own problems, which are big enough and hard enough to require all the energy we have to deal with them.

WHAT IS FREE TRADE?[1]

THERE never would have been any such thing to fight for as free speech, free press, free worship, or free soil, if nobody had ever put restraints on men in those matters. We never should have heard of free trade, if no restrictions had ever been put on trade. If there had been any restrictions on the intercourse between the states of this Union, we should have heard of ceaseless agitation to get those restrictions removed. Since there are no restrictions allowed under the Constitution, we do not realize the fact that we are enjoying the blessings of complete liberty, where, if wise counsels had not prevailed at a critical moment, we should now have had a great mass of traditional and deep-rooted interferences to encounter.

Our intercourse with foreign nations, however, has been interfered with, because it is a fact that, by such interference, some of us can win advantages over others. The power of Congress to levy taxes is employed to lay duties on imports, not in order to secure a revenue from imports, but to prevent imports — in which case, of course, no revenue will be obtained. The effect which is aimed at, and which is attained by this device, is that the American consumer, when he wants to satisfy his needs, has to go to an American producer of the thing he wants, and has to give to him a price for the product which is greater than that which some foreigner would have charged. The object of this device, as stated on the best protectionist authority, is: "To effect the diversion of a part of the labor and capital of the people out of the channels in which it would run otherwise, into

---

[1] In *Good Cheer* for April, 1886, p. 7.

channels favored or created by law." This description is strictly correct, and from it the reader will see that protection has nothing to do with any foreigner whatever. It is purely a question of domestic policy. It is only a question whether we shall, by taxing each other, drive the industry of this country into an arbitrary and artificial development, or whether we shall allow one another to employ each his capital and labor in his own way. Note that there is for us all the same labor, capital, soil, national character, climate, etc., — that is, that all the conditions of production remain unaltered. The only change which is operated is a wrenching of labor and capital out of the lines on which they would act under the impulse of individual enterprise, energy, and interest, and their impulsion in another direction selected by the legislator. Plainly, all the import duty can do is to close the door, shutting the foreigner out and the Americans in. Then, when an American needs iron, coal, copper, woolens, cottons, or anything else in the shape of manufactured commodities, the operation begins. He has to buy in a market which is either wholly or partially monopolized. The whole object of shutting him in is to take advantage of this situation to make him give more of his products for a given amount of the protected articles, than he need have given for the same things in the world's market. Under this system a part of our product is diverted from the satisfaction of our needs, and is spent to hire some of our fellow-citizens to go out of an employment which would pay under the world's competition, into one which will not pay under the world's competition. We, therefore, do with less clothes, furniture, tools, crockery, glassware, bed and table linen, books, etc., and the satisfaction we have for this sacrifice is knowing that some of our neighbors are carrying on business which according to their statement does not pay, and that we are paying their losses and hiring them to keep on.

Free trade is a revolt against this device. It is not a revolt against import duties or indirect taxes as a means of raising revenue. It has nothing to say about that, one way or the other. It begins to protest and agitate just as soon as any tax begins to act protectively, and it denounces any tax which one citizen levies on another. The protectionists have a long string of notions and doctrines which they put forward to try to prove that their device is not a contrivance by which they can make their fellow-citizens contribute to their support, but is a device for increasing the national wealth and power. These allegations must be examined by economists, or other persons who are properly trained to test their correctness, in fact and logic. It is enough here to say, over a responsible signature, that no such allegation has ever been made which would bear examination. On the contrary, all such assertions have the character of apologies or special pleas to divert attention from the one plain fact that the advocates of a protective tariff have a direct pecuniary interest in it, and that they have secured it, and now maintain it, for that reason and no other. The rest is all afterthought and excuse. If any gain could possibly come to the country through the gains of the beneficiaries of the tariff, obviously the country must incur at least an equal loss through the losses of that part of the people who pay what the protected win. If a country could win anything that way, it would be like a man lifting himself by his boot straps.

The protectionists, in advocating their system, always spend a great deal of effort and eloquence on appeals to patriotism, and to international jealousies. These are all entirely aside from the point. The protective system is a domestic system, for domestic purposes, and it is sought by domestic means. The one who pays, and the one who gets, are both Americans. The victim and the beneficiary are amongst ourselves. It is just as unpatriotic to oppress one American as it is patriotic to favor another. If we make one American pay taxes to another American, it will neither vex nor please any foreign nation.

The protectionists speak of trade with the contempt of feudal nobles, but on examination it appears that they have something to sell, and that they mean to denounce trade with their rivals. They denounce cheapness, and it appears that they do so because they want to sell dear. When they buy, they buy as cheaply as they can. They say that they want to raise wages, but they never pay anything but the lowest market rate. They denounce selfishness, while pursuing a scheme for their own selfish aggrandizement, and they bewail the dominion of self-interest over men who want to enjoy their own earnings, and object to surrendering the same to them. They attribute to government, or to "the state," the power and right to decide what industrial enterprises each of us shall subscribe to support.

Free trade means antagonism to this whole policy and theory at every point. The free trader regards it as all false, meretricious, and delusive. He considers it an invasion of private rights. In the best case, if all that the protectionist claims were true, he would be taking it upon himself to decide how his neighbor should spend his earnings, and — more than that — that his neighbor shall spend his earnings for the advantage of the men who make the decision. This is plainly immoral and corrupting; nothing could be more so. The free trader also denies that the government either can, or ought to regulate the way in which a man shall employ his earnings. He sees that the government is nothing but a clique of the parties in interest. It is a few men who have control of the civic organization. If they were called upon to regulate business, they would need a wisdom which they have not. They do not do this. They only turn the "channels" to the advantage of themselves and their friends. This corrupts the institutions of government and continues under our system all the old abuses by which the men who could get control of the governmental machinery have used it to aggrandize themselves at the expense of others. The free trader holds that the people will employ their labor and capital to the best advantage when each man employs his own in his own way, according to the maxim that "A fool is wiser in his own house than a sage in another man's house"; — how much more, then, shall he be wiser than a politician? And he holds, further, that by the nature of the case, if any governmental coercion is necessary to drive industry in a direction in which it would not otherwise go, such coercion must be mischievous.

The free trader further holds that protection is all a mistake and delusion to those who think that they win by it, in that it lessens their self-reliance and energy and exposes their business to vicissitudes which, not being incident to a natural order of things, cannot be foreseen and guarded against by business skill; also that it throws the business into a condition in which it is exposed to a series of heats and chills, and finally, unless a new stimulus is applied, reduced to a state of dull decay. They therefore hold that even the protected would be far better off without it.

PROTECTIONISM

THE –ISM WHICH TEACHES THAT WASTE MAKES WEALTH [1]

PREFACE

DURING the last fifteen years we have had two great questions to discuss: the restoration of the currency and civil-service reform. Neither of these questions has yet reached a satisfactory solution, but both are on the way toward such a result. The next great effort to strip off the evils entailed on us by the Civil War will consist in the repeal of those taxes which one man was enabled to levy on another, under cover of the taxes which the government had to lay to carry on the war. I have taken my share in the discussion of the first two questions, and I expect to take my share in the discussion of the third.

I have written this book as a contribution to a popular agitation. I have not troubled myself to keep or to throw off scientific or professional dignity. I have tried to make my point as directly and effectively as I could for the readers whom I address, *viz.*, the intelligent voters of all degrees of general culture, who need to have it explained to them what protectionism is and how it works. I have therefore pushed the controversy just as hard as I could, and have used plain language, just as I have always done before in what I have written on this subject. I must therefore forego the hope that I have given any more pleasure now than formerly to the advocates of protectionism.

[1] First published as a small volume by Henry Holt & Co., 1885.

Protectionism seems to me to deserve only contempt and scorn, satire and ridicule. It is such an arrant piece of economic quackery, and it masquerades under such an affectation of learning and philosophy, that it ought to be treated as other quackeries are treated. Still, out of deference to its strength in the traditions and lack of information of many people, I have here undertaken a patient and serious exposition of it. Satire and derision remain reserved for the dogmatic protectionists and the sentimental protectionists; the Philistine protectionists and those who hold the key of all knowledge; the protectionists of stupid good faith and those who know their dogma is a humbug and are therefore irritated at the exposure of it; the protectionists by birth and those by adoption; the protectionists for hire and those by election; the protectionists by party platform and those by pet newspaper; the protectionists by "invincible ignorance" and those by vows and ordination; the protectionists who run colleges and those who want to burn colleges down; the protectionists by investment and those who sin against light; the hopeless ones who really believe in British gold and dread the Cobden Club, and the dishonest ones who storm about those things without believing in them; those who may not be answered when they come into debate, because they are "great" men, or because they are "old" men, or because they have stock in certain newspapers, or are trustees of certain colleges. All these have honored me personally, in this controversy, with more or less of their particular attention. I confess that it has cost me something to leave their cases out of account, but to deal with them would have been a work of entertainment, not of utility.

Protectionism arouses my moral indignation. It is a subtle, cruel, and unjust invasion of one man's rights by another. It is done by force of law. It is at the same time a social abuse, an economic blunder, and a political

evil. The moral indignation which it causes is the motive
which draws me away from the scientific pursuits which
form my real occupation, and forces me to take part in a
popular agitation. The doctrine of a "call" applies in
such a case, and every man is bound to take just so great a
share as falls in his way. That is why I have given more
time than I could afford to popular lectures on this subject, and it is why I have now put the substance of those lectures into this book.

W. G. S.

Chapter I

DEFINITIONS: STATEMENT OF THE QUESTION TO BE INVESTIGATED

(A) The System of which Protection is a Survival.

1. The statesmen of the eighteenth century supposed
that their business was the art of national prosperity.
Their procedure was to form ideals of political greatness
and civil prosperity on the one hand, and to evolve out of
their own consciousness grand dogmas of human happiness
and social welfare on the other hand. Then they tried to
devise specific means for connecting these two notions with
each other. Their ideals of political greatness contained,
as predominant elements, a brilliant court, a refined and
elegant aristocracy, well-developed fine arts and *belles
lettres*, a powerful army and navy, and a peaceful, obedient,
and hard-working peasantry and artisan class to pay the
taxes and support the other part of the political structure.
In this ideal the lower ranks paid upward, and the upper
ranks blessed downward, and all were happy together.
The great political and social dogmas of the period were
exotic and incongruous. They were borrowed or accepted
from the classical authorities. Of course the dogmas were

chiefly held and taught by the philosophers, but, as the century ran its course, they penetrated the statesman class. The statesman who had had no purpose save to serve the "grandeur" of the king, or to perpetuate a dynasty, gave way to statesmen who had strong national feeling and national ideals, and who eagerly sought means to realize their ideals. Having as yet no definite notion, based on facts of observation and experience, of what a human society or a nation is, and no adequate knowledge of the nature and operation of social forces, they were driven to empirical processes which they could not test, or measure, or verify. They piled device upon device and failure upon failure. When one device failed of its intended purpose and produced an unforeseen evil, they invented a new device to prevent the new evil. The new device again failed to prevent, and became a cause of a new harm, and so on indefinitely.

2. Among their devices for industrial prosperity were (1) export taxes on raw materials, to make raw materials abundant and cheap at home; (2) bounties on the export of finished products, to make the exports large; (3) taxes on imported commodities to make the imports small, and thus, with No. 2, to make the "balance of trade" favorable, and to secure an importation of specie; (4) taxes or prohibition on the export of machinery, so as not to let foreigners have the advantage of domestic inventions; (5) prohibition on the emigration of skilled laborers, lest they should carry to foreign rivals knowledge of domestic arts; (6) monopolies to encourage enterprise; (7) navigation laws to foster ship-building or the carrying trade, and to provide sailors for the navy; (8) a colonial system to bring about by political force the very trade which the other devices had destroyed by economic interference; (9) laws for fixing wages and prices to repress the struggle of the non-capitalist class to save themselves in the social press; (10) poor-laws

to lessen the struggle by another outlet; (11) extravagant
criminal laws to try to suppress another development of
this struggle by terror; and so on, and so on.

(B) OLD AND NEW CONCEPTIONS OF THE STATE.

3. Here we have a complete illustration of one mode of
looking at human society, or at a state. Such society is,
on this view, an artificial or mechanical product. It is an
object to be molded, made, produced by contrivance.
Like every product which is brought out by working up to
an ideal instead of working out from antecedent truth and
fact, the product here is haphazard, grotesque, false. Like
every other product which is brought out by working on
lines fixed by *a priori* assumptions, it is a satire on human
foresight and on what we call common sense. Such a
state is like a house of cards, built up anxiously one upon
another, ready to fall at a breath, to be credited at most
with naïve hope and silly confidence; or, it is like the long
and tedious contrivance of a mischievous schoolboy, for
an end which has been entirely misappreciated and was
thought desirable when it should have been thought a
folly; or, it is like the museum of an alchemist, filled with
specimens of his failures, monuments of mistaken industry
and testimony of an erroneous method; or, it is like the
clumsy product of an untrained inventor, who, instead of
asking: "what means have I, and to what will they serve?"
asks: "what do I wish that I could accomplish?" and
seeks to win steps by putting in more levers and cogs, increasing friction and putting the solution ever farther off.

4. Of course such a notion of a state is at war with the
conception of a state as a seat of original forces which
must be reckoned with all the time; as an organism whose
life will go on anyhow, perverted, distorted, diseased,
vitiated as it may be by obstructions or coercions; as a

seat of life in which nothing is ever lost, but every antecedent combines with every other and has its share in the immediate resultant, and again in the next resultant, and so on indefinitely; as the domain of activities so great that they should appall any one who dares to interfere with them; of instincts so delicate and self-preservative that it should be only infinite delight to the wisest man to see them come into play, and his sufficient glory to give them a little intelligent assistance. If a state well performed its functions of providing peace, order, and security, as *conditions* under which the people could live and work, it would be the proudest proof of its triumphant success that it had nothing to do — that all went so smoothly that it had only to look on and was never called to interfere; just as it is the test of a good business man that his business runs on smoothly and prosperously while he is not harassed or hurried. The people who think that it is proof of enterprise to meddle and "fuss" may believe that a good state will constantly interfere and regulate, and they may regard the other type of state as "non-government." The state can do a great deal more than to discharge police functions. If it will *follow* custom, and the growth of social structure to provide for new social needs, it can powerfully aid the production of structure by laying down lines of common action, where nothing is needed but *some* common action on conventional lines; or, it can systematize a number of arrangements which are not at their maximum utility for want of concord; or, it can give sanction to new rights which are constantly created by new relations under new social organizations, and so on.

5. The latter idea of the state has only begun to win way. All history and sociology bear witness to its comparative truth, at least when compared with the former. Under the new conception of the state, of course liberty means breaking off the fetters and trammels which the

"wisdom" of the past has forged, and *laissez-faire*, or "let alone," becomes a cardinal maxim of statesmanship, because it means: "Cease the empirical process. Institute the scientific process. Let the state come back to normal health and activity, so that you can study it, learn something about it from an observation of its phenomena, and then regulate your action in regard to it by intelligent knowledge." Statesmen suited to this latter type of state have not yet come forward in any great number. The new radical statesmen show no disposition to let their neighbors alone. They think that they have come into power just because they know what their neighbors need to have done to them. Statesmen of the old type, who told people that they knew how to make everybody happy, and that they were going to do it, were always far better paid than any of the new type ever will be, and their failures never cost them public confidence either. We have got tired of kings, priests, nobles and soldiers, not because they failed to make us all happy, but because our *a priori* dogmas have changed fashion. We have put the administration of the state in the hands of lawyers, editors, *littérateurs*, and professional politicians, and they are by no means disposed to abdicate the functions of their predecessors, or to abandon the practice of the art of national prosperity. The chief difference is that, whereas the old statesmen used to temper the practice of their art with care for the interests of the kings and aristocracies which put them in power, the new statesmen feel bound to serve those sections of the population which have put them where they are.

6. Some of the old devices above enumerated (§ 2) are, however, out of date, or are becoming obsolete.[1] Number

---

[1] February 4, 1884, Mr. Robinson of New York proposed, in the House of Representatives, an amendment to the Constitution, so as to allow Congress to lay an export duty on cotton for the encouragement of home manufactures. (Record, 862.)

3, taxes on imports for other than fiscal purposes, is not among this number. Just now such taxes seem to be coming back into fashion, or to be enjoying a certain revival. It is a sign of the deficiency of our sociology as compared with our other sciences that such a phenomenon could be presented in the last quarter of the nineteenth century, as a certain revival of faith in the efficiency of taxes on imports as a device for producing national prosperity. There is not a single one of the eleven devices mentioned above, including taxes on the exportation of machinery and prohibitions on emigration, which is not quite as rational and sound as taxes on imports.

I now propose to analyze and criticize protectionism.

(C) Definition of Protectionism — Definition of "Theory."

7. By protection*ism* I mean the doctrine of protective taxes as a device to be employed in the art of national prosperity. The protectionists are fond of representing themselves as "practical" and the free traders as "theorists." "Theory" is indeed one of the most abused words in the language, and the scientists are partly to blame for it. They have allowed the word to come into use, even among themselves, for *a conjectural explanation*, or *a speculative conjecture*, or *a working hypothesis*, or *a project which has not yet been tested by experiment*, or *a plausible and harmless theorem about transcendental relations*, or *about the way in which men will act under certain motives*. The newspapers seem often to use the word "theoretical" as if they meant by it imaginary or fictitious. I use the word "theory," however, not in distinction from fact, but, in what I understand to be the correct scientific use of the word, to denote *a rational description of a group of coördinated facts in their sequence and relations*. A theory may, for a special purpose, describe only certain features of facts and disre-

gard others. Hence "in practice," where facts present themselves in all their complexity, he who has carelessly neglected the limits of his theory may be astonished at phenomena which present themselves; but his astonishment will be due to a blunder on his part, and will not be an imputation on the theory.

8. Now free trade is not a theory in any sense of the word. *It is only a mode of liberty;* one form of the assault (and therefore negative) which the expanding intelligence of the present is making on the trammels which it has inherited from the past. Inside the United States, absolute free trade exists over a continent. No one thinks of it or realizes it. No one "feels" it. We feel only constraint and oppression. If we get liberty we reflect on it only so long as the memory of constraint endures. I have again and again seen the astonishment with which people realized the fact when presented to them that they have been living under free trade all their lives and never thought of it. When the whole world shall obtain and enjoy free trade there will be nothing more to be said about it; it will disappear from discussion and reflection; it will disappear from the text-books on political economy as the chapters on slavery are disappearing; it will be as strange for men to think that they might *not* have free trade as it would be now for an American to think that he might not travel in this country without a passport, or that there ever was a chance that the soil of our western states might be slave soil and not free soil. It would be as reasonable to apply the word "theory" to the protestant reformation, or to law reform, or to anti-slavery, or to the separation of church and state, or to popular rights, or to any other campaign in the great struggle which we call liberty and progress, as to apply it to free trade. The pro-slavery men formerly did apply it to abolition, and with excellent reason, if the use of it which I have criticized ever was correct; for it re-

quired great power of realizing in imagination the results of social change, and great power to follow and trust abstract reasoning, for any man bred under slavery to realize, in advance of experiment, the social and economic gain to be won — *most of all for the whites* — by emancipation. It now requires great power of "theoretical conception" for people who have no experience of the separation of church and state to realize its benefits and justice. Similar observations would hold true of all similar reforms. Free trade is a revolt, a conflict, a reform, a reaction and recuperation of the body politic, just as free conscience, free worship, free speech, free press, and free soil have been. It is in no sense a theory.

9. Protectionism is not a theory in the correct sense of the term, but it comes under some of the popular and incorrect uses of the word. It is purely dogmatic and *a priori*. It is desired to attain a certain object — wealth and national prosperity. Protective taxes are proposed as a means. It must be assumed that there is some connection between protective taxes and national prosperity, some relation of cause and effect, some sequence of expended energy and realized product, between protective taxes and national wealth. If then by theory we mean a speculative conjecture as to occult relations which have not been and cannot be traced in experience, protection would be a capital example. Another and parallel example was furnished by astrology, which assumed a causal relation between the movements of the planets and the fate of men, and built up quite an art of soothsaying on this assumption. Another example, paralleling protectionism in another feature, was alchemy, which, accepting as unquestionable the notion that we want to transmute lead into gold if we can, assumed that there was a philosopher's stone, and set to work to find it through centuries of repetition of the method of "trial and failure."

10. *Protectionism, then, is an* ISM; that is, it is a doctrine or system of doctrine which offers no demonstration, and rests upon no facts, but appeals to faith on grounds of its *a priori* reasonableness, or the plausibility with which it can be set forth. Of course, if a man should say: "I am in favor of protective taxes because they bring gain to me. That is all I care to know about them, and I shall get them retained as long as I can" — there is no trouble in understanding him, and there is no use in arguing with him. So far as he is concerned, the only thing to do is to find his victims and explain the matter to them. The only thing which can be discussed is the doctrine of national wealth by protective taxes. This doctrine has the forms of an economic theory. It vies with the doctrine of labor and capital as a part of the science of production. Its avowed purpose is impersonal and disinterested — the same, in fact, as that of political economy. It is not, like free trade, a mere negative position against an inherited system, to which one is led by a study of political economy. It is a species of political economy, and aims at the throne of the science itself. If it is true, it is not a corollary, but a postulate, on which, and by which, all political economy must be constructed.

11. But then, lo! if the dogma which constitutes protectionism — *national wealth can be produced by protective taxes and cannot be produced without them* — is enunciated, instead of going on to a science of political economy based upon it, the science falls dead on the spot. What can be said about production, population, land, money, exchange, labor and all the rest? What can the economist learn or do? What function is there for the university or school? There is nothing to do but to go over to the art of legislation, and get the legislator to put on the taxes. The only questions which can arise are as to the number, variety, size, and proportion of the taxes. As to these questions the economist can offer no light. He has no method of investigating them. He can deduce no principles, lay down no laws in regard to them. The legislator must go on in the dark and experiment. If his taxes do not produce the required result, if there turn out to be "snakes" in the tariff which he has adopted, he has to change it. If the result still fails, change it again. Protectionism bars the science of political economy with a dogma, and the only process of the art of statesmanship to which it leads is eternal trial and failure — the process of the alchemist and of the inventor of perpetual motion.

(D) Definition of Free Trade and of a Protective Duty.

12. What then is a protective tax? In order to join issue as directly as possible, I will quote the definitions given by a leading protectionist journal,[1] of both free trade and protection. "The term 'free trade,' although much discussed, is seldom rightly defined. It does not mean the abolition of custom houses. Nor does it mean the substitution of direct for indirect taxation, as a few American disciples of the school have supposed. It means such an adjustment of taxes on imports as will cause no diversion of capital, from any channel into which it would otherwise flow, into any channel opened or favored by the legislation which enacts the customs. A country may collect its entire revenue by duties on imports, and yet be an entirely free trade country, so long as it does not lay those duties in such a way as to lead any one to undertake any employment, or make any investment he would avoid in the absence of such duties: thus, the customs duties levied by England — with a very few exceptions — are not inconsistent with her profession of being a country which be-

[1] Philadelphia *American*, August 7, 1884.

lieves in free trade. They either are duties on articles not produced in England, or they are exactly equivalent to the excise duties levied on the same articles if made at home. They do not lead any one to put his money into the home production of an article, because they do not discriminate in favor of the home producer."

13. "A protective duty, on the other hand, has for its object to effect the diversion of a part of the capital and labor of the people out of the channels in which it would run otherwise, into channels favored or created by law."

I know of no definitions of these two things which have ever been made by anybody which are more correct than these. I accept them and join issue on them.

(E) Protectionism Raises a Purely Domestic Controversy.

14. It will be noticed that this definition of a protective duty says nothing about foreigners or about imports. According to this definition, a protective duty is a device for effecting a transformation in our own industry. If a tax is levied at the port of entry on a foreign commodity which is actually imported, the tax is paid to the treasury and produces revenue. A protective tax is one which is laid to act as a bar to importation, in order to keep a foreign commodity out. It does not act protectively unless it does act as a bar, and is not a tax on imports but an obstruction to imports. Hence a protective duty is a wall to inclose the domestic producer and consumer, and to prevent the latter from having access to any other source of supply for his needs, in exchange for his products, than that one which the domestic producer controls. The purpose and plan of the device is to enable the domestic producer to levy on the domestic consumer the taxes which the government has set up as a barrier, but has not col-

lected at the port of entry. Under this device the government says: "I do not want the revenue, but I will lay the tax so that you, the selected and favored producer, may collect it." "I do not need to tax the consumer for myself, but I will hold him for you while you tax him."

(F) "A Protective Duty is not a Tax."

15. There are some who say that "a tariff is not a tax," or as one of them said before a Congressional Committee: "We do not like to call it so!" That certainly is the most humorous of all the funny things in the tariff controversy. If a tariff is not a tax, what is it? In what category does it belong? No protectionist has ever yet told. They seem to think of it as a thing by itself, a Power, a Force, a sort of Mumbo Jumbo whose special function it is to produce national prosperity. They do not appear to have analyzed it, or given themselves an account of it, sufficiently to know what kind of a thing it is or how it acts. Any one who says that it is not a tax must suppose that it costs nothing, that it produces an effect without an expenditure of energy. They do seem to think that if Congress will say: "Let a tax of —— per cent be laid on article A," and if none is imported, and therefore no tax is paid at the custom house, national industry will be benefited and wealth secured, and that there will be no cost or outgo. If that is so, then the tariff is magic. We have found the philosopher's stone. Our congressmen wave a magic wand over the country and say: "Not otherwise provided for, one hundred and fifty per cent," and, presto! there we have wealth. Again they say: "Fifty cents a yard and fifty per cent *ad valorem*"; and there we have prosperity! If we should build a wall along the coast to keep foreigners and their goods out, it would cost something. If we maintained a navy to blockade our own coast for the same

purpose, it would cost something. Yet it is imagined that if we do the same by a tax it costs nothing.

16. This is the fundamental fallacy of protection to which the analysis will bring us back again and again. Scientifically stated, it is that *protectionism sins against the conservation of energy.* More simply stated, it is that *the protectionist either never sees or does not tell the other side of the account, the cost, the outlay for the gains which he alleges from protection, and that when these are examined and weighed they are sure vastly to exceed the gains, if the gains were real,* even taking no account of the harm to national growth which is done by restriction and interference.

17. There are only three ways in which a man can part with his product, and different kinds of taxes fall under different modes of alienating one's goods. First, he may exchange his product for the product of others. Then he parts with his property voluntarily, and for an equivalent. Taxes which are paid for peace, order, and security, fall under this head. Secondly, he may give his product away. Then he parts with it voluntarily without an equivalent. Taxes which are voluntarily paid for schools, libraries, parks, etc., fall under this head. Thirdly, he may be robbed of it. Then he parts with it involuntarily and without an equivalent. Taxes which are protective fall under this head. The analysis is exhaustive, and there is no other place for them. Protective taxes are those which a man pays to his neighbor to hire him (the neighbor) to carry on his own business. The first man gets no equivalent (§ 108). Hence any one who says that a tariff is not a tax would have to put it in some such category as tribute, plunder, or robbery. In order, then, that we may not give any occasion for even an unjust charge of using hard words, let us go back and call it a tax.

18. In any case it is plain that *we have before us the case of two Americans.* The protectionists who try to discuss

the subject always go off to talk English politics and history, or Ireland, or India, or Turkey. I shall not follow them. I shall discuss the case between two Americans, which is the only case there is. Whether Englishmen like our tariff or not is of no consequence. As a matter of fact, Englishmen seem to have come to the opinion that if Americans will take their own home market as their share, and will keep out of the world's market, they (the Englishmen) will agree to the arrangement; but it is immaterial whether they agree, or are angry. The only question for us is: What kind of an arrangement is it for one American to tax another American? How does it work? Who gains by it? How does it affect our national prosperity? These and these only are the questions which I intend to discuss.

19. I shall adopt *two different lines of investigation.* First, I shall examine protectionism on its own claims and pretensions, taking its doctrines and claims for true, and following them out to see whether they will produce the promised results; and secondly, I shall attack protectionism adversely, and controversially. If any one proposes a device for the public good, he is entitled to candid and patient attention, but he is also under obligation to show how he expects his scheme to work, what forces it will bring into play, how it will use them, etc. The joint stock principle, credit institutions, coöperation, and all similar devices must be analyzed and the explanation of their advantage, if they offer any, must be sought in the principles which they embody, the forces they employ, the suitableness of their apparatus. We ought not to put faith in any device (*e.g.*, bi-metalism, socialism) unless the proposers offer an explanation of it which will bear rigid and pitiless examination; for, if it is a sound device, such examination will only produce more and more thorough conviction of its merits. I shall therefore first take up protectionism

just as it is offered, and test it, as any candid inquirer might do, to see whether, as it is presented by its advocates, it has any claims to confidence.

CHAPTER II

PROTECTIONISM EXAMINED ON ITS OWN GROUNDS

20. It is the peculiar irony in all empirical devices in social science that they not only fail of the effect expected of them, but that they produce the exact opposite. Paper money is expected to help the non-capitalist and the debtor and to make business brisk. It ruins the non-capitalists and the debtors, and reduces industry and commerce to a standstill. Socialistic devices are expected to bring about equality and universal happiness. They produce despotism, favoritism, inequality, and universal misery. The devices are, in their operation, true to themselves. They act just as an unprejudiced examination of them should have led any one to expect that they would act, or just as a limited experience has shown that they must act. If protectionism is only another case of the same kind, an examination of it on its own grounds must bring out the fact that it will issue in crippling industry, diminishing capital, and lowering the average of comfort. Let us see.

(A) ASSUMPTIONS IN PROTECTIONISM.

21. Obviously the doctrine includes two assumptions. The first is, that if we are left to ourselves, each to choose, under liberty, his line of industrial effort, and to use his labor and capital, under the circumstances of the country, as best he can, we shall fail of our highest prosperity. Secondly, that, if Congress will only tax us (properly) we can be led up to higher prosperity. Hence it is at once

evident that free trade and protection here are not on a level. No free trader will affirm that he has a device for making the country rich, or saving it from hard times, any more than a respectable physician will tell us that he can give us specifics and preventives to keep us well. On the contrary, so long as men live they will do foolish things, and they will have to bear the penalty; but if they are free, they will commit only the follies which are their own, and they will bear the penalties only of those. The protectionist begins with the premise that we shall make mistakes, and that is why he, who knows how to make us go right, proposes to take us in hand. He is like the doctor who can give us just the pill we need to "cleanse our blood" and "ward off chills." *Hence either prosperity in a free-trade country, or distress in a protectionist country, is fatal to protectionism,* while distress in a free-trade country, or prosperity in a protectionist country proves nothing against free trade. Hence the fallacy of all Mr. R. P. Porter's letters is obvious. (§§ 52, 92, 102, 154.)

22. The device by which we are to be made better than ourselves is to select some of ourselves, who certainly are not the best business men among ourselves, to go to Washington, and there turn around and tax ourselves blindly, or, if not blindly, craftily and selfishly. Surely this would be the triumph of stupidity and ignorance over intelligent knowledge, enterprise and energy. The motive which would control each of us, if we were free, would be the hope of the greatest gain. We should have to put industry, prudence, economy, and enterprise into our business. If we failed, it would be through error. How is the congressional interference to act? How is it to meet and correct our error? It can appeal to no other motive than desire for profit, and can only offer us a profit where there was none before, if we will turn out of the industry which we have selected, into one which we do not know. It offers a

greater profit there only by means of what it takes from somebody else and somewhere else. Or, is congressional interference to correct the errors of John, James and William, and to make the idle, industrious, and the extravagant prudent? Any one who believes it must believe that the welfare of mankind is not dependent on the reason and conscience of the interested persons themselves, but on the caprices of blundering ignorance, embodied in a selected few, or on the trickery of lobbyists, acting impersonally and at a distance.

(B) Necessary Conditions of Successful Protective Legislation.

23. Suppose, however, that it were true that Congress had the power (by some exercise of the taxing function) to influence favorably the industrial development of the country: is it not true that men of sense would demand to be satisfied on three points, as follows?

24. (a) If Congress can do this thing, and is going to try it, *ought it not, in order to succeed, to have a distinct idea of what it is aiming at and proposes to do?* Who would have confidence in any man who should set out on an enterprise and who did not satisfy this condition? Has Congress ever satisfied it? Never. They have never had any plan or purpose in their tariff legislation. Congress has simply laid itself open to be acted upon by the interested parties, and the product of its tariff legislation has been simply the resultant of the struggles of the interested cliques with each other, and of the log-rolling combinations which they have been forced to make among themselves. In 1882 Congress did pay some deference, real or pretended, to the plain fact that it was bound, if it exercised this mighty power and responsibility, to bring some intelligence to bear on it, and it appointed a Tariff Commission which

spent several months in collecting evidence. This Commission was composed, with one exception, of protectionists. It recommended a reduction of twenty-five per cent in the tariff, and said: "Early in its deliberations the Commission became convinced that a substantial reduction of tariff duties is demanded, not by a mere indiscriminate popular clamor, but by the best conservative opinion of the country." "Excessive duties are positively injurious to the interests which they are supposed to benefit. They encourage the investment of capital in manufacturing enterprises by rash and unskilled speculators, to be followed by disaster to the adventurers and their employees, and a plethora of commodities which deranges the operations of skilled and prudent enterprise." (§ 111.) This report was entirely thrown aside, and Congress, ignoring it entirely, began again in exactly the old way. The Act of 1883 was not even framed by or in Congress. It was carried out into the dark, into a conference committee,[1] where new and gross abuses were put into the bill under cover of a pretended revision and reduction. When a tariff bill is before Congress, the first draft starts with a certain rate on a certain article, say twenty per cent. It is raised by amendment to fifty, the article is taken into a combination and the rate put up to eighty per cent; the bill is sent to the other house, and the rate on this article cut down again to forty per cent; on conference between the two houses the rate is fixed at sixty per cent. He who believes in the protectionist doctrine must, if he looks on at that proceeding, believe that the prosperity of the country is being kicked around the floor of Congress, at the mercy of the chances which are at last to determine with what per cent of tax these articles will come out. And what is it that determines with what tax any given article will come out? Any intelligent knowledge of industry? Not a word of it. Nothing

[1] Taussig: "History of the Existing Tariff," 78 ff.

in the case of a given tax on a given article, but just this: "Who is behind it?" The history of tariff legislation by the Congress of the United States throws a light upon the protective doctrine which is partly grotesque and partly revolting.

25. (b) If Congress can exert the supposed beneficent influence on industry, *ought not Congress to understand the force which it proposes to use?* Ought it not to have some rules of protective legislation so as to know in what cases, within what limits, under what conditions, the device can be effectively used? Would that not be a reasonable demand to make of any man who should propose a device for any purpose? Congress has never had any knowledge of the way in which the taxes which it passed were to do this beneficent work. It has never had, and has never seemed to think that it needed to get, any knowledge of the mode of operation of protective taxes. It passes taxes, as big as the conflicting interests will allow, and goes home, satisfied that it has saved the country. What a pity that philosophers, economists, sages, and moralists should have spent so much time in elucidating the conditions and laws of human prosperity! Taxes can do it all.

26. (c) If Congress can do what is affirmed and is going to try it, is it not the part of common sense to demand that *some tests be applied to the experiment after a few years to see whether it is really doing as was expected?* In the campaign of 1880 it was said that if Hancock was elected we should have free trade, wages would fall, factories would be closed, etc. Hancock was not elected, we did not get any reform of the tariff, and yet in 1884 wages were falling, factories were closed, and all the other direful consequences which were threatened had come to pass. *Bradstreet's* made investigations in the winter of 1884–1885 which showed that 316,000 workmen, thirteen per cent of the number employed in manufacturing in 1880, were out of work, 17,550 on strike,

and that wages had fallen since 1882 from ten to forty per cent, especially in the leading lines of manufacturing which are protected. What did these calamities all prove then? If we had had any revision of the tariff, should we not have had these things alleged again and again as results of it? Did they not, then, in the actual case, prove the folly of protection? Oh, no! that would be attacking the sacred dogma, and the sacred dogma is a matter of faith, so that, as it never had any foundation in fact or evidence, it has just as much after the experiment has failed as before the experiment was made.

27. If, now, it were possible to devise a scheme of legislation which should, according to protectionist ideas, be just the right jacket of taxation to fit this country to-day, *how long would it fit?* Not a week. Here are certain millions of people on three and a half million square miles of land. Every day new lines of communication are opened, new discoveries made, new inventions produced, new processes applied, and the consequence is that the industrial system is in constant flux and change. How, if a correct system of protective taxes was a practicable thing at any given moment, could Congress keep up with the changes and readaptations which would be required?   The notion is preposterous, and it is a monstrous thing, even on the protectionist hypothesis, that we are living under a protective system which was set up in 1864. The weekly tariff decisions by the treasury department may be regarded as the constant attempts that are required to fit that old system to present circumstances, and, as it is not possible that new fabrics, new compounds, and new processes should find a place in schedules which were made twenty years before they were invented, those decisions carry with them the fate of scores of new industries which figure in no census, and are taken into account by no congressman.   Therefore, even if we believed that the protective doctrine was sound

and that some protective system was beneficial, and that the one which we have was the right one when it was made, we should be driven to the conclusion that one which is twenty years old is sure to be injurious to-day.

28. There is nothing then in the legislative machinery by which the tariff is to be made which is calculated to win the confidence of a man of sense, but everything to the contrary; and the experiments of such legislation which have been made have produced nothing but warnings against the device. Instead of offering any reasonable ground for belief that our errors will be corrected and our productive powers increased, an examination of the tariff as a piece of legislation offers to us nothing but a burden, which must cripple any economic power which we have.

(C) Examination of the Means Proposed, *viz.*, Taxes.

29. Every tax is a burden, and in the nature of the case can be nothing else. In mathematical language, every tax is a quantity affected by a minus sign. If it gets peace and security, that is, if it represses crime and injustice and prevents discord, which would be economically destructive, then it is a smaller minus quantity than the one which would otherwise be there, and that is the gain by good government. Hence, like every other outlay which we make, taxes must be controlled by the law of economy — to get the best and most possible for the least expenditure. Instead of regarding public expenditure carelessly, we should watch it jealously. Instead of looking at taxation as conceivably a good, and certainly not an ill, we should regard every tax as on the defensive, and every cent of tax as needing justification. If the statesman exacts any more than is necessary to pay for good government economically administered, he is incompetent, and fails in his

duty. I have been studying political economy almost exclusively for the last fifteen years, and when I look back over that period and ask myself what is the most marked effect which I can perceive on my own opinion, or on my standpoint, as to social questions, I find that it is this: I am convinced that nobody yet understands the multiplied and complicated effects which are produced by taxation. I am under the most profound impression of the mischief which is done by taxation, reaching, as it does, to every dinner-table and to every fireside. *The effects of taxation vary with every change in the industrial system and the industrial status*, and they are so complicated that it is impossible to follow, analyze, and systematize them; but out of the study of the subject there arises this firm conviction: taxation is crippling, shortening, reducing all the time, over and over again.

30. Suppose that a man has an income of one thousand dollars, of which he has been saving one hundred dollars per annum with no tax. Now a tax of ten dollars is demanded of him, no matter what kind of a tax or how laid. Is he to get the tax out of the nine hundred dollars expenditure or out of the one hundred dollars savings? If the former, then he must cut down his diet, or his clothing, or his house accommodation, that is, lower his standard of comfort. If the latter, then he must lessen his accumulation of capital, that is, his provision for the future. Either way his welfare is reduced and cannot be otherwise affected, and, through the general effect, the welfare of the community is reduced by the tax. Of course it is immaterial that he may not know the facts. The effects are the same. In this view of the matter it is plain what mischief is done by taxes which are laid to buy parks, libraries, and all sorts of grand things. The tax-layer is not providing public order. He is spending other people's earnings for them. He is deciding that his neighbor shall have less clothes and

more library or park. But when we come to protective taxes the abuse is monstrous. The legislator who has in his hands this power of taxation uses it to say that one citizen shall have less clothes in order that he may contribute to the profits of another citizen's private business.

31. Hence if we look at the nature of taxation, and if we are examining protectionism from its own standpoint, under the assumption that it is true, instead of finding any confirmation of its assumptions, in the nature of the means which it proposes to use, we find the contrary. Granting that people make mistakes and fail of the highest prosperity which they might win when they act freely, we see plainly that more taxes cannot help to lift them up or to correct their errors; on the contrary, *all taxation, beyond what is necessary for an economical administration of good government, is either luxurious or wasteful,* and if such taxation could tend to wealth, waste would make wealth.

(D) EXAMINATION OF THE PLAN OF MUTUAL TAXATION.

32. Suppose then that the industries and sections all begin to tax each other as we see that they do under protection. Is it not plain that the taxing operation can do nothing but *transfer* products, never by any possibility create them? The object of the protective taxes is to "effect the diversion of a part of the capital and labor of the country from the channels in which it would run otherwise." To do this it must find a fulcrum or point of reaction, or it can exert no force for the effect it desires. The fulcrum is furnished by those who pay the tax. Take a case. Pennsylvania taxes New England on every ton of iron and coal used in its industries. Ohio taxes New England on all the wool obtained from that state for its

industries.[1] New England taxes Ohio and Pennsylvania on
all the cottons and woolens which it sells to them. What
is the net final result? It is mathematically certain that
the only result can be that (1) New England gets back
just all she paid (in which case the system is nil, save for
the expense of the process and the limitation it imposes on
the industry of all), or, (2) that New England does not get
back as much as she paid (in which case she is tributary to
the others), or, (3) that she gets back more than she paid
(in which case she levies tribute on them). Yet, on the
protectionist notion, this system extended to all sections,
and embracing all industries, is the means of producing
national prosperity. When it is all done, what does it
amount to except that *all Americans must support all
Americans?* How can they do it better than for each to
support himself to the best of his ability? Then, however,
all the assumptions of protectionism must be abandoned
as false.

33. In 1676 King Charles II granted to his natural son,
the Duke of Richmond, a tax of a shilling a chaldron on
all the coal which was exported from the Tyne. We regard such a grant as a shocking abuse of the taxing power.
It is, however, a very interesting case because the mine
owner and the tax owner were two separate persons, and
the tax can be examined in all its separate iniquity. If,
as I suppose was the case, the Tyne Valley possessed such
superior facilities for producing coal that it had a qualified
monopoly, the tax fell on the coal mine owner (landlord);
that is, the king transferred to his son part of the property
which belonged to the Tyne coal owners. In that view the

---

[1] The wool growers held a convention at St. Louis May 28, 1885, at which they
estimated their loss by the reduction of the tax on wool in 1883, or the *difference*
between what they got by this tax before that date and after, at ninety million
dollars (New York *Times*, May 29). If that sum is what they lost, it is what the
consumers gained. They are very angry, and will not vote for any one who will
not help to re-subject the consumers to this tribute to them.

case may come home to some of our protectionists as it
would not if the tax had fallen on the consumers.   If Congress had pensioned General Grant by giving him seventy-
five cents a ton on all the coal mined in the Lehigh Valley,
what protests we should have heard from the owners of
coal lands in that district! If the king's son, however, had
owned the coal mines, and worked them himself, and if the
king had said: "I will authorize you to raise the price of
your coal a shilling a chaldron, and, to enable you to do it,
I will myself tax all coal but yours a shilling a chaldron,"
then the device would have been modern and enlightened
and American.   We have done just that on emery, copper,
and nickel.   Then the tax comes out of the consumer.
Then it is not, according to the protectionist, harmful, but
the key to national prosperity, the thing which corrects
the errors of our incompetent self-will, and leads us up
to better organization of our industry than we, in our
unguided stupidity, could have made.

(E) Examination of the Proposal to "Create an Industry."

34. The protectionist says, however, that he is going to
create an industry.   Let us examine this notion also from
his standpoint, assuming the truth of his doctrine, and see
if we can find anything to deserve confidence.   A protective tax, according to the protectionist's definition (§ 13),
"has for its object to effect the diversion of a part of the
labor and capital of the people . . . into channels favored or
created by law."   If we follow out this proposal, we shall
see what those channels are, and shall see whether they
are such as to make us believe that protective taxes can
increase wealth.

35. *What is an industry?*   Some people will answer: It
is an enterprise which gives employment.   Protectionists

seem to hold this view, and they claim that they "give work" to laborers when they make an industry. On that notion we live to work; we do not work to live. But we do not want work. We have too much work. We want a living; and work is the inevitable but disagreeable price we must pay. Hence we want as much living at as little price as possible. We shall see that the protectionist does "make work" in the sense of lessening the living and increasing the price. But if we want a living we want capital. If an industry is to pay wages, it must be backed up by capital. Therefore protective taxes, if they were to increase the means of living, would need to increase capital. How can taxes increase capital? Protective taxes only take from A to give to B. Therefore, if B by this arrangement can extend his industry and "give more employment," A's power to do the same is diminished in at least an equal degree. Therefore, even on that erroneous definition of an industry, there is no hope for the protectionist.

36. *An industry is an organization of labor and capital for satisfying some need of the community.* It is not an end in itself. It is not a good thing to have in itself. It is not a toy or an ornament. If we could satisfy our needs without it we should be better off, not worse off. How, then, can we create industries?

37. If any one will find, in the soil of a district, some new power to supply human needs, he can endow that district with a new industry. If he will invent a mode of treating some natural deposit, ore or clay, for instance, so as to provide a tool or utensil which is cheaper and more convenient than what is in use, he can create an industry. If he will find out some new and better way to raise cattle or vegetables, which is, perhaps, favored by the climate, he can do the same. If he invents some new treatment of wool, or cotton, or silk, or leather, or makes a new combination which produces a more convenient or attractive

fabric, he may do the same. The telephone is a new industry. What measures the gain of it? Is it the "employment" of certain persons in and about telephone offices? The gain is in the satisfaction of the need of communication between people at less cost of time and labor. It is useless to multiply instances. It can be seen what it is to "create an industry." It takes brains and energy to do it. How can taxes do it?

38. Suppose that we create an industry even in this sense — *What is the gain of it?* The people of Connecticut are now earning their living by employing their labor and capital in certain parts of the industrial organization. They have changed their "industries" a great many times. If it should be found that they had a new and better chance hitherto undeveloped, they might all go into it. To do that they must abandon what they are now doing. They would not change unless gains to be made in the new industry were greater. Hence the gain is the *difference* only between the profits of the old and the profits of the new. The protectionists, however, when they talk about "creating an industry," seem to suppose that the total profit of the industry (and some of them seem to think that the total expenditure of capital) measures their good work. In any case, then, even of a true and legitimate increase of industrial power and opportunity, the only gain would be a margin. But, by our definition, "a protective duty has for its object to effect the diversion of a part of the capital and labor of the people out of the channels in which it would otherwise run." Plainly this device involves coercion. People would need no coercion to go into a new industry which had a natural origin in new industrial power or opportunity. No coercion is necessary to make men buy dollars at ninety-eight cents apiece. The case for coercion is when it is desired to make them buy dollars at one hundred and one cents apiece. Here the statesman with his

taxing power is needed, and can do something. What?
He can say: "If you will buy a dollar at one hundred
and one cents, I can and will tax John over there two
cents for your benefit; one to make up your loss and the
other to give you a profit." Hence, *on the protectionist's
own doctrine*, his device is not needed, and cannot come
into use, when a new industry is created in the true and
only reasonable sense of the words, but *only when and
because he is determined to drive the labor and capital of
the country into a disadvantageous and wasteful employment.*

39. Still further, it is obvious that the protectionist,
instead of "creating a new industry," has *simply taken one
industry and set it as a parasite to live upon another.* Industry is its own reward. A man is not to be paid a premium by his neighbors for earning his own living. A
factory, an insane asylum, a school, a church, a poorhouse,
and a prison cannot be put in the same economic category.
We know that the community must be taxed to support
insane asylums, poorhouses, and jails. When we come
upon such institutions we see them with regret. They are
wasting capital. We know that the industrious people all
about, who are laboring and producing, must part with a
portion of their earnings to supply the waste and loss of
these institutions. Hence *the bigger they are the sadder they
are.*

40. As for the schools and churches, we know that
society must pay for and keep up its own conservative institutions. They cost capital and do not pay back capital
directly, although they do indirectly, and in the course of
time, in ways which we could trace out and verify if that
were our subject. Here, then, we have a second class of
institutions.

41. But the factories and farms and foundries are the
productive institutions which must provide the support of
these consuming institutions. If the factories, etc., put

themselves on a line with the poorhouses, or even with the schools, what is to support them and all the rest too? They have nothing behind them. If in any measure or way they turn into burdens and objects of care and protection, they can plainly do it only by part of them turning upon the other part, and this latter part will have to bear the burden of all the consuming institutions, *including the consuming industries.* For a protected factory is not a producing industry. *It is a consuming industry!* If a factory is (as the protectionist alleges) a triumph of the tariff, that is, if it would not be but for the tariff (and otherwise he has nothing to do with it), then it is not producing; it is consuming. It is a burden to be borne. *The bigger it is the sadder it is.*

42. If a protectionist shows me a woolen mill and challenges me to deny that it is a great and valuable industry, I ask him whether it is due to the tariff. If he says "no," then I will assume that it is an independent and profitable establishment, but in that case it is out of this discussion as much as a farm or a doctor's practice. If he says "yes," then I answer that the mill is not an industry at all. We pay sixty per cent tax on cloth *simply in order that that mill may be.* It is not an institution for getting us cloth, for if we went into the market with the same products which we take there now and if there were no woolen mill, we should get all the cloth we want. The mill is simply *an institution for making cloth cost per yard sixty per cent more of our products than it otherwise would.* That is the one and only function which the mill has added, by its existence, to the situation. I have called such a factory a "nuisance." The word has been objected to. The word is of no consequence. He who, when he goes into a debate, begins to whine and cry as soon as the blows get sharp, should learn to keep out. What I meant was this: A nuisance is something which by its existence and presence in society works

loss and damage to the society — works against the general interest, not for it. A factory which gets in the way and hinders us from attaining the comforts which we are all trying to get — which makes harder the terms of acquisition when we are all the time struggling by our arts and sciences to make those terms easier — is a harmful thing, and noxious to the common interest.

43. Hence, once more, starting from the protectionist's hypothesis, and assuming his own doctrine, we find that he cannot create an industry. He only fixes one industry as a parasite upon another, and just as certainly as he has intervened in the matter at all, just so certainly has he forced labor and capital into less favorable employment than they would have sought if he had let them alone. When we ask which "channels" those are which are to be "favored or created by law," we find that they are, by the hypothesis, and by the whole logic of the protectionist system, *the industries which do not pay*. The protectionists propose to make the country rich by laws which shall favor or create these industries, but these industries can only waste capital, so that if they are the source of wealth, *waste is the source of wealth*. Hence the protectionist's assumption that by his system he could correct our errors and lead us to greater prosperity than we would have obtained under liberty, has failed again, and we find that he wastes what power we do possess.

(*F*) EXAMINATION OF THE PROPOSAL TO DEVELOP OUR NATURAL RESOURCES.

44. "But," says the protectionist, "do you mean to say that, if we have an iron deposit in our soil, it is not wise for us to open and work it?" "You mean, no doubt," I reply, "open and work it *under protective help and stimulus;* for, if there is an iron deposit, the United States does not

own it. Some man owns it. If he wants to open and work it, we have nothing to do but wish him God-speed." "Very well," he says, "understand it that he needs protection." Let us examine this case, then, and still we will do it assuming the truth of the protectionist doctrine. Let us see where we shall come out.

The man who has discovered iron (on the protectionist doctrine), when there is no tax, does not collect tools and laborers and go to work. He goes to Washington. He visits the statesman, and a dialogue takes place.

Iron man. — "Mr. Statesman, I have found an iron deposit on my farm."

Statesman. — "Have you, indeed? That is good news. Our country is richer by one new natural resource than we have supposed."

Iron man. — "Yes, and I now want to begin mining iron."

Statesman. — "Very well, go on. We shall be glad to hear that you are prospering and getting rich."

Iron man. — "Yes, of course. But I am now earning my living by tilling the surface of the ground, and I am afraid that I cannot make as much at mining as at farming."

Statesman. — "That is indeed another matter. Look into that carefully and do not leave a better industry for a worse."

Iron man. — "But I want to mine that iron. It does not seem right to leave it in the ground when we are importing iron all the time, but I cannot see as good profits in it at the present price for imported iron as I am making out of what I raise on the surface. I thought that perhaps you would put a tax on all the imported iron so that I could get more for mine. Then I could see my way to give up farming and go to mining."

Statesman. — "You do not think what you ask. That would be authorizing you to tax your neighbors, and would be throwing on them the risk of working your mine, which you are afraid to take yourself."

Iron man (aside). — "I have not talked the right dialect to this man. I must begin all over again. (Aloud.) Mr. Statesman, the natural resources of this continent ought to be developed. American industry must be protected. The American laborer must not be forced to compete with the pauper labor of Europe."

Statesman. — "Now I understand you. Now you talk business. Why did you not say so before? How much tax do you want?"

The next time that a buyer of pig iron goes to market to get some, he finds that it costs thirty bushels of wheat per ton instead of twenty.

"What has happened to pig iron?" says he.

"Oh! haven't you heard?" is the reply. "A new mine has been found down in Pennsylvania. We have got a new 'natural resource.'"

"I haven't got a new 'natural resource,'" says he. "It is as bad for me as if the grasshoppers had eaten up one-third of my crop."

45. That is just exactly the significance of a new resource on the protectionist doctrine. We had the misfortune to find emery here. At once a tax was put on it which made it cost more wheat, cotton, tobacco, petroleum, or personal services per pound than ever before. A new calamity befell us when we found the richest copper mines in the world in our territory. From that time on it cost us five (now four) cents a pound more than before. By another catastrophe we found a nickel mine — thirty cents (now fifteen) a pound tax! Up to this time we have had all the tin that we wanted above ground, because beneficent nature has refrained from putting any underground in our territory. In the metal schedule, where the metals which we unfortunately possess are taxed from

forty to sixty per cent, tin alone is free. Every little while a report is started that tin has been found. Hitherto these reports have happily all proved false. It is now said that tin has been found in West Virginia and Dakotah. We have reason devoutly to hope that this may prove false, for, if it should prove true, no doubt the next thing will be forty per cent tax on tin. The mine-owners say that they want to exploit the mine. They do not. They want to make the mine an excuse to exploit the taxpayers.

46. Therefore, when the protectionist asks whether we ought not by protective taxes to force the development of our own iron mines, the answer is that, on his own doctrine, he has developed a new philosophy, hitherto unknown, by which "natural resources" become national calamities, and the more a country is endowed by nature the worse off it is. Of course, if the wise philosophy is not simply to use, with energy and prudence, all the natural opportunities which we possess, but to seek "channels favored or created by law," then this view of natural resources is perfectly consistent with that philosophy, for it is simply saying over again that *waste is the key of wealth.*

(G) Examination of the Proposal to Raise Wages.

47. "But," he says again, "we want to raise wages and favor the poor working man." "Do you mean to say," I reply, "that protective taxes raise wages — that that is their regular and constant effect?" "Yes," he replies, "that is just what they do, and that is why we favor them. We are the poor man's friends. You free-traders want to reduce him to the level of the pauper laborers of Europe." "But here, in the evidence offered at the last tariff discussion in Congress, the employers all said that they wanted the taxes to protect them *because* they had to pay such high wages." "Well, so they do." "Well then, if they

get the taxes raised to help them out when they have high wages to pay, how are the taxes going to help them any unless the taxes *lower* wages? But you just said that taxes raise wages. Therefore, if the employer gets the taxes raised, he will no sooner get home from Washington than he will find that the very taxes which he has just secured have raised wages. Then he must go back to Washington to get the taxes raised to offset that advance, and when he gets home again he will find that he has only raised wages more, and so on forever. You are trying to teach the man to raise himself by his boot straps. Two of your propositions brought together eat each other."

48. We will, however, pursue the protectionist doctrine of wages a little further. It is totally false that protective taxes raise wages. As I will show further on (§ 91 and following), protective taxes lower wages. Now, however, I am assuming the protectionist's own premises and doctrines all the time. He says that his system raises wages. Let us go to see some of the wages class and get some evidence on this point. We will take three wage-workers, a boot man, a hat man, and a cloth man. First we ask the boot man, "Do you win anything by this tariff?" "Yes," he says, "I understand that I do." "How?" "Well, the way they explain it to me is that when anybody wants boots he goes to my boss, pays him more on account of the tax, and my boss gives me part of it." "All right! Then your comrades here, the hat man and the cloth man, pay this tax in which you share?" "Yes, I suppose so. I never thought of that before. I supposed that rich people paid the taxes, but I suppose that when they buy boots they must do it too." "And when you want a hat you go and pay the tax on hats, part of which (as you explain the system) goes to your friend the hat man; and when you want cloth you pay the tax which goes to benefit your friend the cloth man?" "I suppose that it must

be so." We go, then, to see the hat man and have the same conversation with him, and we go to see the cloth man and have the same conversation with him. Each of them then gets two taxes and pays two taxes. Three men illustrate the whole case. If we should take a thousand men in a thousand industries we should find that each paid nine hundred and ninety-nine taxes, and each got nine hundred and ninety-nine taxes, if the system worked as it is said to work. What is the upshot of the whole? Either they all come out even on their taxes paid and received, or *some of the wage receivers are winning something out of other wage receivers to the net detriment of the whole class.* If each man is creditor for nine hundred and ninety-nine taxes, and each debtor for nine hundred and ninety-nine taxes, and if the system is "universal and equal," we can save trouble by each drawing nine hundred and ninety-nine orders on the creditors to pay to themselves their own taxes, and we can set up a clearing house to wipe off all the accounts. Then we come down to this as the net result of the system when it is "universal and equal," that *each man as a consumer pays taxes to himself as a producer.* That is what is to make us all rich. We can accomplish it just as well and far more easily, when we get up in the morning, by transferring our cash from one pocket to the other.

49. One point, however, and the most important of all, remains to be noticed. How about the thousandth tax? How is it when the boot man wants boots, and the hat man hats, and the cloth man cloth? He has to go to the store on the street and buy of his own boss, at the market price (tax on), the very things which he made himself in the shop. He then pays the tax to his own employer, and the employer, according to the doctrine, "shares" it with him. Where is the offset to that part which the employer keeps? There is none. The wages class, even on the protectionist explanation, may give or take from each other,

but to their own employers they give and take not. At election time the boss calls them in and tells them that they must vote for protection or he must shut up the shop, and that they ought to vote for protection, because it makes their wages high. If, then, they believe in the system, just as it is taught to them, they must believe that it causes him to pay them big wages, out of which they pay back to him big taxes, out of which he pays them a fraction back again, and that, but for this arrangement, the business could not go on at all. A little reflection shows that this just brings up the question for a wage-earner: *How much can I afford to pay my boss for hiring me?* or, again, which is just the same thing in other words: *What is the net reduction of my wages, below the market rate under freedom, which results from this system?* (See § 65.)

50. Let it not be forgotten that this result is reached by accepting protectionism and reasoning forward from its doctrines and according to its principles. In truth, the employees get no share in any taxes which the boss gets out of them and others (see § 91 ff. for the truth about wages). Of course, when this or any other subject is thoroughly analyzed, it makes no difference where we begin or what line we follow, we shall always reach the same result if the result is correct. If we accept the protectionist's own explanation of the way in which protection raises wages we find that it proves that protection lowers wages.

(*H*) EXAMINATION OF THE PROPOSAL TO PREVENT COMPETITION BY FOREIGN PAUPER LABOR.

51. The protectionist says that he does not want the American laborer to compete with the foreign "pauper laborer" (see § 99). He assumes that if the foreign laborer is a woolen operative, the only American who may have to compete with him is a woolen operative here. His device

for saving our operatives from the assumed competition is
to tax the American cotton or wheat grower on the cloth
he wears, to make up and offset to the woolen operative
the disadvantage under which he labors. If then, the case
were true as the protectionist states it, and if his remedy
were correct, he would, when he had finished his operation,
simply have allowed the American woolen operative to
escape, by transferring to the American cotton or wheat
grower the evil results of competition with "foreign pauper
labor."

(I) Examination of the Proposal to raise the Standard of Public Comfort.

52. But the protectionist reiterates that he wants to
make our people well off, and to diffuse general prosperity,
and he says that his system does this. He says that the
country has prospered under protection and on account of
it. He brings from the census the figures for increased
wealth of the country, and, to speak of no minor errors,
draws an inference that we have prospered *more than we
should have done under free trade*, which is what he has to
prove, without noticing that the second term of the comparison is absent and unattainable. In the same manner
I once heard a man argue from statistics, who showed by
the *small* loss of a city by fire that its fire department cost
too much. I asked him if he had any statistics of the fires
which we should have had but for the fire department
(see § 102).

53. The people of the United States have inherited an
untouched continent. The now living generation is practicing bonanza farming on prairie soil which has never
borne a crop. The population is only fifteen to the square
mile. The population of England and Wales is four hundred and forty-six to the square mile; that of the British

Islands two hundred and ninety; that of Belgium four hundred and eighty-one; of France one hundred and eighty; of Germany two hundred and sixteen. Bateman [1] estimates that in the better part of England or Wales a peasant proprietor would need from four and a half to six acres, and, in the worse part, from nine to forty-five acres on which to support "a healthy family." The soil of England and Wales, equally divided between the families there, would give only seven acres apiece. The land of the United States, equally divided between the families there, would give two hundred and fifteen acres apiece. These old nations give us the other term of the comparison by which we measure our prosperity. They have a dense population on a soil which has been used for thousands of years; we have an extremely sparse population on a virgin soil. We have an excellent climate, mountains full of coal and ore, natural highways on the rivers and lakes, and a coast indented with sounds, bays, and some of the best harbors in the world. We have also a population of good national character, especially as regards the economic and industrial virtues. The sciences and arts are highly cultivated among us, and our institutions are the best for the development of economic strength. As compared with old nations we are prosperous. Now comes the protectionist statesman and says: "The things which you have enumerated are not the causes of our comparative prosperity. Those things are all vain. Our prosperity is not due to them. I made it with my taxes."

54. (a) In the first place the fact is that we surpass most in prosperity those nations which are most like us in their tax systems, and those compared with whom our prosperity is least remarkable are those which have by free trade offset as much as possible the disadvantage of age and dense population. Since, then, we find greatest difference in

---

[1] Broderick, "English Land and English Landlords," p. 194.

prosperity with least difference in tax, and least difference in prosperity with greatest difference in tax, we cannot regard tax as a cause of prosperity, but as an obstacle to prosperity which must have been overcome by some stronger cause. That such is the case lies plainly on the face of the facts. The prosperity which we enjoy is the prosperity which God and nature have given us *minus what the legislator has taken from it.*

55. (*b*) We prospered with slavery just as we have prospered with protection. The argument that the former was a cause would be just as strong as the argument that the latter is a cause.

56. (*c*) The protectionists take to themselves as a credit all the advance in the arts of the last twenty-five years, because they have not entirely offset it and destroyed it.

57. (*d*) The protectionists claim that they have increased our wealth. All the wealth that is produced must be produced by labor and capital applied to land. The people have wrought and produced. The tax gatherer has only subtracted something. Whether he used what he took well or ill, he subtracted. He could not do anything else. Therefore, whatever wealth we see about us, and whatever wealth appears in the census is what the people have produced, *less* what the tax gatherer has taken out of it.

58. (*e*) If the members of Congress can establish for themselves some ideal of the grade of comfort which the average American citizen ought to enjoy, and then just get it for him, they have used their power hitherto in a very beggarly manner. For, although the average status of our people is high when compared with that of other people on the globe, nevertheless, when compared with any standard of ideal comfort, it leaves much to be desired. If Congress has the power supposed, they surely ought not to measure the exercise of it by only making us better off than Europeans.

59. (*f*) During the late presidential campaign the pro-

tectionist orators assured the people that they meant to make everybody well off, that they wished our people to be prosperous, contented, etc. I wish so too. I wish that all my readers may be millionaires. I freely and sincerely confer on them all the bounty of my good wishes. They will not find a cent more in their pockets on that account. The congressmen have no power to bless my readers which I have not, save one; that is, the power to tax them.

60. (g) If the congressmen are determined to elevate the comfort of the population by taxing the population, then every new ship load of immigrants must be regarded as a new body of persons whom we must "elevate" by the taxes we have to pay. It is said that an Irishman affirmed that a dollar in America would not buy more than a shilling in Ireland. He was asked why then he did not stay in Ireland. He replied that it was because he could not get the shilling there. That is a good story, only it stops just where it ought to begin. The next question is: How does he get the dollar when he comes to America? The protectionist wants us to suppose that he gets it by grace of the tariff. If so he gets it out of those who were here before he came. But plainly no such thing is true. He gets it by earning it, and he adds two dollars to the wealth of the country while earning it. The only thing the tariff does in regard to it is to lower the purchasing power of the dollar, if it is spent for products of manufacture, to seventy cents.

61. Here, again, then, we find that protective taxes, if they do just what the protectionist says that they will do, produce the very opposite effects from those which he says they will produce. They lessen wealth, reduce prosperity, diminish average comfort, and lower the standard of living. (See § 30.)

Chapter III

PROTECTIONISM EXAMINED ADVERSELY

62. I have so far examined protectionism as a philosophy of national wealth, assuming and accepting its own doctrines, and following them out, to see if they will issue as is claimed. We have found that they do not, but that protectionism, on its own doctrines, issues in the impoverishment of the nation and in failure to do anything which it claims to do. On the contrary, an examination in detail of its means, methods, purposes, and plans shows that it must produce waste and loss, so that *if it were true, we should have to believe that waste and loss are means of wealth.* Now I turn about to attack it in face, on an open issue, for if any project which is advocated proves, upon free and fair examination, to be based on errors of fact and doctrine, it becomes a danger and an evil to be exposed and combated, and truth of fact and doctrine must be set against it.

1. *PROTECTIONISM INCLUDES AND NECESSARILY CARRIES WITH IT HOSTILITY TO TRADE OR, AT LEAST, SUSPICION AGAINST TRADE*

(A) Rules for Knowing when it is Safe to Trade.

63. Every protectionist is forced to regard trade as a mischievous or at least doubtful thing. Protectionists have even tried to formulate rules for determining when trade is beneficial and when harmful.

64. It has been said that we ought to trade only on meridians of longitude, not on parallels of latitude.

65. It has been affirmed that we cannot safely trade unless we have taxes to exactly offset the lower wages of foreign countries. But it is plain that if the case stands

so that an American employer says: "I am at a disadvantage compared with my foreign competitor, because he pays less wages than I" — then, by the same token, the American laborer will say: "I am at an advantage, compared with my foreign comrade, for I get better wages than he." If the law interferes with the state of things so that the employer is enabled to say: "I am now at less disadvantage in competition with my foreign rival, because I do not now have to pay as much more wages than he as formerly " — then, by the same token, the American laborer must say: "I am not now as much better off than my foreign comrade as formerly, for I do not now gain as much more than he as I did — there is not now as much advantage in emigrating to this country as formerly." Therefore, whenever the taxes just offset the difference in wages, *they just take away from the American laborer all his superiority over the foreigner*, and take away all reason for caring to come to this country. So much for the laborer. But the employer, if he has arrested immigration, has cut off one source of the supply of labor, tending to raise wages, and is at war with himself again (§ 47).

66. It has been said that two nations cannot trade *if the rate of interest in the two differs by two per cent.* The rate of interest in the Atlantic States and in the Mississippi Valley has always differed by two per cent, yet they have traded together under absolute free trade, and the Mississippi Valley has had to begin a wilderness and grow up to the highest standard of civilization in spite of that state of things.

67. It has been said that we ought to *trade only with inferior nations.* The United States does not trade with any other nation, save when it buys territory. A in the United States trades with B in some foreign country. If I want caoutchouc I want to trade with a savage in the forests of South America. If I want mahogany I want to

trade with a man in Honduras. If I want sugar I want to trade with a man in Cuba. If I want tea I want to trade with a man in China. If I want silk or champagne I want to trade with a man in France. If I want a razor I want to trade with a man in England. I want to trade with the man who has the thing which I want of the best quality and at the lowest rate of exchange for my products. What is the definition or test of an "inferior nation," and what has that got to do with trade any more than the race, language, color, or religion of the man who has the goods?

68. If trade was an object of suspicion and dread, then indeed we ought to have *rules for distinguishing safe and beneficial trade* from mischievous trade, but these attempts to define and discriminate only expose the folly of the suspicion. We find that the primitive men who dwelt in caves in the glacial epoch carried on trade. The earliest savages made footpaths through the forests by which to traffic and trade, winning thereby mutual advantages. They found that they could supply more wants with less effort by trade, which gave them a share in the natural advantages and acquired skill of others. They trained beasts of burden, improved roads, invented wagons and boats, all in order to extend and facilitate trade. They were foolish enough to think that they were gaining by it, *and did not know that they needed a protective tariff to keep them from ruining themselves.* Or, why does not some protectionist sociologist tell us at what stage of civilization trade ceases to be advantageous and begins to need restraint and regulation?

(B) Economic Units not National Units.

69. The protectionists say that their system advances civilization inside a state and makes it great, but the facts are all against them (see § 136 ff). It was by trade that civi-

lization was extended over the earth. It was through the contact of trade that the more civilized nations transmitted to others the alphabet, weights and measures, knowledge of astronomy, divisions of time, tools and weapons, coined money, systems of numeration, treatment of metals, skins, and wool, and all the other achievements of knowledge and invention which constitute the bases of our civilization. On the other hand, the nations which shut themselves up and developed an independent and self-contained civilization (China and Japan) present us the types of arrested civilization and stereotyped social status. It is the penalty of isolation and of withdrawal from the giving and taking which properly bind the whole human race together, that even such intelligent and highly endowed people as the Chinese should find their high activity arrested at narrow limitations on every side. They invent coin, but never get beyond a cast copper coin. They invent gunpowder, but cannot make a gun. They invent movable types, but only the most rudimentary book. They discover the mariner's compass, but never pass the infancy of ship-building.

70. The fact is, then, that *trade has been the handmaid of civilization*. It has traversed national boundaries, and has gradually, with improvement in the arts of transportation, drawn the human race into closer relations and more harmonious interests. The contact of trade slowly saps old national prejudice and religious or race hatreds. The jealousies which were perpetuated by distance and ignorance cannot stand before contact and knowledge. To stop trade is to arrest this beneficent work, to separate mankind into sections and factions, and to favor discord, jealousy, and war.

71. Such is the action of protectionism. The protectionists make much of their pretended "nationalism," and they try to reason out some kind of relationship be-

tween the scope of economic forces and the boundaries of existing nations. The argumentation is fatally broken at its first step. They do not show what they might show, *viz.*, that the scope of economic forces on any given stage of the arts does form economic units. An English county was such a unit a century ago. I doubt if anything less than the whole earth could be considered so to-day, when the wool of Australia, the hides of South America, the cotton of Alabama, the wheat of Manitoba, and the meat of Texas meet the laborers in Manchester and Sheffield, and would meet the laborers in Lowell and Paterson, if the barriers were out of the way. But what the national protectionist would need to show would be that the economic unit coincides with the political unit. He would have to affirm that Maine and Texas are in one economic unit, but that Maine and New Brunswick are not; or that Massachusetts and Minnesota are in one economic unit, but that Massachusetts and Manitoba are not. Every existing state is a product of historic accidents. Mr. Jefferson set out to buy the city of New Orleans. He awoke one morning to find that he had bought the western half of the Mississippi Valley. Since that turned out so, the protectionists think that Missouri and Illinois prosper by trading in perfect freedom.[1] If it had not turned out so, it would have been very mischievous for them to trade

---

[1] Since the above was in type, I have, for the first time, seen an argument from a protectionist, that a tariff between our states is, or may become, desirable. It is from the Chicago *Inter-Ocean*, and marks the extreme limit reached, up to this time, by protectionist fanaticism and folly, although it is thoroughly consistent, and fairly lays bare the spirit and essence of protectionism:

"In the United States the present ominous and overshadowing strike in the iron trade, by which from 75,000 to 100,000 men have been thrown out of work, is an incisive example of the tendency of this country, also, to a condition of trade which will compel individual states and certain sections of the country to ask for legislation, in order to protect them against the cheaper labor and superior natural advantage of others." The remedy for the harm done by taxes on our foreign trade is to lay some on our domestic trade. (See §§ 26, 95.)

in perfect freedom. Nova Scotia did not join the revolt of our thirteen colonies. Hence it is thought ruinous to let coal and potatoes come in freely from Nova Scotia. If she had revolted with us, it would have been for the benefit of everybody in this union to trade with her as freely as we now trade with Maine. We tried to conquer Canada in 1812–1813 and failed. Consequently the Canadians now put taxes on our coal and petroleum and wheat, and we put taxes on their lumber, which our coal and petroleum industries need. We did annex Texas, at the cost of war, in 1845. Consequently we trade with Texas now under absolute freedom, but, if we trade with Mexico, it must be only very carefully and under stringent limitations. Is this wisdom, or is it all pure folly and wrongheadedness, by which men who boast of their intelligence throw away their own chances? [1]

72. *Trade is a beneficent thing.* It does not need any regulation or restraint. There is no point at which it begins to be dangerous. It is mutually beneficent. If it ceases to be so, it ceases entirely, because he who no longer gains by it will no longer carry it on. (See § 125.)

II. *PROTECTIONISM IS AT WAR WITH IMPROVEMENT*

73. The cities of Japan are built of very combustible material, and when a fire begins it is rarely arrested until the city is destroyed. It was suggested that a steam fire-engine would there reach its maximum of utility. One was imported and proved very useful on several occasions.

---

[1] Since the above was in type, a treasury order has subjected all goods from Canada to the same taxes as imported goods, although they may be going from Minnesota to England. Nature has made man too well off. The inhabitants of North America will not simply use their chances, but they divide into two artificial bodies so as to try to harm each other. Millions are spent to cut an isthmus where nature has left one, and millions more to set up a tax-barrier where nature has made a highway.

Thereupon the carpenters got up a petition to the government to send the fire-engine away, because it ruined their business.

74. The instance is grotesque and exaggerated, but it is strictly true to the principle of protectionism. The southern counties of England, a century ago, protested against the opening of the great northern turnpike, because that would bring the products of the northern counties to the London market, of which the southern counties had had a monopoly. After the St. Gothard tunnel was opened the people of southern Germany petitioned the Government to lay higher taxes on Italian products to offset the cheapness which the tunnel had produced. In 1837 the first two steamers which ever made commercial voyages across the Atlantic arrived at the same time. A grand celebration was held in New York. The foolish people rejoiced as if a new blessing had been won. Man had won a new triumph over nature. What was the gain of it? It was that he could satisfy his needs with less labor than before; or, in plain language, get things cheaper. But in 1842 a Home Industry Convention was held in New York, at which it was alleged as the prime reason why more taxes were needed, that this steam transportation had made things cheap here.[1] Taxes were needed to neutralize the improvement.

(A) TAXES TO OFFSET CHEAPENED TRANSPORTATION.

75. For the last twenty-five years, to go no farther back, we have multiplied inventions to facilitate transportation. Ocean cables, improved marine engines, and screw steamers, have been only improved means of supplying the wants of people on two continents more abundantly with the products each of the other. The

[1] 62, Niles's "Register," 132.

scientific journals and the daily papers boast of every step in this development as a thing to be proud of and rejoice in, but in the meantime the legislators on both sides of the water are hard at work to neutralize it by taxation. We, in the United States, have multiplied monstrous taxes on all the things which others make and which we want, to prevent them from being brought to us. The statesmen of the European continent are laying taxes on our meat and wheat, lest they be brought to their people. The arts are bringing us together; the taxes are needed to keep us apart. In France, for instance, the agriculturist complains of American competition — not "pauper labor," but gratuitous soil and sunlight. He does not want the French artisan to have the benefit of our prairie soil. The government yields to him and lays a tax on our meat and wheat. This raises the price of bread in Paris, where the reconstruction of the city has collected a large artisan population. The government then finds itself driven to fix the price of bread in Paris, to keep it down. But the reconstruction of the city was accomplished by contracting a great debt, which means heavy taxes. These taxes drive the population out into the suburbs. At least one voice has been raised by an owner of city property that a tax ought to be laid on suburban residents to drive them back to the city,[1] and not let them escape the efforts of the city landlord to throw his taxes on them. Then, again, France has been subsidizing ships, and when the question of renewing the subsidy came up, it was argued that the ships subsidized at the expense of the French taxpayer had lowered freight on wheat and made wheat cheap; that is, as somebody justly replied, had wrought the very mischief against which the increased tax had just been demanded on wheat. Therefore the taxpayer had been taxed first to make wheat cheap, and then again to make it dear.

[1] *Journal des Economistes*, March, 1885, page 496.

76. Tax A to favor B. If A complains, tax C to make it up to A. If C complains, tax B to favor C. If any of them still complain, begin all over again. Tax them as long as anybody complains, or anybody wants anything. This is the statesmanship of the last quarter of the nineteenth century.

77. Bismarck, too, is going into the business. He has to rule a people who live on a poor soil and have to bear a crushing military system. The consequence is that the population is declining. Emigration exceeds the natural increase. Bismarck's cure for it is to lay protective taxes against American pork and wheat and rye. This will protect the German agriculturist. If it lowers still more the comfort of the buyers of food, and drives more of them out of the country, then he will go and buy or fight for colonies at the expense of the German agriculturists whom he has just "protected," although the surplus population of Germany has been taking itself away for thirty years without asking help or giving trouble. What can Germany gain by diverting her emigrants to her own colony unless she means to bring the able-bodied men back to fight her battles? If she means that, the emigrants will not go to her colony.

78. France is also reviving the old colonial policy with discriminating favors and compensatory restraints. She already owns a possession in Algeria, which is the best example of a colony for the sake of a colony. It has been asserted in the French Chambers that each French family now in Algeria has cost the Government (*i.e.*, the French taxpayer) 25,000 francs.[1] The longing of these countries for "colonies" is like the longing of a negro dandy for a cane or a tall hat so as to be like the white gentlemen.

[1] Paris correspondent of the New York *Evening Post*, February 9, 1884.

(B) Sugar Bounties.

79. The worst case of all, however, is sugar. The protectionists long boasted of beet-root sugar as a triumph of their system. It is now an industry in which an immense amount of capital is invested on the Continent, but cheap transportation for cane sugar, and improvements in the treatment of the latter, are constantly threatening it. Mention is made in *Bradstreet's* for June 28, 1885, of a very important improvement in the treatment of cane which has just been invented at Berlin. Germany has an excise tax on beet-root sugar, but allows a drawback on it when exported which is greater than the tax. This acts as a bounty paid by the German taxpayer on the exportation. Consequently, beet-root sugar has appeared even in our market. The chief market for it, however, is England. The consequence is that the sugar, which is nine cents a pound in Germany, and seven cents a pound here, is five cents a pound in England, and that the annual consumption of sugar per head in the three countries [1] is as follows: England, sixty-seven and a half pounds; United States, fifty-one pounds; Germany, twelve pounds. I sometimes find it difficult to make people understand the difference between wanting an "industry" and wanting goods, but this case ought to make that distinction clear. Obviously *the Germans have the industry and the Englishmen have the sugar.*

80. No sooner, however, does Germany get her export bounty in good working order than the Austrian sugar refiners besiege their government to know whether Germany is to have the monopoly of giving sugar to the Englishmen.[2]

---

[1] *Economist,* Commercial Review, 1884, p. 15.

[2] The Vienna correspondent of the *Economist* writes, June 15, 1885, "The representatives of the sugar trade addressed a petition to the Finance Minister, asking, above all things, that the premium on export should be retained, without which, they say, they cannot continue to exist, and which is granted in all countries where beet-root sugar is manufactured."

They get a bounty and compete for that privilege. Then the French refiners say that they cannot compete, and must be enabled to compete in giving sugar to the Englishmen. I believe that their case is under favorable consideration.

80 *a*. I have found it harder (as is usually the case) to get recorded information about the trade and industry of our own country than about those of foreign nations. However, we too, although we do not raise beet-sugar, have our share in this bounty folly, as may be seen by the following statement, which comes to hand just in time to serve my purpose.[1] "The export of refined sugar [from the United States] is entirely confined to hard sugars, or, to be more explicit, loaf, crushed, and granulated. This is because the drawback upon this class of sugar is so large that refiners are enabled to sell them at less than cost. The highest collectable duty upon sugar testing as high as 99° is but 2.36, but the drawback upon granulated testing the same, and in the case of crushed and loaf less, is 2.82 less 1 per cent. This is exactly 43 cents per one hundred pounds more than the government receives in duty. But it rarely happens that raw sugar is imported testing 99°, and never for refining purposes. The following table gives the rates of duty upon the average grades used in refining:

	Degrees	Duty
Fair refining testing..................................	89	1.96
Fair refining testing..................................	90	2.00
Centrifugal testing....................................	96	2.28
Beet-sugar testing....................................	88	1.92

It will be clearly seen from the above figures that with a net drawback upon hard sugar of 2.79 our refiners are able to sell to foreigners, through the assistance of our Treasury, sugar at less than cost. Taking, for instance, the net price of centrifugal testing only 97° and the net price less drawback of granulated:

[1] *Bradstreet's*, July 25, 1885.

Centrifugal raw sugar testing 97°...................... 6.00
Less duty... 2.28
   Net... ——— 3.72
Granulated refined testing 99°........................ 6.37½
Less drawback....................................... 2.71
   Net... ——— 3.66½

                                                    6½

Nothing could demonstrate the absurdity of the present rate of drawback more clearly than the above. A refiner pays 6½ cents per hundred more for raw sugar testing 2° less saccharine than he sells refined for. Not, however, to the American consumers, but to foreigners. After paying the expenses necessary to refining by the assistance of a drawback, which clearly amounts to a subsidy of about 50 cents a hundred pounds, our large sugar monopolists are assisted by the government to increase the cost of sugar to American consumers. One firm controls almost the entire trade of the east; at all events it is safe to say that the trade of the entire country is controlled by three firms, and the Treasury assists this monopoly in sustaining prices against the interest of the country at large. Up to date the exports of refined sugar have amounted to 83,340 tons, which, taken at 50 cents a hundred, has cost the treasury over $830,000. All this may not have gone into the pockets of the refiners, as the ship owners have obtained a share, but the fact remains that the Treasury is the loser by this amount. Besides this bounty presses hard upon the consumers. They not only have to pay the tax, but during the late rise they were compelled to pay more for their sugar than they otherwise would have done had not the export demand caused by selling sugar to foreigners at less than cost, the Treasury paying the difference, increased prices. While an American consumer is charged 6½ cents for granulated, foreign buyers, through the liberality of our government, can buy it under 3¾ cents. Certainly it is time that the Secretary of the Treasury asked the sugar commission to commence a comprehensive and impartial inquiry."

81. Of course the story would not be complete if the English refiners did not besiege their government for a tax to keep out this maleficent gift of foreign taxpayers. This, say they, is not free trade. This is protection turned the other way around. We might hold our own on an equal footing, but we cannot contend against a subsidized industry. A superficial thinker might say that this protest was conclusive. The English government set on foot an investigation, not of the sugar refining, but of *those other interests which were in danger of being forgotten.* There was a tariff investigation which was worth something and was worthy of an enlightened government. It was found that the consumers of sugar had gained more than all the wages paid in sugar refining. But, on the side of the producers, it was found that 6,000 persons are employed and 45,000 tons of sugar are used annually in the neighborhood of London in manufacturing jam and confectionery. In Scotland there are eighty establishments, employing over 4,000 people and using 35,000 tons of sugar per annum in similar industries. In the whole United Kingdom, in those industries, 100,000 tons of sugar are used and 12,000 people are employed, three times as many as in sugar refining. Within twenty years the confectionery trade of Scotland has quadrupled and the preserving trade — jam and marmalade — has practically been originated. In addition, refined sugar is a raw material in biscuit making and the manufacture of mineral waters, and 50,000 tons are used in brewing and distilling. Hence the *Economist* argues (and this view seems to have controlled the decision): "It may be that the gain which we at present realize from the bounties may not be enduring, as it is impossible to believe that foreign nations will go on taxing themselves to the ex-

tent of several millions a year in order to supply us and others with sugar at less than its fair price, but that is no reason for refusing to avail ourselves of their liberality so long as it does last." [1]   (See § 83, note.)

82. One point in this case ought not to be lost sight of. If the English government had yielded to the sugar refiners without looking further, all these little industries which are mentioned, and which in their aggregate are so important, would have been crushed out. Ten years later they would have been forgotten. It is from such an example that one must learn to form a judgment as to *the effect of our tariff in crushing out industries* which are now lost and gone, and cannot even be recalled for purposes of controversy, but which would spring into existence again if the repeal of the taxes should give them a chance.

83. On our side the water efforts have been made to get us into the sugar struggle by the proposed commercial treaties with Spain and England, which would in effect have extended our protective tariff around Cuban and English West Indian sugar.[2] The sugar consumers of the United States were to pay to the Cuban planters the twenty-five million dollars revenue which they now pay to the treasury on Cuban sugar, on condition that the Cubans should bring back part of it and spend it among our manufacturers. It was a new extension of the plan of taxing some of us for the benefit of others of us. Let it be noticed, too, that when it suited their purpose, the protectionists were ready to sacrifice the sugar industry of Louisiana without the least concern. We have been trying for twenty-five years to secure the home market and keep

---

[1] *Economist,* 1884, p. 1052.

[2] A friend has sent me a report (Barbados *Agricultural Report,* April 24, 1885) of an indignation meeting at Bridgetown to protest because the English Government refused to ratify the commercial treaty with the United States. The islanders feel the competition of the "bounty-fed" sugar in the English market; a new complication, a new mischief.

everybody else out of it. *As soon as we get it firmly shut, so that nobody else can get in, we find that it is a question of life and death with us to get out ourselves.* The next device is to tax Americans in order to go and buy a piece of the foreign market. At the last session of Congress Senator Cameron proposed to allow a drawback on raw materials used in exported products. On that plan the American manufacturer would have two costs of production, one when he was working for the home market, and another much lower one when working for the foreign market. As it is now, the exports of manufactured products, of which so much boasting is heard, are for the most part articles sold abroad lower than here so as not to break down the home monopoly market. The proposed plan would raise that to a system, and we should be giving more presents to foreigners.

84. To return to sugar, our treaty with the Sandwich Islands has produced anomalous and mischievous results on the Pacific coast. In the southern Pacific New Zealand is just going into the plan of bounties and protection on sugar.[1] It would not, therefore, be very bold to predict a worldwide catastrophe in the sugar industry within five years.

85. Now what is it all for? What is it all about? Napoleon Bonaparte began it in a despotic whim, when he determined to force the production of beet-root sugar to show that he did not care for the supremacy of England at sea which cut him off from the sugar islands. In order not to lose the capital engaged in the industry, protection was continued. But this led to putting more capital into it and further need of protection. The problem has tormented financiers for seventy-five years. There are two natural products, of which the cane is far richer in sugar. But the processes of the beet-sugar industry have been

[1] *Economist,* Commercial Supplement, February 14, 1885, p. 7.

improved, until recently, far more rapidly than those of the cane industry. Then the refining is a separate interest. If, then, a country has cane-sugar colonies which it wants to protect against other colonies, and a beet-sugar industry which it wants to protect against neighbors who produce beet-sugar, and refiners to be protected against foreign refiners, and if the relations of its own colonial cane-sugar producers to its own domestic beet-sugar producers must be kept satisfactorily adjusted, in spite of changes in processes, transportation, and taxation, and if it wants to get a revenue from sugar, and to use the colonial trade to develop its shipping, and if it has two or three commercial treaties in which sugar is an important item, the statesman of that country has a task like that of a juggler riding several horses and keeping several balls in motion. Sugar is the commodity on which the effects of a world-embracing commerce, produced by modern inventions, are most apparent, and it is the commodity through which all the old protectionist anti-commercial doctrines will be brought to the most decisive test.

(C) Forced Foreign Relations to Regulate Improvement which can no Longer be Defeated.

86. If we turn back once more to our own case, we note the rise in 1883–1884 of the policy of commercial treaties and of a "vigorous foreign policy." For years a "national policy" for us has meant "securing the home market." The perfection of this policy has led to isolation and ostentatious withdrawal from cosmopolitan interests. I may say that I do not write out of any sympathy with vague humanitarianism or cosmopolitan sentiments. It seems to me that local groupings have great natural strength and obvious utility so long as they are subdivisions of a higher organization of the human race, or so long as they are

formed freely and their relations to each other are developed naturally. But now suddenly rises a clap-trap demand for a "national policy," which means that we shall force our way out of our tax-created isolation by diplomacy or war. The effort, however, is to be restrained carefully and arbitrarily to the western hemisphere, and we have anxiously disavowed any part or lot in the regulation of the Congo, although we shall certainly some day desire to take our share in the trade of that district. Our statesmen, however, if they are going to let us have any foreign trade, cannot bear to let us go and take it where we shall make most by it. They must draw *a priori* lines for it. They have taxed us in order to shut us up at home. This has killed the carrying trade, for, if we decided not to trade, what could the shippers find to do? Next ship-building perished, for if there was no carrying trade why build ships, especially when the taxes to protect manufactures were crushing ships and commerce? (§ 101.) Next the navy declined, for with no commerce to protect at sea, we need no navy. Next we lost the interest which we took thirty years ago in a canal across the isthmus, because we have now, under the no-trade policy, no use for it. Next diplomacy became a sinecure, for we have no foreign relations.

87. Now comes the "national policy," not because it is needed, but as an artificial and inflated piece of political bombast. We are to galvanize our diplomacy by contracting commercial treaties and meddling in foreign quarrels. No doubt this will speedily make a navy necessary. In fact our proposed "American policy" is only an old, cast-off, eighteenth-century, John Bull policy, which has forced England to keep up a big army, a big navy, heavy debt, heavy taxes, and a constant succession of little wars. Hence we shall be taxed some more to pay for a navy. Then it is proposed to tax us some more to pay for canals through

which the navy can go. Then we are to be taxed some more to subsidize merchant ships to go through the canal. Then we are to be taxed some more to subsidize voyages, *i.e.*, the carrying trade. Then we are to be taxed some more to provide the ships with cargoes (§ 83).

88. All this time, the whole West Indian, Mexican, and Central and South American trade is ours if we will only stand out of the way and let it come. It is ours by all geographical and commercial advantage, and would have been ours since 1825 if we had but taken down the barriers. Instead of that we propose to tax ourselves some more to lift it over the barriers. Take the taxes off goods, let exchange go on, and the carrying trade comes as a consequence. If we have goods to carry, we shall build or buy ships in which to carry them. If we have merchant ships, we shall need and shall keep up a suitable navy. If we need canals, we shall build them, as, in fact, private capital is now building one and taking the risk of it. If we need diplomacy we shall learn and practice diplomacy of the democratic, peaceful, and commercial type.

89. Thus, under the philosophy of protectionism, the very same thing, if it comes to us freely by the extension of commerce and the march of improvement, is regarded with terror, while, if we can first bar it out, and then only let a little of it in at great cost and pains, it is a thing worth fighting for. Such is the fallacy of all commercial treaties. The crucial criticism on all the debates at Washington in 1884–1885 was: *Have these debaters made up their minds to any standard by which to measure what you get and what you give under a commercial treaty?* It was plain that they had not. A generation of protectionism has taken away the knowledge of what trade is (§§ 125, 139), and whence its benefits arise, and has created a suspicion of trade (§§ 63 ff.). Hence when our public men came to compare what we should get and what we should give, they set

about measuring this by things which were entirely foreign
to it. Scarcely two of them agreed as to the standards by
which to measure it. Some thought that it was the number
of people in one country compared with the number in the
other. Others thought that it was the amount sold to as
compared with the amount bought from the country in
question. Others thought that it was the amount of
revenue to be sacrificed by us as compared with the amount
which would be sacrificed by the other party. If any one
will try to establish a standard by which to measure the
gain by such a treaty to one party or the other, he will be
led to see the fallacy of the whole procedure. The greatest gain to both would be if the trade were perfectly free.
If it is obstructed more or less, that is a harm to be corrected as far and as soon as possible. If then either party
lowers its own taxes, that is a gain and a movement toward
the desirable state of things. No state needs anybody's
permission to lower its own taxes, and entanglements
which would impair its fiscal independence would be a new
harm.[1]

---

[1] Since the above was in type, a report from the "South American Commission"
has been received and published. This Commission submitted certain propositions to the President of Chili on behalf of the United States. The report says:

"The second proposition involved the idea of a reciprocal commercial treaty
between the two countries under which special products of each should be admitted free of duty into the other when carried under the flag of either nation.
This did not meet with any greater favor with President Santa Maria, who was
not disposed to make reciprocity treaties. His people were at liberty to sell where
they could get the best prices and buy where goods were the cheapest. In his
opinion commerce was not aided by commercial treaties, and Chili neither asked
from nor gave to other nations especial favors. Trade would regulate itself, and
there was no advantage in trying to divert it in one direction or the other. So
far as the United States was concerned, there could be very little trade with Chili,
owing to the fact that the products of the two countries were almost identical.
Chili produced very little that we wanted, and although there were many industrial
products of the United States that were used in Chili, the merchants of the latter
country must be allowed to buy where they sold and where they could trade to
the greatest advantage. With reference to the provision that reduced duties

90. Protectionism, therefore, is at war with improvement. It is only useful to annul and offset the effects of those very improvements of which we boast. In time, the improvements win power so great that protectionism cannot withstand them. *Then it turns about and tries to control and regulate them at great expense by diplomacy or war.* The greater and more worldwide these improvements are, the more numerous are the efforts in different parts of the world to revive or extend protection. No doubt there is loss and inconvenience in the changes which improvement brings about. A notable case is the loss and inconvenience of a laborer where a machine is first introduced to supplant him. Patient endurance and hope, in the confidence that he will in the end be better off, has long been preached to him. It is true that he will be better off; but why not apply the same doctrine in connection with the other inconveniences of improvement, where it is equally true?

3. PROTECTION LOWERS WAGES

91. On a pure wages system, that is, where there is a class who have no capital and no land, wages are determined by supply and demand of labor. The demand for labor is measured by the capital in hand to pay for it just as the demand for anything else is measured by the supply of goods offered in exchange for it. In Cobden's language: "When two men are after one boss, wages are low; when two bosses are after one man, wages are high."

should be allowed only upon goods carried in Chilian or American vessels, he said that Chili did not want any such means to encourage her commerce: her ports were open to all the vessels of the world upon an equality, and none should have especial privileges." — (N. Y. *Times*, July 3, 1885.)

If this is a fair specimen of the political and economic enlightenment which prevails at the other end of the American Continent, it is a great pity that the "Commission" is not a great deal larger. They are like the illiterate missionaries who found themselves unawares in a theological seminary. We would do well to send our whole Congress out there.

(A) No True Wages Class in the United States.

92. The United States, however, have never yet been on a pure wages system because there is no class which has no land or cannot get any. In fact, the cheapening of transportation which is going on is making the land of this continent, Australia, and Africa available for the laborers of Europe, and is breaking down the wages system there. This is the real reason for the rise of the proletariat and the expansion of democracy which are generally attributed to metaphysical, sentimental, or political causes. A man who has no capital and no land cannot live from day to day except by getting a share in the capital of others in return for services rendered. In an old society or dense population, such a class comes into existence. It has no reserves; no other chances; no other resource. In a new country no such class exists. The land is to be had for going to it. On the stage of agriculture which is there existing very little capital and very little division of labor are necessary. Hence he who has only unskilled manual strength can get at and use the land, and he can get out of it an abundant supply of the rude primary comforts of existence for himself and his family. If it is made so cheap and easy to get from the old centers of population to the new land that the lowest class of laborers can save enough to pay the passage, then the effect will reach the labor market of the old countries also. Such is now the fact.

93. The weakness of a true wages class is in the fact that they have no other chance. Obviously, however, *a man is well off in this world in proportion to the chances which he can command.* The advantage of education is that it multiplies a man's chances. *Our* noncapitalists have another chance on the land, and the chance is near and easy to grasp and use. It is not necessary that all or any number should use it. Every one who uses it leaves more room behind,

lessens the supply and competition of labor, and helps his class as a class. The other chance which the laborer possesses is also a *good* one, and consequently sets the minimum of unskilled wages high. Here we have the reason for high wages in a new country.

94. The relation of things was distinctly visible in the early colonial days. Winthrop tells how the General Court in Massachusetts Bay tried to fix the wages of artisans by law. It is obvious that artisans were in great demand to build houses, and that they would not work at their trades unless the wages would buy as good or better living than the farmers could get out of the ground, for these artisans could go and take up land and be farmers too. The only effect of the law was that the artisans "went West" to the valley of the Connecticut, and the law became a dead letter. The same equilibration between the gains from the new land and the wages of artisans and laborers has been kept up ever since.

95. In 1884 an attempt was made to unite the Eastern and Western Iron Associations for common effort in behalf of higher wages. The union could not be formed because the Eastern and Western Associations *never had had the same rate of wages*. The latter, being farther west, where the supply of labor is smaller and the land nearer, have obtained higher wages. It may be well to anticipate a little right here in order to point out that this difference in wages has not prevented the growth of the industry in the West, and has not made competition in a common market impossible.[1] The fact is of the first importance to controvert the current assumption of the protectionists. They say that an industry cannot be carried on in one place if the wages there are higher than must be paid by somebody in the same industry in another place. This

---

[1] This is the case for which the *Inter-Ocean* proposed the remedy described in § 71 note.

proposition has no foundation in fact at all. Farm laborers in Iowa get three times the wages of farm laborers in England. The products of the former pay 5,000 miles transportation, and then drive out the products of the latter. Wages are only one element, and often they are far from being the most important element, in the economy of production. *The wages which are paid to the men who make an article have nothing to do with the price or value of that article.* This proposition, I know, has a startling effect on the people who hold to the monkish notions of political economy, but it is only a special case of the theorem that *"Labor which is past has no effect on value,"* which is the true cornerstone of any sound political economy. Wages are determined by the supply and demand of labor. Value is determined by the supply and demand of the commodity. These two things have no connection. Wages are one element in the capitalist's outlay for production. If the total outlay in one line of production, when compared with the return obtained in that line, is not as advantageous as the total outlay in another line when compared with the return available in the second line, then the capital is withdrawn from the first line and put into the second; but the rate of wages in either case or any case is the market rate, determined by the supply and demand of labor, for that is what the employers must pay if they want the men, whether they are making any profits or not.

96. The facts and economic principles just stated above show plainly why wages are high, and put in strong light the assertion of the protectionists that their device makes wages high (§ 47), that is, higher than they would be otherwise, or higher here than they are in Europe. Wages are not arbitrary. They cannot be shifted up and down at anybody's whim. They are controlled by ultimate causes. If not, then what has made them fall during the last eighteen months, ten to forty per cent, most in the most pro-

tected industries (§ 26)? Why are they highest in the least
protected and the unprotected industries, *e.g.*, the building trades? Hod-carriers recently struck in New York for
three dollars for nine hours' work. Where did the tariff
touch their case? *Why does not the tariff prevent the fall in
wages?* It is all there, and now is the time for it to come
into operation, if it can keep wages up. Now it is needed.
When wages were high in the market, and it was not
needed, it claimed the credit. Now when they fall and it is
needed, it is powerless.

97. Wages are capital. If I promise to pay wages I
must find capital somewhere with which to fulfill my contract. If the tariff makes me pay more than I otherwise
would, where does the surplus come from? Disregarding
money as only an intermediate term, a man's wages are his
means of subsistence — food, clothing, house rent, fuel,
lights, furniture, etc. If the tariff system makes him get
more of these for ten hours' work in a shop than he would
get without tariff, *where does the "more" come from?* Nothing but labor and capital can produce food, clothing, etc.
Either the tax must make these out of nothing, or it can
only get them by taking them from those who have made
them, that is by subtracting them from the wages of somebody else. Taking all the wages class into account, then
the tax cannot possibly increase, but is sure by waste and
loss to decrease wages.

(B) How Taxes Do Act on Wages.

98. If taxes are to raise wages they must be laid not on
goods but on men. Let the goods be abundant and the
men scarce. Then the average wages will be high, for the
supply of labor will be small and the demand great. If
we tax goods and not men, the supply of labor will be great,
the demand will be limited, and the wages will be low.

Here we see why employers of labor want a tariff. For it is an obvious inconsistency and a most grotesque satire that the same men should tell the workmen at home that the tariff makes wages high, and should go to Washington and tell Congress that they want a tariff because the wages are too high. We have found that the high wages of American laborers have independent causes and guarantees, outside of legislation. They are provided and maintained by the economic circumstances of the country. This is against the interest of those who want to hire the laborers. No device can serve their interest unless it lowers wages. From the standpoint of an employer the fortunate circumstances of the laborer become an obstacle to be overcome (§ 65). The laborer is too well off. Nothing can do any good which does not make him less well off. The competition which troubles the employer is not the "pauper labor" of Europe.

99. "Pauper labor" had a meaning in the first half of this century, in England, when the overseers of the poor turned over the younger portion of the occupants of the poorhouses to the owners of the new cotton factories, under contracts to teach them the trade and pay them a pittance. Of course the arrangement had shocking evils connected with it, but it was a transition arrangement. The "pauper laborers'" children, after a generation, became independent laborers; the system expired of itself, and "pauper laborer" is now a senseless jingle.

100. The competition which the employers fear *is the competition of those industries in America which can pay the high wages and which keep the wages high because they do pay them.* These draw the laborer away. These offer him another chance. If he had no other way of earning more than he is earning, it would be idle for him to demand more. The reason why he demands more and gets it is because he knows where he can get it, if he cannot get it

where he is. If, then, he is to be brought down, the only way to do it is *to destroy, or lessen the value of, his other chance.* This is just what the tariff does.

101. The taxes which are laid for protection must come out of somebody. As I have shown (§§ 32 ff.) the protected interests give and take from each other, but, if they as a group win anything, they must win from another group, and that other group must be the industries which are not and cannot be protected. In England these were formerly manufactures and they were taxed, under the corn laws, for the benefit of agriculture. In the United States, of course, the case must be complementary and opposite. We tax agriculture and commerce to benefit manufactures. Commerce, *i.e.*, the ship-building and carrying trade, has been crushed out of existence by the burden (§ 86). But the burden thus thrown on agriculture and commerce lowers the gains of those industries, lessens the attractiveness of them to the laborer, lessens the value of the laborer's other chance, lessens the competition of other American industries with manufacturing, and so, by taking away from the blessing which God and nature have given to the American laborer, enable the man who wants to hire his services to get them at a lower rate. The effect of taxes is just the same as such a percentage taken from the fertility of the soil, the excellence of the climate, the power of tools, or the industrious habits of the people. Hence it reduces the average comfort and welfare of the population, and with that average comfort it carries down the wages of such persons as work for wages.

(*C*) Perils of Statistics, Especially of Wages.

102. Any student of statistics will be sure to have far less trust in statistics than the uninitiated entertain. The bookkeepers have taught us that figures will not lie, but

that they will tell very queer stories. Statistics will not lie, but they will play wonderful tricks with a man who does not understand their dialect. The unsophisticated reader finds it difficult, when a column of statistics is offered to him, to resist the impression that they must prove *something*. The fact is that a column of statistics hardly ever proves anything. It is a popular opinion that anybody can use or understand statistics. The fact is that a special and high grade of skill is required to appreciate the effect of the collateral circumstances under which the statistics were obtained, to appreciate the limits of their application, and to interpret their significance. The statistics which are used to prove national prosperity are an illustration of this, for they are used as absolute measures when it is plain that they have no use except for a comparison. Sometimes the other term of the comparison is not to be found and it is always ignored (§ 52).

103. A congressional committee in the winter of 1883–1884, dealing with the tariff, took up the census and proceeded to reckon up the wages in steel production by adding all the wages from the iron mine up. Then they took bar iron and added all the wages from the bottom up again, in order to find the importance of the wages element in that, and so on with every stage of iron industry. They were going to add in the same wages six or eight times over.

104. The statistics of comparative wages which are published are of no value at all.[1] It is not known how, or by whom, or from what selected cases, they were collected. It is not known how wide, or how long, or how thorough was the record from which they were taken. The facts about various classifications of labor in the division of labor, and about the rate at which machinery is run, or about the allowances of one kind and another which vary from mill

[1] I except those of Mr. Carroll Wright. He has sufficiently stated of how slight value his are.

to mill and town to town are rarely specified at all. Protected employers are eager to tell the wages they pay per day or week, which are of no importance. The only statistics which would be of any use for the comparison which is attempted would be such as show the proportion of wages to total cost per unit. Even this comparison would not have the force which is attributed to the other. Hence the statistics offered are worthless or positively misleading. In the nature of the case such statistics are extremely hard to get. If application is made to the employers, the inquiry concerns their private business. They have no interest in answering. They cannot answer without either spending great labor on their books (if the inquiry covers a period), or surrendering their books to some one else, if they allow him to do the labor. If inquiry is made of the men, it becomes long and tedious and full of uncertainties. Do United States Consuls take the trouble involved in such an inquiry? Have they the training necessary to conduct it successfully?

105. The fact is generally established and is not disputed that wages are higher here than in Europe. The difference is greatest on the lowest grade of labor — manual labor, unskilled labor. The difference is less on higher grades of labor. For what the English call "engineers," men who possess personal dexterity and creative power, the difference is the other way, if we compare the United States and England. The returns of immigration reflect these differences exactly (§ 122, note). The great body of the immigrants consists of farmers and laborers. The "skilled laborers" are comparatively a small class, and, if the claims of the individuals to be what they call themselves were tested by English or German trade standards, the number would be very small indeed. Engineers emigrate from Germany to England. Men of that class rarely come to this country, or, if they come, they come under special con-

tracts, or soon return. Each country, spite of all taxes and other devices, gets the class of men for which its industrial condition offers the best chances. The only thing the tariff does in the matter is to take from those who have an advantage here a part of that advantage.

4. PROTECTIONISM IS SOCIALISM

106. Simply to give protectionism a bad name would be to accomplish very little. When I say that protectionism is socialism I mean to classify it and bring it not only under the proper heading but into relation with its true affinities. *Socialism is any device or doctrine whose aim is to save individuals from any of the difficulties or hardships of the struggle for existence and the competition of life by the intervention of "the State."* Inasmuch as "the State" never is or can be anything but some other people, socialism is a device for making some people fight the struggle for existence for others. The devices always have a doctrine behind them which aims to show why this *ought* to be done.

107. The protected interests demand that they be saved from the trouble and annoyance of business competition, and that they be assured profits in their undertakings, by "the State," that is, at the expense of their fellow-citizens. If this is not socialism, then there is no such thing. If employers may demand that "the State" shall guarantee them profits, why may not the employees demand that "the State" shall guarantee them wages? If we are taxed to provide profits, why should we not be taxed for public workshops, for insurance to laborers, or for any other devices which will give wages and save the laborer from the annoyances of life and the risks and hardships of the struggle for existence? The "we" who are to pay changes all the time, and the turn of the protected employer to pay will surely come before long. The plan of all living on each

other is capable of great expansion. It is, as yet, far from being perfected or carried out completely. The protectionists are only educating those who are as yet on the "paying" side of it, but who will certainly use political power to put themselves also on the "receiving" side of it. The argument that "the State" must do something for me because my business does not pay, is a very far-reaching argument. If it is good for pig iron and woolens, it is good for all the things to which the socialists apply it.

CHAPTER IV

SUNDRY FALLACIES OF PROTECTIONISM

108. I can now dispose rapidly of a series of current fallacies put forward by the protectionists. They generally are fanciful or far-fetched attempts to show some equivalent which the taxpayer gets for his taxes.

(A) THAT INFANT INDUSTRIES CAN BE NOURISHED UP TO INDEPENDENCE AND THAT THEY THEN BECOME PRODUCTIVE.

109. I know of no case where this hope has been realized, although we have been trying the experiment for nearly a century. The weakest infants to-day are those whom Alexander Hamilton set out to protect in 1791. As soon as the infants begin to get any strength (if they ever do get any) the protective system forces them to bear the burden of other infants, and so on forever. The system superinduces hydrocephalus on the infants, and instead of ever growing to maturity, the longer they live, the bigger babies they are. It is the system which makes them so, and on its own plan it can never rationally be expected to have any other effect. (See further, under the next fallacy, §§ 111 ff.)

110. Mill [1] makes a statement of a case, as within the bounds of conceivability, where there might be an advantage for a young country to protect an infant industry. He is often quoted without regard to the limitation of his statement, as if he had affirmed the general expediency of protection in new countries and for infant industries. It amounts to a misquotation to quote him without regard to the limitations which he specified. The statement which he did make is mathematically demonstrable.[2] The doctrine so developed is very familiar in private enterprise. A business enterprise may be started which for some years will return no profits or will occasion losses, but which is expected later to recoup all these. *What are the limits within which such an enterprise can succeed?* It must either call for sinking capital only for a short period (like building a railroad or planting an orange grove), or it must promise enormous gains after it is started (like a patented novelty). The higher the rate of interest, as in any new country, the more stringent and narrow these conditions are. Mill said that it was conceivable that a case of an industry might occur in which this same calculation might be applied to a protective tax. If, then, anybody says that he can offer an industry which meets the conditions, let it be examined to see if it does so. If protection is never applied until such a case is offered, it will never be applied at all. A thing which is mathematically conceivable is one which is not absurd; but a thing which is practically possible is quite another thing. For myself, I strenuously dissent from Mill's doctrine even as he limits it. In the first place the state cannot by taxes work out an industrial enterprise of a character such that it, as any one can see, *demands the most intense and careful oversight by persons whose capital is*

---

[1] Bk. V, ch. 10, § 1.

[2] It has been developed mathematically by a French mathematician (*Journal des Economistes*, August and September, 1873, pp. 285 and 464).

at stake in it, and, in the second place, the state would bear the loss, while it lasted, but private interests would take the gain after it began.

(B) That Protective Taxes do not Raise Prices but Lower Prices.

111. To this it is obvious to reply: what good can they then do toward the end proposed? Still it is true that, under circumstances, protective taxes do lower prices. The protectionist takes an infant industry in hand and proposes to rear it by putting on taxes to ward off competition, and by giving it more profits than the world's market price would give. This raises the price. But the consumer then raises a complaint. The protectionist turns to him and promises that by and by there will be "overproduction," and prices will fall. This arrives in due time, for every protected industry is organized as a more or less limited monopoly, and a monopoly which has overproduced its market, *at the price which it wants,* is the weakest industry possible (§ 24). The consumer now wins, but a wail from the cradle calls the protectionist back to the infant industry, which is in convulsions from "overproduction." Some of the infants die. This gives a new chance to the others. They combine for more effective monopoly, put the prices up again by limiting production, and go on until "overproduction" produces a new collapse. This is another reason why infants never win vitality. The net result is that the market is in constant alternations of stringency and laxity, and nothing at all is gained.

112. Whenever we talk of prices *it should be noticed that our statements involve money* — the rate at which goods exchange for money. If then we want to raise prices, we must *restrict the supply* of goods, so that on the doctrine of money also we shall come to the same result as before, that protective taxes lessen production and diminish wealth.

113. The problem of managing any monopoly is to dose
the market with just the quantity which it will take at the
price which the monopolist wants to get. In a qualified
monopoly, that is, one which is shared by a number of
persons, the difficulty is to get agreement about the management. They may not have any communication with
each other and may compete. If so they will overdose the
market and the price will fall. Then they meet, to establish communication; form an "association," to get harmonious action, and agree to divide the production among
them and limit and regulate it, to prevent the former mistake and restore prices (§ 24).

(C) That we should be a Purely Agricultural Nation under Free Trade.

114. A purely agricultural nation covering a territory as
large as that of the United States is inconceivable. The
distribution of industries now *inside* the United States is
a complete proof that no such thing would come to pass,
for we have absolute free trade inside, and manufactures
are growing up in the agricultural states just as fast as
circumstances favor, and just as fast as they can be profitably carried on. Under free trade there would be a sub-
division of cotton, woolen, iron and other industries, and
we should both export and import different varieties and
qualities of these goods. The southern states are now manufacturing coarse cottons in competition with New England.
The western states manufacture coarse woolens, certain
grades of leather and iron goods, etc., in competition with
the East. Here we see the exact kind of differentiation
which would take place under free trade, and we can see
the mischief of the tariff, whether on the one hand it strikes
a whole category with the same brutal ignorance, or tries,
by cunning sub-classification, to head off every effort to

save itself which the trade makes.[1] If, however, it was conceivable that we should become a purely agricultural nation, the only legitimate inference would be that our whole population could be better supported in that way than in any other. If there was a greater profit in something else some of them would go into it.

(D) That Communities which Manufacture are More Prosperous than those which are Agricultural.

115. This is as true as if it should be said that all tall men are healthy. It would be answered that some are and some are not; that tallness and health have no connection. Some manufacturing communities are prosperous and some not. The self-contradiction of protectionism appears in one of its boldest forms in this fallacy. We are told that manufactures are a special blessing. The protectionist says that he is going to give us some. Instead of that he makes new demands on us, lays a new burden on us, gives us nothing but more taxes. He promises us an income and increases our expenditure; promises an asset and gives a liability; promises a gift and creates a debt; promises a blessing and gives a burden. The very thing which he boasts of as a great and beneficial advantage gives us nothing, but takes from us more. Prosperity is no more connected with one form of industry than another. If it were so, some of mankind would have, by nature, a permanently better chance than others, and no one could emigrate to a new, that is agricultural country, without injuring his interests. The world is not made so.

[1] See a fallacy under this head: Cunningham, "Growth of English Industry," 410, note.

(*E*) That it is an Object to Diversify Industry, and that Nations which have Various Industries are Stronger than Others which have not Various Industries.

116. It is not an object to diversify industry, but to multiply and diversify our satisfactions, comforts, and enjoyments. If we can do this by unifying our industry, in greater measure than by diversifying it, then we should do, and we will do, the former. It is not a question to be decided *a priori*, but depends upon economic circumstances. If a country has a supremacy in some one industry it will have only one. California and Australia had only one industry until the gold mines declined in productiveness, that is, until their supreme advantage over other countries was diminished: they began to diversify when they began to be less well off. The oil region of Pennsylvania has a chance of three industries, the old farming industry, coal, and oil. It will have only one industry so long as oil gives chances superior to those enjoyed by any other similar district. When it loses its unique advantage by nature it will diversify. The "strongest" nation is the one which brings products into the world's market which are of high demand, but which cost it little toil and sacrifice to get; for it will then have command of all the good things which men can get on earth at little effort to itself. Whether the products which it offers are one or numerous is immaterial. All the tariff has to do with it is that when the American comes into the world's market with wheat, cotton, tobacco, and petroleum, all objects of high demand by mankind and little cost to him, it forces him to forego a part of his due advantage (§§ 125, 134).

(F) That Manufactures Give Value to Land.

117. This doctrine issued from the Agricultural Bureau. It has been thought a grand development of the protectionist argument. It is a simple logical fallacy based on some misconstrued statistics. The value of land depends on supply and demand. The demand for land is population. Hence where the population is dense the value of land is great. Manufactures can be carried on only where there is a supply of labor, that is, where the population is dense. Hence high value of land and manufacturing industry are common results of dense population. The statistician of the Agricultural Bureau connected them with each other as cause and effect, and the New York *Tribune* said that it was the grandest contribution to political economy since "the fingers of Horace Greeley stiffened in death"; which was true.

118. If manufactures spring up spontaneously out of original strength, and by independent development, of course they "add value to land," that is to say, the district has new industrial power and every interest in it is benefited; but if the manufactures have to be protected, paid for, and supported, they do not do any good as manufactures but only as a device for drawing capital from elsewhere, as tribute. In this way, protective taxes do alter the comparative value of land in different districts. This effect can be seen under some astonishing phases in Connecticut and other manufacturing states. The farmers are taxed to hire some people to go and live in manufacturing villages and carry on manufacturing there. This displacement of population, brought about at the expense of the rural population, diminishes the value of agricultural land and raises that of city land right here within the same state. The hillside population is being impoverished, and the hillside farms are being abandoned on account of the

tribute levied on them to swell the value of mill sites and adjoining land in the manufacturing towns (§§ 120, 137).

(G) That the Farmer, if he Pays Taxes to Bring into Existence a Factory, which would not otherwise Exist, will Win more than the Taxes by Selling Farm Produce to the Artisans.

119. This is an arithmetical fallacy. It proposes to get three pints out of a quart. The farmer is out for the tax and the farm produce and he can not get back more than the tax because, if the factory owes its existence to the protective taxes, it cannot make any profit outside of the taxes. The proposition to the farmer is that he shall pay taxes to another man who will bring part of the tax back to buy produce with it. This is to make the farmer rich. The man who owned stock in a railroad and who rode on it, paying his fare, in the hope of swelling his own dividends, was wise compared with a farmer who believes that protection can be a source of gain to him.

120. Since, as I have shown (§ 101), protective taxes act like a reduction in the fertility of the soil, they lower the "margin of cultivation," and raise rent. They do not, however, raise it in favor of the agricultural land owner, for, by the displacement just described, they take away from him to give to the town land owner. Of course, I do not believe that the protective taxes have really lowered the margin of cultivation in this country, for they have not been able to offset the greater richness of the newest land, and the advance in the arts. What protection costs us comes out of the exuberant bounty of nature to us. Still I know of very few who could not stand it to be a great deal better off than they are, and the New England farmer is the one who has the least chance, and the fewest advantages, with which to endure protection.

(H) That Farmers Gain by Protection, because it
Draws so many Laborers out of Competition with
Them.

121. Since the farmers pay the taxes by which this
operation is supposed to be produced, a simple question is
raised, *viz.*, how much can one afford to pay to buy off competition in his business? He cannot afford to pay anything
unless he has a monopoly which he wants to consolidate.
Our farmers are completely open to competition on every
side. The immigration of farmers every three or four years
exceeds all the workers in all the protected trades. Hence
the farmers, if they take the view which is recommended
to them, instead of gaining any ground, are face to face
with a task which gets bigger and bigger the longer they
work at it. If one man should support another in order
to get rid of the latter's competition as a producer, that
would be the case where the taxpayer supports soldiers,
idle pensioners, paupers, etc. A protected manufacturer,
however, by the hypothesis, is not simply supported in
idleness, but he is carrying on a business the losses of which
must be paid by those who buy off his competition in their
own production. On the other hand, when farmers come
to market, they are in free competition with several other
sources of supply. Hence, if they did any good to agricultural industry by hiring the artisans to go out of competition with them, they would have to share the gain
with all their competitors the world over while paying all
the expense of it themselves.

122. The movement of men over the earth and the
movement of goods over the earth are complementary
operations. Passports to stop the men and taxes to stop
the goods would be equally legitimate. Since it is, once
for all, a fact that some parts of the earth have advantages
for one thing and other parts for other things, men avail

themselves of the local advantages either by moving themselves to the places, or by trading what they produce where
they are for what others produce in the other places. The
passenger trains and the freight trains are set in motion
by the same ultimate economic fact. Our exports are all
bulky and require more tonnage than our imports. On
the westward trip, consequently, bunks are erected and
men are brought in space where cotton, wheat, etc., were
taken out. The tariff, by so much as it lessens the import
of goods, leaves room which the ship owners are eager to
fill with immigrants. To do this they lower the rates.
Hence the tariff is a premium on immigration. The protectionists have claimed that the tariff does favor immigration. But nine-tenths of the immigrants are laborers,
domestic servants, and farmers.[1] Probably more than one-
third of the total number, including women, find their way
to the land. As we have seen, the tariff also lowers the
profits of agriculture, which discourages immigration and
the movement to the land. Therefore, if the farmer believes what the protectionist tells him, he must understand
that the taxes he pays bring in more people, and raise the
value of land by settling it, and that they also bring more
competition, which the farmer must buy off by lowering
the profits of his own (the farming) industry. Then, too,
so far as the immigrants are artisans, the premium on immigration is a tax paid to increase the supply of labor, that is,

[1] IMMIGRATION IN 1884

	Males	Females	Total
Professional occupations......................	2,184	100	2,284
Skilled occupations.........................	50,905	4,156	55,061
Occupations not stated......................	19,778	11,887	31,665
No occupation.............................	75,483	169,904	245,387
Miscellaneous occupations...................	160,159	24,036	184,195
Total.................................	308,509	210,083	518,592

Under miscellaneous were 106,478 laborers and 42,050 farmers.

to lower wages, although the protectionists say that the tariff raises wages. Hence we see that when a tax is laid, in our modern complicated society, instead of being a simple and easy means or method to be employed for a specific purpose, its action and reaction on transportation, land, wages, etc., will produce erratic, contradictory, and confused effects, which cannot be predicted or analyzed thoroughly, and the protectionist, when he pleads three or four arguments for his system, is alleging three or four features of it which, if properly analyzed and brought together, are found to be mutually destructive, and cumulative only as to the mischief they do (see §§ 29, 101).

(*I*) That our Industries would Perish without Protection.

123. Those who say this think only of manufacturing establishments as "industries." They also talk of "our" industries. They mean those we support by the taxes we pay; not those from which we get dividends. No industry will ever be given up except in order to take up a better one, and if, under free trade, any of our industries should perish, it would only be because the removal of restrictions enabled some other industry to offer so much better rewards that labor and capital would seek the latter. It is plain that, if a man does not know of any better way to earn his living than the one in which he is, he must remain in that, or move to some other place. If any one can suppose that the population of the United States could be forced, by free trade, to move away, he must suppose that this country cannot support its population, and that we made a mistake in coming here. This argument is especially full of force if the articles to be produced are coal, iron, wool, copper, timber, or any other primary products of the soil. For, if it is said that we cannot raise these products of the

soil in competition with some other part of the earth's surface, all it proves is that we have come to the wrong spot to seek them. If, however, the soil can support the population under an arrangement by which certain industries support themselves, and those which do not pay besides, then it is plain that the former are really supporting the whole population — part directly and part indirectly, through a circuitous and wasteful organization. Hence the same strong and independent industries could certainly still better support the whole population, if they supported it directly.

124. I have been asked whether we should have had any steel works in this country, if we had had no protection. I reply that I do not know; neither does anybody else, but it is certain that we should have had a great deal more steel, if we had had no protection.

125. "But," it is said, "we should import everything." Should we import everything and give nothing? If so, foreigners would make us presents and support us. Should we give equal value in exchange? If so, there would be just as much "industry" and a great deal less "work" in that way of getting things than in making them ourselves. The moment that ceased to be true we should make and not buy. Suppose that a district, A, has two million inhabitants, one million of whom produce a million bushels of wheat, and one million produce a million hundredweight of iron; and suppose that a bushel of wheat exchanges for a hundredweight of iron. Now, by improved transportation and emigration, suppose that a new wheat country, B, is opened, and that its people bring wheat to the first district, offering two bushels for a hundredweight of iron. Plainly they must offer more than one bushel for one hundredweight, or it is useless for them to come. Now the people of A, by putting all their labor and capital in iron production, produce two million hundredweight. They

keep one million hundredweight, and exchange one million hundredweight of iron for two million bushels of wheat. The destruction of their wheat industry is a sign of a change in industry (unifying and not diversifying) by which they have gained a million bushels of wheat. Such is the gain of all trade. If the gain did not exist, trade would not be a feature of civilization.

(*J*) That it would be Wise to Call into Existence Various Industries, even at an Expense, if we could thus Offer Employment to all Kinds of Artisans, etc., who might Come to us.

126. This would be only maintaining public workshops at the expense of the taxpayers, and would be open to all the objections which are conclusive against public workshops. The expense would be prodigious, and the return little or nothing. This argument shows less sense of comparative cost and gain than any other which is ever proposed.

(*K*) That we Want to be Complete in ourselves and Sufficient to ourselves, and Independent, as a Nation, which State of Things will be Produced by Protection.

127. I will only refer to what I have already said about China and Japan (§ 69) as types of what this plan produces. If a number of families from among us should be shipwrecked on an island, their greatest woe would be that they could not trade with the rest of the world. They might live there "self-contained" and "independent," fulfilling the ideal of happiness which this proposition offers, but they would look about them to see a surfeit of things which, as they know, their friends at home would like to

have, and they would think of all the old comforts which they used to have, and which they could not produce on their island. They might be contented to live on there and make it their home, if they could exchange the former things for the latter. If now a ship should chance that way and discover them and should open communication and trade between them and their old home, a protectionist philosopher would say to them: "You are making a great mistake. You ought to make everything for yourselves. The wise thing to do would be to isolate yourselves again by taxes as soon as possible." We sent some sages to the Japanese to induct them into the ways of civilization, who, as a matter of fact, did tell them that the first step in civilization was to adopt a protective tariff and shut up again by taxes the very ports which they had just opened.

(L) That Protective Taxes are Necessary to Prevent a Foreign Monopoly from Getting Control of our Market.

128. It is said that English manufacturers once combined to lower prices in order to kill out American manufactures, and that they then put up their prices to monopoly rates. If they did this, why did not their other customers send to the United States and buy the goods here in the first instance, and why did not the Americans go and buy the goods of the Englishmen's other customers in the second instance? If the Englishmen put down their prices for their whole market in the first instance, why did they not incur a great loss? and, if they raised it for their whole market in the second instance, why did they not yield the entire market to their competitors? The Englishmen are said to be wonderfully shrewd, and are here credited with the most stupid and incredible folly.

129. The protective system puts us certainly in the

hands of a home monopoly for fear of the impossible chance that we may fall into the hands of a foreign monopoly. Before the war we made no first quality thread. We got it at four cents a spool (retail) of an English monopoly. Under the tariff we were saved from this by being put into the hands of a home monopoly which charged five cents a spool. In the meantime the foreign monopoly lowered thread to three cents a spool (retail) for the Canadians, who were at its mercy. Lest we should have to buy nickel of a foreign monopolist, Congress forced us to buy it of the owner of the only mine in the United States, and added thirty cents a pound to any price the foreigner might ask.

(*M*) That Free Trade is Good in Theory but Impossible in Practice; that it would be a Good Thing if All Nations would have it.

130. That a thing can be true in theory and false in practice is the most utter absurdity that human language can express. For, if a thing is true in practice (protectionism, for instance) the theory of its truth can be found, and that theory will be true. But it was admitted that free trade is true in theory. Hence two things which are contradictory would both be true at the same time about the same thing. The fact is, that *protectionism is totally impracticable.* It does not work as it is expected to work; it does not produce any of the results which were promised from it; it is never properly and finally established to the satisfaction of its own votaries. They cannot let it alone. They always want to "correct inequalities," or revise it one way or another. It was they who got up the Tariff Commission of 1882. Their system is not capable of construction so as to furnish a normal and regular status for industry. One of them said that the tariff would be all right if it could only be made stable; another said that it ought to be revised

every two years. One said that it ought to include everything; another said that it would be good "if it was only laid on the right things."

131. If all nations had free trade, no one of them would have any special gain from it, just as, if all men were honest, honesty would have no commercial value. Some say that a man cannot afford to be honest unless everybody is honest. The truth is that, if there was one honest man among a lot of cheats, his character and reputation would reach their maximum value. So the nation which has free trade when the others do not have it gains the most by comparison with them. It gains while they impoverish themselves. If all had free trade all would be better off, but then no one would profit from it more than others. If this were not true, if the man who first sees the truth and first acts wisely did not get a special premium for it, the whole moral order of the universe would have to be altered, for no reform or improvement could be tried until unanimous consent was obtained. If a man or a nation does right, the rewards of doing right are obtained. They are not as great as could be obtained if all did right, but they are greater than those enjoy who still do wrong.

(N) That Trade is WAR, so that Free Trade Methods
are Unfit for it, and that Protective Taxes are
Suited to it.

132. It is evidently meant by this that trade involves a struggle or contest of competition. It might, however, as well be said that practicing law is war, because it is contentious; or that practicing medicine is war, because doctors are jealous rivals of each other. The protectionists do, however, always seem to think of trade as commercial war. One of them was reported to have said in a speech, in the late campaign, that nations would not fight any more with

guns but with taxes. The nations are to boycott each other. One would think that the experience our Southerners made of that notion in the Civil War, upon which they entered in the faith that "cotton is king," would have sufficed to banish forever that antique piece of imbecility, a commercial war. If trade is war, all the tariff can do about it is to make A fight B's battles, although A has his own battles to fight besides.

(O) That Protection Brings into Employment Labor and Capital which would otherwise be Idle.

133. If there is any labor or capital which is idle, that fact is a symptom of industrial disease; especially is this true in the United States. If a laborer is idle he is in danger of starving to death. If capital is idle it is producing nothing to its owner, who depends on it, and is suffering loss. Therefore, if labor or capital is idle, some antecedent error or folly must have produced a stoppage in the industrial organization. The cure is, not to lay some more taxes, but to find the error and correct it. If then things are in their normal and healthy condition, the labor and capital of the country are employed as far as possible under the existing organization. We are constantly trying to improve our exchange and credit systems so as to keep all our capital all the time employed. Such improvements are important and valuable, but to make them cost more thought and skillful labor than to invent machines. Hence Congress cannot do that work by discharging a volley of taxes at selected articles, and leaving those taxes to find out the proper points to affect, and to exert the proper influence. It takes intelligent and hard-working men to do it. The faith that anything else can do it is superstition.

(P) That a Young Nation Needs Protection and will Suffer some Disadvantage in Free Exchange with an Old One.

134. The younger a nation is the more important trade is to it (cf. §§ 127 ff.). The younger a nation is the more it wins by trade, for it offers food and raw materials which are objects of greatest necessity to old nations. The things England buys of us are far more essential to her than what she buys of France or Germany. The strong party in an exchange is not the rich party, or the old party, but the one who is favored by supply and demand — the one who brings to the exchange the thing which is more rare and more eagerly wanted.[1] If a poor woman went into Stewart's store to buy a yard of calico, she did not have to pay more because Stewart was rich. She paid less because he used his capital to serve her better and at less price than anybody else could. England takes 60 per cent of all our exports. We sell, first, wheat and provisions, prime articles of food; second, cotton, the most important raw material now used by mankind; third, tobacco, the most universal luxury and the one for which there is the intensest demand; fourth, petroleum, the lighting material in most universal use. These are things which are rare and of high demand. We are, therefore, strong in the market. Protection only robs us of part of our advantage (§ 116).

(Q) That we Need Protection to Get Ready for War.

135. We have no army, or navy, or fortifications worth mentioning. We are wasting more by protective taxes in a year than would be necessary to build a first-class navy

[1] See a fallacy under this point: Cunningham, "Growth of English Industry," 410 note.

and fortify our whole seacoast. It is said that, in some way, the taxes get us ready for war, and yet in fact we are not ready for war. It is plain that this argument is only a pretense put forward to try to cover the real motives of protection. If we prefer to go without army, navy, and fortifications, as we now do, then the best way to get ready for war, consistently with that policy, is *to get as rich as we can*. Then we can count on buying anything in the world which anybody else has got and which we need. Protection, then, which lessens our wealth, is only diminishing our power for war.

(R) That Protectionism Produces some Great Moral Advantages.

136. It is a very suspicious thing when a man who sets out to discuss an economic question shifts over on the "moral" ground. Not because economics and morals have nothing to do with each other. On the contrary, they meet at a common boundary line, and, when both are sound, straight and consistent lines run from one into the other. Capital is the first requisite of all human effort for goods of any kind, and the increase of capital is therefore the expansion of *chances* that intellectual, moral, and spiritual good may be won. The moral question is: How will the chances be used? If, then, the economic analysis shows that protective taxes lessen capital, it follows that those taxes lessen the regular chances for all higher good.

137. It is argued that hardship disciplines a man and is good for him; hence, that the free traders, who want people to do what is easiest, would corrupt them, and that protectionists, by "making work," bring in salutary discipline for the people. This is the effect upon those who pay the taxes. The counter-operation on the beneficiaries of the system I have never seen developed. Bastiat said

that the model at which the protectionist was aiming was
Sisyphus, who was condemned in Hades to roll a stone to
the top of a hill, from which, as soon as he got it there, it
rolled down again to the bottom. Then he rolled it up
again, and so on to all eternity. Here then was infinity of
effort, zero of result; the ultimate type to which the protectionist system would come. Somebody pitied Sisyphus,
to whom he replied: "Thou fool! I enjoy everlasting
hope!" If Sisyphus could extract moral consolation from
his case, I am not prepared to deny but that a New England farmer, ground between the upper millstone of free
competition, in his production, with the Mississippi Valley,
and the nether millstone of protective taxes on all his consumption, may derive some moral consolation from his
case. There are a great many people who are apparently
ready to inflict salutary chastisement on the American
citizen for his welfare — and their own advantage.

138. The protectionist doctrine is that *if my earnings are
taken from me and given to my neighbor, and he spends them on
himself, there will be important moral gains to the community
which will be lost if I keep my own earnings, and spend them
on myself.* The facts of experience are all to the contrary.
When a man keeps his own earnings he is frugal, temperate, prudent, and honest. When he gets and lives on
another man's earnings, he is extravagant, wasteful, luxurious, idle, and covetous. The effects on the community
in either case correspond.

139. The truth is that protectionism demoralizes and
miseducates a people (§§ 89, 153, 155). It deprives them
of individual self-reliance and energy, and teaches them
to seek crafty and unjust advantages. It breaks down the
skill of great merchants and captains of industry, and develops the skill of lobbyists. It gives faith in monopoly,
combinations, jobbery, and restriction, instead of giving
faith in energy, free enterprise, public purity, and freedom.

Illustrations of this occur all the time. Objection has been made to the introduction of machines to stop the smoke nuisance because they would interfere in the competition of anthracite and bituminous coal. People have resisted the execution of ordinances against gambling houses because said houses "make trade" for their neighbors. The theater men recently made an attempt to get regulations adopted against skating rinks — purely on moral grounds. The industries of the country all run to the form of combinations.[1] Our wisdom is developed, not in the great art of production, but in the tactics of managing a combination, and while we sustain all the causes and all the great principles of this system of business we denounce "monopoly" and "corporations."

(S) That a "Worker may Gain More by Having his Industry Protected than he will Lose by Having to Pay Dearly for what he Consumes. A System which Raises Prices all round — like that in the United States at present — is Oppressive to Consumers, but is Most Disadvantageous to those who Consume without Producing anything, and Does Little, if Any, Injury to those who Produce More than they Consume."

140. This is an English contribution to the subject dropped in passing by a writer on economic history.[2] It is a noteworthy fact that the "historical economists" and others who deride political economy as a science do not desist from it, but at once set to work to make very bad political economy of the "abstract" or "deductive" sort.

[1] See an interesting collection of illustrations in an article on "Lords of Industry" in the *North American Review* for June, 1884. The futile criticisms at the end of the article do not affect the value of the facts collected.

[2] Cunningham, "Growth of English Industry and Commerce," 316, note 2. (See also §§ 114, 134.)

The passage quoted involves three or four fallacies already noticed, and an assumption of the truth of protectionism as a philosophy. As we have abundantly established, "workers" gain nothing by protection in their production (§ 48). Also, "a system which raises prices all around" must either lessen the demand and requirement for money, *i.e.*, restrict business and the supply of goods (§ 112), or it must increase the amount of money. In the former case it could not but injure "workers"; in the latter case we should find ourselves dealing with a greenback fallacy. But passing by that, who are they who consume more than they produce? I can think only of (1) princes, pensioners, sinecurists, protected persons, and paupers, who draw support from taxes, and (2) swindlers, confidence men, and others who live by their wits on the produce of others. Those under (1), if they receive fixed money grants or subsidies, find an advance in price most disadvantageous. So the protected, of course, as consumers of others' products, when they spend what they have received by protection, suffer. Who are they who produce more than they consume? I can think only of (1) taxpayers, and (2) victims of fraud and of those economic errors which give one man's earnings to another's use. Rise in price is just as advantageous to this class as it was disadvantageous to the other, on the same hypothesis, *viz.*, if they pay fixed money taxes to the parasites, and can sell their products for more money. Evidently the writer did not understand correctly what his two classes consisted of, and he put the protected "workers" in the wrong one. If in industry a person should produce more than he consumes, he could give it away, or it would decay on his hands. If he should consume more than he produced, he would run in debt and become bankrupt.[1] Protection has nothing to do with that.

[1] Mill, "Political Economy," Bk. I, ch. 5, § 5. Cairnes, "Leading Principles," ch. I, § 5.

(T) That "A Duty may at once Protect the Native Manufacturer Adequately, and Recoup the Country for the Expense of Protecting him."

141. This is Professor Sidgwick's doctrine.[1] It has given great comfort to our protectionists because it is put forward by an Englishman and a Cambridge professor. It is offered under the "art" of political economy. It is a new thing; an *a priori* art. The "may" in it deprives it of the character of a doctrine or dogma such as our less cultivated protectionists give us — "Protective taxes come out of the foreigner" — but it is not a maxim of art. It has the air of a very astute contrivance (see § 3), and is therefore very captivating to many people, and it is very difficult to dissect and to expose in a simple and popular way. It has therefore given great trouble and done great mischief. It is, however, a complete error. It is not possible in any way or in any degree to use duties so as to make the foreigner pay for protection.

142. Professor Sidgwick states the hypothetical instance which he sets up to prove by illustration that there "may" be such a case, as follows: "Suppose that a five per cent duty is imposed on foreign silks, and that, in consequence, after a certain interval, half the silks consumed are the product of native industry, and that the price of the whole has risen 2½ per cent. It is obvious that, under these circumstances, the other half, which comes from abroad, yields the state five per cent, while the tax levied from the consumers on the whole is only 2½ per cent; so that the nation, in the aggregate, is at this time losing nothing by protection, except the cost of collecting the tax, while a loss equivalent to the whole tax falls on the foreign producer."

143. It is necessary, in the first place, to complete the hypothesis which is included in this case. Let us assume

---

[1] "Political Economy," 491-492.

that the consumption of silk, when all was imported, was 100 yards and that the price was $1 per yard. Then the following points are taken for granted, although not stated in the case as it is put: (1) That the state needs $5 revenue; (2) that it has determined to get this out of *the consumers of silk;* (3) that the advance in price does not diminish the consumption; (4) that the tax forces a reduction of price for the silk in the whole outside market; (5) that the *"silk"* in question is the same thing after the tax is laid as before. Of these assumptions, 3, 4, and 5 are totally inadmissible, but, if they be admitted in the first instance, and if the doctrine of the case which is put be deduced, it is this: If the part imported multiplied by the tax is equal to the total consumption multiplied by the advance in price, the consumers can pay the latter in protection, for it is equal to the former, and the former, which is paid to the government by the foreigner, is what the consumers of silk must otherwise have paid.

144. Obviously this deduction is arithmetically incorrect, even on the hypothesis. In the first place, the government has not obtained $5 revenue which it needed, but $2.50 (5 cents on 50 yards). In the second place, the foreigner sells at $1.02½ (net 97½) the silk which he used to sell for $1. He therefore gets back from the consumers 2½ cents per yard on 50 yards, or $1.25 out of the $2.50 which he has paid to the government. Also, the domestic silk to compete must be equal to the dollar imported silk which now sells for $1.02½. Hence, the consumers really pay in protection only 2½ cents on 50 yards, *.i.e* $1.25. This case, then, is, that the foreigner pays $1.25 revenue, and the consumers pay $1.25 revenue and $1.25 protection. Hence the result is not at all what is asserted, and there is no such operation of the contrivance as was expected. But the government needs $2.50 more revenue, the operation of its tax having been interfered with by

protection. As there is no equivalence or compensation in the case as it already stands, it is evident that the effect of any further tax, instead of bringing about equivalence or compensation, will be to depart from such a result still further.

145. It is, however, impossible to admit assumptions 3, 4, and 5 above, or to deal with any economic problem by any arithmetical process. The result above reached is totally incorrect and only serves to clear the ground for a correct analysis. The producer may have to bear part of a tax, if he is under the tax jurisdiction, or if he has a monopoly. If he has no monopoly, and is not under the tax jurisdiction, and works for the world's market, he cannot lower his price in order to assume part of the tax. What he does is that he differentiates his commodity. This is the fact in the art of production which is established by abundant experience. It is the explanation of the constant complaint, under the protective system, of "fraud" and of the constant demand for subclassification in the tariff schedules. The protected product never is, at least at first, as good in quality as the imported article which it aims to supersede. Hence the foreigner, if he desires to retain the protected market, can prepare a special quality for that market. The "silk" after the tax is laid is not the same silk as before. It nets to the foreign producer $97\frac{1}{2}$ cents, and pays him business profits at that price. Therefore when he sells it at $1.02\frac{1}{2}$ he gets back the whole tax from the consumers. The domestic silk sold at $1.02\frac{1}{2}$ is no better than might have been obtained for $97\frac{1}{2}$ cents. Hence the consumers are paying a tax for protection which is full and equal to the revenue rate. The fact that the price has fallen to $1.02\frac{1}{2}$, and is not $1.05, evidently proves that instead of disproving it, as many believe.

146. Thus this case falls to pieces. It gains a momentary plausibility from the erroneous assumptions which

are implicit in it. The foreign producer may suffer a narrowing of his market and a reduction of his aggregate profits, but there is no way to make him tributary (unless he has a monopoly) either to the treasury or the protected interests of the taxing country.[1] If it was true in general, or in any limited number of cases, that a country which lays protective taxes can make foreigners pay those taxes, then England, which has had no protective taxes since (say) 1850, and has been surrounded by countries which have had more or less protective taxes, must have been paying tribute to them all this time and must have been steadily impoverished accordingly.

CHAPTER V

SUMMARY AND CONCLUSION

147. I have now examined protectionism impartially on its own grounds, assuming them to be true, and adversely from ground taken against it, and have reviewed a series of the commonest arguments put forward in its favor. If now we return, with all the light we have obtained, to test the assumptions which we found in protectionism, that the people would not organize their industry wisely under liberty, and that protective taxes are the correct device for bringing about a better organization, we find that those two assumptions are totally false and have no semblance of claim upon our confidence. At every step the dogmas of protectionism, its claims, its apparatus, have proved fallacious, absurd, and impracticable. We can now group together some general criticisms of protectionism which our investigation suggests.

[1] I published a criticism of this case in the London *Economist*, December 1, 1883.

148. We have taken the protectionist's own definition
of a protective duty, and have found that such a duty,
instead of increasing national wealth, must, at every step,
and by every incident of its operation, waste labor and
capital, lower the efficiency of the national industry, weaken
the country in trade, and consequently lower the standard
of comfort of the whole population. We have found that
protected industries, according to the statement of the
protectionists, do not produce, but consume. If then these
industries are *the* ones which make us rich, *consumption is
production and destruction produces.* The object of a protective duty is "to effect the diversion of a part of the
capital and labor of the people out of the channels in which
it would run otherwise, into channels favored or created
by law" (§ 13). We have seen that the channels *into* which
the labor and capital of the people are to be diverted are
offered by *the industries which do not pay.* Hence protectionism is found to mean that national prosperity is to be
produced by forcing labor and capital into employments
where the capital cannot be reproduced with the same
increase which could be won by it elsewhere. If that is
so, then capital in those employments will be wasted, and
the final outcome of our investigation, which must be made
the primary maxim of the art of national prosperity under
protectionism, is that *Waste makes Wealth.* Such is its
outcome when regarded as an economic philosophy.

149. As regards the social and jural relations which are
established between citizen and citizen, protectionism is
proved by a half-dozen independent analyses of it to be
simply a device for forcing us to levy tribute on each other.
If the law brings a cent to A it must have taken it from B,
or else it must have produced it out of nothing, that is, it
must be magic. Every soul pays protective taxes. If,
then, anybody gets anything from them, he needs to remember what they cost him, and *he should insist on casting*

up both sides of the account. If anybody gets nothing from them, then *he pays the taxes and gets no equivalent.*

150. During the anti-corn-law campaign in England, a writer in the *Westminster Review* illustrated protectionism by the story of the monkeys in a cage, each of whom received for his dinner a piece of bread. Each monkey dropped his own piece of bread and grabbed his neighbor's. The consequence was that soon the floor of the cage was strewn with fragments, and each monkey had to make the best dinner he could from these. It is a good and fair illustration. I saw a story recently in a protectionist newspaper about the peasants in the Soudan. Each owns pigeons, and at evening, when the pigeons come home, each tries to entice as many of his neighbors' pigeons as he can into his own pigeon house. "All of them do the same thing, and therefore each gets caught in his turn. They know this perfectly well, but no Egyptian fellah could resist the temptation of cheating his neighbor." They ought to *tax* each other's pigeons all around. Then they would put themselves at once on the level of free and enlightened Americans. The protectionist assures me that it is for the good of the community and for my good that he should tax me. I reply that, in his language, "these are fine theories," but that whether it is good for the community or not, and whether it is good for me or not, that he should tax me, I can see that it is for his good that he should tax me. Then he says: "Now you are abusive."

151. *If protectionism is anything else than mutual tribute, then it is magic.* The whole philosophy of it comes down to questions like this: How much can I afford to pay a man for hiring me? How much can I afford to pay a man for trading with me? How much can I afford to pay a man to cease to compete with me in my production? How much can I afford to pay a man to go and compete with those who supply me my consumption? It is only *an expensive way to*

get what we could get for nothing if it was worth having (§ 89).
It is admitted that one man cannot lift himself by his boot
straps. Suppose that a thousand men stand in a ring and
each takes hold of the other's boot straps reciprocally and
they all lift, can the whole group lift itself as a group?
That is what protection comes to just as soon as we have
drawn out into light the other side, the *cost side* of it. Whatever we win on one side, we must pay for by at least equal
cost on another. The losses will all be distributed as net
pure injury to the community. The harm of protection lies
here. It is not measured by the tax. *It is measured by the
total crippling of the national industry.* We might as well
say that it would be a good thing to put snags in the rivers,
to fell trees across the roads, to dull all our tools, as to say
that unnecessary taxation could work a blessing. Men
have argued that to destroy machines was to do a beneficial
thing, and I have recently read an article in a Boston paper,
quoting a Massachusetts man who thinks that what we
need is another war in the United States. Such men may
believe that protective taxes work a blessing, but to those
who will see the truth, it is plain that, when the whole
effect of the protective system is distributed, it benefits
nobody. It is a dead weight and loss upon everybody,
and those who think that they win by it would be far better
off in a community where no such system existed, but where
each man earned what he could and kept what he earned.

152. There is a school of political science in this country
in whose deed of foundation it is provided that the professors shall teach how "by suitable tariff legislation, a
nation may keep its productive industry alive, cheapen the
cost of commodities, and oblige foreigners to sell to it at
low prices, while contributing largely toward defraying the
expenses of the government." [1] Is not that a fine thing?
Those professors ought to likewise provide us a panacea,

[1] Quoted by Taussig: "History of the Existing Tariff," 73.

the philosopher's stone, a formula for squaring the circle, and all the other desiderata of universal happiness. It would be only a trifle for them. The only fear is that they may write the secret which they are to teach in books, and that other nations to whom we are "foreigners," may learn it. Then while Englishmen, Frenchmen, and Germans work for us at low prices and pay our taxes, we shall be forced to work for them at low prices and pay their taxes, and the old somber misery will settle down upon the world again the same as ever.

153. Some years ago we were told that protection was necessary because we had a big debt to pay. Well, we have paid the debt until we have reduced it from $78.25 per head to $28.41 per head. We, the people, have also raised our credit until the annual debt charge has been reduced from $4.29 per head to 95 cents per head. Now it is necessary to keep up the debt in order to keep up the taxes, and protectionism is now most efficient in forcing wasteful and corrupting expenditures to get rid of revenue, lest a surplus should furnish an argument for reducing taxation. This is right on the doctrine that waste makes wealth.

154. They tell us that protection has produced prosperity, and when we ask them to account for hard times in spite of the tariff, they say that hard times are caused by the free traders who will not keep still. Therefore *the prosperity produced by protection is so precarious that it can be overthrown by only talking about free trade.* They denounce *laissez-faire,* or "let alone," but the only question is *when* to let alone, *when* to keep still. They do not let the tariff alone if they want to revise it to suit them, or want to make it "equitable." When they get it "equitable" they will let it alone, but that insures agitation, and makes sure that they will cause it, for an indefinite time to come. On the other hand the victims of the tariff will not keep still. Their time to "let alone" is when it is repealed. If the

tariff did not hurt somebody somewhere it would not do
any good to anybody anywhere, and the victims will resist.[1]
Mr. Lincoln used to tell a story about hearing a noise in
the next room. He looked in and found Bob and Tad
scuffling. "What is the matter, boys?" said he. "It is
Tad," replied Bob, "who is trying to get my knife." "Oh,
let him have it, Bob," said Mr. Lincoln, "just to keep him
quiet." "No!" said Bob, "it is my knife and I need it to
keep me quiet." Mr. Lincoln used the story to prove that
there is no foundation for peace save truth and justice.
Now, in this case, *the man whose earnings are being taken
from him needs them to keep him quiet.* Our fathers fought
for free soil, and if we are worthy to be their sons we shall
fight for free trade, which is the necessary complement of
free soil. If a man goes to Kansas to-day and raises corn
on "free soil," how does he get the good of it, unless he can
exchange that corn for any product of the earth that he
chooses on the best terms that the arts and commerce of
to-day can give him?

155. The history of civil liberty is made up of campaigns against abuses of taxation. Protectionism is the
great modern abuse of taxation; the abuse of taxation
which is adapted to a republican form of government.
*Protectionism is now corrupting our political institutions just
as slavery used to do,* viz., it allies itself with every other
abuse which comes up. Most recently it has allied itself

---

[1] Illustrations of this are presented without number. Here is the most recent
one: "The [silk] masters [of Lyons, France] look to the government for relief
by a reduction of the duty on cotton yarn, or the right to import all numbers duty
free for export after manufacture. With the present tariffs, they maintained,
which is no doubt true, that they cannot compete with the Swiss and German
makers. But the Rouen cotton spinners oppose the demand of the Lyons silk
manufacturers, and protest that they will be ruined if the latter are allowed to
procure their material from abroad. The Lyons weavers assert that they are
being ruined because they cannot." — (*Economist*, 1885, p. 815.) The cotton
men won in the Chamber of Deputies, July 23, 1885.

with the silver coinage, and it is now responsible, in a great measure, for that calamity. The silver coinage law would have been repealed three years ago if the silver mining interest had not served notice on the protectionists that that was their share of protection, and the price of their coöperation. The silver coinage is the chief cause of the "hard times" of the last two or three years. In a well-ordered state it is the function of government to repress every selfish interest which arises and endeavors to encroach upon the rights of others. The state thus maintains justice. Under protectionism *the government gives a license to certain interests to go out and encroach on others.* It is an iniquity as to the victims of it, a delusion as to its supposed beneficiaries, and a waste of the public wealth. There is only one reasonable question now to be raised about it, and that is: How can we most easily get rid of it?

LAISSEZ-FAIRE [1]

AMONG the many terms and phrases of social science which are ill-understood and lightly and incorrectly used, no instance is more remarkable than *laissez-faire*. It will be profitable to define and illustrate its meaning.

The story goes that a certain French minister of state, desiring to exert himself for the benefit of the governed, called the merchants of Paris to a conference. He asked them what he could do for them. His idea of doing something for them was not as new as he supposed it was. In fact, they had had a large experience of that sort of thing already. They therefore answered "*Laissez-nous faire.*" Their answer has passed into a proverb and a maxim.

It seems to be widely believed that this phrase means "Do not do anything at all to interfere with nature." The current English translation of it is "Let alone." The translation, however, is so inadequate as to be incorrect and the lack of any equally terse expression in English which will render all the force of the original is the reason why the French phrase has been retained and naturalized.

A fair rendering of the answer of the French merchants would be: "Let us manage for ourselves." They did not propose to do without management. There is no sign in what they said or in what they did that they thought that brains could not be applied to trade and industry so as to develop and improve them. What they dreaded and declined with thanks was the proposition to define

[1] A fragment from a hitherto unpublished essay written toward the end of the 1880's.

lines of action for them according to the wisdom of a statesman. Even if he took them into counsel they could not be induced to coöperate in the work of laying down rules for themselves which must, in the nature of the case, be rigid, arbitrary, hard to change, dictated by some dogma or ideal, and not such as the development of trade and industry would from time to time call for.

What the merchants meant by *laissez-faire* is a matter of only historical importance, but I know of no scientific writer who maintains the doctrine of *laissez-faire* in any other sense than that in which it was originally used. Anyone who gets his notion of *laissez-faire* from the rendering of it in the writings of the professorial socialists may well suppose that it is something very different from this, but that is only one of the features of the situation of political economy at the moment.

Laissez-faire is so far from meaning the unrestrained action of nature without any intelligent interference by man, that it really means the only rational application of human intelligence to the assistance of natural development. The best illustration of the perfect application of *laissez-faire* is a garden in which art has done its utmost to aid nature in that course of development which fits the interests and purposes of man. If we find such a garden anywhere and investigate the methods by which it has been brought into existence, do we find that the gardener has first made up his mind what he wants nature to give and has then proceeded by the method of trial and failure to try to make her come up to his ideal? There have been such gardeners and their successes have been more complete demonstrations of the folly of their method than even the failures. The Dutch gardeners who trimmed trees to represent beasts and birds, spoiling trees without making animals, illustrate very fairly what those statesmen have done to society who have tried to proceed by first forming ideals and then devising schemes to realize them. The gardener who wants a good garden and not a miserable imitation of a menagerie guards himself well against forming any ideals at all, and still more against putting any coercion on nature. He begins with a submission of himself to the investigation of nature. He abstains most carefully from meddling with her until he has observed her lines of independent action, because he knows that if he interferes sooner he will spoil the clearness and distinctness of the information which she will give him. He wants to find out her laws and he knows that, if he interferes with her action before the manifestation of the law is complete, he will not get that pure and simple expression of it which is his most priceless acquisition. His attitude therefore is one of obedience, of subordination, of following, and his chief folly would be conceit and "regulation." When he has a fund of information about the laws of nature, however, he does not use it to impose any purposes of his own on nature. He has only found out what is the range and what are the limitations of the plant world and by what laws nature produces her results within that range. He then selects, not what is better for the plant, but what suits his purposes. Then his whole task consists in furnishing to nature what she needs to help her and in removing all the obstacles which would hinder her in concentrating her forces on the things which men like to the exclusion of the things they do not like.

This illustration furnishes a complete parallel to what art may do to aid nature in society. The social case is infinitely more difficult for a great variety of reasons, but there are plenty of people who, while they would never dream of laying down rules for the management of a garden, are ready enough to prescribe regulations for society. Others propose to get some "statistics" and solve the problem at once. This is in some respects the funniest superstition of our time. A gardener might as well hope to learn how to raise cabbages by learning how many cabbages were raised in the country in a year. The fallacy would be the same.

Laissez-faire is the only true corrective of dogmatism and *a priori* reasoning. History and statistics are not the opposites or the correctives of those abuses. On the contrary, history and statistics are the very best cloaks of dogmatism. I have a large collection of passages from the writings of the "historical school," as it calls itself, in proof of this. An uncritical reader, having in hand an historical or statistical treatise, is likely to accept generalizations or assertions as in some way guaranteed by the positive material in the context, when a moment's examination would show that it stands entirely upon itself.

To give one instance: Jannasch,[1] in an article on the movement of population into the great cities of Germany at the expense of the small cities and rural districts, says that the German great cities do not have specialized industries like those of England, but have a "higher mission on behalf of culture." He then tries to work out his pronouncement by a few assertions about the class of small independent handicraftsmen who migrate into German cities and by generalizations about independent craftsmen as compared with wage-earners. All this is absolutely without foundation or evidence. The assertions are only part of the articles of faith of a pseudo-patriotism. They are open to plain contradiction on appropriate evidence. These generalizations are only the accepted and certainly erroneous commonplaces of an

[1] Zeitschrift des Preuss. Stat. Bureaus, 1878, p. 269.

economic sect. Especially, however, I desire to point out that the alleged comparison of German and English cities, in a statistical article of a statistical periodical, is as purely dogmatic as if it appeared in a treatise on metaphysics.

Did space permit I should be glad to go into an analysis to show what dogmatism is and to distinguish its mischievous from its useful and necessary forms. A similar analysis needs to be made of speculation and generalization. These terms are all used nowadays in a flippant way by ill-educated men, to the great harm of science.

The doctrine and precept of *laissez-faire* do not preclude the attainment of positive results from investigation, nor the formulation of accurate statements of those results, nor the most elaborate verification of those results. The students of the *laissez-faire* school have done nearly all that ever has yet been done in the way of actual achievement under all these heads. *Laissez-faire* means: Do not meddle; wait and observe. Do not regulate; study. Do not give orders; be teachable. Do not enter upon any rash experiments; be patient until you see how it will work out.

The contrary temper is plainly manifested in our day on every hand. A man who has studied into any social question far enough to be nonplussed by its difficulties will propose some form of legislation about it. *Laissez-faire* would teach: At this time and under such a state of the question, the last thing to do is to legislate about it. When a half-dozen large and delicate interests are involved in a matter like transportation, in such a way that no human intelligence can possibly comprehend and adjust them, least of all by a piece of legislation which must be inelastic and arbitrary, this state of things is made a reason, not for letting the matter alone, but for passing some legislation by way of experiment. Nothing could reveal more astoundingly the prevailing ignorance of what a society is and what methods of dealing with it are rational; for it is not possible to experiment with a society and just drop the experiment whenever we choose. The experiment enters into the life of the society and never can be got out again. Therefore, whenever there is a mania for interference, the doctrine of non-interference is the highest wisdom. It does not involve us in any argument with the people who know that the way to national prosperity is through plenty of greenbacks, or another dose of tariff, or who see what direful results will flow from lack of money if we do not have a "double standard." It does not compel us to argue that everything now is ideally good. It simply means that, whatever may be unsatisfactory in the world, we know we would rather take our chances of managing for ourselves than to submit our interests to the manipulation of social doctors.

The social doctor who, having become possessed by a pet notion, has deduced from it a world of bliss is not the worst variety of the species. The Germans have invented a thing which they call *Socialpolitik*. The cruelest blow that can be aimed at one of these German phrases is to translate it into English, for then all the flatulency is let out of it. I early learned that when a German notion was stated in compound and abstract nouns in *heit* and *keit*, so that it seemed to say something very profound, it was well, before accepting it, to sit down and translate it into everyday English. It is astonishing how often what seemed a profound piece of philosophy turned out to be a bathos. "Social policy" in English does not mean anything. "Statecraft," says Bamberger, "has been defined as the science of the possible. This new 'craft' [*Socialpolitik*], consisting in statecraft plus a new series of social functions which the state is to assume, constitutes a science of the impossible, so long as it is a science of the unproved," *i.e.*, of ends whose attainability has not been shown and whose appropriate means have not been ascertained or tested.

A man who has become interested in some one scheme of social improvement, although in his general standpoint unfavorable to interference, will resist the seduction of state interference as a means of accomplishing his object. A man who has been employed in administering some form of government interference is almost sure to become an advocate of that form of interference.

Let anyone notice, whenever a social question is brought into discussion, how inevitably the conversation or debate will run to the aspect of the matter which comes under the question: What can we do about it? or What can we make the tax-payer do about it? It is scarcely possible to get attention for an economic or sociological analysis of the matter which would aim to answer the question: What is the trouble? Is there any trouble? What are the social and economic causes of it? By what free coöperation of the parties concerned, under better knowledge and better temper, could any evil which exists be remedied? The greatest obstacle to any rational and true social improvement at this moment is the well-founded alarm excited by every proposition to do something by legislation — which compels all sober men to insist upon *laissez-faire* as an absolute principle of safety. In the face of those who are elaborating a social policy for us, there is often nothing to do but prevent anything from being done. Nearly all the machinery of Congress is an elaborate mechanism for preventing anything from being done, and although it stops many measures which a great many of us might think it very advisable to pass, we cheerfully do without them lest some of the others should get through likewise. The only fault with the mechanism is that it is not perfect enough. It fails when there is great clamor out of doors, for there is always cowardice inside, and then a Bland Bill or something of that sort can get a two-thirds vote and rise above the barrier of obstruction.

Laissez-faire is a maxim of policy. It is not a rule of science. Here we have another point of cardinal importance in the social wrangle of the day. No sound thinking is possible if we fail to distinguish correctly the domain of art from that of science. Science deals with what is true. The laws which it discovers admit of no exceptions, and when correctly stated cannot be overstated. The scientific man has reached the limit of his domain when he has laid down what he has found to be true. It is immaterial whether anybody believes it or profits by it or not. Here there is no room for maxims. There is nothing approximate or rough that is not imperfect, needing more work put on it. When, however, we go over to the domain of art, that is, of the application of scientific laws by human intelligence to the fulfillment of our purposes, we have come upon an entirely different domain. The limitations of our intelligence and the complications of natural phenomena as they actually occur prevent all clear, absolute, and unmodified rules. Maxims alone are in order over the whole domain of art. They embody long experience of mankind in the work or art, that is, in getting along as well as is practically possible towards the goal we want to reach under the circumstances in which we find ourselves and with the means at our disposal. For instance, if we are dealing with the phenomena of exchange, it belongs to science to analyze those phenomena and find out their laws. We talk about supply and demand very easily, but supply and demand are less understood today than the most difficult and abstruse laws of physics. The text-books present a weary waste of contradiction and whimsical assertion. I am ashamed of political economy whenever I put the chapter on value in Laughlin's "Mill" before my students. Sidgwick's treatment of the same subject is a "mush of concession" to every notion which has ever been put forward in sufficiently metaphysical form to strike the mind of the author. If the economists have no other function than to tell the public that there is no such thing as political economy, and to wrangle with each other about the method by which they shall prove this, whether deductively or inductively, then a man of common sense would best cease to be an economist and seek a respectable means of livelihood. If they say to the statesman: We have no laws of the industrial order which we can give you as the results of our science to guide you in your work; we have no science and cannot get any results which we can affirm with confidence; the field is open for your experiments — if this, I say, is their position, then all men of sense will send political economy to Saturn as Mr. Gladstone did before he began his colossal experiment in Ireland. If, however, there are laws of exchange and value, it is the duty of economists to find them out. The laws which they may discover will be laws in the only scientific sense of the word. When we go over to statecraft, we go over to art — to the domain, not of truth but of expediency, not of scientific laws but of maxims. The statesman then may well be guided by maxims drawn from history and experience. No maxim is more than approximately wise, for wisdom cannot be put into absolute statements and injunctions.

Statecraft is to be guided all the time by the active

reason and intelligent conscience. This is the domain of ethics also. *Laissez-faire* belongs here, where it had its birth and where alone, so far as I know, the English economists, who have given us all the political economy we possess, have used it. If the statesman proposes to interfere with exchange, then *laissez-faire* comes in as a general warning, not as an absolute injunction: Let them manage for themselves. *Laissez-faire* is the only maxim which allows of the correct use of history and statistics to secure such knowledge as shall properly guide the statesman in his task.

BIBLIOGRAPHY

BIBLIOGRAPHICAL NOTE

The following bibliography is as nearly exhaustive as we have been able to make it. There are doubtless other articles which have not come to our attention; and there are certainly a number of contributions to the press, signed and unsigned, to which we have no clue. The distribution of those which we have found will indicate the task of anyone who should aim at exhaustiveness.

It has seemed best to us to include the titles of certain unpublished writings, especially where these are to be made accessible to students by the deposit of the manuscripts with the Yale University Library (under Sumner Estate). Sumner had a way of writing something out very carefully, perhaps as a lecture, and then laying it away with apparently no thought of publishing it; a number of such manuscripts have been printed for the first time in the series of essays published by the Yale University Press. There are also a few of Sumner's printed utterances which we possessed in the form of clippings, but could not locate; the titles of such have been included as accessible at the Yale University Library, under the following two entries: (a) "Sumner, W. G., Miscellanea, 1877–1891. Newspaper clippings mounted. 24 × 31 cm." (b) "Sumner, W. G., newspaper clippings collected by W. G. Sumner. The articles relate chiefly to Prof. Sumner and to subjects connected with political economy. Mounted and bound. 41 cm." The latter includes data from 1885 to 1909. In both cases much of the material consists of attacks on Sumner and his views — matters in which he seemed to be particularly interested. There are also numerous references to his public lectures and debates.

There is a good deal of Sumner's writing in the reports of the Connecticut State Board of Education. We have been informed that his services to that Board, extending over twenty years, included much committee work and many carefully written reports. As these are of a somewhat special nature, we refer simply to the documents of the Board.

The most complete set of Sumner's essays consists of the four volumes published by the Yale University Press between 1911 and 1919. Numerous essays were here printed for the first time; others through their reprinting have thus been made more accessible. Such inclusion is noted below where, for the sake of brevity, the four volumes are referred to as the Collected Essays, as follows:

War and Other Essays as Collected Essays, I,

Earth Hunger and Other Essays as Collected Essays, II,

The Challenge of Facts and Other Essays as Collected Essays, III,

The Forgotten Man and Other Essays as Collected Essays, IV.

Translations of Sumner's articles and books into foreign languages have been noted in so far as they have come to our attention.

At the end is appended a list of the more important biographical sketches of Sumner.

A. G. K.
M. R. D.

1864–66. NOTES OF LECTURES ON THEOLOGY, PHILOSOPHY, ETC., by Ewald, Wiesinger et al., Göttingen. 4 vols., 28½ cm. Manuscripts, Yale University Library.

1869–70. Note: Sumner was one of the editors of *The Living Church*, a periodical published in New York from May, 1869 to April, 1870, Vol. I, Nos. 1–12. The following articles in this short-lived journal were signed by him:

ECCLESIASTICAL TRIALS. September, 1869, Vol. I, No. 5, pp. 71–73.

THE GENERAL THEOLOGICAL SEMINARY. October, 1869, Vol. I, No. 6, pp. 87–88.

THE EVANGELICAL CONFERENCE AND THE CRISIS. December, 1869, Vol. I, No. 8, pp. 116–118.

THE PUBLIC SCHOOL QUESTION. January, 1870, Vol. I, No. 9, pp. 133–135.

THE STUDY OF THE BIBLE. April, 1870, Vol. I, No. 12, pp. 182–184.

AN ESSAY TOWARDS UNITY. April, 1870, Vol. I, No. 12, pp. 186–187.

1871. "REFORM AT YALE. VIEWS OF REV. WILLIAM G. SUMNER." Letter to the editor of the New York Standard, March 22, in reply to an editorial of March 18 regarding Sumner's championship of the "Young Yale" movement.

1872. THE BOOKS OF THE KINGS, by K. C. W. F. Bähr. Translated, Enlarged, and Edited . . . Book 2, by W. G. Sumner, in Lange, J. P., A commentary on the Holy Scripture . . . New York, Scribner, Armstrong & Co., 1866–1882, 26 vols., VI, 312 pp.

THE CHURCH'S LAW OF THE INTERPRETATION OF SCRIPTURE. Unpublished manuscript on scientific criticism of the Bible. April 3. 61 pp. (Sumner Estate.)

MEMORIAL DAY ADDRESS. Delivered at Morristown, New Jersey, May 30. Printed for the first time in Collected Essays, III, pp. 347–362.

1873. THE SOLIDARITY OF THE HUMAN RACE. Unpublished manuscript of an address on the influence of ideas and events in one country on conditions in other countries, delivered at the Sheffield Scientific School, January 11. 40 pp. (Sumner Estate.)

RELATION OF PHYSICAL TO MORAL GOOD. An address. Unpublished manuscript probably of this date, 35 pp. (Sumner Estate.)

INTRODUCTORY LECTURE TO COURSES IN POLITICAL AND SOCIAL SCIENCE. Printed for the first time in Collected Essays, III, pp. 391–403.

HISTORY OF PAPER MONEY. Paper money in China, England, Austria, Russia, and the American Colonies. Unpublished manuscript, 109 pp. (Sumner Estate.)

SOCIALISM. Three unpublished manuscripts written between 1873 and 1880 which appear to be preliminary sketches to the essay entitled The Challenge of Facts. 38, 12, and 31 pp. respectively. (Sumner Estate.)

1874. A HISTORY OF AMERICAN CURRENCY, with chapters on the English Bank Restriction and Austrian Paper Money, to which is appended "The Bullion Report." New York, H. Holt & Co., 391 pp., twofold diagram.

1874. THE LESSON OF THE PANIC (of 1873). Unpublished manuscript advocating a return to a sound currency, 20 pp. (Sumner Estate.)

HAVE WE HAD ENOUGH? Unpublished manuscript on the evils of paper money, written soon after the panic of 1873, 15 pp. (Sumner Estate.)

POLITICAL ECONOMY. From 300 to 400 pages of lecture notes for classroom use. (Sumner Estate.)

TAXATION. What it is, what its relation to other departments of political economy is, and what are the general principles by which it must be controlled. Unpublished manuscript probably of this date, 24 pp. (Sumner Estate.)

AMERICAN FINANCE. Journal of Social Science, July, No. VI, pp. 181–189.

THE CURRENCY QUESTION. An address delivered about this time opposing the issue of irredeemable paper money. Unpublished manuscript, 96 pp. (Sumner Estate.)

1875. "WALL ST. JARGON AT COLLEGE. Commentations on Financial Matters." Report of Sumner's use of a newspaper financial page as the basis of a lecture to his college class. New York Daily Tribune, February 18.

THE ADMINISTRATION OF ANDREW JACKSON. Address before the Kent Club of the Yale Law School, reported rather completely in the New York Daily Tribune, May 3. Printed in full for the first time in Collected Essays, IV, pp. 337–367.

CONSTITUTION OF THE AMERICAN REPUBLIC. Lecture in a series on political topics to Yale graduates. Reported rather fully under the caption, "The American Republic," in the New York Daily Tribune, May 8.

MONETARY DEVELOPMENT. Eleventh paper in a series entitled The First Century of the Republic. Harper's New Monthly Magazine, September, Vol. 51, No. 304, pp. 552–570. The series appeared in book form in 1876.

1876. MONETARY DEVELOPMENT. In Woolsey, T. D., and others, The First Century of the Republic. New York, Harper & Bros., pp. 238–259.

1876. POLITICS IN AMERICA, 1776–1876. North American Review, January, Vol. CXXII, Centennial number, pp. 47–87. Reprinted in Collected Essays, IV, pp. 285–333.

THE CURRENCY QUESTION. Address before the New Haven Chamber of Commerce, February 26. A full abstract is given in the New York Daily Tribune, February 28.

"THE REFORM CAMPAIGN." Remarks of Prof. W. G. Sumner before the Independent Reform Conference, New York City. The New York Daily Tribune, May 17.

SHALL THE "HARD TIMES" CONTINUE? A review of the address of Professor Sumner before the New Haven Chamber of Commerce. The Woonsocket Patriot, May 19.

FREE PIG-IRON. Letter to the New York Mercantile Journal, June 3.

FOR PRESIDENT? New Haven Palladium, September 12. Reprinted in Collected Essays, III, pp. 365–379.

IS THE WAR OVER? "Real Issues of the Day." New York World, October 9.

FEARS OF A SOLID SOUTH. "Real Issues of the Day." New York World, October 10.

BOURBONISM. "Real Issues of the Day." New York World, October 16.

WHAT HAS BECOME OF REFORM? "Real Issues of the Day." New York World, October 23.

THE DEMOCRATIC REPLY. To the visiting Republicans in New Orleans who refused to enter into a conference upon the subject of the counting of the election returns. New York Tribune, November 17.

"PROFESSOR SUMNER ON LOUISIANA." Letter in answer to Governor Ingersoll's request to express his views on the political situation in Louisiana after his visit to New Orleans at the request of Abram S. Hewitt, chairman of the Democratic National Committee. New York World, November 21, New York Daily Tribune, November 22, New York Herald, November 22.

1877. LECTURES ON THE HISTORY OF PROTECTION IN THE
UNITED STATES. Delivered before the International
Free-trade Alliance in the first half of 1876. Reprinted
from "The New Century." Published for the International Free-trade Alliance by G. P. Putnam's Sons,
New York, 64 pp. Contents: The National Idea and
the American System, Broad Principles Underlying
the Tariff Controversy, The Origin of Protection in
this Country, The Establishment of Protection in this
Country, Vacillation of the Protective Policy in this
Country.

REPUBLICAN GOVERNMENT. The Chicago Tribune,
January 1. Reprinted in Collected Essays, III, pp.
223–240.

YALE'S COURSE OF STUDY. Address before the New
York Yale alumni. Briefly mentioned in the New
York Daily Tribune, January 20.

PROTECTION AND PIG-IRON. Letter to the New Haven
Courier, February 12.

DEMOCRACY AND RESPONSIBLE GOVERNMENT. Address
at Providence, R. I., June 19, before the Phi Beta
Kappa Society of Brown University. Appeared in
somewhat abridged form in the New York Daily
Tribune, June 20; printed in full in the Providence
Evening Press, June 21. Reprinted in Collected Essays, III, pp. 243–286.

SILVER. Address before the Senior Class of Yale University. The New Haven Union, December 12; the
New York Daily Tribune, December 13.

THE SILVER QUESTION. What it is and how to deal
with it. New York World, December 12.

THE COMMERCIAL CRISIS OF 1837. Written in 1877 or
1878. (There are indications on the manuscript that
it was once printed, but efforts to find where have
failed.) Published, probably for the first time, in
Collected Essays, IV, pp. 371–398.

1878. OUR REVENUE SYSTEM, by A. L. Earle. Preface by
W. G. Sumner. New York, published for the New
York Free-trade Club by G. P. Putnam's Sons, 47 pp.
(Economic Monograph No. V.)

1878. MONEY AND ITS LAWS. International Review, January
and February, Vol. V, pp. 75–81.
WHAT IS FREE TRADE? Chicago News, January 7.
SILVER. Address in Chicago. The Chicago Tribune,
January 9.
THE SILVER QUESTION. Lecture before the Manhattan
Club of New York City, January 25, on the disastrous
results of remonetization. The New York World,
January 26. Abstract in the New York Times,
January 26.
A FEW PLAIN ANSWERS. Letter to the New Haven
Register, February 28, on the tariff.
PROTECTION AND REVENUE IN 1877. Lecture delivered
before the New York Free-trade Club, April 18. New
York, published for the New York Free-trade Club
by G. P. Putnam's Sons, 38 pp. (Economic Mono-
graph No. VIII.)
"PROF. SUMNER'S TESTIMONY on the general and local
causes of the depression," before the Congressional
Committee on Labor and Business Depression. New
York Daily Tribune, August 23.
SOCIALISM. Scribner's Monthly, October, Vol. XVI, No.
6, pp. 887–893.
THE NATIONAL BANK CIRCULATION. Scribner's Magazine, December, Vol. XVII, No. 2, pp. 205–209.
RELATION OF LEGISLATION TO CURRENCY. Unpublished
manuscript written about this time dealing with the
nature of money, coining, paper money, legal tender
acts, the monetary experience of England and France,
etc., and opposing the abuses of legislation in regard
to currency. 45 pp. (Sumner Estate.)
A CONCURRENT CIRCULATION OF GOLD AND SILVER.
Printed for the first time in Collected Essays, IV,
pp. 183–210.
1879. THE INFLUENCE OF COMMERCIAL CRISES ON OPINIONS
ABOUT ECONOMIC DOCTRINES. An address before the
Free-trade Club, New York City, May 15. Printed
for the first time in Collected Essays, IV, pp. 213–235.
BIMETALLISM. Princeton Review, November, pp. 546–
578.

486 BIBLIOGRAPHY

1879. AMORTIZATION OF PUBLIC DEBTS. Unpublished manuscript, chiefly historical, written about this time. 35 pp. (Sumner Estate.)

THE COÖPERATIVE COMMONWEALTH. Written in the seventies or early eighties. Extracts printed for the first time in Collected Essays, IV, pp. 441–462.

1880. WHAT OUR BOYS ARE READING. Combined with "Books and Reading for the Young," by J. H. Smart. Chas. Scribner's Sons. Reprinted in Collected Essays, II, pp. 367–377.

THE TRUE AIM OF LIFE. Address to the Seniors in Yale University. The New Haven Register, February 1. (Not in form for reprinting.)

THE THEORY AND PRACTICE OF ELECTIONS. Princeton Review, March, pp. 262–286, and July, pp. 24–41.

TWO LETTERS TO THE NEW YORK TIMES, April 3 and 4, giving his reasons for using Spencer's "Study of Sociology" as a text-book.

THE REVIVAL OF OCEAN COMMERCE. A free-trade letter to the American Railroad Journal, September 10.

THE TARIFF QUESTION. A series of short articles in the New Haven Register, October 9, 12, 14, and 19.

THE FINANCIAL QUESTIONS NOW BEFORE US. Unpublished manuscript written about this time, 8 pp. (Sumner Estate.)

1881. POLITICAL ECONOMY AND POLITICAL SCIENCE. A priced and classified list of books recommended for general reading and as an introduction to special study of subjects of economic and political importance. Compiled by W. G. Sumner, D. A. Wells, W. E. Foster, R. L. Dugdale, and G. H. Putnam. New York Society for Political Education. Cover title, 36 pp., 20 cm. Economic Tracts No. 2.

PRESIDENTIAL ELECTIONS AND CIVIL-SERVICE REFORM. Princeton Review, January, pp. 129–148.

PANIC WITHOUT CAUSE. Lecture in Brothers' Hall, New Haven, on the recent panic in Wall Street. New Haven Register, January 14.

THE ARGUMENT AGAINST PROTECTIVE TAXES. Princeton Review, March, pp. 241–259.

1881. SHALL AMERICANS OWN SHIPS? North American Review, June, Vol. 132, No. CCXCV, pp. 559–566. Reprinted in Collected Essays, IV, pp. 273–282.

SOCIOLOGY. Princeton Review, November, pp. 303–323. Reprinted in Collected Essays, I, pp. 167–192.

1882. ANDREW JACKSON AS A PUBLIC MAN. What he was, what chances he had, and what he did with them. Boston, New York, Houghton Mifflin Company. 402 pp. (American Statesmen Series.)

PROTECTIVE TAXES AND WAGES. Philadelphia Tariff Commission, 21 pp. Caption title.

PROTECTION AND FREE TRADE. Lecture before the Revenue Reform Club of Brooklyn, briefly reported in the New York Daily Tribune, March 2.

THE NECESSITY FOR TARIFF REFORM. Address before the mass meeting held by the Free-trade Club in Chickering Hall, New York City. New York Times, April 15.

BANK CHECKS AND BLANKETS. A free-trade letter to the New Haven Register, June 2.

THE "AMERICAN SYSTEM." A letter to the American Free-trade League, June.

FORTUNES MADE IN THREAD. Letter to the New York Times, June 5, on the peculiar protection given to the manufacturers of thread.

WHY SHOULD THE MEN OF IOWA LEVY TAXES ON THEMSELVES TO BENEFIT PENNSYLVANIA? Iowa State Leader, September 4.

THE FREE PLAY OF ECONOMIC FORCES. Letter to the Nation regarding Jevons's "State in Relation to Labor," September 30.

LUMBER PRICES. Letter to the Northwestern Lumberman, October 14.

THE SCIENCE OF SOCIOLOGY. A toast given at a dinner for Herbert Spencer, November 9. Reported in full under the caption, "Evolutionists at Dinner," in the New York Daily Tribune, November 10. All the speeches were published in book form in 1883, entitled Herbert Spencer on the Americans and the Americans on Herbert Spencer.

1882. Professor Sumner's speech before the Tariff Commission, reviewed by George Basil Dixwell. Cambridge, J. Wilson & Son, 43 pp.

Professor Sumner's "Argument against Protective Taxes," reviewed by George Basil Dixwell. Cambridge, J. Wilson & Son, 13 pp.

WAGES. Princeton Review, November, pp. 241–262.

1883. THE FORGOTTEN MAN. The original lecture on this subject, delivered January 30, in the Brooklyn Historical Society rooms. 28 pp. typewritten. Printed for the first time in Collected Essays, IV, pp. 465–495. Reprinted separately as a pamphlet in 1933.

WHAT SOCIAL CLASSES OWE TO EACH OTHER. First appeared in Harper's Weekly, February–May, Vol. XXVII, Nos. 1366–1376. New York, Harper & Brothers, 169 pp. Republished by the Yale University Press, 1925, with a foreword by A. G. Keller, 169 pp.

ON THE CASE OF A CERTAIN MAN WHO IS NEVER THOUGHT OF. Reprinted in Collected Essays, I, pp. 247–253, from "What Social Classes Owe to Each Other," pp. 123–133. Also reprinted in Modern Essays, selected and edited by J. M. Berdan, J. R. Schultz, and H. E. Joyce, New York, the Macmillan Co., 1916, pp. 341–348, and (with the title The Forgotten Man) in Points of View for College Students, compiled by Paul Kaufman, New York, Doubleday, Doran, 1926, pp. 335–342.

THE CASE OF THE FORGOTTEN MAN FURTHER CONSIDERED. Reprinted in Collected Essays, I, pp. 257–268, from "What Social Classes Owe to Each Other," pp. 134–152.

THE SCIENCE OF SOCIOLOGY. A Speech at the Farewell Banquet to Herbert Spencer. Delivered November 9, 1882, published in "Herbert Spencer on the Americans and the Americans on Herbert Spencer," pp. 35–40. New York, D. Appleton & Company, 96 pp. Reprinted in Collected Essays, IV, pp. 401–405.

BEST PUBLIC OPINION. Letter to the Gazette and Free Press, January 12, in reply to T. K. Beecher.

1883. LET COMMERCIAL RELATIONS ALONE. Letter to W. H. Knight in the Gazette and Free Press, January 16.

Letter to Mr. Earle of the American Free-trade League regarding a speech of Mr. William M. Evarts's. Printed in the New York Times, February 6.

"PROFESSOR SUMNER ON MONETARY SCIENCE." Letter to the editor of Bradstreet's in which he disagrees with the theory of H. C. Adams that money laws in economics are dependent on the nation's sentiment as expressed in its legislative enactments. February 10.

"PROFESSOR SUMNER REPLIES." Letter to the New Haven Register, February 10, referring to his remarks about the protective tax on thread in his lecture on the "Forgotten Man."

"PROFESSOR SUMNER'S PRESUMPTION." A defense of his letter to Mr. Earle regarding a speech of Mr. Evarts's. New York Times, February 14.

WILLIMANTIC LINEN MILLS. Letter to the New York Times, February 16, defending his position as taken against the protective tax on thread.

SOME FACTS ABOUT THREAD. Unpublished manuscript, 14 pp., referring to the controversy with the Willimantic Linen Co. (Sumner Estate.) An address before the Revenue Reform Club of Montclair, New Jersey, February 23, briefly reported in the New York Daily Tribune, February 24.

A THEORIST ANSWERED. A free-trade letter to the New Haven Register, February 26, in reply to a letter signed "Hardpan."

THE GAIN TO THE COUNTRY BY PROTECTION. Some conclusions as to the cost of our protective system. Letter to the New York Times, February 27.

"PROFESSOR SUMNER INSTRUCTS HIS CRITICS." A letter to the editor in reply to criticism of his earlier letter on The Gain to the Country by Protection. New York Times, March 2.

THAT CENSUS PUZZLE. Letter to the editor. New York Times, March 3.

PROTECTIVE TAXES AND WAGES. North American Review, March, Vol. 136, No. CCCXVI, pp. 270–276.

1883. A Course of Reading in Political Economy. Prepared for The Critic, March, 4 pp.

Sociology. Paper read before the Nineteenth Century Club in New York City, briefly reported in the New York Daily Tribune, March 7.

Tariff Statistics and Protection. Letter to the editor. New York Times, March 9.

Protection Arguments from the Willimantic Linen Company's Business. Letter to the editor. New York Times, April 16.

Thread. Letter to the Boston Transcript, April 25, regarding the Willimantic Linen Co.

The Willimantic Mills' Profit. Letter to the Boston Transcript, April 30.

Letter to the Palladium (New Haven), April 30, regarding the controversy with the Willimantic Linen Co.

Thread at Three Cents a Spool. Letter to the editor. New York Times, May 3.

"Professor Sumner's Views." Letter to the New Haven Register, May 26, in answer to Mr. Barrows of the Willimantic Linen Co.

The Philosophy of Strikes. Harper's Weekly, September 15, Vol. XXVII, No. 1395, p. 586. Reprinted in Collected Essays, IV, pp. 239–246.

Letter to the New Haven Register, October 18, regarding the development of our industries.

"Mixed Up Mr. Sheldon." Letter to the New Haven Register, October 30, showing Mr. Sheldon's ignorance of tariff laws.

Suggestions on Social Subjects. Passages selected from "What Social Classes Owe to Each Other," in the Popular Science Monthly, December, Vol. XXIV, pp. 160–169.

An American Criticism of British Protectionist Theories. A criticism of Professor Sidgwick's doctrine that protective taxes come out of the foreigner. The London Economist, December 1, Vol. XLI, No. 2,101, pp. 1397–1398.

The Democratic Theory of Public Offices. Address before the Civil Service Reform Association, Roches-

1883. ter, N. Y. Reasons for reform in the manner of select-
ing public officers. What would be gained by the
change. Printed in the Rochester newspapers of the
time. (Sumner Estate.)

1884. PROBLEMS IN POLITICAL ECONOMY. New York, 12mo.,
125 pp. H. Holt & Co. A series of questions for
students.

DES DEVOIRS RESPECTIFS DES CLASSES DE LA SOCIÉTÉ.
Traduit de l'anglais par J.-G. Courcelle-Seneuil.
Paris, Guillaumin et Cie., 236 pp., 13½ cm.

OUR COLLEGES BEFORE THE COUNTRY. Princeton Review, March, pp. 127–140. Reprinted in Collected
Essays, I, pp. 355–373.

SOCIOLOGICAL FALLACIES. North American Review,
June, Vol. 138, No. CCCXXXI, pp. 574–579. Reprinted in Collected Essays, II, pp. 357–364.

EVILS OF THE TARIFF SYSTEM. North American Review,
September, Vol. 139, No. CCCXXXIV, pp. 293–299.

1885. PROTECTIONISM. The -Ism which Teaches that Waste
Makes Wealth. New York, H. Holt & Company,
12mo., 170 pp. Reprinted in Collected Essays, IV,
pp. 9–111.

"SHOULD THE TARIFF LAWS OF THE UNITED STATES BE
FOR REVENUE ONLY?" Debate with Gen. Stewart L.
Woodford, February 20 and 21, in Brooklyn, reported
with short excerpts in the New York Times, February
21 and 22.

THE ETHICAL ASPECTS OF THE PROTECTION SYSTEM.
Address delivered April 26; possessed in form of
galley proof. (Sumner Estate.)

THE SILVER QUESTION. In reply to an inquiry as to
whether existing supplies of gold are sufficient for
banking and commercial wants. New York Daily
Commercial Bulletin, October 19.

COLLECTED ESSAYS IN POLITICAL AND SOCIAL SCIENCE.
New York, H. Holt & Company, 173 pp. Contents:
Bimetallism, Wages, The Argument against Protective
Taxes, Sociology, Theory and Practice of Elections,
Presidential Elections and Civil Service Reform, Our
Colleges before the Country.

1885. OUR CURRENCY FOR THE LAST TWENTY-FIVE YEARS.
Harper's Weekly, January 10–February 7, Vol.
XXIX, Nos. 1464–1468, pp. 23, 43, 58, 78, 91.
SHALL SILVER BE DEMONETIZED? North American Re-
view, June, Vol. 140, No. CCCXLIII, pp. 485–489.

1886. LE PROTECTIONNISME. Traduit de l'anglais par Joseph
Chailley. Paris, Guillaumin et Cie., 256 pp., 14½ cm.
REGULATION OF CONTRACTS. How far have modern im-
provements in production and transportation changed
the principle that men should be left free to make their
own bargains? Science, March 5, Vol. VII, No. 161,
pp. 225–228.
WHAT IS FREE TRADE? In Good Cheer for April, p. 7.
Reprinted in Collected Essays, IV, pp. 123–127.
CAN PROTECTION INCREASE THE WEALTH OF THE COUN-
TRY? The Tax-gatherer, May 22, No. 19.
INDUSTRIAL WAR. Forum, September, Vol. II, pp. 1–8.
Reprinted in Collected Essays, III, pp. 93–102.
MR. BLAINE ON THE TARIFF. North American Review,
October, Vol. 143, No. CCCLIX, pp. 398–405.
WHAT IS THE "PROLETARIAT"? The Independent, Octo-
ber 28. Reprinted in Collected Essays, III, pp. 161–
165.
WHO WIN BY PROGRESS? The Independent, Novem-
ber 25. Reprinted in Collected Essays, III, pp. 169–
174.
THE NEW SOCIAL ISSUE. The Independent, December
23. Reprinted in Collected Essays, III, pp. 207–212.
SUBJECTS FOR THESES AND COMPOSITIONS. Prepared
with notes and references attached to the subjects
for Senior and Junior Classes, Yale College. I. Honor
Theses in Political Science. II. Subjects for Required
Compositions. 9 pp. (Sumner Estate.)
HISTORY OF THE UNITED STATES OF AMERICA, 1824–
1876. Notes of Sumner's lectures taken by J. C.
Schwab, 1886–1887. MS 17½ × 25½ cm. Yale Uni-
versity Library.
POLITICAL ECONOMY. Notes of Sumner's lectures taken
by J. C. Schwab, 1886–1887. MS 17½ × 25½ cm.
Yale University Library.

1887. SOCIALE PFLICHTEN ODER WAS DIE KLASSEN DER GE-
SELLSCHAFT EINANDER SCHULDIG SIND. Autorisirte
Uebersetzung von M. Jacobi. Mit einem Vorwort von
Dr. Th. Barth. Berlin, Elwin Staude, 96 pp., 21 cm.
WHAT MAKES THE RICH RICHER AND THE POOR POORER?
Popular Science Monthly, January, Vol. XXX, pp.
289-296. Reprinted in Collected Essays, III, pp.
65-77.
SOCIALISM. Speech before the Massachusetts Reform
Club, Boston, January 8. Boston Sunday Record,
January 9.
FEDERAL LEGISLATION ON RAILROADS. The Independ-
ent, January 20. Reprinted in Collected Essays, III,
pp. 177-182.
LEGISLATION BY CLAMOR. The Independent, February
24. Reprinted in Collected Essays, III, pp. 185-190.
THE SHIFTING OF RESPONSIBILITY. The Independent,
March 24. Reprinted in Collected Essays, III, pp.
193-198.
SOME POINTS IN THE NEW SOCIAL CREED. The Inde-
pendent, April 21. Reprinted in Collected Essays, II,
pp. 207-211.
THE INDIANS IN 1887. Forum, May, Vol. III, pp. 254-
262.
SPECULATIVE LEGISLATION. The Independent, May 19.
Reprinted in Collected Essays, III, pp. 215-219.
UNRESTRICTED COMMERCE. Chautauquan, June, Vol.
VII, pp. 541-543.
THE BANQUET OF LIFE. The Independent, June 23.
Reprinted in Collected Essays, II, pp. 217-221.
SOME NATURAL RIGHTS. The Independent, July 28.
Reprinted in Collected Essays, II, pp. 222-227.
STRIKES AND THE INDUSTRIAL ORGANIZATION. Popular
Science News, July, Vol. XXI, No. 7, pp. 93-94. Re-
printed in Collected Essays, IV, pp. 249-253.
STATE INTERFERENCE. North American Review, Au-
gust, Vol. 145, No. CCCLXIX, pp. 109-119. Re-
printed in Collected Essays, I, pp. 213-226.
THE ABOLITION OF POVERTY. The Independent, August
25. Reprinted in Collected Essays, II, pp. 228-232.

494   BIBLIOGRAPHY

1887. THE STATE AS AN "ETHICAL PERSON." The Independent, October 6. Reprinted in Collected Essays, III, pp. 201–204.

THE BOON OF NATURE. The Independent, October 27. Reprinted in Collected Essays, II, pp. 233–238.

CIVIL SERVICE REFORM. Chautauquan, November, Vol. VIII, pp. 78–80.

IS LIBERTY A LOST BLESSING? The Independent, November 24. Reprinted in Collected Essays, II, pp. 131–135.

ADVANTAGES OF FREE TRADE. The Christian Secretary, Vol. XLVI. (Clipping in Sumner Estate.)

1888. LAND MONOPOLY. The Independent, January 12. Reprinted in Collected Essays, II, pp. 239–244.

A GROUP OF NATURAL MONOPOLIES. The Independent, February 16. Reprinted in Collected Essays, II, pp. 245–248.

THE FALL IN SILVER AND INTERNATIONAL COMPETITION. Rand McNally's Banker's Monthly, February, pp. 47–48.

THE FIRST STEPS TOWARDS A MILLENNIUM. Cosmopolitan, March, Vol. V, pp. 32–36. Reprinted in Collected Essays, II, pp. 93–105.

ANOTHER CHAPTER ON MONOPOLY. The Independent, March 15. Reprinted in Collected Essays, II, pp. 249–253.

TRUSTS AND TRADES-UNIONS. The Independent, April 19. Reprinted in Collected Essays, IV, pp. 257–262.

THE FAMILY MONOPOLY. The Independent, May 10. Reprinted in Collected Essays, II, pp. 254–258.

AN EIGHT-HOUR DAY. The Popular Science News and Boston Journal of Chemistry, June, Vol. XXII, No. 6, p. 83.

THE FAMILY AND PROPERTY. The Independent, June 14 and July 19. Reprinted in Collected Essays, II, pp. 259–269.

TARIFF REFORM. The Independent, August 16. Reprinted in Collected Essays, IV, pp. 115–120.

THE STATE AND MONOPOLY. The Independent, Sep-

1888. tember 13 and October 11. Reprinted in Collected Essays, II, pp. 270–279.

"A CONDITION NOT A THEORY." On free trade. Belford's Monthly Magazine, October, Vol. I, No. 5.

DEMOCRACY AND PLUTOCRACY. The Independent, November 15. Reprinted in Collected Essays, II, pp. 283–289.

DEFINITIONS OF DEMOCRACY AND PLUTOCRACY. The Independent, December 20. Reprinted in Collected Essays, II, pp. 290–295.

1889. THE CONFLICT OF PLUTOCRACY AND DEMOCRACY. The Independent, January 10. Reprinted in Collected Essays, II, pp. 296–300.

PEASANT EMANCIPATION IN DENMARK. Based on a review of Stavnsbaands-løsningen og landboreformerne. Set fra nationaløkonomiens Standpunkt. Af V. Falbe Hansen, Copenhagen: Gad. 1888. The Nation, February 7, No. 1232, pp. 123–124.

PEASANTS AND LAND TENURE IN SCANDINAVIA. Unpublished manuscript, 20 typewritten pages, written in 1889 or later, covering the period from the earliest times to the eighteenth century. (Sumner Estate.)

SEPARATION OF STATE AND MARKET. The Independent, February 14. Reprinted in Collected Essays, II, pp. 306–311.

DEMOCRACY AND MODERN PROBLEMS. The Independent, March 28. Reprinted in Collected Essays, II, pp. 301–305.

SOCIAL WAR IN DEMOCRACY. The Independent, April 11. Reprinted in Collected Essays, II, pp. 312–317.

AN EXAMINATION OF A NOBLE SENTIMENT. The Independent, May 16. Reprinted in Collected Essays, II, pp. 212–216.

SKETCH OF WILLIAM GRAHAM SUMNER. Based largely on Sumner's reply to questions put by the editor. The Popular Science Monthly, June, Vol. XXXV, pp. 261–268. Reprinted in Collected Essays, III, pp. 3–13.

AN OLD "TRUST." The Independent, June 13. Reprinted in Collected Essays, IV, pp. 265–269.

1889. WHAT IS CIVIL LIBERTY? The Popular Science Monthly, July, Vol. XXXV, pp. 289–303. Reprinted in Collected Essays, II, pp. 109–130.

WHO IS FREE? IS IT THE SAVAGE? The Independent, July 18. Reprinted in Collected Essays, II, pp. 136–140.

WHO IS FREE? IS IT THE CIVILIZED MAN? The Independent, August 15. Reprinted in Collected Essays, II, pp. 140–145.

WHO IS FREE? IS IT THE MILLIONAIRE? The Independent, September 12. Reprinted in Collected Essays, II, pp. 145–150.

WHO IS FREE? IS IT THE TRAMP? The Independent, October 17. Reprinted in Collected Essays, II, pp. 150–155.

LIBERTY AND RESPONSIBILITY. The Independent, November 21. Reprinted in Collected Essays, II, pp. 156–160.

LIBERTY AND LAW. The Independent, December 26. Reprinted in Collected Essays, II, pp. 161–166.

DO WE WANT INDUSTRIAL PEACE? Forum, December, Vol. VIII, pp. 406–416. Reprinted in Collected Essays, I, pp. 229–243.

FREE TRADE. Unpublished manuscript of about this date. I. Definitions of Protection and Protectionism. II. The Medieval Doctrine of Commerce. III. The Sixteenth Century. IV. The Dynastic States. V. Mercantilism and the Colonial System. VI. The New Doctrine. VII. Smithianismus. VIII. Protection in the United States. IX. Nineteenth-century Protectionism. X. The Present Situation. About 64 typewritten pages. (Sumner Estate.)

1880–89. THE STRIKES. Unpublished manuscript written sometime in the eighties, 21 typewritten pages. A general survey of the "labor question." (Sumner Estate.)

A PARABLE. Written in the eighties. Printed for the first time in Collected Essays, III, pp. 105–107.

THE SPHERE OF ACADEMICAL INSTRUCTION. Address delivered at the celebration of a school anniversary. To judge "what an academy is, what it ought to do,

1880–89. and how it ought to do it; and to judge of its achievements by true standards." Unpublished manuscript of the eighties, 27 pages. (Sumner Estate.)

LAISSEZ-FAIRE. A fragment of a hitherto unpublished manuscript written toward the end of the eighties.

INTEGRITY IN EDUCATION. An address delivered in Hartford probably in the eighties. Printed for the first time in Collected Essays, IV, pp. 409–419.

DISCIPLINE. Probably in the eighties. Printed for the first time in Collected Essays, IV, pp. 423–438.

THE CHALLENGE OF FACTS. Written sometime in the eighties. Original title was Socialism. Printed for the first time in Collected Essays, III, pp. 17–52.

1890. ALEXANDER HAMILTON. ("Makers of America.") New York, Dodd, Mead & Co., 12mo., 280 pp.

LIBERTY AND DISCIPLINE. The Independent, January 16. Reprinted in Collected Essays, II, pp. 166–171.

DOES LABOR BRUTALIZE? The Independent, February 20. Reprinted in Collected Essays, II, pp. 187–193.

LIBERTY AND PROPERTY. The Independent, March 27. Reprinted in Collected Essays, II, pp. 171–176.

LIBERTY AND OPPORTUNITY. The Independent, April 24. Reprinted in Collected Essays, II, pp. 176–181.

WHY I AM A FREE TRADER. Twentieth Century, April 24, pp. 8–10.

CAN WE GET MORE MONEY? Frank Leslie's Illustrated Newspaper, May 3, Vol. LXX, No. 1807, pp. 274–275.

LIBERTY AND LABOR. The Independent, May 22. Reprinted in Collected Essays, II, pp. 181–187.

PROPOSED SILVER LEGISLATION. Frank Leslie's Illustrated Newspaper, May 24, Vol. LXX, No. 1810, p. 330.

LIBERTY AND MACHINERY. The Independent, June 12. Reprinted in Collected Essays, II, pp. 193–198.

THE DISAPPOINTMENT OF LIBERTY. The Independent, July 17. Reprinted in Collected Essays, II, pp. 198–203.

WHAT EMANCIPATES. The Independent, August 14. Reprinted in Collected Essays, III, pp. 137–142.

498 BIBLIOGRAPHY

1890. THE DEMAND FOR MEN. The Independent, September
11. Reprinted in Collected Essays, III, pp. 111–116.
THE SIGNIFICANCE OF THE DEMAND FOR MEN. The
Independent, October 16. Reprinted in Collected
Essays, III, pp. 119–123.
WHAT THE "SOCIAL QUESTION" Is. The Independent,
November 20. Reprinted in Collected Essays, III,
pp. 127–133.
1891. THE FINANCIER AND THE FINANCES OF THE AMERICAN
REVOLUTION. New York, Dodd, Mead & Co., 2 vols.,
8vo., 309 and 330 pp.
LIBERTÉ DES ÉCHANGES. Nouveau Dictionnaire d'Éco-
nomie Politique, Vol. 2, pp. 138–166. Guillaumin et
Cie., Paris.
POWER AND PROGRESS. The Independent, January 15.
Reprinted in Collected Essays, III, pp. 145–150.
CONSEQUENCES OF INCREASED SOCIAL POWER. The In-
dependent, August 13. Reprinted in Collected Essays,
III, pp. 153–158.
1892. ROBERT MORRIS ("Makers of America"). New York,
Dodd, Mead & Co., 12mo., 172 pp.
1893. PROPOSED CLASSIFICATION OF THE SOCIAL SCIENCES. A
chart printed for distribution to the classes in Social
Science in Yale University. "Not published."
PROTECTIONISM. The -Ism which Teaches that Waste
makes Wealth. Translated into Russian by ÎA A.
Novikov. S.-Peterburg, Sklad izdaniîa v knizhnom
magazinîe F. V. Shchepanskago.
1894. THE ABSURD EFFORT TO MAKE THE WORLD OVER.
Forum, March, Vol. XVII, pp. 92–102. Reprinted
in Collected Essays, I, pp. 195–210.
1895. THE VENEZUELA MESSAGE. Letter to the New York
Times, December 18.
1896. A HISTORY OF BANKING IN THE UNITED STATES. Being
Vol. I of A History of Banking in all the Leading
Nations. New York, The Journal of Commerce and
Commercial Bulletin, 485 pp.
"PROFESSOR SUMNER ON YALE." Letter to The Yale
News, January 20. Learning is more appreciated here
now than thirty years ago.

1896. THE CURRENCY CRISIS. A course of six lectures given at the house of Mr. John E. Parsons, 30 East 36th St., New York City, February 13 and 27 and March 5, 12, 19, and 26. What the lecturer said, as well as the questions and answers at the end of his lectures, was taken down in shorthand and typewritten. Mr. Herbert Parsons has the transcript in bound form, and the Yale University Library also has a copy. (Sumner Estate.)

THE TREASURY AS A BANK OF ISSUE AND A SILVER WAREHOUSE. The Bond Record, March, Vol. IV, No. 2, pp. 87–89.

AN ANSWER TO MR. TIGHE'S LETTER ON YALE'S VENEZUELAN ATTITUDE. Letter to the Yale Alumni Weekly, May 20, Vol. V, No. 30, pp. 1–2.

THE FALLACY OF TERRITORIAL EXTENSION. Forum, June, Vol. XXI, pp. 416–419. Reprinted in Collected Essays, I, pp. 285–293.

A FEW WORDS. Short address as member of the State Board of Education at the graduating exercises of the New Haven Normal School, June 18. (Sumner Estate.)

THE POLICY OF DEBASEMENT. "The Battle of the Standards." New York Journal, July 29.

THE PROPOSED DUAL ORGANIZATION OF MANKIND. The Popular Science Monthly, August, Vol. XLIX, pp. 433–439. Reprinted in Collected Essays, I, pp. 271–281.

PROSPERITY STRANGLED BY GOLD. Leslie's Weekly, August 20. Reprinted in Collected Essays, IV, pp. 141–145.

CAUSE AND CURE OF HARD TIMES. Leslie's Weekly, September 3. Reprinted in Collected Essays, IV, pp. 149–153.

THE FREE-COINAGE SCHEME IS IMPRACTICABLE AT EVERY POINT. Leslie's Weekly, September 10. Reprinted in Collected Essays, IV, pp. 157–162.

DELUSION OF THE DEBTORS. Leslie's Weekly, September 17. Reprinted in Collected Essays, IV, pp. 165–170.

1896. THE CRIME OF 1873. Leslie's Weekly, September 24. Reprinted in Collected Essays, IV, pp. 173–180.

THE SINGLE GOLD STANDARD. Chautauquan, October, Vol. XXIV, pp. 72–77.

BANKS OF ISSUE IN THE UNITED STATES. Forum, October, Vol. XXII, pp. 182–191.

EARTH HUNGER OR THE PHILOSOPHY OF LAND GRABBING. Printed for the first time in Collected Essays, II, pp. 31–64.

A FREE COINAGE CATECHISM. Reprinted from The Evening Post, The Evening Post Publishing Co., New York, 16 pp.

LECTURES ON AMERICAN HISTORY, Yale University, 1896–1897. Notes taken by J. C. Schwab. MS. 13 × 21 cm. Yale University Library.

ADVANCING SOCIAL AND POLITICAL ORGANIZATION IN THE UNITED STATES. 1896 or 1897. Printed for the first time in Collected Essays, III, pp. 289–344.

1897. THE TEACHER'S UNCONSCIOUS SUCCESS. Address given at a dinner held in honor of Mr. Henry Barnard, at Jewel Hall, Hartford, January 25. Printed for the first time in Collected Essays, II, pp. 9–13.

MONEY AND CURRENCY. A course of four lectures delivered in Boston. I. The Anxiety Lest there be not Money Enough. II. How We Resumed Specie Payments in 1879. What We Did Not Do. III. The Single Gold Standard — A Beneficent and Accomplished Fact. IV. Where We now Stand and what We Have to Do. Syllabus.

SOCIOLOGY. A course of six lectures given in Albany, February 27, March 6, 13, 20, 27, and April 3. Introduction. Individuality and Sociality. Property. Industrialism and Militarism. Population. Mental Reaction on Experience. Suggested Books for a Course of Reading. Syllabus.

THE ORIGIN OF THE DOLLAR. Paper read at meeting of the British Association for the Advancement of Science, at Toronto, August 19–25. (Sumner Estate.)

OUTLINE OF A PROPOSED CURRICULUM (for Yale College). 4 pages typewritten manuscript. (Sumner Estate.)

1898. THE SPANISH DOLLAR AND THE COLONIAL SHILLING.
American Historical Review, Vol. III, No. 4, pp. 607–
619.

SYLLABUS of six lectures given during January and
February in Plainfield, N. J. I. What is a Free
Man and a Free State? II. What is Democracy?
III. Aggregations of Wealth and Plutocracy. IV.
The Rich and the Poor. V. Woman. VI. Immi-
gration.

LEITER HAS BEEN A HERO. Letter to The World, New
York, June 15, on the Joseph Leiter deal.

THE COIN SHILLING OF MASSACHUSETTS BAY. Yale Review, November, Vol. VII, pp. 247–264, and February,
1899, Vol. VII, pp. 405–420.

1899. THE CONQUEST OF THE UNITED STATES BY SPAIN. A
lecture before the Phi Beta Kappa Society of Yale
University, January 16. Yale Law Journal, Vol. VIII,
No. 4, pp. 168–193. Boston, D. Estes & Co., 32 pp.
23 cm. Reprinted in Collected Essays, I, pp. 297–
334.

THE POWER AND BENEFICENCE OF CAPITAL. Proceed-
ings of the Sixth Annual Convention of The Savings
Banks Association of the State of New York, held at
the Rooms of the Chamber of Commerce, 32 Nassau
Street, New York, May 10; pp. 77–95. J. S. Babcock,
New York, printer. Reprinted in Collected Essays,
II, pp. 337–353.

1900. "PROF. SUMNER'S VIEWS ON MARRIAGE." Editorial
with excerpts indicating what he actually did say in
a lecture to Yale seniors widely referred to in the
press and consistently misconstrued. New York
Times, February 18.

FIRST FRUITS OF EXPANSION. New York Evening Post,
April 14, p. 13.

THE PREDICAMENT OF SOCIOLOGICAL STUDY. Printed
for the first time in Collected Essays, III, pp. 415–
425. Original title of manuscript was Sociology.
Written about 1900.

1901. THE ANTHRACITE COAL INDUSTRY, by Peter Roberts.
Introduction by W. G. Sumner. New York, London,

1901. Macmillan Co., 261 pp. Reprinted in Collected Essays, III, pp. 387–388.

TYPES OF INVESTMENT SECURITIES FOR CLASS ROOM USE. New Haven, The Tuttle, Morehouse and Taylor Co., 22 pp., 27 × 35½ cm. Verbatim reprints of a large number of shares, certificates, bonds, and other evidences of ownership of debt, without independent text or comment: collected for use in college instruction.

TRUSTS. I. The Economics of Trusts. II. Policy in regard to Trusts. Journal of Commerce and Commercial Bulletin, June 24 and 25.

THE PREDOMINANT ISSUE. Burlington, Vt., 14 pp. Reprinted from the International Monthly, November, 1900, Vol. 2, pp. 496–509. Reprinted in Collected Essays, I, pp. 337–352.

THE YAKUTS. Abridged from the Russian of Sieroshevski. Journal of the Anthropological Institute of Great Britain and Ireland, Vol. 31, pp. 65–110.

THE BEQUESTS OF THE NINETEENTH CENTURY TO THE TWENTIETH. Written about this time. First published in the Yale Review, June, 1933, Vol. XXII, No. 4, pp. 732–754.

1902. SUICIDAL FANATICISM IN RUSSIA. The Popular Science Monthly, March, Vol. LX, pp. 442–447.

THE CONCENTRATION OF WEALTH: ITS ECONOMIC JUSTIFICATION. The Independent, April–June. Reprinted in Collected Essays, III, pp. 81–90.

STATEMENT IN "A Series of Forecasts from well-known Financiers and Critics for the year 1903." In reply to an inquiry from the editor. New York Evening Post, December 31.

1903. AUTOBIOGRAPHICAL SKETCH OF WILLIAM GRAHAM SUMNER. A History of the Class of 1863, Yale College, pp. 165–167. New Haven, The Tuttle, Morehouse & Taylor Co., 1905. Reprinted in Collected Essays, II, pp. 3–5.

WAR. Printed for the first time in Collected Essays, I, pp. 3–40.

MODERN MARRIAGE. Written about this time. Printed

1903. posthumously in the Yale Review, January, 1924,
       Vol. XIII, No. 2, pp. 249–275.
1904. REPLY TO A SOCIALIST (THE FALLACIES OF SOCIALISM).
       Collier's Weekly, October 29, pp. 12–13. Reprinted
       in Collected Essays, III, pp. 55–62.
1905. LYNCH-LAW, by James Elbert Cutler. Foreword by
       W. G. Sumner. New York, Longmans, Green, and
       Co., 287 pp. Reprinted in Collected Essays, III, pp.
       383–384.
       ECONOMICS AND POLITICS. Printed for the first time in
       Collected Essays, II, pp. 318–333.
       THE SCIENTIFIC ATTITUDE OF MIND. Address to initiates
       of the Sigma Xi Society, Yale University, on March 4.
       Printed for the first time in Collected Essays, II, pp.
       17–28.
       THE UNITED STATES AS A WORLD POWER. Address
       before the Friday Evening Club, Morristown, New
       Jersey, briefly reported under the caption, "Resent
       Navy Attack," in the New York Daily Tribune,
       March 18.
1906. THE TREND OF SOCIALISM IN THIS COUNTRY. New York
       Herald, January 1.
       PROTECTIONISM TWENTY YEARS AFTER. (Title given
       by editor.) Address at a dinner of the Committee
       on Tariff Reform of the Tariff Reform Club in the
       City of New York, June 2. Published by the Reform
       Club Committee on Tariff Reform, 42 Broadway, New
       York, N. Y. Series 1906, No. 4, 7 pp., August 15.
       Reprinted in Collected Essays, IV, pp. 131–138.
1900–06. PURPOSES AND CONSEQUENCES. Printed for the first
       time in Collected Essays, II, pp. 67–75. Written
       sometime between 1900 and 1906.
       RIGHTS. Printed for the first time in Collected Essays, II,
       pp. 79–83. Written sometime between 1900 and 1906.
       EQUALITY. Printed for the first time in Collected Essays,
       II, pp. 87–89. Written sometime between 1900 and
       1906.
1907. FOLKWAYS: A Study of the Sociological Importance of
       Usages, Manners, Customs, Mores, and Morals. Bos-
       ton, Ginn & Co., 692 pp.

1907. THE SPREAD OF SOCIALISTIC NOTIONS AND FAITH IN
SOCIALISTIC DEVICES. Appeared under different cap-
tions in the St. Louis Republic, the New York Herald,
and other newspapers, January 2.

SOCIOLOGY AS A COLLEGE SUBJECT. American Journal
of Sociology, March, Vol. 12, No. 5, pp. 597–599.
Reprinted in Collected Essays, III, pp. 407–411.

"LAYS PANIC TO ROOSEVELT. PROF. SUMNER OF YALE
ON THE FINANCIAL CRISIS." Article in the form of
an interview, under New Haven date line, November 1,
published in the New York Times, the New York Sun,
and other papers.

INDISCREET DENUNCIATION AND LAWS. Article in a
symposium on "What Caused the Panic." Everybody's Magazine, December, Vol. XVII, No. VI, pp.
832 b–832 c.

1908. DECLINE OF CONFIDENCE DUE TO RECKLESS DENUN-
CIATION. Article on the causes of the panic. Annual
Financial and Commercial Review, New York Herald,
January 2.

1909. WHAT IS SANE TARIFF REFORM? Annual Financial and
Commercial Review, New York Herald, January 4.

THE FAMILY AND SOCIAL CHANGE. American Journal
of Sociology, March, Vol. XIV, No. 5, pp. 577–591.
Reprinted in Collected Essays, I, pp. 43–61.

WITCHCRAFT. Forum, May, Vol. XLI, pp. 410–423.
Reprinted in Collected Essays, I, pp. 105–126.

AUTOBIOGRAPHY and List of Books Published. Facsimile
of letter and photograph in The Yale Courant, May,
Vol. XLV, No. 7, on occasion of Sumner's retirement.

THE STATUS OF WOMEN IN CHALDEA, EGYPT, INDIA,
JUDEA, AND GREECE TO THE TIME OF CHRIST. Forum,
August, Vol. XLII, pp. 113–136. Reprinted in Col-
lected Essays, I, pp. 65–102.

THE MORES OF THE PRESENT AND THE FUTURE. Yale
Review, November, Vol. XVIII, pp. 233–245. Reprinted in Collected Essays, I, pp. 149–164.

1910. RELIGION AND THE MORES. American Journal of
Sociology, March, Vol. XV, No. 5, pp. 577–591.
Reprinted in Collected Essays, I, pp. 129–146.

POSTHUMOUS

1911. WAR. Yale Review (New Series), October, Vol. I, No. 1, pp. 1–27. Printed in Collected Essays, I, pp. 3–40. WAR AND OTHER ESSAYS. Edited by Albert Galloway Keller. New Haven, Yale University Press, 381 pp.

1913. EARTH HUNGER OR THE PHILOSOPHY OF LAND GRABBING. Yale Review (New Series), October, Vol. III, No. 1, pp. 3–32. Printed in Collected Essays, II, pp. 31–64. EARTH HUNGER AND OTHER ESSAYS. Edited by Albert Galloway Keller. New Haven, Yale University Press, 377 pp.

1914. THE CHALLENGE OF FACTS AND OTHER ESSAYS. Edited by Albert Galloway Keller. New Haven, Yale University Press, 450 pp.

1919. THE FORGOTTEN MAN AND OTHER ESSAYS. Edited by Albert Galloway Keller. New Haven, Yale University Press, 559 pp.

1920. THE ENGLISH BANK RESTRICTION AND THE BULLION REPORT OF JUNE 8, 1810. Reprinted from Sumner's History of American Currency (1874), with an introduction by Stuyvesant Fish. New York, H. Holt & Co., 162 pp.

1923. DISCIPLINE AND OTHER ESSAYS, from the Collected Works of William Graham Sumner. New Haven, Yale University Press, 38 pp. Contents: Discipline, Purposes and Consequences, Power and Progress, Liberty and Responsibility.

1924. SELECTED ESSAYS OF WILLIAM GRAHAM SUMNER. Edited by Albert Galloway Keller and Maurice Rea Davie. New Haven, Yale University Press, 356 pp. MODERN MARRIAGE. Yale Review, January, Vol. XIII, No. 2, pp. 249–275. EL MATRIMONIO MODERNO. Inter-América, July, Español, Vol. VIII, No. 2, pp. 161–179.

1925. WHAT SOCIAL CLASSES OWE TO EACH OTHER (1883, Harper & Brothers). Republished by the Yale University Press, with a foreword by A. G. Keller, 169 pp.

1927. THE SCIENCE OF SOCIETY. Co-author with Albert Galloway Keller, Vol. IV also with Maurice R. Davie.

1927. New Haven, Yale University Press, 4 vols., first three volumes of text numbered consecutively, 2251 pp., fourth volume or case book, 1331 pp.
1933. THE FORGOTTEN MAN — REDISCOVERED AFTER FIFTY YEARS. New Haven, Yale University Press, 31 pp.
THE BEQUESTS OF THE NINETEENTH CENTURY TO THE TWENTIETH. Yale Review, June, Vol. XXII, No. 4, pp. 732–754.
1934. ESSAYS OF WILLIAM GRAHAM SUMNER. Edited by Albert Galloway Keller and Maurice Rea Davie. New Haven, Yale University Press, 2 vols., 499 and 534 pp.

BIOGRAPHICAL SKETCHES OF SUMNER

"Sketch of William Graham Sumner." Based largely on Sumner's reply to questions put by the editor. The Popular Science Monthly, June, 1889, Vol. XXXV, pp. 261–268. Reprinted in Collected Essays, III, pp. 3–13.
"Autobiographical Sketch of William Graham Sumner." In A History of the Class of 1863, Yale College, pp. 165–167. New Haven, The Tuttle, Morehouse & Taylor Co., 1905. Reprinted in Collected Essays, II, pp. 3–5.
"William Graham Sumner." By Albert G. Keller. The Nation, April 21, 1910, Vol. 90, No. 2338, pp. 397–398.
"William Graham Sumner." By Robert W. DeForest. The Survey, April 30, 1910, Vol. XXIV, pp. 167–170.
"William Graham Sumner." By A. G. Keller. The American Journal of Sociology, May, 1910, Vol. XV, No. 6, pp. 832–835. (Sumner as a sociologist).
"Comment on William Graham Sumner." The Pioneer, by Henry W. Farnam. The Teacher, by J. C. Schwab. The Inspirer, by Irving Fisher. The Idealist, by Clive Day. The Man, by Albert G. Keller. The Veteran, by Richard T. Ely. Yale Review, May, 1910, Vol. XIX, pp. 1–12.
"Memorial Addresses." Delivered June 19, 1910, in Lampson Lyceum, Yale University, by Otto T. Bannard, Henry DeForest Baldwin, and Albert Galloway Keller. Printed in Collected Essays, III, pp. 429–450.
"Talks with a Great Teacher. Intimate hours with the late Professor William Graham Sumner, of Yale." By J. Pease

Norton, The World's Work, August, 1910, Vol. XX, No. 4, pp. 13290–13292.

"Obituary. William Graham Sumner." The Economic Journal, London, September, 1910, Vol. XX, pp. 496–497.

William Graham Sumner. By Harris E. Starr. New York, H. Holt & Co., 1925, 557 pp.

"William Graham Sumner, Class of 1863, Sociologist, 1840–1910." By Wayland Wells Williams, in The Memorial Quadrangle, a book about Yale compiled by Robert Dudley French, including biographies of forty-three eminent Yale men written by various hands. New Haven, Yale University Press, 1929, 459 pp., pp. 295–299.

Reminiscences (Mainly Personal) of William Graham Sumner. By A. G. Keller. New Haven, Yale University Press, 1933, 110 pp.

INDEX

509

Outlying continents, I, 186; the exploitation of, I, 190–193; the opening up of, I, 433, 462–463; II, 245; the settlement of, I, 451.
Overpopulation, I, 88, 135, 252, 431–432; II, 92–93, 274–275.
Overproduction, II, 438.
Overwork, I, 347.

Pain, I, 382; II, 242.
Paine, Thomas, II, 321.
Pair-marriage, I, 245–246, 266, 279.
Panama Congress, the, I, 200–201, 203.
Paper currency a natural monopoly, I, 398.
Paper money, II, 340–341, 381.
Papuans, war among the, I, 137.
PARABLE, A, I, 497–499.
Parents, II, 88–89; and children, I, 273–275, 277.
Party, the Democratic, I, 84; the Federal, II, 343–344; the Republican, I, 84.
Passport, II, 373, 444.
Patents as artificial monopolies, I, 398.
Paternal theory, I, 495–496.
Pathos, I, 219.
"Patrimony of the Disinherited," the, I, 384.
Patriotism, I, 52, 145; II, 270–271, 362.
Pauperization, I, 377.
Paupers, I, 476, 477; II, 161–165, 457.
Peace, and religion, I, 157–159; -element, development of the, I, 149; for women, I, 154; -group, the, I, 144, 150–152, 156–161, 168; -institutions, I, 149–157; -institutions of civilized nations, I, 153–157; -institutions of the West Australians, I, 151; makes war, I, 144; of God, I, 154; of the house, I, 149–150, 154; -pacts, I, 140, 143; -rules, I, 149; -taboo, I, 149, 151, 159; the king's, I, 154–156; the triumphs of, II, 284; universal, I, 168–169.
Peaceful access, I, 150.
Peacefulness and militancy, I, 161.
Pearson, Karl, I, 43–44.
Peasant-proprietors, II, 310, 316, 404.

Peasants, II, 222, 242–245.
Penalties, I, 334–335.
Pennsylvania, II, 389, 398.
Pensions, I, 490; II, 457.
People, the, I, 216 ff., 470–471; II, 145, 147, 195–198, 220–223, 237, 323, 343; see Man-on-the-curbstone.
Personal superiority a natural monopoly, I, 398–399.
Persons and capital, II, 97–98.
Pessimism, I, 52, 265; see Optimism.
"Pest of glory," the, I, 193; II, 282.
Pestilence, I, 466.
Pets, social, I, 495.
Phantasm, I, 51; definition of, I, 44; of the Middle Ages, I, 44–47; political, I, 343.
Philanthropists, II, 476, 477, 494.
Philanthropy, I, 435, 436; II, 118.
Philippines, the, I, 13, 86; II, 269–271, 279–281.
Philosophers, I, 484, 494; social, II, 15–16, 26, 118.
Philosophies, new, I, 444–445.
Philosophizing, I, 468.
Philosophy, I, 57, 88, 454, 458–459; II, 124–125, 127; eighteenth century, II, 169; of colonization, I, 186–187; of optimism, I, 83; political, I, 82–83, 86; II, 279; religious, I, 82–83; sentimental, II, 101–102, 106; social, II, 16–17, 102–105, 153–154; the new, II, 262–263; world-, I, 55, 59, 60, 69.
Phrases, high-sounding, II, 131.
Plunder, II, 151, 156–158, 379.
Plutocracy, I, 103, 220; II, 219, 223–225, 240, 246; definition of, II, 223; and democracy, the antagonism of, I, 84, 100; II, 229–230, 294–295; and imperialism and militarism, II, 294–295; and political institutions, II, 228–229.
PLUTOCRACY, DEFINITIONS OF DEMOCRACY AND, II, 220–225.
PLUTOCRACY, DEMOCRACY AND, II, 213–219.
PLUTOCRACY AND DEMOCRACY, THE CONFLICT OF, II, 226–230.
Plutocrat, definition of a, II, 228.